NATIONAL
SECURITY

ISSN 1543-5407

NATIONAL SECURITY

Anjali Bhattacharjee

INFORMATION PLUS® REFERENCE SERIES
Formerly published by Information Plus, Wylie, Texas

GALE®

THOMSON
™
GALE

Detroit • New York • San Diego • San Francisco • Cleveland • New Haven, Conn. • Waterville, Maine • London • Munich

National Security

Anjali Bhattacharjee and Bill Becker

Project Editor
Ellice Engdahl

Editorial
Paula Cutcher-Jackson, Kathleen Edgar,
Debra Kirby, Prindle LaBarge, Elizabeth Manar,
Charles B. Montney, Heather Price

Permissions
Shalice Shah-Caldwell

Product Design
Cynthia Baldwin

Composition and Electronic Prepress
Evi Seoud

Manufacturing
Keith Helmling

LIBRARY OF CONGRESS CATALOGING-IN-PUBLICATION DATA

ISBN 0-7876-5103-6 (set)
ISBN 0-7876-6546-0
ISSN 1543-5407

Printed in the United States of America
10 9 8 7 6 5 4 3 2 1

TABLE OF CONTENTS

CHAPTER 1

National security may be defined as protection from threats to a country's territory, people, or values and policies. During the Cold War from the 1940s through the 1980s, America's national security policy relied on containment and a shifting balance between conventional and nuclear forces. Though an uncontested global leader since the Soviet Union's fall in 1991, the U.S. currently faces many threats: international terrorism, weapons of mass destruction, reliance on imported oil and gas, the Arab-Israeli conflict, and the war on drugs, among them. The so-called "transition states" (Russia, China, and India) and "states of concern" (Iraq, North Korea, Iran, Libya, Syria, Sudan, and Cuba) also influence U.S. security planning. Entrusted with formulating national security are the president, National Security Council, intelligence infrastructure, military, and Congress.

CHAPTER 2

Though in decline since 1987, transfers of major conventional weapons (any armaments that don't fall into the "weapons of mass destruction" category), remain sizable. U.S. arms sales are regulated by legislation and the State Department's Office of Defense Trade Controls. Foreign nations, particularly European countries, compete with the United States as arms suppliers; and the demand for weapons is especially strong in the Persian Gulf area. On the other hand, many international and nongovernmental organizations work to limit the small arms, light weapons, and landmines that have killed so many civilians around the world. Also, many nations have signed international agreements (such as the Convention on Anti-Personnel Mines, the CFE and CFE 1A treaties, and the Wassenaar Arrangement) intended to restrain the development and use of conventional weapons.

CHAPTER 3

Weapons of mass destruction include biological, chemical, and nuclear agents, as well as conventional weapons capable of inflicting widespread casualties. Throughout history the inventory of such weapons has grown. Currently they are of great concern in China, Egypt, India, Iran, Israel, Libya, North Korea, Pakistan, and Syria. Iraq, which has secretly developed and stockpiled all three kinds of WMD despite the 1991 Gulf War and United Nations inspections, provides a case study. During the early- and mid-1990s, illicit trafficking in nuclear and fissile materials posed another serious threat, which was addressed by a U.S-Russian accord in 1995. At least 12 other nonproliferation regimes and treaties currently cover WMD.

CHAPTER 4

The federal government funds both research and preparedness efforts to battle bioterrorism, spending much of its budget in this area on the National Guard and the Centers for Disease Control and Prevention (CDC). To assist state and local health departments, the CDC has prioritized various biological and chemical weapons by threat level and it has created a laboratory response network. The Animal and Plant Health Inspection Service (APHIS), another federal agency important in guarding against bioattack, monitors potential threats to U.S. agricultural products and livestock.

CHAPTER 5

Terrorism is generally motivated by religious and/or political conflicts and, though tactics vary, is almost always violent. Because of tensions in the Middle East, many states currently sponsoring anti-American terrorism are Islamic: Iran, Iraq, Syria, and Libya. The U.S. also accuses Sudan, North Korea, and Cuba of state-sponsored violence, while some of its own international actions have been labeled terrorist by other nations. Though anti-American terrorism by Middle Eastern extremists dates back to the 1980s, the September 11, 2001 attacks of Osama bin Laden and al-Qaeda have been the most devastating. The federal government reacted by trying to cut off financing for terrorist operations, reorganizing its bureaucracy, improving transportation security, passing the Patriot Act of 2001, and declaring war on terrorism. Several opinion polls captured the public's reactions to 9/11 and its aftermath.

CHAPTER 6

Terrorist attacks carried out by groups or individuals operating exclusively in the U.S. have involved guns, bombs, and germs; targeted Congressmen, churchgoers, federal workers, spectators at Olympic games, and employees of abortion clinics; and have occurred at locations ranging from Washington, D.C., to Oklahoma City, Oklahoma. Some have been attributed to left-wing organizations espousing socialist ideologies, others to anti-government right-wing extremists. Special-interest/single-issue terrorism often falls into the categories of ecoterrorism and anti-abortion activism. In response to hate crimes, watchdog groups such as the Anti-Defamation League and Southern Poverty Law Center monitor domestic extremists.

PREFACE

National Security is one of the latest volumes in the Information Plus Reference Series. Previously published by the Information Plus company of Wylie, Texas, the Information Plus Reference Series (and its companion set, the Information Plus Compact Series became a Gale Group product when Gale and Information Plus merged in early 2000. Those of you familiar with the series as published by Information Plus will notice a few changes. Gale has adopted a new layout and style that we hope you will find easy to use. Other improvements include greatly expanded indexes in each book, and more descriptive tables of contents.

While some changes have been made to the design, the purpose of the Information Plus Reference Series remains the same. Each volume of the series presents the latest facts on a topic of pressing concern in modern American life. These topics include today's most controversial and most studied social issues: abortion, capital punishment, care for the elderly, crime, health care, energy, the environment, immigration, minorities, national security, social welfare, women, youth, and many more. Although written especially for the high school and undergraduate student, this series is an excellent resource for anyone in need of factual information on current affairs.

By presenting the facts, it is Gale's intention to provide its readers with everything they need to reach an informed opinion on current issues. To that end, there is a particular emphasis in this series on the presentation of scientific studies, surveys, and statistics. These data are generally presented in the form of tables, charts, and other graphics placed within the text of each book. Every graphic is directly referred to and carefully explained in the text. The source of each graphic is presented within the graphic itself. The data used in these graphics are drawn from the most reputable and reliable sources, in particular from the various branches of the U.S. government and from major independent polling organizations. Every effort was made to secure the most recent information available. The reader

should bear in mind that many major studies take years to conduct, and that additional years often pass before the data from these studies are made available to the public. Therefore, in many cases the most recent information available in 2003 dated from 2000 or 2001. Older statistics are sometimes presented as well, if they are of particular interest and no more-recent information exists.

Although statistics are a major focus of the Information Plus Reference Series, they are by no means its only content. Each book also presents the widely held positions and important ideas that shape how the book's subject is discussed in the United States. These positions are explained in detail and, where possible, in the words of their proponents. Some of the other material to be found in these books includes: historical background; descriptions of major events related to the subject; relevant laws and court cases; and examples of how these issues play out in American life. Some books also feature primary documents, or have pro and con debate sections giving the words and opinions of prominent Americans on both sides of a controversial topic. All material is presented in an even-handed and unbiased manner; the reader will never be encouraged to accept one view of an issue over another.

HOW TO USE THIS BOOK

National security has been foremost on the minds of many Americans since the September 11, 2001, terrorist attacks. The United States has taken many measures as a result, including the formation of the Department of Homeland Security, increased security measures at airports, and the enactment of the Patriot Act of 2001. This book covers all of these topics and more, providing the history of national security in the United States; descriptions of the various conventional and nonproliferation treaties and regimes; and information on countries of proliferation concern to the United States. Nuclear, chemical, and biological weapons are discussed in detail, as are domestic and international terrorism and Americans' feelings regarding national security after the September 11, 2001, terrorist attacks.

National Security consists of ten chapters and three appendixes. Each of the chapters is devoted to a particular aspect of U.S. national security. For a summary of the information covered in each chapter, please see the synopses provided in the Table of Contents at the front of the book. Chapters generally begin with an overview of the basic facts and background information on the chapter's topic, then proceed to examine sub-topics of particular interest. For example, Chapter 4: Preparing for Biological and Chemical Attacks begins with a description of the federal role in preparing for chemical and/or biological attacks, including funding for research and preparedness. The chapter then moves into a discussion of various chemical and biological agents, including the possible threat and preparedness activities for each agent. One such biological attack in the United States, the Dalles Incident, is covered in detail. Finally the chapter examines the protection of animals and plants. Readers can find their way through a chapter by looking for the section and sub-section headings, which are clearly set off from the text. Or, they can refer to the book's extensive index, if they already know what they are looking for.

Statistical Information

The tables and figures featured throughout *National Security* will be of particular use to the reader in learning about this topic. These tables and figures represent an extensive collection of the most recent and valuable statistics on national security, as well as related issues—for example, graphics in the book cover common chemical warfare agents, U.S. State Department–designated foreign terrorist organizations, the organization of the U.S. Department of Defense, the numbers and locations of "patriot" groups, and world oil transit "chokepoints." Gale believes that making this information available to the reader is the most important way in which we fulfill the goal of this book: to help readers understand the issues and controversies surrounding national security in the United States and reach their own conclusions.

Each table or figure has a unique identifier appearing above it, for ease of identification and reference. Titles for the tables and figures explain their purpose. At the end of each table or figure, the original source of the data is provided.

In order to help readers understand these often complicated statistics, all tables and figures are explained in the text. References in the text direct the reader to the relevant statistics. Furthermore, the contents of all tables and figures are fully indexed. Please see the opening section of the index at the back of this volume for a description of how to find tables and figures within it.

In addition to the main body text and images, *National Security* has three appendices. The first is the Important Names and Addresses directory. Here the reader will find contact information for a number of government and private organizations that can provide further information on aspects of national security. The second appendix is the Resources section, which can also assist the reader in conducting his or her own research. In this section, the author and editors of *National Security* describe some of the sources that were most useful during the compilation of this book. The final appendix is the index. It has been greatly expanded from previous editions, and should make it even easier to find specific topics in this book.

ADVISORY BOARD CONTRIBUTIONS

The staff of Information Plus would like to extend their heartfelt appreciation to the Information Plus Advisory Board. This dedicated group of media professionals provides feedback on the series on an ongoing basis. Their comments allow the editorial staff who work on the project to continually make the series better and more user-friendly. Our top priorities are to produce the highest-quality and most useful books possible, and the Advisory Board's contributions to this process are invaluable.

The members of the Information Plus Advisory Board are:

- Kathleen R. Bonn, Librarian, Newbury Park High School, Newbury Park, California

- Madelyn Garner, Librarian, San Jacinto College—North Campus, Houston, Texas

- Anne Oxenrider, Media Specialist, Dundee High School, Dundee, Michigan

- Charles R. Rodgers, Director of Libraries, Pasco-Hernando Community College, Dade City, Florida

- James N. Zitzelsberger, Library Media Department Chairman, Oshkosh West High School, Oshkosh, Wisconsin

In addition, Information Plus staff owe special thanks to Dr. Harold Molineu, Professor of Political Science at Ohio University, for his particular assistance as an acting advisor on *National Security*. Dr. Molineu's substantial background in the field allowed him to provide expert advice and indispensable recommendations on content and organization.

COMMENTS AND SUGGESTIONS

The editors of the Information Plus Reference Series welcome your feedback on *National Security*. Please direct all correspondence to:

Editors
Information Plus Reference Series
27500 Drake Rd.
Farmington Hills, MI 48331-3535

ACKNOWLEDGMENTS

The editors wish to thank the copyright holders of material included in this volume and the permissions managers of many book and magazine publishing companies for assisting us in securing reproduction rights. We are also grateful to the staffs of the Detroit Public Library, the Library of Congress, the University of Detroit Mercy Library, Wayne State University Purdy/Kresge Library Complex, and the University of Michigan Libraries for making their resources available to us.

Following is a list of the copyright holders who have granted us permission to reproduce material in National Security. *Every effort has been made to trace copyright, but if omissions have been made, please let us know.*

For more detailed source citations, please see the sources listed under each individual table and figure.

BP Amoco: Table 9.1, Table 9.2

Center for Nonproliferation Studies: Table 3.1, Table 3.2

Centers for Disease Control and Prevention: Figure 4.2, Table 4.5, Table 4.6, Table 4.7, Table 4.8, Table 4.9

Central Intelligence Agency: Figure 1.2, Figure 7.4

Congressional Research Service: Table 8.3

Council for a Livable World, Arms Trade Oversight Project: Table 2.3

Harris Interactive®, Rochester, NY. Reproduced by permission: Table 5.4, Table 5.5, Table 5.6

Intelligence Community: Figure 7.3

Hays, Peter, Brenda J. Vallance, and Alan R. Van Tassell, eds. AMERICAN DEFENSE POLICY, **pp. 65, 66, 68, 69, 70, 436, 437, 438, 440, 441. © 1996 Johns Hopkins University Press. Reprinted with permission of The Johns Hopkins University Press.** Table 2.6, Table 2.7, Table 2.8, Table 2.9, Table 3.14, Table 3.15

Henry Holt and Company, LLC: Figure 9.5

National Archives and Records Administration, Office of the Federal Register: Figure 7.1

National Defense University: Figure 10.2, Figure 10.3, Figure 10.5, Figure 10.6

National Defense University, Institute for National Strategic Studies: Table 1.1

National Security Council: Figure 10.1

Stockholm International Peace Research Institute: Figure 2.1, Table 2.1, Table 2.2, Table 2.4, Table 2.5

U.S. Department of Defense: Figure 8.1, Figure 8.2, Figure 8.4, Figure 8.5

U.S. Department of Defense, Joint Chiefs of Staff: Figure 8.3

U.S. Department of Defense, Office of the Secretary of Defense: Figure 3.1, Figure 3.2, Figure 3.3, Figure 3.4, Figure 3.5, Table 3.3, Table 3.5, Table 3.6, Table 3.7, Table 3.8, Table 3.9, Table 3.10, Table 3.11, Table 3.12, Table 3.13, Table 4.10

U.S. Department of Defense, Washington Headquarters Services, Directorate for Information Operations and Reports: Table 5.3

U.S. Department of Energy, Energy Information Administration: Figure 9.1, Figure 9.2, Figure 9.3, Table 9.3

U.S. Department of Justice, Immigration and Naturalization Service: Figure 7.5, Table 7.1

U.S. Department of State: Figure 2.2, Figure 5.1, Figure 5.2, Figure 5.3, Figure 5.4, Table 5.2, Figure 7.2

U.S. Department of State, Office of the Coordinator for Counterterrorism: Table 5.1

U.S. General Accounting Office: Figure 4.1, Table 4.1, Table 4.2, Table 4.3, Table 4.4, Table 8.2, Table 8.4, Figure 10.4, Table 10.1, Table 10.2, Table 10.3, Table 10.4

Wirthlin Worldwide, Reston, VA. Reproduced by permission: Figure 5.5, Figure 5.6, Figure 5.7, Figure 9.4

CHAPTER 1

AN INTRODUCTION TO NATIONAL SECURITY

In a global society where states are becoming increasingly interconnected and interdependent, national security is of utmost importance to most countries. As a consequence of America's "War on Terrorism," military presence in Afghanistan, and increasingly tenuous ties with Arab countries, national security issues continue to dominate U.S. foreign policy. After the attacks of September 11, 2001, the terms "terrorism" and "national security"—words that spent over a decade on the backburner in popular political debate and policymaking—have taken on a whole new dimension of importance.

What exactly does "national security" mean, as used by the United States government? The word "national" stresses that the whole nation faces an intentional threat. The word "security" connotes a condition of simple law and order, peace, and safety that does not sacrifice Americans' free exercise of their constitutional rights and liberties. But while the terms "national" and "security" are easy to comprehend, analysts find it hard to come up with a conclusive definition, since issues pertaining to U.S. national security can vary widely. Diplomacy, trade, arms control, military intervention, espionage, money laundering, the environment, and migration are all elements that can play a role in national security. The following definitions are from various sources in the field:

- "National security is the confidence held by the great majority of the nation's people that the nation has the military capability and effective policy to prevent its adversaries from effectively using force in preventing the nation's pursuit of its national interests." —Sam Sarkesian, *U.S. National Security: Policy Makers, Processes, and Politics* (2nd ed.), Lynne Reiner Publishers, Colorado, 1995

- "The ability of a nation to protect its internal values from external threats." —David L. Sills, Robert K. Merton (eds.), *International Encyclopedia of Social Sciences, Vol. 19,* Free Press, New York, 1968

- "Security, in an objective sense, measures the absence of threats to acquired values, in a subjective sense, the absence of fear that such values will be attacked." —Arnold Wolfers, *Discord and Collaboration,* Johns Hopkins University Press, Baltimore, 1962

- "The U.S. national security strategy will be based on a distinctly American internationalism that reflects the union of our values and our national interests. The aim of this strategy is to help make the world not just safer but better. Our goals on the path to progress are clear: political and economic freedom, peaceful relations with other states, and respect for human dignity." —President George W. Bush, *The National Security Strategy of the United States of America,* 2002

Though these definitions of national security vary, there are some common themes. To simplify matters for the reading of this text, the following definition of national security is offered. National security is the name given to a leadership's collective efforts to protect its nation from all threats that could significantly harm its territory or populace, or that could affect its fundamental values and policies.

Another method of defining national security is by looking at threats to national security. Typically, one can categorize threats to national security as separate from other common crimes, because the former:

1) Generally promise to take more lives or cause much more damage and disruption

2) Arise from a source in the international arena, usually as a reaction against a state's foreign policy

3) Are designed to make a political, ideological, or religious statement

4) Are customarily larger, more menacing, and perceived as a greater threat than those generally handled by local law enforcement authorities

FIGURE 1.1

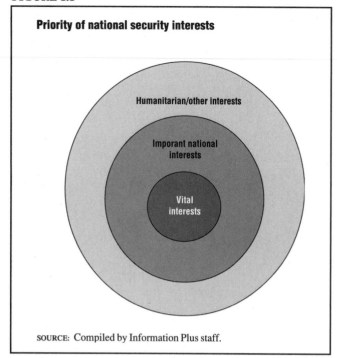

Priority of national security interests

Humanitarian/other interests

Imporant national interests

Vital interests

SOURCE: Compiled by Information Plus staff.

These national security threats may come from governments (also called "states" in security terminology), subnational entities (such as terrorist groups, organized-crime networks, companies practicing industrial espionage, etc.), external intelligence-gathering agencies (private individuals or agencies that are often hired to gather information), or even U.S. citizens. In the international arena, the following entities are usually considered prime targets for threats against U.S. national security:

1) U.S. citizens outside the country (tourists traveling abroad, soldiers deployed on active duty, and the diplomatic community)

2) U.S. property outside the country, including U.S. embassies, military facilities, naval ships, factories, and offices

3) U.S. citizens, U.S. government, and physical structures within American borders

Generally, the U.S. government has not been hesitant to engage itself in initiatives to defend national security. Usually such actions, whether preemptive (actions taken in advance to try to avoid a potential threat) or defensive (actions taken in reaction to a real and present threat), are taken when there are significant risks to national interests. These risks are usually classified in three main groups, as shown in Figure 1.1. They are:

1) Vital interests, or issues directly concerning the survival and safety of the country. These threats could involve physical territory, safety of citizens, or even danger to a close ally. To defend vital interests, the military is fully mobilized and significant resources are committed to the resolution of the conflict.

2) Important national interests, or those in which national survival is not at stake, but there may be a menace to the world at large that could potentially escalate into a vital interest problem. Military mobilization and resource commitment generally depend on the situation itself.

3) Humanitarian or other interests, or those where the primary focus is on containing the problem and fighting any chance of escalation rather than defending national security interests.

POWER AND NATIONAL SECURITY

A state's power plays a strong role in its ability to fulfill its national security agenda. As the term "power" is a highly dynamic and subjective term, measuring it can be complicated. In their book *Foundations of National Power* (Van Nostrand, New York, 1951), Harold and Margaret Sprout state that a nation's power can be roughly measured by using the following equation: national power = human resources + physical habitat + foodstuffs and raw materials + tools and skills + organization + morale and political behavior + external conditions and circumstances. Nation-states (a political designation containing a relatively homogenous population or people with a feeling of common nationality) apply power in order to bring about the things they most want, whether those are in the political, economic, or military realm.

THE HISTORICAL DEVELOPMENT OF U.S. NATIONAL SECURITY

From the 1940s to the 1980s

Modern American national security policy has evolved through several stages since the end of World War II (WWII; 1939–45). After WWII, the United States emerged as the most powerful nation in the world. However, most of the globe was ideologically and politically divided between the Democratic camp, headed by the United States, and the Soviet Union-led Communist bloc. The primary concern for the United States during this time was the containment of the Communist threat, which laid the foundation for national security policy for decades to come.

Although the Soviet Union had a stronger military land force, America's naval predominance and its possession of the atomic bomb gave it unrivaled power. To continue its rise as a superpower, the United States infused significant financial resources into a large-scale military buildup. This was primarily called for under an evaluation conducted by a joint Department of State/Department of Defense committee, which delivered its findings to the National Security Council in 1950 in a document labeled NSC 68.

The U.S. containment policies were further abetted by the Truman Doctrine and the Marshall Plan. The 1947

Truman Doctrine had been a direct response to the growing Communist threat in Greece and Turkey and marked the beginning of U.S. intervention around the globe in the name of democracy. President Truman declared that totalitarian governments (those that put the fate of the state above the fate of its citizens; such governments are often run by despots or dictators) could not be imposed on free people and that any attempts to do so would be countered by the United States, which considered them violations of individual rights and sovereignty. The Marshall Plan, on the other hand, was a substantial economic aid package geared toward helping restore the economies of post-WWII Europe. Implemented in 1948, the plan was designed to establish stability in Europe and promote American agendas.

In the 1950s, the Korean War (1950–52) and advances in Soviet nuclear technology led the United States to reassess its strategic national security policies. Enormous military buildup by the Soviets and Americans in the mid-1950s led then-President Eisenhower to try to find a balance between military spending and the delicate domestic economy. The Joint Chiefs of Staff (consisting of the Chairman, the Vice Chairman, the Chief of Staff of the Army, the Chief of Naval Operations, the Chief of Staff of the Air Force, and the Commandant of the Marine Corps) came up with the Sequoia Study, which examined U.S. strategic forces and made several recommendations:

- Withdrawal of some U.S. troops from abroad

- Creation of a mobile strategic reserve (a well-prepared, -trained, and -equipped military unit on reserve—not active duty—that can be mobilized within a short period of time if the president deems that there is a threat to national security

- Strengthening alliances while allowing allied forces to rely primarily on their own defenses

- Further investment in U.S. air defenses

This was also a time when science and technology began to play an increasing role in American strategy. In 1954 President Eisenhower introduced the "New Look" policy, which focused on massive retaliation as a deterrent against the Soviet threat, the reduction of conventional ground forces, and an increase in air-defense capabilities. "Massive retaliation" involved instantaneous defense against any threat by employing any means necessary, including nuclear weapons. The thinking behind this concept was that the Soviet Union would not attack the United States, even if it knew it could do major damage, if it feared the same damage to itself.

The rapid arms buildup by both the Soviets and Americans later led the United States to question its heavy reliance on nuclear weapons and to explore other policy options. By the late 1960s, both the Soviet Union

and the United States had acquired second-strike nuclear capability, meaning each country was able to seriously retaliate against a nuclear strike on its territory. Under the administration of President John F. Kennedy, the 1960s witnessed the initiation of yet another national security doctrine, called "flexible response." It was developed as the United States began to reexamine its diminishing reliance on conventional weapons and the increasing role played by tactical nuclear weapons in Europe. Many U.S. policymakers and military leaders felt that if tensions heightened considerably, there was not much of a leap between using tactical (used for a specific purpose or goal, rather than as an all-out attack) and strategic (used to strike at an enemy's military, economic, or political power sources) nuclear weapons. Thus the world might become engaged in an all-out nuclear war. They also realized that the doctrine of massive retaliation would not be effective when dealing with lower-intensity conflicts, such as clashes with Soviet proxies in smaller countries.

Flexible response policy gave the president the ability to choose the appropriate level of force required to deal with a variety of different challenges. The president could opt for a massive nuclear retaliation, or a limited counterforce (attacking only the opponent's force structure) or countervalue (attacking the opponent's cities and populace) nuclear strike. Conventional forces were also strengthened and improved under this doctrine in order to shift away from heavy reliance on nuclear weapons. The military reserves and National Guard were boosted, the number of Navy warships was increased, army divisions were increased, and counterinsurgency (antirevolution or antirevolt) forces were enlarged.

It was not until the 1970s that U.S. national security policy again began to be seriously questioned, prompted by the unsuccessful American intervention in the Vietnam conflict. The necessity for U.S. involvement to protect democracy and contain the Soviet threat was coming under increasing scrutiny by both U.S. critics and the world at large. Meanwhile, U.S. policymakers had come up with the idea of "strategic sufficiency" (maintaining enough military prowess to deter the enemy from coercing a country or its allies) in order to keep the doctrine of flexible response alive, along with enough retaliatory power to guarantee mutually assured destruction (MAD) in case of a war. In order to limit tensions and the possibility of a conflict between the United States and the Soviet Union, the Nixon administration introduced the concept of "détente." These efforts paid off when the two parties sat down for the Strategic Arms Limitations Talks (SALT I) in 1972.

The State of the World since the Breakup of the Soviet Union

The 1991 breakup of the Soviet Union brought an end to the bipolar global structure in which most world power rested in the hands of the U.S. and Soviet blocs. However, defining what has happened to the balance of power in the world since then is a matter of great debate. One theory is that the world has primarily been engaged in following an unrivaled U.S. leadership, or "unipolar hegemony." This notion of unipolarity was strongly validated when the United States led a forceful alliance against Iraq during the Gulf War in 1991.

However, other international analysts claim that in this theory, American dominance is grossly overstated and that, in fact, the world is much more "multipolar" in nature. A multipolar global order relies on international interdependence, in which each region finds its own optimal power structure. In a multipolar world, power—whether military, economic, or political—varies from nation to nation, and each uses its strength to fight for survival and dominance.

Joseph Nye, a prominent political scientist and theorist, brought forth yet another theory—the idea of "multilateral interdependence," in which the world power structure can be compared to a three-layer cake. The top military layer is mainly unipolar (since not many states can rival the military might of the United States); the middle economic layer is tripolar (consisting primarily of the strong U.S., Western European, and Japanese economies); and the bottom layer is made up of transnational interdependence among a number of states. As the idea of interdependence grows, states realize that cooperation is the essential ingredient to realize their respective policies, especially in the realm of national security.

For the United States, this notion is most apparent in the country's participation in a multitude of international organizations and regional alliances under the broad umbrella of "collective security." Collective security is the idea that a bloc (or group) of states sharing common interests ally against any potential aggression or opposition. A threat to one means a threat to all. This is not a recent phenomenon and can be traced back centuries to medieval times. Currently, the United Nations (UN) and the North Atlantic Treaty Organization (NATO) are the primary bodies that actively engage in collective security. Bilateral military alliances (between the United States and one other country) or multilateral alliances (between several countries) are other avenues for ensuring national security.

CHANGING GLOBAL DYNAMICS: THE UNITED STATES AS A GLOBAL LEADER

To understand national security, it is necessary to see a country's policies within the context of its history, ideology, and existing political governance. As societies and states continue to evolve, so do the relationships between these entities. Each passing generation bears witness to its own set of global conflicts, political alliances, and other shifts in interstate dynamics.

The world today is very different from what it was a few decades ago. For instance, until 1991 a significant part of the globe was involved in the so-called Cold War, which was fought along ideological lines. Countries found themselves allying with either the Soviet or U.S.-led blocs.

The twentieth century witnessed a host of political phenomena, such as the fall of colonialism, the rise of capitalistic economies, the growth of industry, growing concern for human rights, and the spread of nuclear weapons. Countries like the United States constantly find themselves adapting their policies as shifts in global power occur. Today, the United States finds itself a leading superpower both in economic and military might. The economic, social, cultural, and military trends that accompany globalization impel the United States to adopt policies that optimize its position as a global leader. This global presence and prominence can lead to conflicts and make the United States a target.

UNDERSTANDING THE THREAT

Self-preservation is sought by all states, and ultimately it is up to each country to use its security infrastructure to ensure its own survival. Though the details have varied, the goals of American national security have always been to protect the sovereignty of the United States and to protect U.S. interests. The country's political leadership (both executive and legislative), military, and intelligence community are all primary actors involved in establishing and executing a sound national security policy. These actors employ tools such as diplomacy, military intervention, trade agreements, and alliances to carry out the U.S. national security agenda.

Besides the currently pressing dilemma of dealing with international terrorist networks and strengthening U.S. homeland security, some other international concerns that have occupied America's national security agenda for at least the past decade include:

- The United States depends on oil and gas imports from the Persian Gulf. The erratic prices for such imports, combined with declining U.S. oil production, are problematic for the United States. In addition, U.S. and UN sanctions against Iran and Iraq do not allow them to increase their oil output, and lead to hostility against those imposing the sanctions.

- Iraq's weapons of mass destruction (WMD) programs, which were supposed to have ended after the Persian Gulf War, are almost certainly continuing.

- There are significant political and ideological differences between the United States and other countries, including U.S. allies, in the Middle East as well as Southeast Asia.

- The United States is worried by the ongoing Arab-Israeli conflict and rising anti-U.S. extremism around the world.

- WMD and small arms threaten to proliferate worldwide.

- The war against drugs drains millions of dollars each year and commits national resources and personnel to a fight that may have no imminent conclusion.

- There exist various "transition states" and "states of concern," two types of geopolitical entities that may be either potential allies or may work overtly or covertly to undermine U.S. national security. Transition states and states of concern are explained in greater detail in the next two sections.

Transition States

During the Cold War, two of the main national security threats to the United States were the two most powerful Communist nations—the Soviet Union and China. The United States and these two countries squared off, faced each other down, and tried to use deterrence to avoid war. To the United States, the smaller Communist nations, such as Cuba and North Korea, were important, but secondary, threats.

In the years following the demise of the Soviet Union in 1991 and the end of the Cold War, U.S. fear of the spread of Communism waned, but Communist nations like China continued to pose a threat in terms of economic and military competition. In addition, despite the weakening of the former Soviet Union as a global superpower, the confederation of states that emerged from the fractured superpower was still problematic in many ways. Such countries are considered "transition states."

A transition state is a country that is slowly becoming more like a traditional Western capitalist society. Eastern European countries and, more recently, certain Middle Eastern and Asian states such as China and India would fall into this category. To encourage countries to make the transition to democracy, the United States promotes a) the growth of market democracy in the country; and b) increases in the country's per capita gross domestic product (GDP), or the total value of the goods and services it produces. This policy often involves the United States in actions in parts of the world that are unstable. Often, American involvement in such countries is perceived by certain groups to be evidence of increasing Western interference with their cultures and ways of life.

RUSSIA, CHINA, AND INDIA. The phenomenon of transnationalism, or ties that go beyond national boundaries, is relatively new and is gaining significance in world politics. With each of the three transition states on the Eurasian landmass—Russia, China, and India—the

TABLE 1.1

Population and gross national product (GNP) in China, India, and Russia

	Population (in millions)	GNP (billions of U.S. dollars)	GNP per capita (U.S. dollars)
China	1,232.7	$639	$518
India	983.4	385	392
Russia	146.6	1,100	7,483

SOURCE: Hans Binnendijk, et al., eds., "Population and Gross National Product in China, India and Russia," in *Strategic Assessment 1999: Priorities for a Turbulent World,* National Defense University, Institute for National Strategic Studies, Washington, DC, 1999. Data from the International Institute for Strategic Studies

United States knows that it faces potential opportunity in terms of economics and strategic alliances. However, the United States also wants to maintain a balance of power and prevent the regional dominance, or hegemony, of any one of these countries. Following its established national security policy guidelines, America strives to counter the proliferation of conventional weapons and WMD in these countries and their export from them.

Russia, China, and India are not strong U.S. allies like some Western European nations, and their transition to free-market economies is far from complete. Among these transition states, China has the best chance to fulfill the promise of its potential. A 1999 comparison of the population and Gross National Product (GNP) of China, India, and Russia shows Russian per capita GNP more than 14 times China's and more than 19 times India's. (See Table 1.1.) Still, China has tripled its GNP since launching reforms in 1979, and from 1979 through 1999 it had the world's fastest-growing economy.

With its population of almost 1.5 billion people, and an expanding role in Asia, China is a rising power. The Soviet Union's collapse permitted China to reduce its forces in the north and devote greater military resources to the south and southeast. China has also expanded its participation in the Association of Southeast Asian Nations (ASEAN) and the ASEAN Regional Forum. In the late 1990s, its economic success allowed it to provide a $1 billion loan to Thailand through the International Monetary Fund. It is one of the four powers (along with North Korea, South Korea, and the United States) negotiating the future of the Korean peninsula.

China is also becoming more assertive regionally. It claims the Senakaku Islands, which Japan also claims, and the Spratly Islands in the South China Sea, which are also claimed by the Philippines, Vietnam, Brunei, Malaysia, and Taiwan. To reinforce the latter claim, China seized Mischief Reef in the Spratlys in 1995. In May 1996 China formally expanded its claimed sea area from 370,000 to 3,000,000 square kilometers.

Perhaps most importantly, China claims that the island of Taiwan is an inalienable part of China, since it was considered Chinese territory until the end of WWII, when military leader Chiang Kai-shek defected to the island to form a separate non-Communist state. Taiwan, which is richer, more confident, and more democratic than China, but much smaller, challenges the assertion that it should be considered part of mainland China.

The world got a glimpse of China's ambitions in 1996, when it fired ballistic missiles into the waters around Taiwan. The Taiwan issue is a precarious subject in Sino-American relations. Officially, the United States calls for a "one-China" policy, which recognizes the rights of the mainland government, based in the capital of Beijing. However, the United States also stated that it will defend Taiwan at all costs if the island nation is militarily forced to unify with mainland China. For American policymakers, the ultimate goal is to seek a peaceful reunification between the two countries.

In the late 1990s the administration of President Bill Clinton called for a strategy of "engagement" in U.S.-China relations that would reflect the principles of "taming the dragon." At that time, President Clinton stated that "bringing China into the community of nations, rather than trying to shut it out, is plainly the best way to advance both our interests and our values."

Russia, China, and India remain mainstays in Asia in terms of conventional and nuclear weapons status. Russia is India's leading arms supplier, though Britain, France, Germany, and Israel have contributed to the development of its weapons arsenal as well. India has been engaged in a dispute with its neighbor, Pakistan, over the region of Kashmir since the two countries split in 1948. Each nation blames the other country for the consequent arms buildup, which includes nuclear weapons. Both countries have tested nuclear weapons, creating further tensions and animosity. Pakistan continues to engage in significant weapons transactions with China and North Korea.

India exercises regional influence over such surrounding states as Bangladesh, Sri Lanka, Nepal, and Bhutan. China, however, like Pakistan, presents a serious obstacle to India and is a serious strategic rival. In late 1996 Chinese president Jiang Zemin's visit to India led to a significant thaw in India-China relations. The two sides agreed to set aside border disputes, but the relationship between the two countries continues to be one of serious rivalry over regional influence, global status, energy access, foreign investment, and trade. Senior Indian officials identified China, not Pakistan, as the key reason for their May 1998 nuclear tests.

Relations between India and China are of strategic concern to the United States, since both countries are now nuclear weapons states and both possess ambitions to regional hegemony. Good relations between India and China are perceived as necessary by the United States in order to maintain regional stability for both economic and political purposes.

All three transition states—Russia, India, and China—have the military potential to greatly upset their regions of the world. In Eurasia, Russia has only 1.2 million troops, representing a decaying military, and its offensive forces no longer menace Europe, but it is still far stronger than its immediate neighbors. In South Asia, India has twice as many troops as its rival, Pakistan, but both are equipped with nuclear weapons, and the two countries' animosity over disputed Kashmir is intensifying.

In any case, every security problem that involves the United States in and around Eurasia will be made much more manageable by cooperation with and among these states. The United States cannot dictate policies to sovereign nations, but can offer diplomatic channels and mediation opportunities to try to enhance the countries' transitions to free-market economies and democratic societies.

States of Concern

States of concern (also known as "rogue states") are a group of countries perceived as dangerous by and to the United States. States such as Iran, Iraq, North Korea, Libya, Syria, Sudan, and Cuba, which have demonstrated anti-American sentiment and maintain a hostile relationship with the United States, fall under this category. The U.S. Department of State claims that these countries have established links to terrorist networks. The Clinton administration defined such states as "recalcitrant and outlaw states that not only choose to remain outside the family of democracies, but also that assault democratic values" (*Strategic Assessment 1999: Priorities for a Turbulent World,* Institute for National Strategic Studies, National Defense University, Washington, D.C.). This definition is debatable, given its Western bias, but it currently applies to countries that threaten U.S. interests by unconventional and violent means. It is generally agreed that such states can swiftly destabilize their respective regions and other regimes in surrounding areas, and also threaten vital U.S. interests and national security.

Many states of concern are ruled by long-standing leaders, since they are not democratically elected.

- Cuba's leader, Fidel Castro, seized power in 1959 and has led the Communist-controlled government ever since.

- Communist leader Kim Jong-Il appears to have consolidated power in North Korea after the death of his father, Kim Il Sung (who led the country from 1948 until his death in 1994).

- Libya's Muammar Qadhafi, who took control in a military coup in 1969, does not face any organized opposition, nor is there a more moderate leadership capable of replacing him.

- Syria's leader, Bashar al-Assad, inherited the reins of control of the country after his father, President Hafez al-Assad, who had ruled for 30 years, died in 2000.

- Iraq's Saddam Hussein came to power as president in 1979. He survived the Gulf War of 1991 and the more than a decade of UN sanctions that followed, and still continues to be a problem for the United States.

- Iran's Muslim cleric leadership, which came to power in the Islamic Revolution of 1979, remains in power, with its current chief of state (supreme leader), Ayatollah Ali Khamenei, at the helm since 1989. Though the more liberal government of Iran's elected president, Mohammad Khatami, has made overtures toward reform and has been seeking more democracy in the Islamic republic, Khamenei and his allies have opposed many of the changes.

These states seek to gain military strength to support their regimes by buying weapons and materials from sympathetic states manufacturing conventional weaponry or WMD. This makes U.S. efforts to isolate such countries by utilizing sanctions on weapons and other imports and exports ineffectual. Some transition states, as well as some of America's closest allies, do not support U.S. policies like sanctions to isolate states of concern. For example, most of America's European allies reject U.S. efforts to punish companies doing business with Cuba, Libya, or Iran. France's oil consortium openly challenged such U.S. sanctions by investing in Iranian oil fields, and Canadian companies regularly invest in Cuban businesses. Other countries continue to sell weapons to states considered "rogues" by the United States.

States of concern to the United States may alter the regional status quo by violence, if necessary. Both Iran and Iraq aspire to control the Persian Gulf region, with Iraq having attacked both Iran and Kuwait in the last few decades. North Korea seeks control of the Korean peninsula, which is also claimed by South Korea. Syria seeks to intimidate Israel and to control its sector of the Middle East. All such states of concern may threaten their neighbors, who may be U.S. allies, or control local resources, such as petroleum, that are of vital interest to the West.

NATIONAL SECURITY POLICYMAKERS

As new conflicts emerge and geostrategic power shifts occur worldwide, the shape of the post-Cold War world is still not quite clear-cut, and as a result, America's role within this new world is also evolving. Being positioned as a global leader, the United States finds itself revisiting its fundamental values and resetting its national interest agenda accordingly. Within the structure of the U.S. government, there are those entrusted with protecting U.S. citizens from acts of war, terrorism, and other types of violence. Some of the most important follow.

TABLE 1.2

National Security Council, January 2003

Core Members

President	George W. Bush
Vice-President	Richard Cheney
Secretary of State	Colin Powell
Secretary of the Treasury	(Vacant)
Secretary of Defense	Donald Rumsfeld
Assistant to the President on National Security Affairs	Condoleezza Rice
Director of Central Intelligence	George J. Tenet
Chairman of the Joint Chiefs of Staff	General Richard B. Myers

Other Members

Chief of Staff	Andrew H. Card, Jr.
Counsel to the President	Albert Gonzales
Attorney General	John Ashcroft

SOURCE: Created by Information Plus staff from data published on the White House's web site (http://www.whitehouse.gov)

The President

The president is the highest executive leader of the United States. All decisions regarding national security reside within his office.

The National Security Council (NSC)

Established by the National Security Act of 1947 (and later amended by the National Security Act Amendments of 1949), the National Security Council (NSC) is a part of the Executive Office of the President. Its primary function is to assist the president on all matters pertaining to foreign policy and national security. The NSC is headed by the president and its regular participants include the vice president, secretary of state, secretary of the treasury, secretary of defense, assistant to the president for national security affairs, the chairman of the Joint Chiefs of Staff, and the director of central intelligence. (See Table 1.2.) Other key personnel, such as the president's chief of staff, counsel to the president, attorney general, and the assistant to the president for economic policy, are also invited to attend NSC meetings when necessary.

The Intelligence Infrastructure

Headed by the director of central intelligence (DCI), the U.S. intelligence infrastructure includes the Central Intelligence Agency, Defense Intelligence Agency, National Security Agency, Army Intelligence, Navy Intelligence, Air Force Intelligence, Marine Corps Intelligence, National Imagery and Mapping Agency, National Reconnaissance Office, Federal Bureau of Investigation, Department of the Treasury (including the Secret Service and the Bureau of Alcohol, Tobacco, and Firearms), Department of Energy, and Department of State. (See Figure 1.2.) The main goal of this entity is to keep a finger on the national threat-level pulse for both immediate and long-term concerns. The DCI is aided by another group, called the National Intelligence Council, which is

FIGURE 1.2

The intelligence community

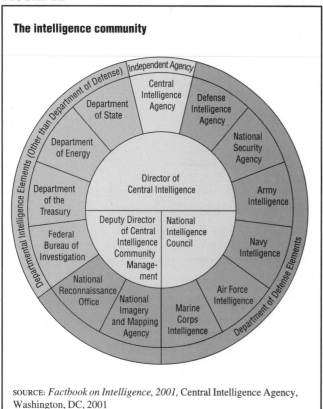

SOURCE: *Factbook on Intelligence, 2001,* Central Intelligence Agency, Washington, DC, 2001

composed of government intelligence officers as well as members of the public (academia or nonprofit organizations) and private sectors.

The Military

The U.S. Air Force, Army, Coast Guard, Marine Corps, and Navy all play an integral role in safeguarding the country's national security. The armed forces are also called in to enforce or defend U.S. security policies when needed.

The Legislative Assemblies

The U.S. House of Representatives and Senate, which, combined, make up the Congress, are crucial to any national security policy adopted by the country. The U.S. Constitution does not assign the executive branch supreme authority—it must have the support of its legislature. All laws and resolutions must be passed through both houses of Congress before the president can act upon them. Various committees within Congress (such as the Committee on International Relations and the Subcommittee on Intelligence) also serve as important overseers of policies related to national security and international affairs.

CHAPTER 2

THE THREAT OF CONVENTIONAL WEAPONS

Weapons are an integral part of any military, especially since the evolution of the nation-state (a political designation containing a relatively homogenous population or people with a feeling of common nationality). Today conventional weapons are accurate and deadly enough to destroy almost all types of military targets, including buried command centers, hardened aircraft shelters, and tanks and other armored vehicles. Challenging and combating the proliferation of weapons that can be used against the United States and its allies is a top priority on the national security agenda.

Weapons proliferation involves both the spread of arms across national borders and the buildup of states' arsenals. An increase in weapons sales and production is not always associated with wars or other conflicts. Factors such as power, prestige, ideology, and perceived threats can be significant influences on a state's decision to buy, sell, or produce weapons. Oftentimes companies and states end up increasing their weapons production and export levels because of political and economic factors or the need to stay ahead of the technological innovation curve.

Both conventional arms and weapons of mass destruction (WMD) pose their own set of unique problems in the realm of weaponry. Conventional weapons include all types of armaments that do not fall under the WMD category. Small arms, machine guns, grenades, landmines, armored vehicles, radar equipment, aircraft, submarines, and ships are all included in the conventional arms discussion. Key players in arms trafficking are individuals, transnational groups (which may include terrorists, organized crime, religious groups, drug traffickers, multinational businesses, or others), defense contractors, and governments themselves. Trade in surplus weapons is a significant source of revenue for several states, including the United States.

Several factors have played a role in conventional weapons proliferation over the past few years. The dissolution of the Soviet Union introduced several weapons systems no longer needed by the newly independent states, also known as "states of the former Soviet Union." Iraqi aggression against Kuwait in 1990 made several Persian Gulf states increasingly insecure about the state of their national security. Technological innovation in most developed countries has created a rapid turnover period between a weapon's development and its replacement by a newer system, thereby creating an increasing military surplus that needs to be eliminated.

WEAPONS SALES

Though international transfers of major conventional weapons have been generally in decline since 1987, a healthy trade in such weapons continues, and some recent increases have occurred. From 1987 until 1995 there was a significant general decrease, followed by a slight increase from 1996 to 1997. In 1998 the decline began again, with a sharp fall in 2000, yet the total rose slightly in 2001. (See Figure 2.1.)

Table 2.1 and Table 2.2 show the export and import of major conventional weapons by selected regions and organizations. The world totals in both the export and import of arms have decreased from 1992 to 2001. For example, Table 2.1 shows a decrease of almost two-thirds in the amount of arms exported by North America during this time. Countries of the North Atlantic Treaty Organization (NATO) also showed a sharp decline, from $15.7 billion worth of weapons exported in 1992 to less than $9 billion in 2001. Table 2.2 shows a high of over $1 billion worth of weapons imported into North America in 1994, and a low of $139 million in 1998, a figure that more than quadrupled (to $584 million) by 2001. In 2000, 69 percent of all arms sales were headed toward developing countries.

Trends and Players

In previous decades, the Cold War saw the increased export of arms from the U.S. and Soviet blocs to countries

FIGURE 2.1

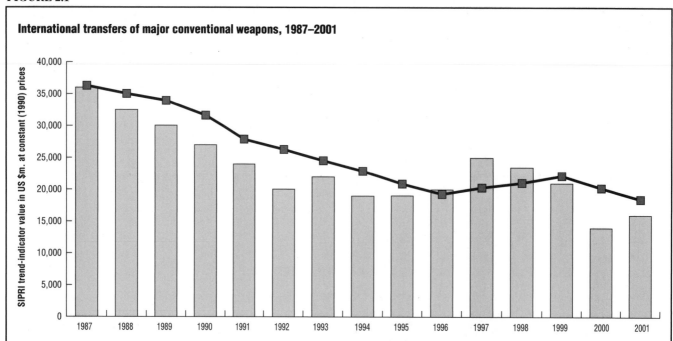

International transfers of major conventional weapons, 1987–2001

Note: The histogram shows annual totals and the curve denotes the five-year moving average. Five-year averages are plotted at the last year of each five-year period.

The SIPRI data on arms transfers refer to actual deliveries of major conventional weapons. To permit comparison between the data on such deliveries of different weapons and identification of general trends, SIPRI uses a *trend-indicator value*. The SIPRI values are only an indicator of the volume of international arms transfers and not of the actual financial values of such transfers. Thus they are not comparable to economic statistics such as gross domestic product or export/import figures.

SOURCE: "The trend in international transfers of major conventional weapons, 1987–2001," in *SIPRI Yearbook 2002,* Stockholm International Peace Research Institute, Stockholm, Sweden, June 2002. Reprinted by permission.

around the world to help maintain regional strongholds and, thereby, the balance of power. Both sides also rushed to ship weapons to their Third World allies to support various "national movements" or to suppress insurgent (rebel) activities. Regional hotspots like Iran/Iraq and Afghanistan proved valuable markets for arms sales. Unfortunately, these weapons were often used by corrupt regimes to remove a specific ethnic group or to perpetrate other human rights violations. Several developing countries spent millions of dollars acquiring weapons and weapons systems, that often were purchased at the expense of diverting resources from critical social programs.

The end of the Cold War somewhat disrupted the worldwide arms flow, but did not bring an end to global hostilities. Conflicts in the Balkans and Africa, as well as intrastate and interstate tensions in the newly independent states, continued to demand the inflow of weapons. Although the disintegration of the Soviet Union put a temporary halt to arms sales, the immediate need for hard currency in the newly independent states, as well as the abundance of Soviet-made weapons and weapons systems, forced them onto the arms market.

The current global market sees an interesting pattern of buyers and sellers that is quite different from traditional Cold War sales. Key Western allies, such as Turkey and the

United Arab Emirates (UAE), have turned to the newly independent states for certain weapons systems, as have China and Iran. Russia aggressively marketed its defense equipment in order to raise funds to help stabilize its fledgling economy and finance its oil sector. Despite Russia's internal political upheavals and problems within the military, certain countries such as Kuwait, India, the UAE, and Malaysia still view it as a strong military supplier. Among its advanced weaponry, Russia sold T-72 tanks to Syria and Su-27 fighter jets and surface-to-air missiles to China, much to the displeasure of the American government.

The U.S. Role

U.S. ARMS EXPORTS. Western arms sales not only go to developing countries but also flow into key U.S. allies such as Israel, Taiwan, certain Persian Gulf states, and NATO countries. Frequently U.S. military assistance programs to countries such as Pakistan and Israel are used by these countries to finance the purchase of American military equipment. These high-quality, American-made weapons, though sold to U.S. allies, can eventually find their way into various states of concern and into the hands of dangerous transnational groups (terrorists and organized crime) after the initial exchange. U.S. armed forces are accustomed to using these weapons, not facing them in the hands of opposing armed forces. This is a source of concern to defense planners.

TABLE 2.1

Volume of exports of major conventional weapons, 1992–2001

Figures are SIPRI trend-indicator values expressed in US $m. at constant (1990) prices. Regional and group figures include transfers between countries/non-state actors in the same region or organization, unless otherwise noted. Figures may not add up because of the conventions of rounding.

	1992	1993	1994	1995	1996	1997	1998	1999	2000	2001
World total	20,216	21,868	19,045	19,272	20,291	24,832	23,325	21,179	15,165	16,231
Intl organizations	–	–	–	–	–	–	–	–	–	–
Africa	103	63	19	18	36	12	28	17	23	20
Sub-Saharan	103	63	11	18	36	9	28	17	23	20
Americas	12,363	11,891	9,726	9,634	9,425	11,468	13,077	10,088	6,168	4,771
North	12,215	11,827	9,684	9,586	9,364	11,440	13,061	10,087	6,163	4,714
Central	86	23	–	5	–	–	–	–	–	–
South	62	41	43	43	61	28	17	1	4	58
Asia	861	1,395	835	1,042	719	449	380	440	201	768
Central	–	–	–	85	12	..	2	..	16	9
North-East	852	1 370	801	925	707	360	336	192	166	738
South-East	8	22	31	30	–	88	42	68	1	20
South	..	3	3	2	–	–	–	–	19	1
Europe	6,764	8,275	8,160	8,373	9,784	12,227	9,583	10,181	8,445	10,411
Middle East	116	216	223	164	232	328	252	150	279	252
Oceania	8	28	24	20	14	330	3	298	–	–
Rebel groups	1	–	–	–	–	–	–	–	–	–
ASEAN	8	22	31	30	–	88	42	68	1	20
EU	3,430	4,270	5,584	4,381	5,627	7,709	6,759	4,688	3,822	4,310
EU to non-EU	2,455	3,192	4,342	3,548	4,981	6,851	5,635	3,922	3,258	3,599
CIS	2,530	3,176	1,569	3,477	3,678	4,225	2,709	5,168	4,351	5,755
CIS Europe	2,530	3,176	1,569	3,392	3,667	4,225	2,707	4,988	4,336	5,747
Framework	3,313	3,926	4,944	3,717	5,053	7,015	6,157	4,308	3,589	3,942
Framework to non-Framework	3,142	3,810	4,599	3,381	4,845	6,648	5,699	3,967	3,274	3,770
NATO	15,650	16,195	15,454	13,811	14,867	19,119	19,693	14,666	9,744	8,631
NATO Europe	3,436	4,370	5,770	4,224	5,502	7,680	6,633	4,711	3,686	4,055
OECD	16,145	16,492	15,706	14,131	15,314	19,690	19,913	15,231	10,182	9,462
OSCE/CSCE	18,979	20,102	17,844	18,043	19,160	23,668	22,649	20,491	14,645	15,136
P5	16,493	17,719	13,227	14,930	16,222	29,841	19,487	16,487	11,880	12,542
Wassenaar	18,746	20,174	17,783	17,927	19,024	23,311	22,623	20,062	14,271	14,943

ASEAN = Association of South-East Asian Nations
EU = European Union
CIS = Commonwealth of Independent States
Framework = Framework Agreement Concerning Measures to Facilitate the Restructuring and Operation of the European Defense Industry
NATO = North Atlantic Treaty Organization
OECD = Organisation for Economic Co-operation and Development
OSCE/CSCE = Organisation for Security and Co-operation in Europe/Conference on Security and Co-operation in Europe
P5 = 5 Permanent members of the UN Security Council
Wassenaar = Wassenaar Arrangement

SOURCE: "Table 8B.2. Volume of exports of major conventional weapons," in *SIPRI Yearbook 2002*, Stockholm International Peace Research Institute, Stockholm, Sweden, June 2002. Reprinted by permission.

Despite U.S. concern about American-made weapons being used against U.S. troops, the United States was the world's largest weapons supplier during the late 1990s. (See Table 2.3.) According to the Stockholm International Peace Research Institute, from 1997 to 2001 the United States sold $44.8 billion worth of major conventional weapons to other countries. (See Table 2.4.) Still, U.S. arms exporting has markedly decreased since 1997, falling from $11.3 billion in 1997 to $4.6 billion in 2001. This decrease led to the United States being ranked second to Russia in 2001.

In a report entitled "U.S. Policy on Small/Light Arms Export" prepared by Lora Lumpe of the Federation of American Scientists for the Academy of Arts and Sciences Conference on Controlling Small Arms in Washington, D.C. on December 11-12, 1997, five primary channels through which arms leave the United States were identified:

1) Foreign military sales (FMS), which are negotiated at a state level between governments

2) Excess defense weapons under the Foreign Assistance Act

3) Direct industry sales

4) Covert government operations

5) Illegal markets

According to the Congressional Research Service's report *Conventional Arms Transfers to Developing Nations*,

TABLE 2.2

Volume of imports of major conventional weapons, 1992–2001

Figures are SIPRI trend-indicator values expressed in US $m. at constant (1990) prices. Regional and group figures include transfers between countries/non-state actors in the same region or organization, unless otherwise noted. Figures may not add up because of the conventions of rounding.

	1992	1993	1994	1995	1996	1997	1998	1999	2000	2001
World total	20,216	21,868	19,045	19,272	20,291	24,832	23,325	21,179	15,165	16,231
Intl organizations	–	10	29	11	–	–	50	8	51	22
Africa	386	322	565	553	468	596	787	1,164	736	807
Sub-Saharan	310	196	259	122	256	387	669	668	437	425
Americas	1,082	1,242	1,867	1,401	1,524	2,121	962	1,027	1,330	1,824
North	537	721	1,031	514	473	649	139	143	517	584
Central	17	158	121	50	81	195	266	39	257	14
South	529	363	715	837	969	1,277	557	844	557	1,226
Asia	5,251	5,678	5,403	8,049	8,047	11,064	8,912	9,252	5,336	6,689
Central	–	–	24	99	170	163	–	62	113	36
North-East	3,809	3,602	2,811	4,855	5,261	7,632	6,637	5,799	3,261	4,320
South-East	271	780	1,266	1,720	1,153	1,114	1,068	1,294	778	213
South	1,172	1,294	1,304	1,376	1,462	2,154	1,208	2,096	1,270	2,053
Europe	6,325	5,175	4,462	3,013	3,409	3,802	4,570	3,988	3,710	3,976
Middle East	6,843	9,031	6,426	6,109	6,699	6,888	7,916	5,079	3,680	2,156
Oceania	316	392	291	129	141	359	123	654	324	747
Rebel groups	1	1	148	2	7	1	–	–	14	68
ASEAN	614	669	1,919	2,368	1,865	2,024	1,299	1,613	869	449
CIS	106	62	360	154	273	171	59	127	122	115
CIS Europe	106	62	337	54	103	8	59	65	9	80
EU	4,976	2,989	3,184	2,183	2,155	2,847	3,728	2,773	3,169	3,246
EU from non-EU	4,119	2,068	1,976	1,346	1,508	1,988	2,603	2,005	2,605	2,525
NATO	7,170	5,822	5,535	3,834	3,347	3,917	4,778	3,247	4,019	4,218
NATO Europe	6,634	5,102	4,506	3,319	2,874	3,268	4,639	5,348	3,159	3,737
GCC	2,423	3,844	1,765	2,268	3,975	4,639	3,827	1,842	890	533
OECD	9,566	8,178	7,078	5,148	6,541	6,925	8,827	7,693	6,139	5,822
OSCE/CSCE	8,202	7,844	6,791	4,948	5,091	5,498	6,472	5,348	5,024	5,038
P5	2,948	1,538	882	960	1,663	1,322	865	1,795	2,778	4,461
Wassenaar	10,352	9,921	7,938	7,115	6,827	6,854	8,749	7,900	6,297	6,080

Note: Table shows the volume of arms transfers for different geographical regions and subregions, selected groups of countries, rebel groups and international organizations. Countries/rebel groups can belong to only one region. Since many countries are included in more than one group or organization, totals cannot be derived from these figures. Countries are included in the values for the different international organizations from the year of joining.

SOURCE: "Table 8B.1. Volume of imports of major conventional weapons," in *SIPRI Yearbook 2002*, Stockholm International Peace Research Institute, Stockholm, Sweden, June 2002. Reproduced by permission.

TABLE 2.3

Arms deliveries to the world by supplier, 1993–2000

(expressed as % of total, by year)

	1993	1994	1995	1996	1997	1998	1999	2000
U.S.	47.16%	45.32%	44.43%	41.37%	39.14%	45.43%	49.09%	48.28%
Russia	10.57%	5.77%	9.72%	8.65%	6.25%	6.06%	8.49%	11.91%
France	4.66%	4.42%	7.78%	10.05%	15.15%	18.74%	8.49%	5.10%
United Kingdom	14.30%	17.66%	14.73%	18.15%	16.36%	10.47%	13.96%	17.35%
China	3.73%	2.04%	1.94%	1.68%	2.41%	1.65%	0.82%	1.70%
Germany	5.28%	5.77%	5.56%	5.30%	2.89%	3.86%	5.20%	2.72%
Italy	1.24%	0.68%	0.56%	0.28%	1.68%	0.55%	0.82%	1.02%
All Other European	7.15%	11.55%	9.72%	9.49%	10.58%	8.82%	7.39%	6.81%
All Others	5.91%	6.79%	5.56%	5.03%	5.53%	4.41%	5.75%	5.10%
Major West European	25.49%	28.53%	28.62%	33.78%	36.08%	33.63%	28.47%	26.20%
TOTAL	100%	100%	100%	100%	100%	100%	100%	100%

SOURCE: "Arms Deliveries to the World, by Supplier 1993–2000," in *Conventional Arms Transfers to Developing Nations, 1993–2000,* Council for a Livable World, Arms Trade Oversight Project, Washington, DC, August 2001

TABLE 2.4

Countries supplying major conventional weapons to other countries, 1997–2001

The list includes all countries/non-state actors with imports of major conventional weapons in the period 1997–2001. Ranking is according to the 1997–2001 aggregate exports. Figures are trend-indicator values expressed in US $m. at constant (1990) prices. Figures may not add up because of the conventions of rounding.

Rank order 1997–2001	Rank order 1996–2000	Supplier	1997	1998	1999	2000	2001	1997–2001
1	1	USA	11,277	12,930	9,957	6,095	4,562	44,821
2	2	Russia	2,837	1,885	3,874	3,779	4,979	17,354
3	3	France	2,963	3,340	1,474	743	1,288	9,808
4	4	UK	2,441	1,040	990	1,103	1,125	6,699
5	5	Germany (FRG)	542	1,147	1,261	1,196	675	4,821
6	6	Ukraine	671	765	568	193	430	2,627
7	7	Netherlands	548	545	340	204	225	1,862
8	8	Italy	368	345	404	196	358	1,671
9	9	China	323	292	192	160	588	1,555
10	10	Belarus	401	57	474	253	333	1,518
11	13	Sweden	83	112	146	296	486	1,123
12	11	Israel	247	168	98	259	203	975
13	12	Spain	619	167	29	51	4	870
14	14	Canada	163	131	130	68	152	644
15	15	Australia	317	3	298	0	0	618
16	16	Slovakia	81	10	141	83	21	336
17	18	Moldova	316	0	0	3	5	324
18	17	Czech Republic	31	23	65	81	95	295
19	26	Norway	58	2	9	45	156	270
20	21	Bulgaria	4	48	163	4	4	223
21	19	Switzerland	66	31	41	44	36	218
22	30	South Korea	29	31	0	6	150	216
23	20	Belgium	89	23	28	2	72	214
24	22	Kazakhstan	0	2	180	16	9	207
25	23	Georgia	0	0	72	108	0	180
26	24	Poland	20	1	67	26	44	158
27	27	Singapore	78	42	0	1	0	121
28	32	Brazil	28	15	0	0	55	98
29	28	South Africa	9	28	17	22	20	96
30	33	Indonesia	10	0	60	0	20	90
31	29	Greece	52	21	1	0	11	85
32	31	Kuwait	0	82	0	0	0	82
33	41	Austria	5	12	2	2	61	82
34	25	Unknown*	16	1	2	52	8	79
35	34	Turkey	0	3	43	21	2	69
36	35	Qatar	37	0	9	0	0	46
37	63	Lebanon	0	0	0	0	45	45
38	42	Finland	1	8	13	9	3	34
39	37	UAE	33	0	0	0	0	33
40	39	Romania	8	2	19	3	0	32
41	43	Hungary	24	0	0	0	0	24
42	44	Denmark	0	0	0	18	0	18
43	45	India	0	0	0	16	1	17
44	48	New Zealand	13	0	0	0	0	13
45	40	North Korea	0	13	0	0	0	13
46	50	Malaysia	0	0	8	0	0	8
47	51	Taiwan	5	0	0	0	0	5
48	52	Jordan	5	0	0	0	0	5
49	49	Egypt	5	0	0	0	0	5
50	59	Argentina	0	0	0	2	3	5
51	38	Chile	0	2	1	1	0	4
52	53	Pakistan	0	0	0	3	0	3
53	54	Libya	3	0	0	0	0	3
54	46	Japan	3	0	0	0	0	3
55	55	Yugoslavia	2	0	0	0	0	2
56	58	Croatia	0	0	0	2	0	2
57	65	Bahrain	0	0	0	0	2	2
58	60	Uruguay	0	0	0	1	0	1
59	61	Malawi	0	0	0	1	0	1
60	57	Iran	1	0	0	0	0	1
61	62	Syria	0	0	0	0	0	0
62	56	Saudi Arabia	0	0	0	0	0	0

TABLE 2.4

Countries supplying major conventional weapons to other countries, 1997–2001 [CONTINUED]

The list includes all countries/non-state actors with imports of major conventional weapons in the period 1997–2001. Ranking is according to the 1997–2001 aggregate exports. Figures are trend-indicator values expressed in US $m. at constant (1990) prices. Figures may not add up because of the conventions of rounding.

Rank order								
1997–2001	1996–2000	Supplier	1997	1998	1999	2000	2001	1997–2001
63	64	Ireland	0	0	0	0	0	0
64	47	Estonia	0	0	0	0	0	0
65	36	Cyprus	0	0	0	0	0	0
		Total	24,832	23,325	21,179	15,165	16,231	100,732

*One or more unknown supplier(s).

Note: – = between 0 and 0.5.
The SIPRI data on arms transfers refer to actual deliveries of major conventional weapons. To permit comparison between the data on such deliveries of different weapons and identification of general trends, SIPRI uses a *trend-indicator value*. The SIPRI values are only an indicator of the volume of international arms transfers and not of the actual financial values of such transfers. Thus they are not comparable to economic statistics such as gross domestic product or export/import figures.

SOURCE: "Table 8A.2. The suppliers of major conventional weapons," in *SIPRI Yearbook 2002*, Stockholm International Peace Research Institute, Stockholm, Sweden, June 2002. Reproduced by permission.

1993–2000, some of the major weapons sales by the United States in 2000 included:

- Sale of 80 F-16 block 60 fighter jets to the UAE (value = $6.432 billion)

- Reconfiguration of 24 AH-64 Apache helicopters (value = $270 million) and the sale of 35 Blackhawk helicopters along with several helicopter engines (value = $340 million) to Israel

- Upgrade of Egyptian AH-64 Apache helicopters (value = $400 million) as well as the sale of Stinger and Avenger missiles and six SPS-48E 3-D land-based radar systems to Egypt

- Sale of 29 multiple-launch rocket systems to South Korea (value = $260 million) along with parts for F-16 C/D fighter planes (value = $190 million)

THE REGULATION AND CONTROL OF U.S. ARMS SALES. U.S. arms sales are technically governed by regulations that forbid sales to certain countries of concern and regimes known to be oppressive. The 1976 Arms Export Control Act (AECA), overseen by the Office of Defense Trade Controls (ODTC) within the Bureau of Political Military Affairs of the U.S. Department of State, is the primary law dealing with U.S. arms sales. AECA mandates that American weapons must only be exported for United Nations (UN) operations, self-defense purposes, and as responses to internal security threats. It also requires the Departments of Defense and State to produce interval reports and obliges Congress to be notified of any significant arms sales. The ODTC is responsible for the International Traffic in Arms Regulations, which contains a list of all munitions acceptable for export. All companies wishing to sell such equipment need to register with the ODTC and obtain the appropriate export license before concluding any sales.

Another important law regulating U.S. arms sales is the 1961 Foreign Assistance Act, which calls for military and other developmental aid to friendly governments. This law bars any sales to oppressive governments and countries adhering to policies contrary to American values and beliefs.

These regulations have not always proved effective, as demonstrated by arms sales to oppressive regimes such as Iraq (during the Iran-Iraq war) and Indonesia. Perhaps the biggest blow to U.S. credibility on its arms export policies, though, was the Iran-Contra affair. In November 1986 officials of the administration of President Ronald Reagan announced that some of the money earned from arms sales to Iran had been redirected to aid the Nicaraguan Contras, an act that violated the existing Boland Amendment ban on aid to Nicaraguan military and paramilitary activities. The arms sales to Iran had been conducted primarily to secure the release of Americans held hostage in the Middle East. High members of the Reagan administration, including President Reagan himself, Vice President George H. W. Bush, National Security Advisor John Poindexter, Secretary of State George Schultz, Secretary of Defense Caspar Weinberger, and Director of Central Intelligence William Casey were aware of the arms sales, but it is not clear how many members of the administration were directly aware that the money was being rerouted to the Contras. The independent investigation that followed embroiled the Reagan administration in a major scandal; National Security Advisors Robert McFarlane, John Poindexter, and Lt. Col. Oliver North resigned as a result.

The U.S. Department of State initiated the Blue Lantern program in 1990 to strengthen U.S. export controls in order to make sure U.S. arms exports do not end up in the wrong hands or abet any illicit supply networks. The primary function of the program is to perform end-use checks, generally conducted by U.S. personnel abroad to ensure the material was not acquired using fraudulent documentation, on all U.S. arms exports. The Blue Lantern program has promoted the responsible sale of weapons to allies and prevented the transfer of dual-use technology to adversaries. (Dual-use items are controlled commodities that have both military and civilian potential uses.)

According to the State Department, in 2001 the ODTC initiated 410 checks, 71 of which were unfavorable. Of the unfavorable transactions, the majority (about 28 percent) were directed to the East Asia Pacific region, followed by the Western Hemisphere (26 percent), Europe (23 percent), Africa (13 percent), and the Near East (10 percent). (See Figure 2.2.) Most of these sales are believed to be aircraft spare parts that were intended for the Chinese and Iranian militaries. In fiscal year (FY) 2001 cooperation between U.S. Customs and the State Department led to the seizure of over 325 commercial arms, worth over $13 million.

ARMS IMPORTS. On the receiving end of arms sales, the United States obtained less than $1 billion worth of arms from 1997 to 2001, ranking number 26 in the world in arms imports. (See Table 2.5.) Taiwan was the largest arms importer, receiving $11.3 billion worth of major conventional weapons from 1997 to 2001. China ranked second with $7.1 billion worth of imports over the same period, followed by Saudi Arabia ($6.7 billion), Turkey ($5 billion), and India ($4.7 billion). While Taiwan's imports drastically decreased from 1997 to 2001, China's import of arms rose significantly during this period (from $541 million to $3.1 billion).

Other Countries

A number of countries are involved in weapons acquisition to either expand or replace military equipment, and there is intense and increasing competition among weapons suppliers. In addition to the United States, France, Russia, China, the United Kingdom, and Germany are also significant players on the world arms market. Russia's weapon sales, for example, have been on the rise for the past few years, up to about $5 billion in 2001. From 1997 through 2001 Russia was the second-largest supplier of weapons in the world, selling $17.4 billion worth during this period. (See Table 2.4.) France, the United Kingdom, and Germany followed with $9.8, $6.7, and $4.8 billion worth of sales, respectively, over the same period.

Though European countries have seen a decline in weapons sales in the past few years, especially in their sales to developing countries, Western European contractors heavily compete with American companies for sales. Additionally, they have historically served as significant suppliers in the conventional arms market to those countries that are not traditional clients of the United States.

FIGURE 2.2

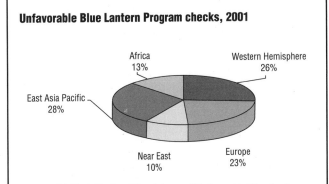

Unfavorable Blue Lantern Program checks, 2001

Africa 13%
Western Hemisphere 26%
East Asia Pacific 28%
Near East 10%
Europe 23%

SOURCE: "Table 1. Regional Breakdown of Unfavorable Blue Lantern Checks in FY 2001," in "End-Use Monitoring of Defense Articles and Defense Services: Commercial Exports," *Congressional Budget Justification Foreign Operations, Fiscal Year 2003*, U.S. Department of State, Washington, DC, April 15, 2002

Russia's increased arms trade is a direct result of the economic and political turmoil Russia has faced since the Soviet breakup. It still continues to supply its past allies and those already familiar with Russian technology, including India, China, and Iran. Post-Soviet conflict also put weapons on the illicit market. In 1992, for example, the Russian ministry of defense claimed that about 25,000 firearms were stolen in the first half of the year alone. The following year, about 450 Russian military personnel were fired and another 3,700 disciplined for violating Russian arms export controls.

In comparison with other states, China entered the arms market somewhat late, in the 1980s. With sales in the vicinity of about $1.6 billion from 1997–2001, China supplies arms to those countries unable to afford newer, more sophisticated technology. It sold antiship missiles to Iran and remains the primary supplier for Pakistan. Its rumored missile technology shipments to Iran and North Korea have raised some concerns within the arms control community.

The Persian Gulf remains one of the most active theaters when it comes to arms sales. Five states surrounding the Gulf (Iran, Iraq, Saudi Arabia, the UAE, and Yemen) and five more in its near vicinity (Egypt, Israel, Libya, Syria, and Turkey) currently possess ballistic missile capabilities and are prime buyers of Western weapons equipment. Along with these missile capabilities, there are several other factors that make this region of particular importance to the West. These include energy resources (there is an abundance of oil and natural gas fields in the region), the Iraqi/Iranian threats (both countries have posed threats to U.S. national security interests through the course of history), and strategic military alliances (Israel, Egypt, and Jordan all serve as important allies in the area). Of late, there have been extensive talks among U.S. and regional policymakers about the implications of deploying

TABLE 2.5

Countries and non-state agents receiving major conventional weapons, 1997–2001

The list includes all countries/non-state actors with imports of major conventional weapons in the period 1997–2001. Ranking is according to the 1997–2001 aggregate imports. Figures are trend-indicator values expressed in US $m. at constant (1990) prices. Figures may not add up because of the conventions of rounding.

Rank order 1997–2001	Rank order 1996–2000	Recipient	1997	1998	1999	2000	2001	1997–2001
1	1	Taiwan	4,863	4,026	1,641	492	375	11,397
2	5	China	541	230	1,500	1,746	3,100	7,117
3	2	Saudi Arabia	2,783	2,507	1,215	69	143	6,717
4	3	Turkey	955	1,767	1,180	684	442	5,028
5	6	India	1,502	551	1,062	531	1,064	4,710
6	7	Greece	820	1,461	573	685	897	4,436
7	4	South Korea	718	941	1,131	740	401	3,931
8	8	Egypt	905	511	530	818	486	3,250
9	9	Japan	575	1,206	1,035	181	206	3,203
10	12	Pakistan	624	588	797	163	759	2,931
11	10	Israel	42	1,296	1,169	283	45	2,835
12	17	UK	74	379	98	882	1,247	2,680
13	13	UAE	678	748	420	278	288	2,412
14	11	Finland	393	558	799	513	10	2,273
15	15	Singapore	159	655	194	520	141	1,669
16	29	Australia	14	109	337	324	687	1,471
17	20	Malaysia	527	37	783	87	20	1,454
18	21	Brazil	449	163	205	40	597	1,454
19	19	Switzerland	388	448	499	27	33	1,395
20	18	Iran	232	287	234	279	335	1,367
21	16	Thailand	830	61	168	83	162	1,304
22	26	Italy	556	10	8	235	428	1,237
23	30	Algeria	35	103	428	175	365	1,106
24	34	Canada	103	21	40	411	470	1,045
25	25	Netherlands	137	259	299	188	153	1,036
26	23	USA	546	119	103	106	114	988
27	24	Norway	198	187	193	286	109	973
28	22	Spain	204	76	318	259	90	947
29	28	Qatar	491	338	97	8	8	942
30	14	Kuwait	438	204	110	133	34	919
31	36	Angola	3	183	350	111	255	902
32	32	Sweden	147	278	165	99	93	782
33	45	Jordan	108	202	47	145	280	782
34	35	New Zealand	322	14	317	0	60	713
35	38	Argentina	88	120	199	184	97	688
36	39	Peru	351	28	114	0	178	671
37	33	Mexico	184	256	33	178	13	664
38	52	Bangladesh	26	0	193	222	180	621
39	44	Denmark	98	171	144	85	116	614
40	54	Colombia	164	99	37	71	222	593
41	31	Chile	122	90	194	169	16	591
42	27	Indonesia	97	95	193	164	38	587
43	40	Myanmar (Burma)	220	203	119	0	0	542
44	37	Viet Nam	101	171	152	8	74	506
45	50	Austria	192	206	48	25	15	486
46	49	Syria	0	20	20	420	0	460
47	48	Germany (FRG)	5	118	136	121	80	460
48	51	France	161	137	94	44	0	436
49	53	Ethiopia	62	194	75	95	0	426
50	42	Bahrain	74	8	0	314	30	426
51	46	Sri Lanka	2	69	44	254	40	409
52	43	Cyprus	113	21	242	2	15	393
53	47	Kazakhstan	163	0	62	113	31	369
54	55	Morocco	135	0	60	124	0	319
55	41	Oman	175	22	0	88	30	315
56	61	Venezuela	32	12	59	82	116	301
57	57	Eritrea	36	180	14	0	60	290
58	60	Belgium	60	67	60	30	33	250
59	62	Yemen	0	0	54	158	33	245
60	64	Romania	25	57	33	17	110	242
61	74	Macedonia	0	7	72	6	126	211
62	59	Poland	0	0	1	135	63	199
63	58	Congo (DRC)	18	0	72	108	0	198
64	63	North Korea	4	2	172	11	2	191
65	56	Hungary	70	31	50	14	14	179
66	82	Georgia	8	18	22	6	80	134
67	69	Philippines	45	51	0	0	13	109

TABLE 2.5

Countries and non-state agents receiving major conventional weapons, 1997–2001 [CONTINUED]

The list includes all countries/non-state actors with imports of major conventional weapons in the period 1997–2001. Ranking is according to the 1997–2001 aggregate imports. Figures are trend-indicator values expressed in US $m. at constant (1990) prices. Figures may not add up because of the conventions of rounding.

Rank order								
1997–2001	1996–2000	Recipient	1997	1998	1999	2000	2001	1997–2001
68	71	Uganda	0	62	39	6	0	107
69	73	Botswana	67	4	2	0	32	105
70	67	Sudan	66	0	36	0	0	102
71	89	Croatia	41	0	0	0	59	100
72	65	Bosnia-Herzegovina	71	3	25	0	0	99
73	70	Ecuador	52	14	20	5	0	91
74	107	Afghanistan/NA[1]	0	0	0	14	68	82
75	75	Belarus	0	41	41	0	0	82
76	66	Tunisia	38	16	9	0	18	81
77	90	Slovenia	8	4	16	0	53	81
78	95	Ireland	0	2	30	0	46	78
79	84	NATO[2]	0	49	0	0	22	71
80	76	Uruguay	19	30	9	4	0	62
81	78	Kenya	61	0	0	0	0	61
82	79	United Nations[2]	0	1	8	51	0	60
83	83	Bahamas	0	0	0	54	0	54
84	86	Czech Republic	5	0	2	18	27	52
85	110	Portugal	0	7	2	2	38	49
86	85	Lithuania	0	18	5	4	19	46
87	87	Rwanda	2	2	26	14	0	44
88	80	Brunei	30	7	5	0	1	43
89	91	Laos	14	20	0	7	0	41
90	77	South Africa	9	0	14	0	17	40
91	93	Estonia	14	2	1	22	0	39
92	97	Zimbabwe	0	1	24	4	7	36
93	117	Namibia	2	7	0	0	25	34
94	88	Nigeria	1	0	0	26	1	28
95	96	Zambia	0	0	0	27	0	27
96	112	Guinea	0	4	0	8	15	27
97	128	Latvia	0	0	4	0	22	26
98	81	Cambodia	22	0	0	0	0	22
99	103	Ghana	4	0	7	1	9	21
100	100	Congo	18	1	2	0	0	21
101	101	Papua New Guinea	20	0	0	0	0	20
102	99	Mauritania	8	3	0	9	0	20
103	92	Lebanon	6	5	4	4	1	20
104	102	Chad	0	7	0	13	0	20
105	113	Unknown[3]	0	3	5	0	9	17
106	105	Cameroon	6	9	0	0	1	16
107	106	Mali	7	3	0	5	0	15
108	104	Dominican Republic	0	0	2	13	0	15
109	108	Trinidad & Tobago	0	2	0	11	1	14
110	109	Sierra Leone	8	0	5	0	0	13
111	111	Panama	12	0	0	0	0	12
112	143	Nepal	0	0	0	0	10	10
113	114	Jamaica	0	5	5	0	0	10
114	115	Cape Verde	0	9	0	1	0	10
115	118	Liberia	0	0	1	8	0	9
116	119	Yugoslavia	8	0	0	0	0	8
117	120	Suriname	0	0	8	0	0	8
118	121	Togo	7	0	0	0	0	7
119	122	Malta	6	0	0	0	0	6
120	68	Bulgaria	0	0	6	0	0	6
121	141	Uzbekistan	0	0	0	0	5	5
122	127	Micronesia	4	0	0	0	0	4
123	124	El Salvador	0	3	0	0	0	3
124	129	Niger	3	0	0	0	0	3
125	130	Azerbaijan	0	0	0	3	0	3
126	131	Albania	0	3	0	0	0	3
127	146	Lesotho	0	0	0	0	2	2
128	72	Armenia	0	0	2	0	0	2
129	132	Lebanon/Hizbollah	1	0	0	0	0	1
130	134	Swaziland	0	0	0	1	0	1
131	135	Northern Cyprus	0	1	0	0	0	1
132	94	Mauritius	1	0	0	0	0	1
133	125	Luxembourg	0	0	1	0	0	1

TABLE 2.5

Countries and non-state agents receiving major conventional weapons, 1997–2001 [CONTINUED]

The list includes all countries/non-state actors with imports of major conventional weapons in the period 1997–2001. Ranking is according to the 1997–2001 aggregate imports. Figures are trend-indicator values expressed in US $m. at constant (1990) prices. Figures may not add up because of the conventions of rounding.

Rank order								
1997–2001	1996–2000	Recipient	1997	1998	1999	2000	2001	1997–2001
134	136	Guatemala	0	1	0	0	0	1
135	148	Djibouti	0	0	0	0	1	1
136	137	Bolivia	0	0	0	1	0	1
137	138	Turkey/PKK[1]	0	0	0	0	0	0
138	139	Sri Lanka/LTTE[1]	0	0	0	0	0	0
139	140	Macedonia/NLA[1]	0	0	0	0	0	0
140	123	Lebanon/SLA[1]	0	0	0	0	0	0
141	142	Tonga	0	0	0	0	0	0
142	98	Slovakia	0	0	0	0	0	0
143	133	Paraguay	0	0	0	0	0	0
144	126	Palau	0	0	0	0	0	0
145	116	Palestinian AA[4]	0	0	0	0	0	0
146	144	Mozambique	0	0	0	0	0	0
147	145	Maldives	0	0	0	0	0	0
148	147	Cote d'Ivoire	0	0	0	0	0	0
149	149	Belize	0	0	0	0	0	0
		Total	**24,832**	**23,325**	**21,179**	**15,165**	**16,231**	**100,732**

[1]Non-state actor: rebel group. SLA = South Lebanese Army; NA = Northern Alliance (UIFSA = United Islamic Front for the Salvation of Afghanistan); NLA = National Liberation Army; PKK = Kurdish Workers' Party; LTTE = Liberation Tigers of Tamil Eelam.
[2]Non-state actor: international organization.
[3]One or more unknown recipient(s).
[4]Non-state actor: Palestine Autonomous Authority.

Note: – = between 0 and 0.5.
The SIPRI data on arms transfers refer to actual deliveries of major conventional weapons. To permit comparison between the data on such deliveries of different weapons and identification of general trends, SIPRI uses a *trend-indicator value*. The SIPRI values are only an indicator of the volume of international arms transfers and not of the actual financial values of such transfers. Thus they are not comparable to economic statistics such as gross domestic product or export/import figures.

SOURCE: "Table 8A.1. The recipients of major conventional weapons," in *SIPRI Yearbook 2002*, Stockholm International Peace Research Institute, Stockholm, Sweden, June 2002. Reproduced by permission.

a theater missile defense in the Gulf. The main purpose of deploying this system would be the protection of U.S. vital strategic interests and those of its main regional allies: member states of the Gulf Cooperation Council (GCC), including Bahrain, Kuwait, Oman, Qatar, Saudi Arabia, and the UAE. Past use of WMD, revelations about Iranian and Iraqi WMD programs, and the instability in other Gulf states and the former Soviet Union, have all contributed to heightened perception of potential threats for most states in this theater. Accordingly, the constant purchasing of top-of-the-line equipment is a strong priority for the defense ministries of these countries.

There is an ongoing Cooperative Defense Initiative between the United States and its GCC allies that, among other things, focuses on improved interoperability (coordination between two separate entities, such as by holding joint exercises and simulations) among these countries. Also, through the Hizam al-Taawun ("belt of cooperation") project, these states are coordinating their shared early warning and air defense systems. This should theoretically allow the GCC states to pool their defense resources, spending less money individually but sharing in collective security. The project was initially undertaken in 1997, when GCC defense ministers collectively agreed to purchase ". . . a $500 million ground-based early warning system that would link the GCC states' radar and communication systems" (Robert Shuey, "Theater Missile Defense: Issues for Congress," *Congressional Research Service*, May 22, 2001). Nevertheless, besides a few Patriot units deployed in Kuwait and Saudi Arabia, a cohesive joint infrastructure to protect against potential future missile attacks is still lacking in the region. (Patriot units consist of the Patriot missile, its launcher, a high-tech radar, and an engagement control station [a station where operators control the missiles and identify targets]. The Patriot missile is a high-velocity missile that focuses on neutralizing incoming missiles before they hit the ground. The missile can achieve supersonic speed within 20 feet of leaving the launcher and has a range of at least 100 kilometers.)

SMALL ARMS SALES AND THE ROLE OF IGOs AND NGOs

Small arms are highly desirable to guerilla and other subnational groups, because they tend to be cheap, easy to conceal, and easily transportable. The World Health Organization (WHO) has estimated that 2.3 million violent deaths across the globe are a consequence of small arms and light weapons. Though definitions vary, examples of small arms include revolvers and self-loading pistols, rifles and carbines, light machine guns, sub-machine guns, and assault rifles. Examples of light weapons include heavy machine-guns, portable anti-aircraft guns, portable anti-tank guns and recoilless rifles, portable launchers of anti-tank missile and rocket systems, portable launchers of anti-aircraft missile systems, and mortars of calibers less than 100 mm. Such weapons are of grave concern to individual states, as well as the international community, but the issue has not been addressed multilaterally (by more than two nations) until quite recently. The definition of terms and concerns about sovereignty, among other things, have impeded a global consensus on small arms proliferation.

Organizations Battle Small Arms Proliferation

International government organizations (IGOs)—organizations made up of various countries, typically represented by government officials of these individual countries—and nongovernmental organizations (NGOs)—organizations that are set up to study particular area(s) of focus and are typically not made up of any government officials—have been very strong proponents of halting weapons proliferation.

THE UNITED NATIONS (UN). The UN organized a platform for debate on conventional weapons sales. After its initial proposition in 1997 and subsequent reiteration in 1999 by a panel of experts, the UN Conference on the Illicit Trade in Small Arms and Light Weapons was held July 9–20, 2001. Representatives from the governments of over 150 countries attended. The stated goal of the conference was to "develop and strengthen international efforts to prevent, combat, and eradicate the illicit trade in small arms and light weapons by creating a Global Programme of Action" and promoting state responsibilities. Efforts toward this goal were hampered, though, by the fact that no consensus on a definition of small arms and light weapons could be reached.

The United States, in particular, had reservations regarding rules and regulations proposed at the conference, because of domestic considerations. The National Rifle Association (NRA), a powerful American gun owners' lobby group, among others, felt that the UN's Programme of Action is a violation of the Second Amendment of the U.S. Constitution. The Second Amendment deals with individual citizens' "right to bear arms" and therefore relates to measures that might constrain the legal manufacture of small arms and prohibit civilian possession of such. The United States would not accept any language that would infringe upon Americans' national right to bear arms as a matter of sovereignty (a nation's right to make its own laws and policies).

The end result of the conference was an 86-paragraph report (the "Programme of Action") dealing with illegal trade in small arms and assistance to affected states. The Programme of Action called for the implementation of an arms embargo, the improvement of interstate cooperation, and the encouragement of cooperation among civil society organizations (another label for NGOs).

The future of the UN conference and the Programme of Action is questionable. Although there is strong support from various international groups, states remain hesitant about endorsing the agreement. Furthermore, the ambiguity in the language used and the conference's inability to agree on definitions leave it susceptible to violations. Verification of states' compliance is also dubious. However, the conference is still viewed by many activists as a step in the right direction.

THE WORLD HEALTH ORGANIZATION (WHO). The WHO is another IGO confronting the problem of arms sales. The WHO feels it has a direct stake in the issue, since thousands of people are killed or injured by violent, armed attacks annually. Violence was declared a public health problem at the 49th World Health Assembly meeting in 1996.

THE INTERNATIONAL CRIMINAL POLICE ORGANIZATION (INTERPOL). The International Criminal Police Organization (Interpol) tackles arms trafficking by creating a platform where countries agree to share information to foster the elimination of firearms trafficking. Interpol has 181 member nations and runs a database to collect information on illegal firearms and track stolen and recovered weapons.

THE ORGANIZATION FOR SECURITY AND COOPERATION IN EUROPE (OSCE). The Organization for Security and Cooperation in Europe (OSCE) has tackled the issue of small arms trafficking and other issues related to post-conflict stabilization. In April 2000 the OSCE Forum for Security and Cooperation held a seminar on small arms proliferation and conventional weapons trafficking. A product of this seminar was the OSCE Document on Small Arms and Light Weapons, which aimed to help the UN combat illicit weapons trafficking. The OSCE document pledges that member states will take extreme precautions when it comes to arms transfers (which are to be undertaken only for legitimate purposes) as well as develop confidence-building and transparency measures. (Confidence building implies unilateral or collective—more than one country—efforts undertaken to boost trust between member parties, while transparency implies openness. Generally, these are achieved by holding joint exercises as well as on-site inspections and data exchanges.) It is important to note that the document does not call for the creation of a new authority to combat small arms trafficking—rather, it relies on the voluntary declaration of participating states to stand by the principles of the document.

THE INTERNATIONAL ACTION NETWORK ON SMALL ARMS (IANSA). The International Action Network on Small

Arms (IANSA) is an umbrella organization representing over 340 NGOs dedicated to combating arms proliferation. IANSA encourages coordination among human rights groups, development agencies, gun control lobby groups, public health organizations, and religious constituencies. These groups also focus on ways to reincorporate former combatants, including child soldiers, into everyday life.

AFRICAN AND LATIN AMERICAN NGOS. Not all NGOs support this international coordination prohibiting arms. African and Latin American NGOs (such as the Vivario—a Brazilian organization that fights to abolish arms and educate the public about their dangers) represent areas of the world marred by small arms violence. They are therefore strong proponents of a regime (administration to enforce) that would fight conventional arms proliferation. Much work remains when it comes to banning the illicit trafficking of weapons, and it appears that initiative must come from individual countries before a global plan can be negotiated.

LANDMINES

Landmines are another type of conventional weapon of concern to the United States. Over 100 countries possess more than 250 million antipersonnel landmines (APMs), and there has been a worldwide grassroots movement to rid the globe of these deadly weapons. Landmines and other unexploded ordnance affect hundreds of thousands of people. According to the U.S. State Department, more than 60 countries have unexploded landmines on their territory. The International Committee of the Red Cross estimates that as many as 26,000 civilians, including up to 10,000 children, are killed and injured each year by mines. The State Department considers these types of weapons especially dangerous, because they:

- Kill and maim thousands of people annually

- Create millions of refugees

- Prevent productive land use, especially for agricultural and industrial purposes

- Deny road/travel access

- Deny access to water and create food scarcities, leading to starvation and malnutrition

- Inflict long-term psychological effects on victims

- Undermine political and economic stability

The global antilandmine campaign is spearheaded by the International Campaign to Ban Landmines (ICBL), the recipient of the 1997 Nobel Peace Prize. The efforts of this group culminated in the 1997 Convention on the Prohibition of the Use, Stockpiling, Production and Transfer of Anti-Personnel Mines and on Their Destruction. The treaty entered into force on March 1, 1999.

The convention has 125 countries as parties, while 18 countries have signed but not ratified the treaty. As of October 2002, 49 countries had not signed the treaty, including China, India, Iran, Iraq, Israel, Pakistan, Russia, and the United States. One of the criticisms of the treaty is the lack of a strong monitoring and verification authority. Most countries that refuse to sign the treaty rely heavily on APMs in their areas of conflict. Increased mine laying by India and Pakistan along their disputed border has caused serious concern among antimine activists. Countries such as Sri Lanka, Russia, and Turkey claim they have not signed in order to defend themselves against mines laid by internal insurgents and terrorists.

The United States meanwhile believes that mines serve an important purpose in the Demilitarized Zone (DMZ) between North and South Korea, where U.S. military personnel are deployed. American officials believe the United States does not have a strong enough military presence along the DMZ to defeat potential North Korean aggression without the help of APMs. The United States had been a leading proponent of the antilandmine treaty, as long as it gained an exception for the Korean issue. When such an exception was refused, the U.S. delegation withdrew from treaty negotiations and refused to sign the treaty.

Though the United States has not signed the ICBL treaty, it has had a moratorium on producing mines since 1996. It has also unilaterally destroyed 3.3 million mines from its arsenal. This moratorium and the number of mines destroyed by the United States, though, are reported by the United States only and are not subject to international laws or regulations, so many critics argue that such measures are not enough.

America has also provided assistance with fighting the landmine problem through the U.S. Humanitarian Demining Program. Operating under the Department of State, demining programs assist countries around the world, both financially and through direct training. Since the demining program's inception in October 1993, it has contributed about $600 million toward demining activities and has recently undertaken a mine-clearance contract with the government of Sri Lanka. A Quick Reaction Demining Force was sent to Sri Lanka to assess the mine threat there and perform short-term clearance tasks, primarily in the heavily mined Jaffna peninsula, as well as the Vanni and Killinochchi regions. The team has previously worked in stabilization efforts in Afghanistan and postconflict Kosovo.

TREATIES AND REGIMES

International treaties are intended to restrain the development and potential use of conventional weapons. They are sometimes limited, either by the types of weapons included in the treaty (for example, a treaty dealing only with landmines) or their application (they may not be signed by all parties with the type or types of weapons concerned). In efforts to reduce the threat to its own security, mainly from the Soviet Union and other Communist countries, the United States has proposed, signed, and ratified many such treaties over the years, particularly during the Cold War era. Many of these treaties are bilateral (involving two parties), but some have been ratified or signed by other countries, especially the Warsaw Pact Organization countries, which were allied with the Soviet Union, and the countries of NATO, which are allied with the United States.

Treaty on Conventional Armed Forces in Europe (CFE)

The Treaty on Conventional Armed Forces in Europe (CFE) was originally drafted primarily for NATO and Warsaw Pact countries and was signed November 19, 1990. Because of the breakup of the Soviet Union and other changes in Europe, 30 states now are parties to this treaty, which aims to restrict the overwhelming number of conventional forces in Europe. Current members of the CFE include Armenia, Azerbaijan, Belarus, Belgium, Bulgaria, Canada, the Czech Republic, Denmark, France, Georgia, Germany, Greece, Hungary, Iceland, Italy, Kazakhstan, Luxembourg, Moldova, the Netherlands, Norway, Poland, Portugal, Romania, Russia, Slovakia, Spain, Turkey, Ukraine, the United Kingdom, and the United States. As new members are added to NATO, each will be asked to comply with CFE requirements. In November 2002, at a NATO conference in Prague, Secretary General George Robertson stated that NATO: "reiterated the goals, principles and commitments contained in the Founding Act on Mutual Relations, Cooperation and Security, and in the Rome Declaration. Reaffirming adherence to the CFE Treaty as a cornerstone of European security, [NATO] agreed to continue to work cooperatively toward ratification by all the States Parties and entry into force of the Agreement on Adaptation of the CFE Treaty, which would permit accession by non-CFE states." He also "welcomed the approach of those non-CFE countries who have stated their intention to request accession to the adapted CFE Treaty upon its entry into force, and agreed that their accession would provide an important additional contribution to European stability and security."

"The Atlantic to the Urals" is the so-called area of application (AOA) for the CFE. This means that parties to the treaty can only deploy a limited number and certain types of weaponry within the AOA. Some signatory countries actually lie outside the AOA or their territories extend beyond it; for them, limits apply only to any of their forces stationed in the zones of Europe established by the treaty. The first negotiations addressed only equipment levels in the AOA; follow-up negotiations addressed troop limits, resulting in the CFE 1A document (discussed below).

Under the CFE, total arms equipment holdings for all parties in the AOA are limited to five categories: tanks, artillery, armored combat vehicles (ACVs), combat air-

TABLE 2.6

Equipment limits under the Conventional Armed Forces in Europe (CFE) Treaty, by zone

Treaty-limited equipment	Overall	One country	Central zone	Expanded central zone	Extended zones	Flank zones
Tanks[1]	20,000	13,300	7,500	10,300	11,800	4,700
Artillery pieces[1]	20,000	13,700	5,000	9,100	11,000	6,000
Armored combat vehicles[1]	30,000	20,000	11,250	19,260	21,400	5,900
Combat aircraft[2]	6,800	5,150				
Attack helicopters[3]	2,000	1,500				

[1]As a result of an agreement announced on June 14, 1991, equipment assigned to naval infantry or coastal defense forces is counted against the total authorized.
[2]No state is permitted to maintain more than 400 permanently land-based naval aircraft; no group total is to exceed 430 aircraft.
[3]No state is permitted to maintain any permanently land-based naval helicopters.

SOURCE: "Table 1. CFE Equipment Limits by Zone," in *American Defense Policy*, 7th ed., Peter L. Hays et al., eds., Johns Hopkins University Press, Baltimore, MD, 1997

craft, and attack helicopters. Limits on the equipment levels allotted to each country are stated in the treaty according to each country's boundaries and according to the zones beyond its sovereign territory in which it may operate. These four zones lie in a concentric fashion that calls for fewer troops and fewer weapons deployed the closer one moves to the center of Europe. The smallest of the zones is the central zone; the largest is the flank zone, on the northern and southern flanks of Europe.

Further limits on the amount a single country could possess altogether are also stated in the treaty. (See Table 2.6.) A restriction to 20,000 tanks, 30,000 ACVs, 20,000 heavy artillery pieces, 2,000 attack helicopters, and 6,800 combat aircraft in the AOA for all NATO and former Warsaw Pact members is also called for. Each alliance divides its "bloc" limit among member parties. (See Table 2.7 and Table 2.8.) One state cannot possess more than one-third of the treaty's allowed maximums.

Russia's continued presence in Chechnya stands starkly in violation of the CFE, but Russia continues to unilaterally destroy military items it inherited from the Soviet Union. Even though its armed forces in Chechnya violate the treaty's flank restrictions, Russia has pledged to comply with the CFE "as soon as possible."

The CFE embraces several methods of compliance, including onsite inspections, information exchanges, and national/multinational technical means. All of these are overseen by the Joint Consultative Group of Vienna, Austria. The types of inspection permitted by the treaty are several: announced inspections of declared sites, challenge inspections within a specified area (for which, if a country refuses the inspection, it is required to issue a reasonable assurance of compliance), and inspections to

TABLE 2.7

Equipment limits for NATO countries under the Conventional Armed Forces in Europe (CFE) Treaty

States	Tanks	Artillery	Armored combat vehicles	Attack helicopters	Combat aircraft
Belgium	334	320	1,099	46	232
Canada	77	38	277	13	90
Denmark	353	553	316	12	106
France	1,306	1,292	3,820	352	800
Germany	4,166	2,705	3,446	306	900
Greece	1,735	1,878	2,534	18	650
Italy	1,348	1,955	3,339	142	650
Netherlands	743	607	1,080	69	230
Norway	170	527	225	0	100
Portugal	300	450	430	26	160
Spain	794	1,310	1,588	71	310
Turkey	2,795	3,523	3,120	43	750
United Kingdom	1,015	636	3,176	384	900
United States	4,006	2,492	5,372	518	784
Total	19,142	18,286	29,822	2,000	6,662
Treaty limits	20,000	20,000	30,000	2,000	6,800

SOURCE: "Table 2. CFE Equipment Limits by State (NATO)," in *American Defense Policy*, 7th ed., Peter L. Hays et al., eds., Johns Hopkins University Press, Baltimore, MD, 1997

TABLE 2.8

Equipment limits for former WTO countries under the Conventional Armed Forces in Europe (CFE) Treaty

States	Tanks	Artillery	Armored combat vehicles	Attack helicopters	Combat aircraft
Armenia[1]	220	285	220	50	100
Azerbaijan[1]	220	285	220	50	100
Belarus[1]	1,800	1,615	2,600	80	260
Bulgaria	1,475	1,750	2,000	67	235
Czech Republic[2]	957	767	1,367	50	230
Georgia[1]	220	285	220	50	100
Hungary	835	840	1,700	108	180
Kazakhstan[1]	0	0	0	0	0
Moldova[1]	210	250	210	50	50
Poland	1,730	1,610	2,150	130	460
Romania	1,375	1,475	2,100	120	430
Russian Federation[1]	6,400	6,415	11,480	890	3,450
Slovakia[2]	478	383	683	25	115
Ukraine[1]	4,080	4,040	5,050	330	1,090
Total	20,000	20,000	30,000	2,000	6,800
Treaty limits	20,000	20,000	30,000	2,000	6,800

[1]As a result of the Tashkent agreement, May 15, 1992.
[2]As a result of the Prague agreement, February 5, 1993.

SOURCE: "Table 3. CFE Equipment Limits by State (Former WTO)," in *American Defense Policy*, 7th ed., Peter L. Hays et al., eds., Johns Hopkins University Press, Baltimore, MD, 1997

verify the destruction or redeployment of equipment. By 2000 over 51,000 pieces of equipment from the AOA were destroyed or converted for civilian purposes.

The Concluding Act of the Negotiation on Personnel Strength of Conventional Armed Forces in Europe, Also Called the Conventional Armed Forces in Europe 1A (CFE 1A) Treaty

The Concluding Act of the Negotiation on Personnel Strength of Conventional Armed Forces in Europe, also called the Conventional Armed Forces in Europe 1A

(CFE 1A) Treaty, was intended as a politically, not legally, binding document, which is not subject to ratification. Signed on July 17, 1992, its point was to limit or reduce personnel levels in the AOA of the CFE treaty. Parties to the treaty are generally members of NATO and the former Warsaw Pact, plus those countries that were part of the former Soviet Union located in the AOA of the CFE. Each country sets its own limits on personnel levels. (See Table 2.9.) Once set, these limits are open to discussion but not negotiation. Personnel counted within the limits can be 1) active-duty land or air forces, including land-based air

TABLE 2.9

Troop limits under the CFE 1A treaty

North Atlantic Treaty Group			Budapest/Tashkent Group		
State	Ceilings	Holdings	State	Ceilings	Holdings
Belgium	70,000	68,688	Armenia	Not reported	32,682
Canada	10,660	1,408	Azerbaijan	Not reported	56,000
Denmark	39,000	29,893	Belarus	100,000	92,664
France	325,000	332,591	Bulgaria	104,000	98,930
Germany	345,000	314,688	Czech Republic	93,333	92,893
Greece	158,621	163,705	Georgia	40,000	Not reported
Italy	315,000	290,224	Hungary	100,000	75,294
Netherlands	80,000	66,540	Kazakhstan	0	0
Norway	32,000	26,100	Moldova	20,000	11,123
Portugal	75,000	42,534	Poland	234,000	269,670
Spain	300,000	168,346	Romania	230,000	230,000
Turkey	530,000	575,963	Russian Federation	1,450,000	1,110,578
United Kingdom	260,000	192,547	Slovakia	46,667	54,223
United States	250,000	137,271	Ukraine	450,000	495,156

SOURCE: "Table 6. CFE 1A Troop Limits," in *American Defense Policy,* 7th ed., Peter L. Hays et al., eds., Johns Hopkins University Press, Baltimore, MD, 1997

defense; 2) command and staff of those units; 3) land-based naval aircraft and naval infantry, coastal defense units, and other forces holding equipment under the CFE treaty; or 4) reserve personnel called up for active duty for more than 90 days. Sea-based naval personnel, internal security units, and forces under UN command are exempt. The treaty sets forth additional measures to stabilize personnel, such as 42-day advance notification required to: increase personnel strength by more than 1,000; increase an air force unit by more than 500; or call up more than 35,000 reservists (except if the reservists are called up for natural disasters or other emergencies).

The Wassenaar Arrangement on Export Controls for Conventional Arms and Dual-Use Goods and Technologies

Signed by 33 countries, the Wassenaar Arrangement on Export Controls for Conventional Arms and Dual-Use Goods and Technologies (often referred to as simply the Wassenaar Arrangement) came about in order to promote transparency and set arms sales limitations on certain weapons and dual-use goods and technologies. Its current signatories include Argentina, Australia, Austria, Belgium, Bulgaria, Canada, the Czech Republic, Denmark, Finland, France, Germany, Greece, Hungary, Ireland, Italy, Japan, Luxembourg, the Netherlands, New Zealand, Norway, Poland, Portugal, the Republic of Korea, Romania, the Russian Federation, Slovakia, Spain, Sweden, Switzerland, Turkey, Ukraine, the United Kingdom, and the United States. The countries have agreed to a control list in terms of their weapons exports.

These countries actively participate in preventative enforcement, follow-up investigations, and information exchanges as means of controlling dual-use equipment. Dual-use items are equipment and materials considered to be controlled commodities that either cannot be exported at all or that require an export license because of the potential for misuse. The items, such as certain telecommunications equipment, chemicals, or even microorganisms and toxins, have potential civilian as well as military uses.

In order to ensure that surplus military equipment does not get into the wrong hands, states party to the Wassenaar Arrangement agreed to increase safeguards on military equipment. They agreed that surplus military equipment should fall under the same export controls as new materials and that the physical security of, and inventory controls on, these materials should be increased. To ensure that its goals are met, the Wassenaar Arrangement requires data exchanges biannually (in April and October) to report on transactions from the previous six months.

CHAPTER 3

PROLIFERATION OF
WEAPONS OF MASS DESTRUCTION (WMD)

HISTORY OF USAGE AND PROLIFERATION

The use of gases, poisons, and toxins by states at war can be traced back centuries. As Table 3.1 shows, there is a long history, dating back to the fifth century B.C., associated with chemical and biological weapons.

One of the first people to contemplate the use of a biological weapon in North America was Lord Jeffrey Amherst. Amherst was the commanding general of British forces in North America during the final battles of the French and Indian War (1754–63). Carl Waldman's *Atlas of the North American Indian* (Facts on File, New York, 1985) describes a siege at Fort Pitt (Pittsburgh) by the forces of Native American leader Chief Pontiac during the summer of 1763. Amherst sent a letter to another British officer, encouraging him to send smallpox-infected blankets and handkerchiefs to the Indians surrounding the fort, in an effort to start an epidemic. Though there were epidemics of smallpox among some of the Indian tribes in the area, it is uncertain if such a plan was executed or if the smallpox was related to this early proposal of "germ warfare."

Yet the transformation of biological, chemical, and nuclear agents into weapons of mass destruction (WMD) is a more recent phenomenon in the history of warfare. What exactly constitutes a weapon of mass destruction? Several explanations exist. Some analysts only include the non–conventional chemical, biological, radiological, and nuclear (CBRN) weapons in this category. According to the definition in the U.S. Code, Title 5, "War and National Defense," a WMD is "any weapon or device that is intended, or has the capability, to cause death or serious bodily injury to a significant number of people through the release, dissemination, or impact of (A) toxic or poisonous chemicals or their precursors; (B) a disease organism; or (C) radiation or radioactivity."

However, several other policy analysts and experts in the field look at WMD as a much broader phenomenon.

Conventional weapons capable of creating widespread casualty or "mass destruction" are also classified as WMD. The Federal Bureau of Investigation, for instance, states that "[a] weapon of mass destruction (WMD), though typically associated with nuclear/radiological, chemical, or biological agents, may also take the form of explosives, such as in the bombing of the Alfred P. Murrah Federal Building in Oklahoma City, Oklahoma, in 1995. A weapon crosses the WMD threshold when the consequences of its release overwhelm local responders." For the purpose of this text, WMD shall here after solely refer to CBRN weapons and their delivery systems.

It was not until World War I (1914–18) that WMD were first used strategically in a battlefield environment to inflict massive casualties. On April 22, 1915, the German army released chlorine gas from cylinders in Ypres, Belgium, causing at least 2,800 casualties. The British retaliated later that year, using the same gas against German troops. In total, about 124,000 tons of chemical weapons were used by all sides during World War I.

World War II (1939–45) saw the introduction of nuclear weapons, as the United States dropped atom bombs on Hiroshima and Nagasaki, Japan. The ensuing Cold War between the United States and the Soviet Union witnessed an alarming buildup of WMD arsenals and the spread of WMD capabilities across borders to developing nations.

Since then, the use and stockpiling of WMD have continued. Though the timeline in Table 3.1 ends in 1998, several additional deployments of WMD have occurred since. In 1998 the United States bombed sites in Iraq that allegedly contained WMD. From 1998 to 2001 several different series of anthrax hoaxes and actual attacks were launched by various individuals and organizations (some still unknown). Media organizations such as NBC and the *Washington Post*; government offices in the U.S. State Department; the White House; congressional offices; U.S. post offices; and abortion clinics across the country were

TABLE 3.1

Chronology of the use and control of biological and chemical weapons, 429 B.C.–1998

- 429 B.C. - Spartans ignite pitch and sulphur to create toxic fumes in the Peloponnesian War (CW)
- 424 B.C. - Toxic fumes used in siege of Delium during the Peloponnesian War (CW)
- 960-1279 A.D. - Arsenical smoke used in battle during China's Sung Dynasty (CW)
- 1346-1347 - Mongols catapult corpses contaminated with plague over the walls into Kaffa (in Crimea), forcing besieged Genoans to flee (BW)
- 1456 - City of Belgrade defeats invading Turks by igniting rags dipped in poison to create a toxic cloud (CW)
- 1710 - Russian troops allegedly use plague-infected corpses against Swedes (BW)
- 1767 - During the French and Indian Wars, the British give blankets used to wrap British smallpox victims to hostile Indian tribes (BW)
- April 24, 1863 - The U.S. War Department issues General Order 100, proclaiming "The use of poison in any manner, be it to poison wells, or foods, or arms, is wholly excluded from modern warfare"
- July 29, 1899 - "Hague Convention (II) with Respect to the Laws and Customs of War on Land" is signed. The Convention declares "it is especially prohibited... To employ poison or poisoned arms"
- 1914 - French begin using tear gas in grenades and Germans retaliate with tear gas in artillery shells (CW)
- April 22, 1915 - Germans attack the French with chlorine gas at Ypres, France. This was the first significant use of chemical warfare in WWI (CW)
- September 25, 1915 - First British chemical weapons attack; chlorine gas is used against Germans at the Battle of Loos (CW)
- 1916-1918 - German agents use anthrax and the equine disease glanders to infect livestock and feed for export to Allied forces. Incidents include the infection of Romanian sheep with anthrax and glanders for export to Russia, Argentinian mules with anthrax for export to Allied troops, and American horses and feed with glanders for export to France (BW)
- February 26, 1918 - Germans launch the first projectile attack against U.S. troops with phosgene and chloropicrin shells. The first major use of gas against American forces (CW)
- June 1918 - First U.S. use of gas in warfare (CW)
- June 28, 1918 - The United States begins its formal chemical weapons program with the establishment of the Chemical Warfare Service (CW)
- 1919 - British use Adamsite against the Bolsheviks during the Russian Civil War (CW)
- 1922-1927 - The Spanish use chemical weapons against the Rif rebels in Spanish Morocco (CW)
- June 17, 1925 - "Geneva Protocol for the Prohibition of the Use in War of Asphyxiating, Poisonous or Other Gases, and of Bacteriological Methods of Warfare" is signed - not ratified by U.S. and not signed by Japan
- 1936 - Italy uses mustard gas against Ethiopians during its invasion of Abyssinia (CW)
- 1937 - Japan begins its offensive biological weapons program. Unit 731, the biological weapons research and development unit, is located in Harbin, Manchuria. Over the course of the program, at least 10,000 prisoners are killed in Japanese experiments (BW)
- 1939 - Nomonhan Incident - Japanese poison Soviet water supply with intestinal typhoid bacteria at former Mongolian border. First use of biological weapons by Japanese (BW)
- 1940 - The Japanese drop rice and wheat mixed with plague-carrying fleas over China and Manchuria (BW)
- 1942 - U.S. begins its offensive biological weapons program and chooses Camp Detrick, Frederick, Maryland as its research and development site (BW)
- 1942 - Nazis begin using Zyklon B (hydrocyanic acid) in gas chambers for the mass murder of concentration camp prisoners (CW)
- December 1943 - A U.S. ship loaded with mustard bombs is attacked in the port of Bari, Italy by Germans; 83 U.S. troops die in poisoned waters (CW)
- April 1945 - Germans manufacture and stockpile large amounts of tabun and sarin nerve gases but do not use them (CW)
- May, 1945 - Only known tactical use of biological weapons by Germany. A large reservoir in Bohemia is poisoned with sewage (BW)
- September, 1950-February, 1951 - In a test of biological weapons dispersal methods, biological simulants are sprayed over San Francisco (BW)
- 1962-1970 - U.S. uses tear gas and four types of defoliant, including Agent Orange, in Vietnam (CW)
- 1963-1967 - Egypt uses chemical weapons (phosgene, mustard) against Yemen (CW)
- June, 1966 - The United States conducts a test of vulnerability to covert biological weapons attack by releasing a harmless biological simulant into the New York City subway system (BW)
- November 25, 1969 - President Nixon announces unilateral dismantlement of the U.S. offensive biological weapons program (BW)
- February 14, 1970 - President Nixon extends the dismantlement efforts to toxins, closing a loophole which might have allowed for their production (BW)
- April 10, 1972 - "Convention on the Prohibition of the Development, Production and Stockpiling of Bacteriological (Biological) and Toxin Weapons and on Their Destruction" (BWC) is opened for signature
- 1975 - U.S. ratifies Geneva Protocol (1925) and BWC
- 1975-1983 - Alleged use of Yellow Rain (trichothecene mycotoxins) by Soviet-backed forces in Laos and Kampuchea. There is evidence to suggest use of T-2 toxin, but an alternative hypothesis suggests that the yellow spots labeled Yellow Rain were caused by swarms of defecating bees (CW)
- 1978 - In a case of Soviet state-sponsored assassination, Bulgarian exile Georgi Markov, living in London, is stabbed with an umbrella that injects him with a tiny pellet containing ricin (BW)
- 1979 - The U.S. government alleges Soviets use of chemical weapons in Afghanistan, including Yellow Rain (CW)
- April 2, 1979 - Outbreak of pulmonary anthrax in Sverdlovsk, Soviet Union. In 1992, Russian president Boris Yeltsin acknowledges that the outbreak was caused by an accidental release of anthrax spores from a Soviet military microbiological facility (BW)
- August, 1983 - Iraq begins using chemical weapons (mustard gas), in Iran-Iraq War (CW)
- 1984 - First ever use of nerve agent tabun on the battlefield, by Iraq during Iran-Iraq War (CW)
- 1985-1991 - Iraq develops an offensive biological weapons capability including anthrax, botulium toxin, and aflatoxin (BW)
- 1987-1988 - Iraq uses chemical weapons (hydrogen cyanide, mustard gas) in its Anfal Campaign against the Kurds, most notably in the Halabja Massacre of 1988 (CW)
- September 3, 1992 - "Convention on the Prohibition of the Development, Production, Stockpiling and Use of Chemical Weapons and on their Destruction" (CWC) approved by United Nations
- April 29, 1997 - Entry into force of CWC
- 1998 - Iraq is suspected of maintaining an active CBW program in violation of the ceasefire agreement it signed with the UN Security Council. Baghdad refuses to allow UNSCOM inspectors to visit undeclared sites (CW/BW)

CW: Chemical Weapons Use
BW: Biological Weapons Use

SOURCE: Adapted from "Chronology of State Use and Biological and Chemical Weapons Control," in "Chemical & Biological Weapons Resource Page," Center for Nonproliferation Studies, Monterey, CA, October 24, 2001 [Online] http://cns.miis.edu/research/cbw/pastuse.html [accessed July 25, 2002]. Reproduced by permission.

targeted. Anthrax exposure, infection, and even deaths resulted from some of the attacks on media organizations and in post offices where anthrax-laced mail was handled. The assumption of intelligence and homeland security planners is that this type of weapon will continue to be used intermittently in the future.

The dangers of modern WMD are significant enough to warrant increasing global concern, especially in light of how many countries possess some sort of WMD capabilities. (See Table 3.2.) Given the complex nature of the subject, it is hard to give a single explanation why countries choose to build WMD capabilities. In most cases, however, the reasons include one or more of the following:

• National security/lack of conventional weapons capability

• Perception of an imminent threat

• Deterrence/balance of power

• Regional stability

• Leadership personalities

• Pride/prestige

• Politically powerful commercial defense industries

• Technological imperatives (the race to acquire the best technological capabilities in order to maintain positions of leadership)

The enormous and widespread damage and costs usually associated with WMD (especially nuclear weapons) have discouraged states from using such weapons during times of conflict. Instead, most stockpile them primarily for purposes of deterrence. Most countries that possess nuclear weapons have a "no first strike" policy that calls on WMD for defensive purposes only (i.e., they will not launch nuclear weapons at another country first, but only in reaction to an attack against their own nation). Recognizing the potential disastrous effects of WMD proliferation, and citing reasons ranging from the fear of retaliation to morality to the difficulty of controlling the effects of WMD, many countries and international organizations have spearheaded arms control initiatives. These are designed to curb WMD buildup, and generally take the form of various treaties and agreements, though compliance with, and adherence to, such treaties has varied. Table 3.1 and Table 3.2 provide information about some treaties and conventions related to WMD. Table 3.3 gives information about adherence to treaties by those countries of particular concern to the United States. (Note: North Korea withdrew from the Nuclear Nonproliferation Treaty [NPT] in January 2003.)

The United States

As early as 1863, the U.S. War Department set what would become the American biological and chemical weapons policy for decades to come: poison would be "wholly excluded from modern warfare." Around the turn of the century, in 1899, much of the rest of the world adopted a similar policy, when the Hague Convention prohibited use of poison-tipped weapons in combat.

Yet U.S. policy on WMD has not always been clear. Several years after the Hague Convention, the United States started using chemical weapons and began a biological weapons program as well. At the end of World War I, in 1918, the United States began to propose and honor treaties against the use of chemical and biological weapons. As one of the war's victors, the United States decided to reaffirm in the Versailles Treaty (1919) the prewar prohibition on the use of poisonous gases, forbidding Germany to manufacture or import them.

Drawing upon the language of these peace treaties, the United States introduced a similar provision regarding submarines and poisonous gases at the Washington Disarmament Conference of 1922. At the 1925 Geneva Conference for the Supervision of the International Traffic in Arms, the United States also took the initiative and sought to prohibit the export of gases for war-making. At the suggestion of the French, it was decided to draw up a protocol on nonuse of poisonous gases. At the suggestion of Poland, the prohibition was extended to bacteriological weapons. Signed on June 17, 1925, the Geneva Protocol thus reinforced the prohibitions previously laid down by the Versailles and Washington treaties, and added a ban on bacteriological warfare.

During World War II, a U.S. "no first use" policy was implemented, but President Franklin D. Roosevelt stated that retaliation in kind would be used if chemical or biological weapons were used against Americans. During the Vietnam War (1961-1975), the United States used tear gas and defoliants such as Agent Orange against the Viet Cong. By 1975 the United States ratified the Geneva Protocol of 1925 against gas agents (though it stated that defoliants or riot-control agents such as tear gas were excluded) and the Biological and Toxin Weapons Convention (BTWC), proposed in 1972. The United States also signed the Chemical Weapons Convention (CWC), sponsored by the United Nations (UN), in 1993, and it went into effect in 1997. However, the United States implemented three unilateral exclusions to the CWC in 1998. In addition, some countries claim the United States has continued to develop chemical and biological weapons in defiance of its stated policies and the numerous treaties and conventions it has signed.

CHEMICAL WEAPONS

Chemical warfare agents are poisonous chemical materials used to kill or incapacitate. They can be delivered in a variety of ways, including canisters, artillery shells, artillery rockets, aerial bombs, mines, missile

TABLE 3.2

Chemical and biological weapons: possession and programs through 2002

Country	Chemical				Biological			
	Program Status	Possible Agents	Signed CWC	Ratified CWC	Program Status	Possible Agents	Signed BWC	Ratified BWC
Algeria	Possible	Unknown	01/13/93	08/14/95	Research effort, but no evidence of production	Unknown	No	No
Canada	Former program	-mustard -phosgene -lewisite	01/13/93	09/26/95	Former program Started: 1941 Ended: 1945	**Past Weaponized Agents** -anthrax **Research** -brucellosis -rocky mountain spotted fever -plague -tularemia -typhoid -yellow fever -dysentery -rinderpest -botulinum toxin -ricin	04/10/72	09/18/72
China	Probable	Unknown	01/13/93	04/25/97	Likely maintains an offensive program	Unknown	—	11/15/84*
Cuba	Possible	Unknown	01/13/93	04/29/97	Probable research program	Unknown	04/10/72	04/21/76
Egypt	Probable	-mustard -phosgene -sarin -VX	No	No	Likely maintains an offensive program	Unknown	No	No
Ethiopia	Probable	Unknown	01/14/93	05/13/96	—	—	04/10/72	05/26/75
France	Former program	-mustard -phosgene	01/13/93	03/02/95	Former program Started: 1921 Ended: 1926 1927-34 (dormant) Started: 1935 Ended: 1940 1940-1945 (German occupation)	**Past Weaponized Agents** -potato beetle **Research** -anthrax -salmonella -cholera -rinderpest -botulinum toxin -ricin	—	09/27/84*
Germany	Former program	-phosgene -cyanide -mustard -tabun -sarin -soman	01/13/93	08/12/94	Former program Started: 1915 Ended: 1918 1919-1939 (dormant) Started: 1940 Ended: 1945	**Past Weaponized Agents** -glanders (WW I) -anthrax (WW I) **Research** -foot and mouth disease -plague -rinderpest -typhus -yellow fever -potato beetle -potato blight	04/10/72	11/28/72
India	Former program	Unknown	01/14/93	09/03/96	Research program, but no evidence of production	Unknown	01/15/73	07/15/74
Iran	Known	-mustard -sarin -hydrogen cyanide -cyanogen chloride -phosgene	01/13/93	11/03/97	Likely maintains an offensive program	-anthrax -foot and mouth disease -botulinum toxin -mycotoxins	04/10/72	08/22/73

warheads, grenades, sprayers, and even release by individuals. Although such weapons are generally frowned upon by the international community, several states have developed fully fledged chemical weapons programs, both in the past and currently.

Besides their use in World War I, chemical weapons were also used by the Italians in Ethiopia, the Egyptians in Yemen, and the Iraqis against Iran. The United States, Russia (or former Soviet Union), North Korea, Libya, Iran, Iraq, Syria, Israel, and North Korea have all been

TABLE 3.2

Chemical and biological weapons: possession and programs through 2002 [CONTINUED]

Country	Chemical				Biological			
	Program Status	Possible Agents	Signed CWC	Ratified CWC	Program Status	Possible Agents	Signed BWC	Ratified BWC
Iraq	Known; probable reconstitution of program in absence of UN inspections and monitoring	-mustard -sarin -tabun -VX -Agent 15	No	No	Previously active research and production program; probable reconstitution of program in absence of UN inspections and monitoring	**Past Weaponized Agents** -anthrax -botulinum toxin -ricin -aflatoxin -wheat cover smut **Research** -brucellosis -hemorrhagic conjuctivitis virus (Enterovirus 70) -rotavirus -camel pox -plague (?) -gas gangrene toxin **Current Research** Unknown	05/11/72	06/19/91**
Israel	Probable	Unknown	01/13/93	No	Research, with possible production of agents	Unknown	No	No
Italy	Former program	-mustard -phosgene	01/13/93	12/08/95	—	—	04/10/72	05/30/75
Japan	Former program	-phosgene -hydrogen cyanide -mustard -lewisite -chloropicrin	01/13/93	09/15/95	Former program Started: 1931 Ended: 1945	**Past Weaponized Agents** -anthrax -plague -glanders -typhoid -cholera -dysentery -typhoid -paratyphoid **Research** -gas gangrene -influenza -tetanus -tuberculosis -tularemia -salmonella -typhus -glanders -tetrodotoxin	04/10/72	06/08/82
Libya	Known	-mustard -sarin -tabun -lewisite -phosgene	No	No	Research, with possible production of agents	Unknown	—	01/19/82*
Myanmar (Burma)	Probable	Unknown	01/14/93	No	—	—	No	No
N. Korea	Known	-adamsite -mustard -hydrogen cyanide -cyanogen chloride -phosgene -sarin -soman -tabun -VX	No	No	Research, with possible production of agents	-anthrax -plague -yellow fever -typhoid -cholera -tuberculosis -typhus -smallpox -botulinum toxin	—	03/13/87*
Pakistan	Probable	Unknown	01/13/93	10/28/97	Possible	Unknown	04/10/72	09/25/74
Russia	Known	-Novichok binary nerve agents	01/13/93	11/05/97	Research, some work beyond legitimate defense activities likely	Unknown	04/10/72	03/26/75

TABLE 3.2

Chemical and biological weapons: possession and programs through 2002 [CONTINUED]

Country	Chemical				Biological			
	Program Status	Possible Agents	Signed CWC	Ratified CWC	Program Status	Possible Agents	Signed BWC	Ratified BWC
Soviet Union	Former program	-sarin -soman -mustard -lewisite -phosgene -VX analogue	01/13/93	11/05/97	Former program Started: 1926 Ended: 1992	**Past Weaponized Agents** -smallpox -plague -tularemia -glanders -Venezuelan equine encephalitis -anthrax -Q fever -Marburg **Research** -Ebola -Bolivian hemorrhagic fever -Argentinian hemorrhagic fever -Lassa fever -Japanese encephalitis -Russian spring-summer encephalitis -brucellosis -Machupo virus -yellow fever -typhus -melioidosis -psittacosis -rinderpest -African swine fever virus -wheat stem rust -rice blast	04/10/72	03/26/75
S. Africa	Former program	-thallium -CR -paraoxon -mustard (WW II)	01/14/93	09/13/95	Former program Started: 1981 Ended: 1993	-anthrax -cholera -plague -salmonella -gas gangrene -ricin -botulinum toxin	04/10/72	11/03/75
S. Korea	Former program	Unknown	01/14/93	04/28/97	—	—	04/10/72	06/25/87
Sudan	Possible	Unknown	No	05/24/99*	Possible research	Unknown	No	No
Syria	Known	-mustard -sarin -VX	No	No	Research, with possible production of agents	-anthrax -botulinum toxin -ricin	04/14/72	No
Taiwan	Probable	Unknown	No	No	Possible research program	Unknown	04/10/72	02/09/73
U.K.	Former program	-phosgene -mustard -lewisite	01/13/93	05/13/96	Former program Started: 1936 Ended: 1956	**Past Weaponized Agents** -anthrax **Research** -plague -typhoid -botulinum toxin	04/10/72	03/26/75

accused at one point or another of having developed chemical weapons.

One of the things that makes chemical weapons programs hard to detect is the dual-use nature of many of the chemicals used—the fact that they can be found in legal industries. The ingredients used to produce chemical weapons may also be used by labs and hospitals, other health and sciences fields, farming and pest control, and so on. Table 3.4 provides some examples of chemicals used both in weapons and other fields.

Categorizing Chemical Weapons

The weaponization of a chemical agent, or the process that turns the ordinary chemical into a weapon, is a laborious process, involving the stabilization of the compound, the creation and implementation of a delivery method, and the storage and transportation of the weapon. The potency of a chemical agent will greatly depend on environmental factors, the quality of the agent, and its means of delivery. The properties of chemical agents vary depending on their intended purpose (for example, a

TABLE 3.2

Chemical and biological weapons: possession and programs through 2002 [CONTINUED]

Country	Chemical				Biological			
	Program Status	Possible Agents	Signed CWC	Ratified CWC	Program Status	Possible Agents	Signed BWC	Ratified BWC
U.S.A.	Former program	-mustard -sarin -soman -VX -lewisite -binary nerve agents	01/13/93	04/25/97	Former program Started: 1943 Ended: 1969	**Past Weaponized Agents** -Venezuelan equine encephalitis -Q fever -tularemia -anthrax -wheat rust -rice blast **Research** -brucellosis -smallpox -Eastern and Western equine encephalitis -Argentinian hemorrhagic fever -Korean hemorrhagic fever -Bolivian hemorrhagic fever -Lassa fever -glanders -melioidodis -plague -yellow fever -psittacosis -typhus -dengue fever -Rift Valley fever -Chikungunya virus -late blight of potato -rinderpest -Newcastle disease -fowl plague -staph enterotoxin B -botulinum toxin -ricin	04/10/72	03/26/75
Viet Nam	Possible	Unknown	01/13/93	No	—	—	—	06/20/80*
Yugoslavia, Federal Republic of (FRY)	Former program	-sarin -mustard -tabun -soman -VX -lewisite -BZ	No	04/20/00*	None/Unknown	None/Unknown	04/10/72	10/25/73

*Denotes countries which acceded to the treaty.

Note: This chart summarizes data available from open sources. Precise assessment of a state's capabilities is difficult because most weapons of mass destruction (WMD) programs were, and/or are, secret and cannot be independently assessed. States have been placed in the following categories:

- **Known** - where states have either declared their programs or there is clear evidence of chemical or biological weapons possession
- **Probable** - where states have been publicly named by government or military officials as "probable" chemical or biological weapons possessors or as producing chemical or biological weapons
- **Possible** - where states have been widely identified as possibly having chemical or biological weapons or a CBW program by sources other than government officials
- **Former** - where states have acknowledged having a chemical or biological weapons stockpile and/or CBW program in the past
- **Weaponized Agents** - where agents are produced in quantity, and/or filled into munitions in a specialized formulation with enhanced shelflife or dissemination properties. The chart distinguishes between past and current activities
- **Research** - possible agents studies; no evidence of weaponization

Only when countries are known to have weaponized agents is a distinction made between weapons and non-weapons research. In all other cases, the agents are classified as "possible" agents because not enough information is available to determine whether or not weaponization has occurred.

SOURCE: Adapted from "Chemical and Biological Weapons: Possession and Programs Past and Present," in "Chemical & Biological Weapons Resource Page," Center for Nonproliferation Studies, Monterey, CA, April 9, 2002 [Online] http://cns.miis.edu/research/cbw/possess.htm [accessed July 24, 2002]. Reproduced by permission.

TABLE 3.3

Adherence to international treaties and regimes for countries of concern

	NPT	CTBT	NSG/ZC	BWC	CWC	AG	MTCR
China	R	S	–/M	R	R	–	*–
India	–	–	–/–	R	R	–	–
Iran	R	S	–/–	R	R	–	–
Iraq	R	–	–/–	R	–	–	–
Libya	R	–	–/–	R	–	–	–
North Korea	R	–	–/–	R	–	–	–
Pakistan	–	–	–/–	R	R	–	–
Russia	R	R	M/M	R	R	–	M
Sudan	R	–	–/–	–	R	–	–
Syria	R	–	–/–	S	–	–	–

* China has agreed to export restrictions for complete missiles but not to the MTCR technical annex that addresses exports of missile technologies.
R—Ratified S—Signed M—Member

Nuclear Nonproliferation Treaty (NPT)
Nonnuclear weapon member states forswear the right to manufacture or acquire nuclear weapons. Exporting nuclear materials to nonnuclear weapon states is prohibited unless the material is safeguarded.
Nonnuclear weapon states that are NPT members agree to International Atomic Energy Agency safeguards at all nuclear sites.

Comprehensive Nuclear Test Ban Treaty (CTBT) (has not entered into force)
Signatories undertake not to carry out any nuclear weapons test explosion or other nuclear explosion.

Nuclear Suppliers Group (NSG)
Members agree informally to control exports of nuclear materials and to establish tight controls on enrichment and reprocessing technologies.

Zangger Committee (ZC)
Developed list of safeguarded trigger items that NPT members will export only to facilities under IAEA safeguards.

Australia Group (AG)
Informal group whose members have adopted export controls on specific chemical precursors, microorganisms, and related production equipment with chemical and biological weapons applications.

Biological and Toxin Weapons Convention (BWC)
Bans development, production, stockpiling, retention, or acquisition of biological agents or toxins that have no justification for peaceful purposes.
Treaty in force but has no verification or monitoring mechanisms.

Chemical Weapons Convention (CWC)
Bans chemical weapons development, production, stockpiling, transfer and use.
Requires adherents to declare and destroy stockpiles and production plants within 10 years. Entered into force in April 1997.

Missile Technology Control Regime (MTCR)
Voluntary regime with 32 members states; no control over nonmembers; no enforcement authority.
Main goal is to halt or slow the spread of missiles and UAVs that can deliver a 500-kilogram or larger payload to 300 or more kilometers.
Members agreed to control two categories of exports related to missile development, production, and operation:
    Category I: whole missiles and UAVs with 500 kilometer/300 kilometer payload/range; and complete subsystems such as guidance and engines.
    Category II: equipment and technology related to warheads and re-entry vehicles, missile engines, guidance technology, propellants and missile and UAVs with a 300km range but less than a 300 kilometer payload.

SOURCE: "Annex B—Adherence to International Treaties and Regimes for Countries of Concern," in *Proliferation: Threat and Response*, U.S. Department of Defense, Office of the Secretary of Defense, Washington, DC, January 2001

battlefield scenario or more tactical use). Usually, chemical weapons are categorized based on factors such as:

1) Toxicity, or the lethality of an agent. Less toxic substances can be used to incapacitate (as in a riot-control situation) rather than kill.

2) Physical state. Whether an agent is in solid, liquid, or gaseous form plays a significant role in its weaponization and delivery.

3) Mode of action, or whether the agent is delivered via inhalation (breathing), ingestion (eating or drinking), or subcutaneous (through the skin) means.

4) Speed, or the amount of time between exposure to an agent and the appearance of symptoms.

5) Ability to persevere. This refers to how long an agent can retain its characteristics in the environment in which it is used and continue to pose a threat. The ability to persevere is relevant for response and decontamination following a chemical attack.

Classes of Chemical Weapons

Chemical weapons fall under one of the following classes: blister agents, blood agents, choking agents, nerve agents, or nonlethal agents. (Table 3.5 provides a summary of common examples of each type and their effects.)

BLISTER AGENTS. Classified as first-generation chemical agents (World War I era agents—some of the first chemical agents used on the battlefield), blister agents are also known as vesicants. Their primary physiological effects include burning sensations to the eyes, skin, and mucous membranes. As the name implies, large, watery blister formations can occur, along with severe damage to the upper pulmonary tract. Lewisite, nitrogen mustard, sulfur mustard, and phosgene oxime are all different types of vesicants. They can be dispersed in aerosol, liquid, or vapor form, and (except for lewisite) cause no immediate pain at the time of exposure. Blister agents are used primarily to incapacitate rather than kill the enemy, but large doses can result in death.

TABLE 3.4

Dual use chemicals

Dual-Use Chemical	Chemical Warfare Agent	Other Uses
Thiodiglycol	Sulfur Mustard	Plastics, dyes, inks
Thionyl chloride	Sulfur Mustard	Pesticides
Sodium sulfide	Sulfur Mustard	Paper
Phosphorus trichloride	Sulfur Mustard	Insecticides
Phosphorus Oxychloride	Tabun	Insecticides
Dimethylamine	Tabun	Detergents
Sodium Cyanide	Tabun	Dyes, Pigments
Dimethyl methylphosphonate	G (nerve) Agents	Fire retardants
Dimethyl hydrochloride	G (nerve) Agents	Pharmaceuticals
Potassium bifluoride	G (nerve) Agents	Ceramics
Diethyl phosphite	G (nerve) Agents	Paint Solvent
Methylphosphonic difluoride	G (nerve) Agents and VX	Organic Chemical Synthesis
Phosphorus pentasulfide	VX	Lubricants, pesticides

SOURCE: Compiled by Information Plus staff based on "United States Efforts in Curbing Chemical Weapons Proliferation," *World Military Expenditures and Arms Transfers*, U.S. Arms Control and Disarmament Agency, Washington, DC, 1990, and *Chemical and Biological Warfare: A Comprehensive Survey for the Concerned Citizen,* Eric Croddy et al., Copernicus Books, New York, NY, 2002

TABLE 3.5

Common chemical warfare agents

Types	Agents	Effects
Blister	Mustard Nitrogen Mustard Lewisite	Causes large skin blisters; respiratory damage; long-term debilitating injuries, including blindness
Choking	Phosgene	Death from lack of oxygen
Blood	Hydrogen Cyanide Cyanogen Chloride	Interferes with body's oxygen supply, causing death
Nerve	Tabun Sarin Soman Cyclosarin VX Fourth generation	Loss of muscular control, respiratory failure, and death
Other	TFNM[1] BZ[2]	Penetrates air filters; Incapacitation

[1]Trifluoronitrosomethane
[2] 3-Quinuclidinyl Benzilate

SOURCE: "Common Chemical Warfare Agents," in *Proliferation: Threat and Response*, U.S. Department of Defense, Office of the Secretary of Defense, Washington, DC, January 2001

BLOOD AGENTS. Blood agents enter the body primarily via inhalation and incapacitate the blood tissues' ability to properly utilize oxygen, causing the target to asphyxiate. Hydrogen cyanide, cyanogen chloride, and arsine are all blood agents that are highly volatile and disperse quickly under normal conditions.

CHOKING AGENTS. Also known as lung irritants, choking agents usually come in the form of heavier gases that tend to settle at ground level or in depressions such as trenches and foxholes. Chlorine, chloropicirin, phosgene, and diphosgene are choking agents that, when inhaled, cause a fluid buildup in the lungs, so that victims die of oxygen deficiency.

NERVE AGENTS. Nerve agents come in various forms, including VX and the G-series agents (so called because their U.S. Army codes all begin with the letter "G") tabun, sarin, soman, and cyclosarin. Highly deadly, these agents block the flow of acetylcholinestrase, an enzyme crucial to the functioning of the nervous system. Effects of exposure to nerve agents include seizures and a loss of body control as the agents exhaust their victims' muscles, including the heart.

NONLETHAL AGENTS. These incapacitants (which can be used separately or in conjunction with other chemical agents) include less potent chemicals that can be further subdivided into psychochemicals, tear gas agents, and vomiting agents. Psychochemicals are mainly hallucinogenic compounds, such as lysergic acid diethylamide (LSD) and 3-quinuclidinyl benzilate, that cause delusions and can render victims incapacitated for a period of time.

Tear gas agents are riot-control agents that are highly irritating to the eyes and respiratory tract. They include orthochlorobenzylidene malononitrile, chloroacetophenonoe, and brombenzyl cyanide. Vomiting agents, such as adamsite, are arsenic-based. They cause vomiting and can also irritate the eyes and respiratory system.

Chemical Weapons Attack in Tokyo, Japan, 1995

A sarin gas attack was perpetrated on civilians at the Kasumigaseki subway station in Tokyo, Japan, on March 20, 1995, by the Japanese cult Aum Shinrikyo ("Supreme Truth"), led by Shoko Asahara. The Aum cult, a religiously motivated apocalyptic terrorist group, had spent the late 1980s and early 1990s experimenting with various warfare agents, seeking out chemical weapon components and other WMD from various states. In one instance they attempted to buy a MIG-29, one of the Soviet Union's most advanced fighter aircraft, and a nuclear warhead from Russia. They succeeded in buying a large Russian military helicopter. Aum also tested anthrax on sheep in Australia.

Sarin, in terms of its symptoms, is in a class with two other deadly nerve agents, soman and tabun. Symptoms of exposure to these chemicals include reduced vision, diarrhea, vomiting, paralysis, and respiratory failure (asphyxiation). Those sufficiently exposed can lapse into a coma and die. With sarin, doses that are potentially life threatening may be only slightly larger than those producing the least effects. Symptoms of overexposure occur within minutes or hours and include constriction of pupils (miosis), visual effects, headaches and pressure sensation, runny nose and nasal congestion, salivation, chest tightness, nausea, vomiting, giddiness, anxiety, difficulty in thinking, difficulty sleeping, nightmares, muscle twitches, tremors, weakness, abdominal and thoracic cramps, diarrhea, and involuntary elimination, with severe exposure symptoms progressing to convulsions, asphyxiation, and death.

During the morning rush hour on March 20, 1995, Aum Shinrikyo cult members carried bags of sarin onto five separate trains in the Tokyo subway system. Each punctured the sarin-filled bags with the tip of a specially sharpened umbrella, then got off at the next stop. The five packages leaked onto the floor of the trains, and the sarin fumes began spreading almost immediately. Soon many passengers were coughing and feeling nauseous. As the trains reached their next stops, some passengers collapsed on the platforms and others ran for the station exits. Within a few hours, 12 commuters were dead and 5,500 others were injured to varying degrees, some permanently. One woman had her contact lenses "welded" to her eyeballs by the nerve gas and had to have both her eyes surgically removed. It was unknown whether the attack had been chemical until military specialists entered the subway in the early afternoon and established that the compound used was sarin.

On July 17, 2000, Toru Toyoda and Kenichi Hirose, two of the perpetrators of the attack, who were charged with murder and attempted murder, were sentenced to death by hanging. Another, Shigeo Sugimoto, was sentenced to life imprisonment. All three claimed that they had been brainwashed by the cult.

BIOLOGICAL WEAPONS

Certain biological organisms and toxins have been developed as weapons that can be used against humans, livestock, and crops. Biological weapons are different from their chemical counterparts because they involve agents that use living organisms (such as viruses or bacteria) or toxins derived from living organisms (such as ricin from the castor bean and mycotoxin produced by certain fungi). Generally abhorred around the globe, biological weapons attack a target by causing a deadly disease via inhalation, injection, ingestion, or cutaneous (via the skin) entry into the body. They can be delivered through a variety of means, including bombs, warheads, sprayers, and individual delivery.

Depending on the agent, the incubation period of biological agents, or the time between when the agent infects and when symptoms first appear, can vary from a few hours to weeks. When it comes to weaponizing biological agents, certain characteristics make some organisms more ideal than others. These include the agent's ability to reliably infect, its contagiousness (whether or not it will spread easily), stability, incubation time, ease of transportation, resistance to common antibiotics, and virulence

(lethality). Weaponizing biological agents can be tricky, since it is important to keep the pathogen alive and virulent through the delivery process and to make sure that the size of the agent is just right for optimum delivery.

Common Classes of Biological Weapons Agents

BACTERIA. Bacteria are single-celled organisms that can vary in lethality. Common bacteria used in biological weapons include bacillus anthracis (causes anthrax), vibrio cholerae (causes cholera), yersina pestis (plague bacteria), and francisella tularensis (causes tularemia). The bacterial incubation period is usually a few days.

RICKETTSIAE. Named after Harold T. Rickettes, rickettsial organisms are similar to bacteria, except that they exist within the intracellular environment and can only reproduce in animal tissue. Rocky Mountain fever, Q fever, and typhus are all diseases brought about by rickettsiae.

VIRUSES. Small in comparison with bacteria, viruses are also intracellular parasites and can affect plants and animals alike. Some diseases caused by viruses include smallpox, encephalitis, ebola, yellow fever, lassa fever, and Venezuelan equine encephalitis.

TOXINS. Toxins differ from the other three classes in that they are mainly poisons produced by living organisms, rather than being living organisms themselves. Toxins can be protein or nonprotein in nature, and exercise their toxicity by disrupting nerve impulse transmissions or blocking protein synthesis. Examples of toxins include clostridium botulinum (causes botulism), found on poorly preserved food; ricinus communis (ricin), found in the castor bean seed; and saxitoxin, found in certain shellfish.

NUCLEAR WEAPONS

Nuclear and other radiological (radioactive) weapons are some of mankind's deadliest creations. In August 1945 two atomic bombs were detonated in Japan by the United States. These bombs were a product of the top-secret Manhattan Project, which cost the U.S. government approximately $2 billion. The attack devastated the cities of Hiroshima and Nagasaki, causing about 70,000 and 40,000 fatalities, respectively. A mile-wide area below the blast point (1,800 feet in the air) was directly affected by the atomic bombs, and people within 500 meters of ground zero died immediately. About 150,000 people were injured by the atomic explosions at Hiroshima and Nagasaki, and the after-effects of the nuclear radiation (such as radiation-induced cancer) have continued for decades. Today, nuclear technology is much cheaper, easier to acquire, and poses one of the gravest threats to U.S. national security.

To achieve nuclear yield, physics relies on fission or fusion technology, with the former being more easy to accomplish in a weapons production process. When the atom of a material is broken into two roughly equal fragments and bombarded by neutrons, it releases energy. This process is called "fission," and the substances that are manipulated to release energy through fission are called "fissile materials." In a nuclear chain reaction, the minimum amount of fissile material required to sustain the reaction is called "critical mass." When additional material is added to the reaction, it results in the creation of a supercritical state (one in which the rate of the reaction constantly increases), where the mass rapidly expands because of the intense heat and pressure. The critical mass of a particular nuclear device depends on the type of fissile material used, its density, and the design of the weapon.

Fission weapons can be delivered in a number of ways, including bombs, several different types of missiles and other dispersal devices. Most nuclear devices are either implosion-type weapons (those that burst inward) or gun-type assemblies (those that propel outward), and the most typical fissile materials used are plutonium and highly enriched uranium. Other fissile isotopes, such as cesium and cobalt, can also create significant damage as radiological weapons. According to explosives experts, the blast effects of a nuclear bomb are similar to those of a conventional bomb, but the results are far more deadly, because of the high temperatures caused by an atomic explosion and because of the nuclear radiation that follows. Illicit trafficking of radiological substances on the black market (especially from the former Soviet Union) is a grave source of concern for authorities.

COUNTRIES OF PROLIFERATION CONCERN

With the end of the Cold War and the breakup of the Soviet Union in the early 1990s, the proliferation of WMD has taken a much more global form. Today's WMD threat no longer focuses solely on two superpowers, but includes a host of nations, among them China, Egypt, India, Iran, Iraq, Israel, Libya, North Korea, Pakistan, Russia, and Syria. Though several countries (including the United States, Russia, the United Kingdom, France, and China) reduced stockpiles from 1986 to 2002, stockpiles of these weapons still remain high in each of these countries and have spread to other nations. North Korea's declaration of an active nuclear weapons program in late 2002 and the renewal of UN inspections in Iraq in November 2002 are recent illustrations of the gravity of this transnational threat. In a June 2000 address to the Asia Society, U.S. Assistant Secretary for Nonproliferation, Robert J. Einhorn of the State Department, called the proliferation of WMD and their missile-delivery systems the gravest threat to world security.

The following sections focus on the status of WMD programs around the world and present one case study (on Iraq) that examines in depth how a country develops such capabilities.

TABLE 3.6

China's nuclear, biological, and chemical weapons and missile programs, January 2001

Nuclear	Has substantial stockpile of nuclear warheads and means for delivery at all ranges—short, medium and long; modernizing nuclear missile force.
	Member of IAEA.
	Member of Zangger Committee.
	Maintains stockpile of fissile material.
	Has pledged no-first-use of nuclear weapons.
	Ratified the NPT and signed the CTBT.
Biological	Possesses infrastructure adequate to develop and produce biological warfare agents.
	Reaffirmed commitment not to develop biological weapons, but China likely retains some elements of an offensive program.
	Acceded to the BWC.
Chemical	Has the ability to quickly mobilize the chemical industry to produce a wide variety of chemical agents and delivery means.
	Probably has not divulged full nature of chemical warfare program.
	Ratified the CWC and has restricted the transfer of selected Australia Group chemicals.
Ballistic missiles	Modernizing and expanding SRBM, MRBM, ICBM, and SLBM force.
	Successfully tested DF-31 ICBM (1999 and 2000).
	Not a member of the MTCR, but pledged to control missile technology items.
Other means of delivery available	Land-, sea-, and air-launched cruise missiles, mostly anti-ship.
	Aircraft: fighters, bombers, helicopters.
	Ground systems: artillery, rocket launchers, mortars.

IAEA = International Atomic Energy Agency
NPT = Nuclear Nonproliferation Treaty
CTBT = Comprehensive Test Ban Treaty
BWC = Biological and Toxin Weapons Convention
CWC = Chemical Weapons Convention
SRBM = Short Range Ballistic Missile (Range: 1000 kilometers or less)
MRBM = Medium Range Ballistic Missile
ICBM = Intercontinental Ballistic Missile (Range: greater than 5,500 kilometers)
SLBM = Submarine-launched Ballistic Missile
MTCR = Military Technology Control Regime

SOURCE: "China: NBC Weapons and Missile Programs," in *Proliferation: Threat and Response,* U.S. Department of Defense, Office of the Secretary of Defense, Washington, DC, January 2001

China

As one of the five nuclear weapon states of the Nuclear Nonproliferation Treaty (NPT), China has been developing WMD since the mid-1950s. It conducted its first nuclear test in 1964 and maintains a nuclear arsenal that consists of missiles and various other munitions. China's missile collection includes intercontinental ballistic missiles (ICBMs), submarine-launched ballistic missiles (SLBMs), and a host of theater missiles. It is estimated to possess around 400 nuclear warheads, and it is believed that China will add additional warheads to missiles primarily targeted at the United States and Taiwan. China has, however, repeatedly pledged a "no first use" policy with its nuclear forces, meaning it would only use nuclear weapons to retaliate for an offensive nuclear attack. Table 3.6 shows China's nuclear, biological, and chemical (NBC) weapons and missile programs.

China acceded to the NPT in 1992 and pledged not to export assembled ground-to-ground missiles (missiles originating from a land-based launcher toward another land-based target) two years later. In 1996 it signed the Comprehensive Test Ban Treaty and the Chemical Weapons Convention (CWC), stating at the time that former chemical weapons production facilities in China had the ability to produce warfare agents such as mustard and lewisite, but that all chemical weapons stockpiles had been destroyed. The U.S. government has been skeptical of such claims. U.S. defense officials also question China's claim that it does not possess biological weapons agents, though China did sign the Biological and Toxin Weapons Convention (BTWC) in 1984.

China remains a key supplier of WMD dual-use technology, primarily to Pakistan and North Korea. It is widely accepted among analysts that Pakistan's short-range ballistic missile and medium-range ballistic missile programs were directly assisted by China in terms of raw materials and technical expertise. China has also entered into a nuclear cooperation deal with Iran with regards to two specific power plants using uranium, including facility development, nuclear mining and fuel fabrication processes that both countries claim will be used toward developing nuclear energy.

Egypt

Over the years, Egypt has served as an ally to the United States in the Middle East, but continues to be on the American list of countries to watch out for in regards to WMD proliferation. In a 2002 unclassified report, the Central Intelligence Agency (CIA) warned the U.S. Congress about Egypt's continued purchase of missiles and technology from North Korea and its ongoing acquisition of various weapon systems. Egypt began its nuclear program in the 1950s with assistance from, first, the Soviet Union and, later, the United States. It also produced its own Scud-B and Scud-C missiles, along with a host of rockets, to deliver WMD. Egypt acceded to the NPT in 1981 and has also called for the creation of a Middle Eastern nuclear weapon–free zone.

Egypt is one of the first countries to have trained its own military in chemical weapons defense, and reportedly used mustard gas against northern Yemen during the mid-1960s. Its chemical weapons arsenal is believed to include mustard and phosgene, which are deliverable through missile warheads, rockets, mines, and artillery shells. Egypt's development of chemical weapons and its refusal to sign the CWC are believed to be in direct response to the development of an Israeli nuclear program. It has nevertheless officially pledged not to acquire and produce chemical warfare agents.

Information on Egypt's biological weapons program is somewhat limited. It signed the BTWC on April 10, 1972, and declares that it does not have biological weapons capability. U.S. experts claim, on the other hand, that Egypt has a strong technological base and the necessary resources for developing a significant biological weapons program, and that its past efforts have been linked to developing diseases such as plague and encephalitis virus.

India

India is one of the most recent players in the nuclear weapons arena, which it entered after conducting a series of five underground nuclear weapons tests in 1998. Table 3.7 demonstrates India's NBC and missile capabilities. India is one of a handful of states that refuses to sign the NPT, and has a strong nuclear power program, for which it receives assistance from a host of countries. It has developed a host of ballistic missiles and advanced conventional weapons to serve as delivery modes for its nuclear warheads.

India ratified the CWC in 1996 and declared an existing stockpile of chemical weapons. Under terms of the CWC, it must destroy this weapons stockpile by 2007.

There is little information on whether India has offensive biological weapons capabilities, though as Table 3.7 illustrates, India possesses a strong civilian biotechnology infrastructure. India has been a signatory of the BTWC since the early 1970s.

Iran

A long-standing threat to the United States, Iran is believed to have developed an active WMD program to counter the Israeli threat, as well as to establish regional dominance. (See Table 3.8.) It acceded to the NPT in 1970, but the U.S. government asserts that Iran is secretly procuring and developing nuclear weapons. The International Atomic Energy Agency (IAEA), which conducts inspections under the NPT, has yet to discover any such illicit activities. Over the years, Iran has engaged in numerous transactions with foreign countries dealing with dual-use materials. It has a strong civilian nuclear power energy program, which could potentially be used as a cover for clandestine weapons programs. With North Korea's help, Iran has worked on producing several Scud-range missiles, and there are conflicting reports that it is currently working on the production of full-range ICBMs. Iran's missiles currently are estimated to be capable of reaching at least 500 kilometers, with the potential to go up to 6000. (See Figure 3.1.)

Iran is one of the few countries that has had chemical weapons used against it (by Iraq, in the 1980–88 war). The United States claims that Iran has been working on developing a chemical weapons program since the war with Iraq, so that it never has to undergo the trauma of having chemical weapons used against it again. Its alleged arsenal is believed to consist of choking, blister, and nerve agents. Iran ratified the CWC in 1997 and strongly denies the existence of a chemical weapons program.

TABLE 3.7

India's nuclear, biological, and chemical weapons and missile program, January 2001

Nuclear	Conducted nuclear experiment tests on 11 and 13 May 1998; claimed a total of five tests.
	Conducted a peaceful nuclear explosive (PNE) in 1974. Capable of manufacturing complete sets of components for plutonium-based nuclear weapons.
	Has small stockpile of nuclear weapons components and probably can deploy a few nuclear weapons within a few days to a week. It can deliver these weapons with fighter aircraft.
	Announced draft nuclear doctrine in August 1999 of no-first-use; stated intent to create triad of air-, land-, and sea-based missile delivery systems.
	Has signed neither the NPT nor the CTBT.
Biological	Has substantial biotechnical infrastructure and expertise, some of which is being used for biological warfare defense research.
	Ratified the Biological and Toxin Weapons Convention.
Chemical	Acknowledged chemical warfare program in 1997 and stated that related facilities would be open for inspection.
	Has sizeable chemical industry, which could be source of dual-use chemicals for countries of proliferation concern.
	Ratified the CWC.
Ballistic missiles	Has development and production facilities for solid- and liquid-propellant fuel missiles.
	Three versions of liquid-propellant Prithvi SRBM: Prithvi I (Army)—150 kilometer range (produced) Prithvi II (Air Force)—250 kilometer range (tested) Dhanush (Navy)—250 kilometer range (unsuccessfully tested)
	Solid-propellant Agni MRBM: Agni tested in 1994 (estimated range 2,000 kilometers) Agni II tested in April 1999 (estimated range 2,000 kilometers)
	SLBM and IRBM also under development.
	Is not a member of the MTCR.
Other means of delivery	Has ship-borne and airborne anti-ship cruise missiles; none have NBC warheads.
	Aircraft: fighter bombers.
	Ground systems: artillery and rockets.

NPT = Nuclear Nonproliferation Treaty
CTBT = Comprehensive Test Ban Treaty
CWC = Chemical Weapons Convention
SRBM = Short Range Ballistic Missile (Range: 1000 kilometers or less)
SLBM = Submarine-launched Ballistic Missile
IRBM = Intermediate Range Ballistic Missile (Range: 3,000–5,000 kilometers)
MTCR = Military Technology Control Regime
MRBM = Medium Range Ballistic Missile
NBC = Nuclear, Biological, or Chemical

SOURCE: "India: NBC Weapons and Missile Program," in *Proliferation: Threat and Response,* U.S. Department of Defense, Office of the Secretary of Defense, Washington, DC, January 2001

TABLE 3.8

Iran's nuclear, biological, and chemical weapons and missile programs, January 2001

Nuclear	Seeking fissile material and related nuclear technology for weapons development, especially from sources in Russia.
	Russia is completing construction of power reactor at Bushehr and recently agreed to additional nuclear cooperation; China has pledged not to sell a key facility and other nuclear technologies.
	Acceded to the NPT and signed the CTBT.
Biological	Possesses overall infrastructure and expertise to support biological warfare program.
	Pursues contacts with Russian entities and other sources to acquire dual-use equipment and technology.
	Believed to be actively pursuing offensive biological warfare capabilities; may have small quantities of usable agent now.
	Ratified the BWC.
Chemical	Began chemical warfare program during Iran-Iraq war; employed limited amounts of agent against Iraqi troops.
	Possesses weaponized stockpile of agents; capable of agent delivery; trains military forces to operate in contaminated environment.
	Seeking to improve chemical precursor production capability.
	Ratified the CWC and made declarations.
Ballistic missiles	Has force of SCUD B, SCUD C and Chinese-made CSS-8 SRBMs; producing SCUDs.
	Main effort is to produce Shahab-3 MRBM, based on North Korean No Dong; effort involves considerable Russian and Chinese assistance.
	Flight tested Shahab-3 in July 1998, and in July and September 2000
	Seeking to develop additional longer-range missiles, such MRBMs, IRBMs and possibly an ICBM.
	Not a member of the MTCR.
Other means of delivery available	Land-, sea-, and air-launched anti-ship cruise missiles; air-launched tactical missiles; none have NBC warheads.
	Aircraft: fighters.
	Ground systems: artillery, rocket launchers.

NPT = Nuclear Nonproliferation Treaty
CTBT = Comprehensive Test Ban Treaty
BWC = Biological and Toxin Weapons Convention
CWC = Chemical Weapons Convention
SRBM = Short Range Ballistic Missile (Range: 1000 kilometers or less)
MRBM = Medium Range Ballistic Missile
IRBM = Intermediate Range Ballistic Missile (Range: 3,000–5,000 kilometers)
ICBM = Intercontinental Ballistic Missile (Range: greater than 5,500 kilometers)
MTCR = Military Technology Control Regime
NBC = Nuclear, Biological, or Chemical

SOURCE: "Iran: NBC Weapons and Missile Programs," in *Proliferation: Threat and Response,* U.S. Department of Defense, Office of the Secretary of Defense, Washington, DC, January 2001

Iran has also ratified the BTWC (in 1973), but is believed to retain the resources and expertise to conduct an offensive biological weapons program.

Israel

Over the years, Israel has received considerable assistance from the West in the form of conventional armaments and financial aid. Nevertheless, Israel has not signed the NPT and has chosen to pursue a nuclear option, because it does not believe that the United States would effectively protect it in the case of a first-strike WMD attack from its immediate neighbors. Even though Israel considers the United States a strong ally, it is strongly independent and believes that it can only rely upon itself for protection. Israel's geographic and demographic position puts it in a rather vulnerable position, in comparison with its Arab neighbors. Israel has not overtly declared its nuclear capability, but there is little disagreement among experts that Israel has a well-developed nuclear program, based out of Dimona.

There has been very little published about Israel's biological and chemical weapons capabilities. According to the Federation of American Scientists, Israel's offensive biological and chemical warfare program is located at Ness Ziona. Several reports published by scientists working at the Department of Pharmacology in the Israel Institute of Biological Research at Ness Ziona have dealt with nerve agents.

FIGURE 3.1

Estimated ranges of current and potential Iranian ballistic missiles, January 2001

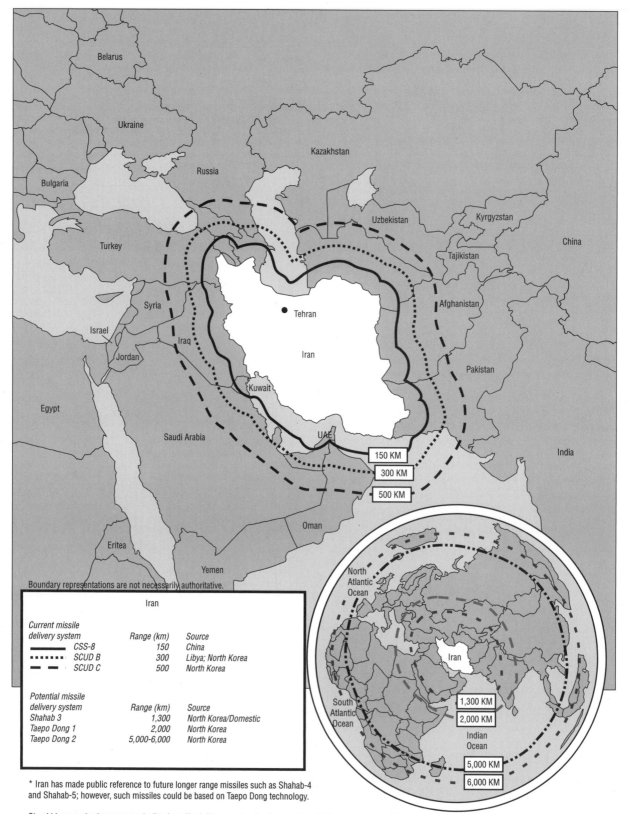

Iran		
Current missile delivery system	Range (km)	Source
CSS-8	150	China
SCUD B	300	Libya; North Korea
SCUD C	500	North Korea
Potential missile delivery system	Range (km)	Source
Shahab 3	1,300	North Korea/Domestic
Taepo Dong 1	2,000	North Korea
Taepo Dong 2	5,000-6,000	North Korea

* Iran has made public reference to future longer range missiles such as Shahab-4 and Shahab-5; however, such missiles could be based on Taepo Dong technology.

Should Iran receive long range missiles from North Korea, or develop its own, it could threaten a much wider area.

SOURCE: "Estimated Ranges of Current and Potential Iranian Ballistic Missiles," in *Proliferation: Threat and Response*, U.S. Department of Defense, Office of the Secretary of Defense, Washington, DC, January 2001

TABLE 3.9

TABLE 3.10

Libya's nuclear, biological, and chemical weapons and missile programs, January 2001

Nuclear	Has made little progress with long-standing goal of acquiring or developing a nuclear weapon; may be trying to recruit foreign experts to assist with effort.
	Ratified the NPT; has not signed the CTBT.
	Signed the African Nuclear Weapon Free Zone Treaty.
Biological	Remains in research and development stage, but may be capable of producing small quantities of agent.
	Ratified the BWC.
Chemical	Produced blister and nerve agents in 1980s at Rabta; employed chemical agents against Chadian troops in 1987; attempted to construct underground chemical agent production facility at Tarhunah.
	Rabta and Tarhunah believed to be inactive, although chemical program not completely abandoned.
	Has not signed the CWC.
Ballistic missiles	Maintains aging SCUD missile force of limited operational utility.
	Has made only limited success with over 20-year indigenous missile production effort; may renew focus on purchasing complete ballistic missile.
	Not a member of the MTCR.
Other means of delivery available	Land- and sea-launched anti-ship cruise missiles; none have NBC warheads.
	Aircraft: fighters, bombers, helicopters, transport planes.
	Ground systems: artillery, rocket launcher.

NPT = Nuclear Nonproliferation Treaty
CTBT = Comprehensive Test Ban Treaty
BWC = Biological and Toxin Weapons Convention
CWC = Chemical Weapons Convention
MTCR = Military Technology Control Regime
NBC = Nuclear, Biological, or Chemical

SOURCE: "Libya: NBC Weapons and Missile Programs," in *Proliferation: Threat and Response,* U.S. Department of Defense, Office of the Secretary of Defense, Washington, DC, January 2001

North Korea's nuclear, biological, and chemical weapons and missile programs, January 2001

Nuclear	Plutonium production at Yongbyon and Taechon facilities frozen by the 1994 Agreed Framework; freeze verified by IAEA.
	Believed to have produced and diverted sufficient plutonium prior to 1992 for at least one nuclear weapon.
	Concerns remain over possible covert nuclear weapons effort.
	Ratified the NPT; later declared it has a special status. This status is not recognized by the United States or the United Nations. Has not signed the CTBT.
Biological	Pursued biological warfare capabilities since 1960s.
	Possesses infrastructure that can be used to produce biological warfare agents; may have biological weapons available for use.
	Acceded to the Biological and Toxin Weapons Convention.
Chemical	Believed to possess large stockpile of chemical precursors and chemical warfare agents.
	Probably would employ chemical agents against U.S. and allied forces under certain scenarios.
	Has not signed the CWC.
Ballistic missiles	Produces and capable of using SCUD B and SCUD C SRBMs, and No Dong MRBM.
	Successfully launched variant of Taepo Dong 1 MRBM in failed attempt to orbit satellite. (August 1998)
	Developing Taepo Dong 2 ICBM-range missile; agreed to flight test moratorium on long-range missiles in September 1999; reaffirmed in June 2000.
	Remains capable of conducting test.
	Not a member of the MTCR.
Other means of delivery available	Land- and sea-launched anti-ship cruise missiles; none have NBC warheads.
	Aircraft: fighters, bombers, helicopters.
	Ground systems: artillery, rocket launchers, mortars, sprayers.
	Special Operations Forces.

IAEA = International Atomic Energy Agency
CTBT = Comprehensive Test Ban Treaty
CWC = Chemical Weapons Convention
SRBM = Short Range Ballistic Missile (Range: 1000 kilometers or less)
MRBM = Medium Range Ballistic Missile
ICBM = Intercontinental Ballistic Missile (Range: greater than 5,500 kilometers)
MTCR = Military Technology Control Regime
NPT = Nonproliferation Treaty
NBC = Nuclear, Biological, or Chemical

SOURCE: "North Korea: NBC Weapons and Missile Programs," in *Proliferation: Threat and Response,* U.S. Department of Defense, Office of the Secretary of Defense, Washington, DC, January 2001

Libya

Libya's potential as a nuclear power is somewhat questionable, as the only major nuclear facility in Libya is a 10-megawatt research reactor. It also lacks the financial and technical expertise to undertake a massive nuclear weapons program. It ratified the NPT in 1975. The United States, however, continues to view Libya as a threat because of that nation's expressed desire to pursue WMD. (See Table 3.9.) It does possess a variety of missiles, including a Scud variant, and has a nascent program to develop the al-Fatah ballistic missile. Figure 3.2 estimates the ranges of Libya's ballistic missiles. Libya also allegedly received a shipment of North Korean No-Dong ballistic missiles and has received technical expertise from Germany, India, Russia, Iran, and China.

Libya refuses to sign the CWC and is believed to have used chemical weapons in its conflict with Chad in 1987. Libya faced significant international pressure in the 1980s when it was believed to have been developing an offensive chemical weapons program at facilities in Tarhuna and Rabta. It was forced to shut down these enterprises, though in 1995 it reopened the Pharma 150 complex in

Rabta as a pharmaceutical plant. It is believed that Libya continues to retain several tons of blister and nerve agents.

Libya acceded to the BTWC in 1982. There have been some unconfirmed rumors that it has been recruiting South African scientists to jump-start its biological weapons program.

North Korea

Table 3.10 demonstrates North Korea's pursuit of various NBC weapons and missile programs. In late 2002 North Korea shocked the world by confirming the existence of its nuclear weapons program. North Korean nuclear research can be traced back to the 1960s, when the country established a research reactor with the help of the Soviet Union. It signed the NPT in 1985, but there

FIGURE 3.2

Estimated ranges of current and potential Libyan ballistic missiles, January 2001

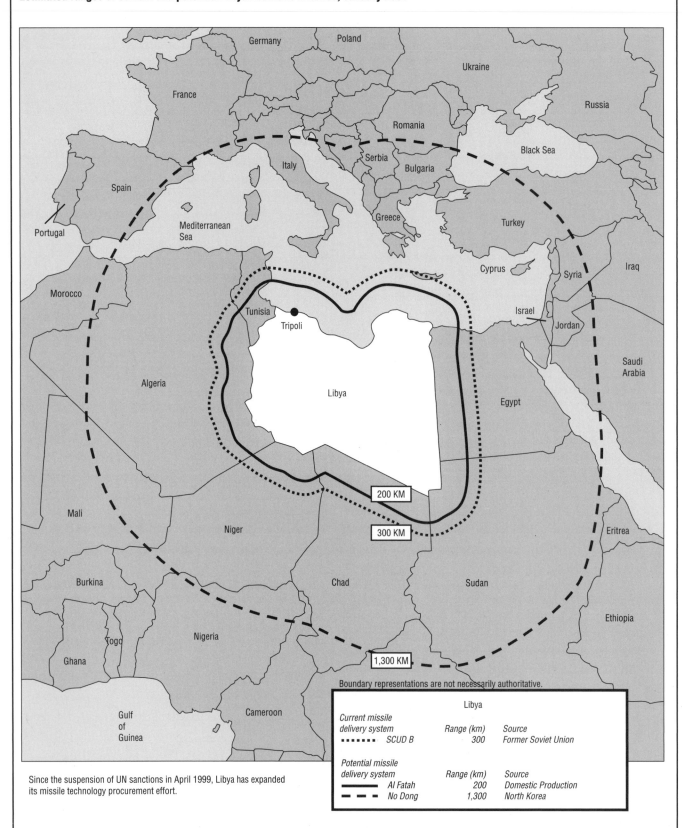

Since the suspension of UN sanctions in April 1999, Libya has expanded its missile technology procurement effort.

Boundary representations are not necessarily authoritative.

Libya		
Current missile delivery system	Range (km)	Source
••••••• SCUD B	300	Former Soviet Union
Potential missile delivery system	Range (km)	Source
—— Al Fatah	200	Domestic Production
– – – No Dong	1,300	North Korea

SOURCE: "Estimated Ranges of Current and Potential Libyan Ballistic Missiles," in *Proliferation: Threat and Response*, U.S. Department of Defense, Office of the Secretary of Defense, Washington, DC, January 2001

were discrepancies between its nuclear declarations and the results of IAEA inspections. North Korea agreed to put a halt to its nuclear program in 1994, when it entered into an agreement with the United States, which pledged to help it develop civilian nuclear energy. North Korea nullified this agreement in 2002, when it revealed its uranium-enrichment program for nuclear weapons. It has also successfully developed a series of Scud missiles and flight-tested an ICBM in 1998. Its stockpile of approximately 600 ballistic missiles reportedly includes about 100 medium-range No-Dong missiles. These missiles could reach an estimated 1,300 kilometers. (See Figure 3.3.)

North Korea has refused to sign the CWC and is believed to maintain a significant chemical weapons capability. Its stockpile of chemical weapons is said to include sarin, phosgene, and mustard, as well as several types of delivery munitions.

North Korea signed the BTWC in 1987, but is suspected by U.S. officials of secretly developing biological weapons agents, including the bacteria that causes anthrax and plague.

Pakistan

Pakistan has pursued various NBC weapons and missile programs. (See Table 3.11.) It officially developed its nuclear weapons program in direct response to a perceived threat from India. It received significant scientific and technical assistance from China and North Korea in developing nuclear and missile capabilities. The nuclear weapons program commenced in the 1970s and resulted in a series of tests immediately following the 1998 Indian tests. Soon thereafter Pakistan commissioned the development of a research reactor capable of producing weapons-grade plutonium. Pakistan owns several ballistic missiles capable of reaching India, most of which are said to be reverse-engineered (copying a design by acquiring a functional device and breaking it down to basics) Chinese and North Korean missiles.

Pakistan signed the CWC in 1993 (and later ratified it in 1997) but there is little information, if any, on declared chemical weapons agents.

While its biotechnology infrastructure is not as developed as that of India, Pakistan has well-established laboratories capable of carrying out biological weapons research. It ratified the BTWC in 1974.

Syria

Syria hosts a nuclear research center at Dyr al-Jajar and has been a signatory to the NPT since 1968. Although it researches civilian uses for nuclear energy, Syria is perceived as a threat by U.S. policy officials. Table 3.12 shows Syria's NBC weapons and missile programs. Its

TABLE 3.11

Pakistan's nuclear, biological, and chemical weapons and missile programs, January 2001

Nuclear	Conducted nuclear weapon tests on 28 and 30 May 1998 in response to India's tests; claimed a total of six tests.
	Capable of manufacturing complete sets of components for highly enriched uranium-based nuclear weapons; developing capability to produce plutonium.
	Has small stockpile of nuclear weapons components and can probably assemble some weapons fairly quickly. It can deliver them with fighter aircraft and possibly missiles.
	Has signed neither the NPT nor the CTBT.
Biological	Believed to have capabilities to support a limited biological warfare research effort.
	Ratified the BWC.
Chemical	Improving commercial chemical industry, which would be able to support precursor chemical production.
	Ratified the CWC but did not declare any chemical agent production. Opened facilities for inspection.
Ballistic missiles	Has development and production facilities for solid- and liquid-propellant fuel missiles.

	Solid-propellant program:
	   Hatf I rocket—80 kilometer range (produced)
	   Hatf III—300 kilometer range; based on M-11 (being developed)
	   Shaheen I—750 kilometer range claimed (tested)
	   Shaheen II/Ghaznavi—2,000 kilometer range claimed (in design)

	Liquid-propellant program: Ghauri—1,300 kilometer range; based on No Dong (tested)
	Is not a member of the MTCR.
Other means of delivery	Has ship-borne, submarine-launched, and airborne anti-ship cruise missiles; none has NBC warheads.
	Aircraft: fighter-bombers.
	Ground systems: artillery and rockets.

NPT = Nuclear Nonproliferation Treaty
CTBT = Comprehensive Test Ban Treaty
BWC = Biological and Toxin Weapons Convention
CWC = Chemical Weapons Convention
MTCR = Military Technology Control Regime

SOURCE: "Pakistan: NBC Weapons and Missile Programs," in *Proliferation: Threat and Response,* U.S. Department of Defense, Office of the Secretary of Defense, Washington, DC, January 2001

missile program can be traced back to the early 1970s, and it currently possesses one of the largest collections of ballistic missiles in the Middle East, though the range of most of the missiles is estimated to be limited to 500 kilometers. (See Figure 3.4.) Over the years it has relied on the Soviet Union, Iran, and North Korea to help develop its missile program.

Syria is also believed to have an extensive collection of chemical weapons, including nerve and blister agents. It allegedly received assistance from Egypt in the chemical weapons arena before the 1973 war against Israel. Syria is not a signatory to the CWC.

It did, however, sign the BTWC in 1972. There is no definite evidence of a Syrian biological weapons program, but the country does have an extensive biotechnology and pharmaceutical infrastructure that employs many dual-use items that could be diverted to a clandestine weapons program.

FIGURE 3.3

Estimated ranges of current and potential North Korean ballistic missiles, January 2001

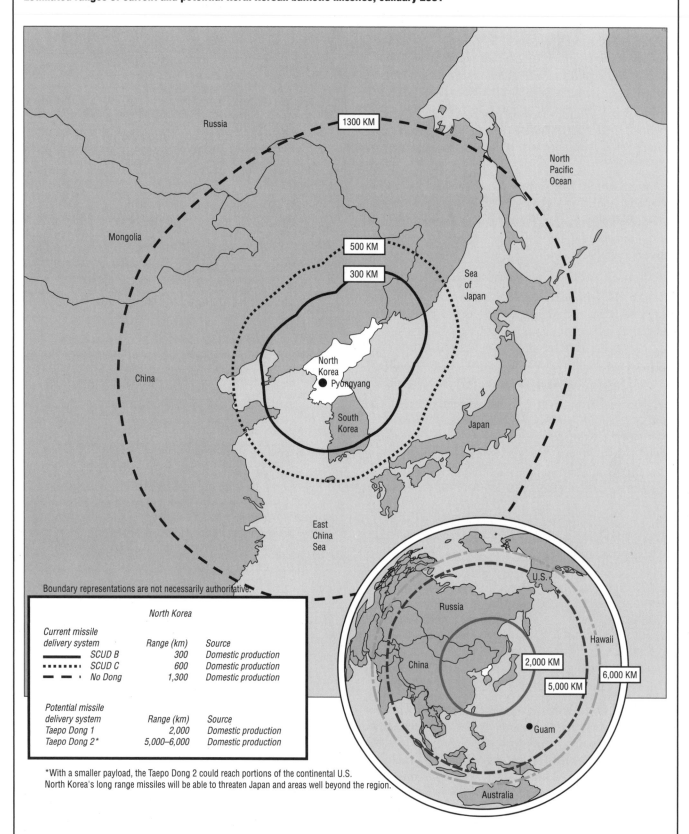

Boundary representations are not necessarily authoritative.

Current missile delivery system	Range (km)	Source
SCUD B	300	Domestic production
SCUD C	600	Domestic production
No Dong	1,300	Domestic production

Potential missile delivery system	Range (km)	Source
Taepo Dong 1	2,000	Domestic production
Taepo Dong 2*	5,000–6,000	Domestic production

*With a smaller payload, the Taepo Dong 2 could reach portions of the continental U.S. North Korea's long range missiles will be able to threaten Japan and areas well beyond the region.

SOURCE: "Estimated Ranges of Current and Potential North Korean Ballistic Missiles," in *Proliferation: Threat and Response*, U.S. Department of Defense, Office of the Secretary of Defense, Washington, DC, January 2001

TABLE 3.12

Syria's nuclear, biological, and chemical weapons and missile programs, January 2001

Nuclear	Is not pursuing the development of nuclear weapons.
	Ratified the NPT; has not signed the CTBT.
Biological	Possesses adequate biotechnical infrastructure to support limited biological warfare program.
	Believed to be pursuing biological agent development, but no major agent production effort likely is underway.
	Signed but not ratified the BWC.
Chemical	Possesses and is capable of delivering nerve agents; may be developing more advanced VX nerve agent.
	Making improvements to chemical infrastructure.
	Has not signed the CWC.
Ballistic missiles	Maintains and is capable of using force of SCUD B, SCUD C, and SS-21 missiles.
	Producing SCUD Cs with North Korean assistance.
	Making improvements to missile production infrastructure.
	Not a member of the MTCR.
Other means of delivery available	Land- and sea-launched anti-ship cruise missiles; none have NBC warheads.
	Aircraft: fighters, helicopters.
	Ground systems: artillery, rockets.

NPT = Nuclear Nonproliferation Treaty
BWC = Biological and Toxin Weapons Convention
CWC = Chemical Weapons Convention
MTCR = Military Technology Control Regime
CTBT = Comprehensive Test Ban Treaty
NBC = Nuclear, Biological, or Chemical

SOURCE: "Syria: NBC Weapons and Missile Programs," in *Proliferation: Threat and Response,* U.S. Department of Defense, Office of the Secretary of Defense, Washington, DC, January 2001

Iraq: A Case Study in WMD

In 2002 the United States once again focused its attention on Iraq, a long-standing thorn in the U.S. side when it comes to WMD and national security policies, due to its consistent attempts to establish NBC and missile programs. (See Table 3.13.) In November 2002 the UN Security Council passed Resolution 1441, which called for the return of UN inspectors to Iraq in order to determine if Iraq had renewed its secret WMD programs since 1998, when members of the UN Special Commission on Iraq (UNSCOM) and the IAEA Action Team had been prohibited from entering Iraq and conducting regular monitoring and verification tasks.

Mandated by UN Security Council Resolution 687 after the Persian Gulf War of the early 1990s, UNSCOM was a multilateral body established to assist the IAEA in verifying and dismantling all of Iraq's nonnuclear WMD capabilities. In the seven years from 1991 to 1998, UNSCOM accounted for 817 of 819 ballistic missiles and both uncovered and destroyed a vast undeclared WMD arsenal, including 48 Scud missiles, 3,000 tons of precursor chemicals, 690 tons of chemical weapons agents, 38,537 munitions, and a biological weapons facility at al-Hakam.

Yet UNSCOM was controversial. The precedent that it established as a verification unit dealing with a sovereign

TABLE 3.13

Iraq's nuclear, biological, and chemical weapons and missile programs, January 2001

Nuclear	Had comprehensive nuclear weapons development program prior to Operation Desert Storm. Infrastructure suffered considerable damage from Coalition bombing and IAEA dismantlement.
	Retains scientists, engineers, and nuclear weapons design information; without fissile material, would need five or more years and significant foreign assistance to rebuild program and produce nuclear devices; less time would be needed if sufficient fissile material were acquired illicitly.
	Ratified the NPT; has not signed the CTBT.
Biological	Produced and weaponized significant quantities of biological warfare agents prior to Desert Storm.
	Admitted biological warfare effort in 1995, after four years of denial; claimed to have destroyed all agents, but offered no credible proof.
	May have begun program reconstitution in absence of UN inspections and monitoring.
	Acceded to the BWC.
Chemical	Rebuilt some of its chemical production infrastructure allegedly for commercial use.
	UNSCOM discovered evidence of VX persistent nerve agent in missile warheads in 1998, despite Iraqi denials for seven years that it had not weaponized VX.
	May have begun program reconstitution in absence of UN inspections and monitoring.
	Has not signed the CWC.
Ballistic missiles	Probably retains limited number of SCUD-variant missiles, launchers, and warheads capable of delivering biological and chemical agents. Retains significant missile production capability.
	Continues work on liquid- and solid-propellant SRBMs (150 kilometers) allowed by UNSCR 687; likely will use technical experience gained for future longer range missile development effort.
	Not a member of the MTCR.
Other means of delivery available	Land-launched anti-ship cruise missiles; air-launched tactical missiles; none have NBC warheads; stockpile likely is very limited.
	Air systems: fighters, helicopters, UAVs.
	Ground systems: artillery, rockets.

IAEA = International Atomic Energy Agency
NPT = Nuclear Nonproliferation Treaty
CTBT = Comprehensive Test Ban Treaty
UN = United Nations
BWC = Biological and Toxin Weapons Convention
UNSCOM = United Nations Special Commission
CWC = Chemical Weapons Convention
SRBM = Short Range Ballistic Missile (Range: 1000 kilometers or less)
MTCR = Military Technology Control Regime
NBC = Nuclear, Biological, or Chemical
UAV = Unmanned Aerial Vehicle

SOURCE: "Iraq: NBC Weapons and Missile Programs," in *Proliferation: Threat and Response,* U.S. Department of Defense, Office of the Secretary of Defense, Washington, DC, January 2001

state's most sensitive security matters, along with evidence that UNSCOM was being used as an intelligence-gathering mechanism by Western governments, eventually led to its demise following the Desert Fox air strikes of December 1998. On December 17, 1999, UN Security Council Resolution 1284 replaced UNSCOM with a newer verification unit called the UN Monitoring, Verification, and Inspections Commission (UNMOVIC), led by former IAEA director Hans Blix. However, Iraq did not accept the agreement. Representatives from the capital, Baghdad, demanded sanctions be lifted before inspections could resume; the

FIGURE 3.4

Estimated ranges of current Syrian ballistic missiles, January 2001

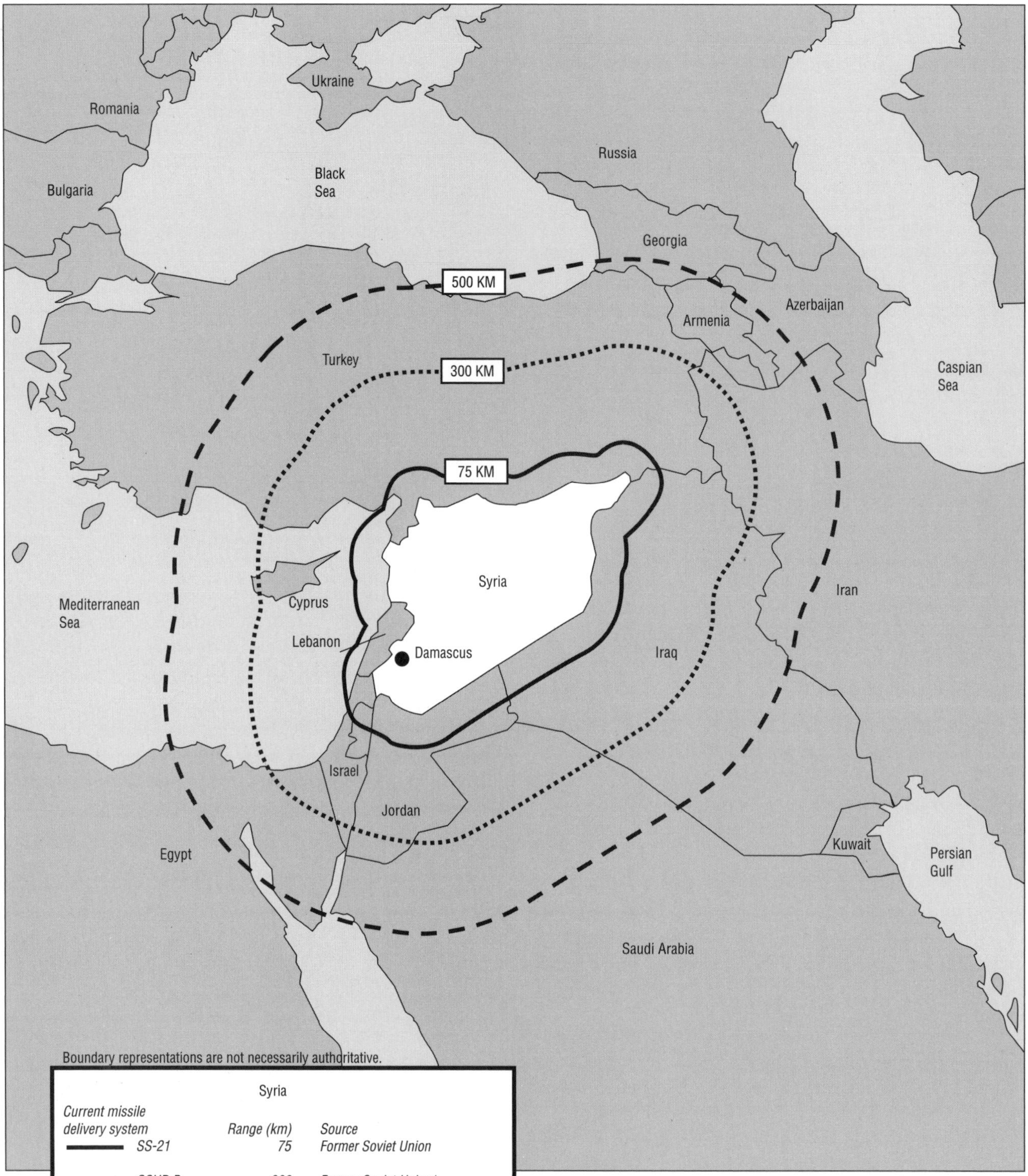

Syria		
Current missile delivery system	*Range (km)*	*Source*
—— SS-21	75	Former Soviet Union
······· SCUD B	300	Former Soviet Union/ Domestic production
- - - SCUD C	500	North Korea/ Domestic production

Boundary representations are not necessarily authoritative.

Syria's SCUD missiles allow it to threaten all of Israel and major portions of Turkey.

SOURCE: "Estimated Ranges of Current Syrian Ballistic Missiles," in *Proliferation: Threat and Response*, U.S. Department of Defense, Office of the Secretary of Defense, Washington, DC, January 2001

United States refused to do so until Iraq demonstrated its complete destruction of all WMD.

Even as the inspectors were allowed to begin their new mission in late 2002, the question remained: What had Iraq been up to in the four years that UN arms inspectors were not allowed into the country? Had there been a resumption in the development of WMD capability? Or had Iraq more or less remained benign because of its economic plight, a result of extensive multilateral sanctions? The answers vary, depending on whom you ask. Iraq and many states that empathize with its plight believe that the ongoing sanctions have caused sufficient damage to the Iraqi people and the domestic economy, that UNSCOM had already uncovered all that was there to be uncovered about Iraq's WMD capability, and that the UN needs to lift the embargo before any inspection teams are allowed in. Proponents of the arms inspection regime, on the other hand, claim that substantial Iraqi WMD capability still remains unaccounted for and that there needs to be further verification that Iraq has met all disarmament conditions before sanctions are eased. Both sides seem unwilling to fully concede or bargain.

BACKGROUND: THE SOURCES OF U.S. INFORMATION ON IRAQI WMD CAPABILITY. Iraq has been extremely careful to hide its WMD procurement activities, and had it not been for the defection of two important Iraqi officials, Dr. Khidir Hamza (in 1994) and General Hussein Kamel (in 1995), much would still remain concealed.

Hamza obtained his training in the United States, receiving degrees from the Massachusetts Institute of Technology and Florida State University, and began working for the Iraqi nuclear program in 1970. He eventually became the director of Iraq's nuclear weaponization program, making him the highest-ranking scientist to defect.

General Hussein Kamel, on the other hand, was a prominent figure in Iraqi politics who was married to one of Saddam Hussein's daughters and defected to Jordan. Kamel was in charge of the Ministry of Industry and Military Industrialization, the primary agency responsible for secretly developing Iraq's WMD. He led the IAEA inspectors to a stash of over 140 boxes of documents detailing this program and matters related to the Iraqi nuclear program. Later Kamel became disenchanted with his situation in Jordan and returned to Iraq after Saddam Hussein promised him asylum. Within days of returning, he was executed.

Much of the information the United States has about possible Iraqi WMD programs comes from these two men.

THE NUCLEAR WEAPONS PROGRAM. Iraq started developing a nuclear program around 1970, by concentrating on acquiring nuclear facilities abroad. Because Iraq was a signatory to the NPT, it was legally prohibited from developing nuclear weapons, so all its efforts had to occur in a highly clandestine manner. As a result, Iraq had some trouble acquiring the materials it needed to develop a successful weapons program, particularly fissile materials. It bought the Tamuz-1 (or Osirak) 40 megawatt test reactor from France in 1976, which used weapons-grade uranium and could produce weapons-grade plutonium. However just before Osirak could go critical and produce sufficient plutonium to test the IAEA safeguards, Israel bombed the facility in 1981. By 1990 Iraq initiated a program to chemically process unirradiated and irradiated research reactor fuel to recover a significant quantity of highly enriched uranium for a low-yield nuclear device. However, the project did not come to fruition, because of the January 1991 allied bombings of the research center at Tuwaitha.

There has been much debate as to how far along Iraq was in developing a nuclear weapon at the time of the Persian Gulf War. One thing is clear, though, from the documents recovered at General Kamel's farm: the Iraqi nuclear program was plagued with bitter infighting, mismanagement, and a dearth of infrastructure capabilities. At the same time, the documents made it clear that Iraq would go to any lengths to pursue nuclear technology. If Iraq had not invaded Kuwait, and in turn been attacked by a UN coalition force that included the United States, in the early 1990s, it is highly probable that it could have developed a small nuclear armory by 1996.

Iraq intended to develop its first nuclear device (an implosion-type) by 1991. In an interview, General Kamel stated that despite repeated attempts, the scientists were never able to test a nuclear device. What Iraq essentially wanted was to fit nuclear devices atop its ballistic missiles, but the size of the nuclear devices they were experimenting with (12-ton and 5-ton) made this tricky. They did not manage to achieve the needed miniaturization before the war.

There is reason to believe that Iraq could potentially develop a nuclear weapon, given the right amount of fissile material. The current political situation has made it extremely difficult for inspectors to ascertain the level of potential WMD infrastructure remaining in the country.

THE CHEMICAL WEAPONS PROGRAM. Unlike its nuclear and biological programs, Iraq could not easily hide its chemical weapons capability from the rest of the world, because it had used such weapons in the past, against Iran and even against its own rebels during the Iran-Iraq war (1980–88). It first used riot-control agents during the early part of the war; by 1984 Iraq progressed to the use of mustard gas and tabun, and later still it added nerve agents such as sarin and cyclosarin. An infamous incident at Halabja remains one of the deadliest chemical weapons attacks on a civilian population. On March 16, 1988, Iraq used an amalgam of chemical weapons, including sarin, tabun, and VX, against the insurgent (rebel) Iraqi Kurds, killing hundreds. According to the Federation of American Scientists, Iraqi use of chemical weapons during the Iran-Iraq war can be divided into three distinct phases:

1) 1983–86: Chemical weapons played a defensive role, in order to deflect Iranian human-wave assaults (human volunteers, wanting to be martyrs, basically went out in masses before the Iranian troops to overwhelm Iraqi forces). Around 5,500 Iranians were killed by tabun-filled aerial bombs, and approximately 16,000 were killed by the blister agent mustard gas.

2) 1986–early 1988: Iraq used chemical weapons to disrupt offensive Iranian maneuvers.

3) Early 1988–conclusion of war: Iraq integrated its nerve agent strikes into its overall offensive, which later that year lead to a cease-fire.

Iraq started producing blister agents in 1981 and disclosed in 1995 that it had a stock of 2,850 tons of mustard. The nerve gases sarin and tabun were not produced till 1984, and the program itself faced several problems with regards to stabilization and storage. In 1995 Iraq declared that it had produced over 210 tons of tabun and 790 tons of sarin. However, it is believed that the quality of these agents was relatively poor. In addition, UNSCOM destroyed about 30 tons of tabun, 30 tons of sarin, and 600 tons of mustard during 1992 and 1994.

Iraq also focused a lot of its resources on developing the deadly nerve agent VX, importing about 500 tons of precursor chemicals (chemicals used in the production of a CW agent) between 1987 and 1988. Iraq admitted to filling aerial bombs with VX, but the program itself was unsuccessful and was eventually abandoned in late 1988. Iraq was accused by the British of developing Agent-15, an incapacitating gas.

Because of the duplicitous nature of many Iraqi declarations submitted to the UN, the entire scope of Iraq's chemical weaponization process was never fully determined. Based on information provided by Iraq, the program did not heavily rely on domestic resources—munitions for the program were procured from abroad through legal or illegal means. Through 1997 UNSCOM helped destroy approximately 38,000 filled and unfilled munitions. Citing UNSCOM reports, the Federation of American Scientists claims on their Web site that the Iraqi chemical weaponization program included the use of "binary artillery munitions and aerial bombs, chemical warheads for short-range missiles, cluster aerial bombs, and spray tanks." Dr. Hamza states that Iraq is fully capable of rebuilding its chemical weapons facilities, and he believes that Saddam Hussein's new determination makes this even more likely.

Recent Western intelligence reports back up Dr. Hamza's statements, strongly indicating that Saddam Hussein is rebuilding and stockpiling his chemical weapons

arsenal. Satellite images reveal that the Republican Guard (a unit within the Iraqi military infrastructure) has been working on shifting weapons to new hiding places, which include schools and hospitals. Tons of precursor chemicals for VX are believed to be hidden. Evidence also suggests that Iraq is working on rebuilding chemical facilities that were destroyed during the bombings.

THE BIOLOGICAL WEAPONS PROGRAM. The Iraqi biological warfare program, begun in 1974, was quite comprehensive and included a range of agents, such as botulinum toxin, anthrax, ricin, and a variety of others. Iraq legitimately acquired much of its seed stock from U.S. and European suppliers under the guise of laboratory research. The American Type Culture Collection in Rockville, Maryland, provided Iraq with most of its anthrax strains since 1985. Bacteria came from Bedford, England, as well as Fluka Chimie, a Swiss firm.

By 1997 UNSCOM determined that 79 sites were providing active support to the Iraqi biological weapons infrastructure. The main biological warfare facilities were located at al-Salman and al-Hakam. Al-Salman conducted experiments on the effects of agents and toxins on larger animals, such as sheep, monkeys, and dogs, within laboratory confines as well as out in the field. There have been some rumors that human subjects were used, but this has never been confirmed. Al-Hakam was a shock to most outsiders. Its existence was known, but its nondescript and insecure appearance led many to initially ignore it. It took UN inspectors four years to uncover that the facility was an integral part of the weapons program, where researchers carried out work on anthrax, botulinum toxin, and aflatoxin.

Iraq still has several medical, university, and veterinary facilities that conduct biological research, which could be used as the basis for a covert biological weapons program. Iraq continues to retain the laboratory equipment, know-how, and means for delivering agents. Since inconsistencies still remain about the quantity of biological agents destroyed, it is estimated that even today, Iraq could produce 350 liters of weapons-grade anthrax per week.

MISSILES. Although missiles are not direct constituents of WMD capability, they play a very significant role in the delivery of these deadly weapons. UN Security Council Resolution 687 calls for the destruction of all Iraqi long-range missiles, forbidding Iraq to have any missiles with a range of more than 150 kilometers. Yet a 1999 intelligence report from the White House to Congress indicates that Iraq might still retain seven or more complete missile systems and their components. Figure 3.5 shows the estimated ranges of current and potential Iraqi ballistic missiles. In 1995 Iraq was caught trying to smuggle in gyroscopes (part of the missile's on-board guidance

FIGURE 3.5

Estimated ranges of current and potential Iraqi ballistic missiles, January 2001

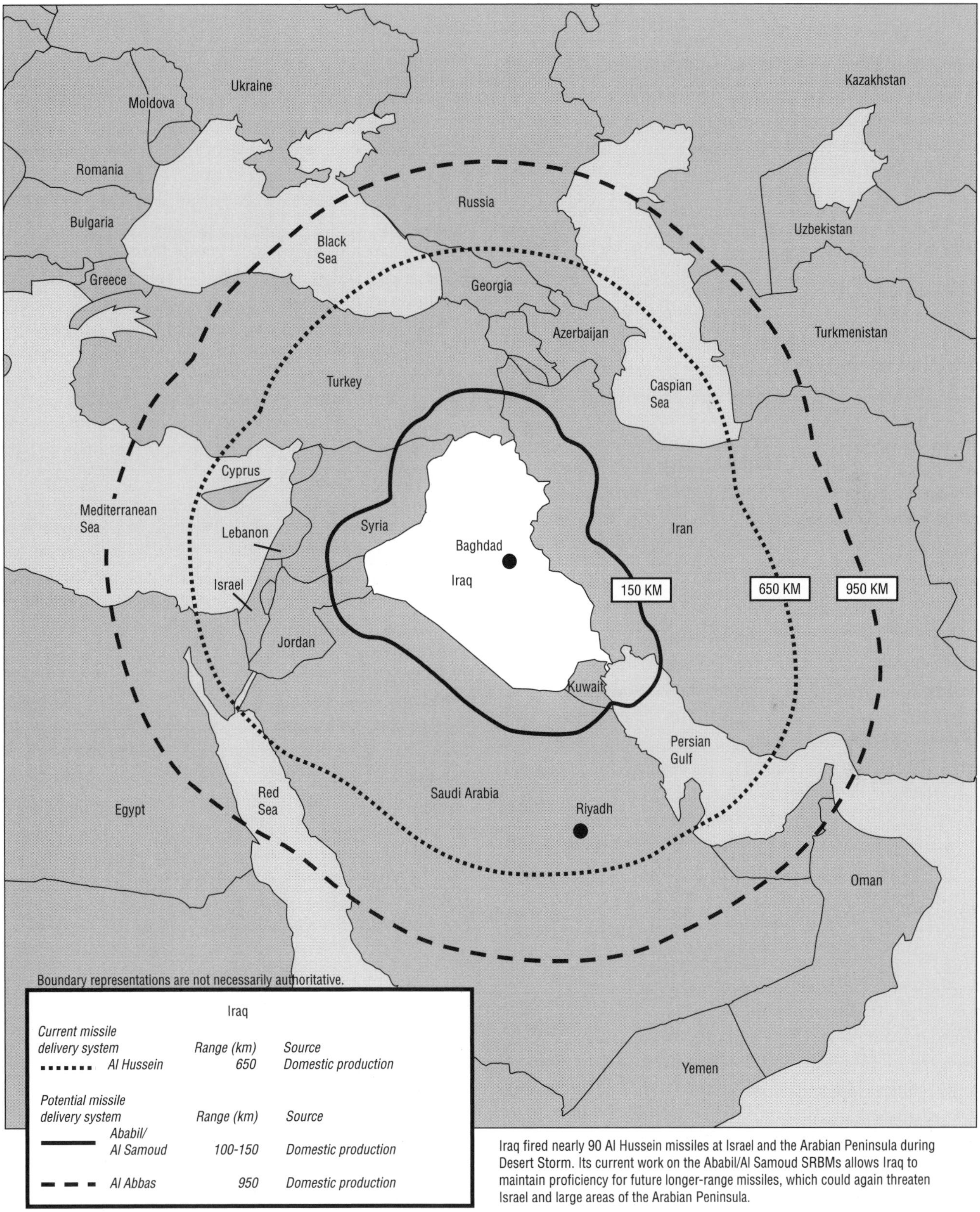

Boundary representations are not necessarily authoritative.

Iraq		
Current missile delivery system	Range (km)	Source
••••••• Al Hussein	650	Domestic production
Potential missile delivery system	Range (km)	Source
——— Ababil/Al Samoud	100-150	Domestic production
– – – Al Abbas	950	Domestic production

Iraq fired nearly 90 Al Hussein missiles at Israel and the Arabian Peninsula during Desert Storm. Its current work on the Ababil/Al Samoud SRBMs allows Iraq to maintain proficiency for future longer-range missiles, which could again threaten Israel and large areas of the Arabian Peninsula.

SOURCE: "Estimated Ranges of Current and Potential Iraqi Ballistic Missiles," in *Proliferation: Threat and Response*, U.S. Department of Defense, Office of the Secretary of Defense, Washington, DC, January 2001

system that guides it toward its intended target) from Russia to bolster its missile capabilities. The Center for Nonproliferation Studies estimates that Iraq still retains certain components of its missile systems and might have started work on al-Hussein and Scud missiles within a year after inspections stopped.

WHAT NOW? Baghdad seems to be applying a high value to its WMD infrastructure. Compliance with UN inspection requirements would likely result in a lifting of sanctions, but Iraq has so far failed to do so consistently, despite the economic cost. It has been estimated that Iraq has lost over $120 billion since the day sanctions were first imposed.

Given its past history of deception and concealment, it would be hard to simply take any present or future declarations from Iraq at face value. Its obstinate refusal to allow inspectors back into the country has also created significant doubt as to its credibility. At the same time, many feel that there is no credible evidence that Iraq has not ended its WMD programs. As of January 2003, the world community stood by Resolution 1441, and the November 2002 return of UNMOVIC inspectors to Iraq was seen as a generally positive step. Whether further actions, such as the preemptive strike being considered by the United States, are necessary is a hotly contested topic of debate, and is likely to remain so.

THE TRAFFICKING OF NUCLEAR AND FISSILE MATERIAL

The illicit trafficking of nuclear and fissile material was a grave U.S. national security threat in the early and mid-1990s. In the aftermath of the Soviet breakup, there was a rapid increase in the amount of this trafficking. Political and economic crises in the newly independent states, and inadequate security and inventory systems at former Soviet nuclear facilities, especially the civilian ones used for energy production, were major factors contributing to this problem. Budget cuts severely reduced salaries for many scientific and security personnel, which increased incentives for such "insiders" to trade material for money.

Between 1992 and 1994 there were seven reported cases involving weapons-usable fissile materials, which are often referred to as "the seven significant cases." These cases are considered significant because of the quantity and/or quality of the material(s) involved. The last of the cases involved the seizure of 2.7 kilograms of highly enriched uranium in Prague, Czech Republic on December 14, 1994. The Prague case has generated much controversy with regards to the origins of the smuggled uranium and the conduct of the investigation by the Czech authorities.

There are several other factors that make this case significant. The highly enriched uranium confiscated in Prague can be traced back to a large criminal network, members of which are also linked to the Landshut, Germany, highly enriched uranium seizure of July 1994 and the Munich, Germany, plutonium-239 seizure of August 1994. Evidence suggests that materials from all three of these cases originated from the Institute for Physics and Power Engineering (IPPE) in Obninsk, Russia, although the Russian authorities continue to deny that the material came from Obninsk.

Although many gaps and uncertainties remain, certain conclusions can be drawn from the events that followed the seizure of the uranium in Prague. All the suspects indicted in connection with this crime were middlemen—no buyer or supplier was ever arrested or even identified. The IPPE is an important research facility in the Russian Federation, and it is very hard to imagine that almost 3 kilograms of uranium was diverted or stolen by a novice—or by a single person. If the uranium did come from IPPE, it suggests the presence of an elaborate network of smugglers.

Identifying an actual buyer would be crucial to this case, since it would prove that a market does exist for illicitly trafficked nuclear material. In the past, intelligence agencies were severely criticized for setting up "sting operations" for smuggled nuclear goods, which enticed economically strapped individuals to steal nuclear materials. Some believe this may have created an artificial market for such substances where none would have existed without the temptation.

Cases such as this one brought to the world's attention the urgent need to improve security inventory procedures in Russia and other republics of the former Soviet Union. According to the Russian-language newspaper *Moskovskiye Novosti,* at the time of the Prague incident, IPPE desperately lacked adequate security and systems of registering, controlling, and physically protecting nuclear materials.

The U.S. and Russian governments jointly initiated the Material Protection, Control, and Accounting Program (MPCA) with nuclear facilities of the former Soviet Union in 1995. The IPPE was one of the first pilot facilities for the program. Under the auspices of the MPCA, U.S. laboratories cooperated with Russian facilities to introduce advanced material protection and accounting systems. This included developing computerized materials inventory and accounting databases, training Russian specialists, and implementing video monitoring systems and portal monitors. To guard against nuclear theft, portal monitors are generally used in facilities such as uranium enrichment plants, weapons manufacturing and storage plants, nuclear laboratories, and nuclear waste disposal sites. They scan vehicular or human traffic and sound off an alarm if they detect a higher radioactivity passing through than that which is originally programmed. The project was successful in securing tons of fissile materials, and by March 1996 the program received more funding from the U.S. Department of Energy, and a new computerized MPCA system was established at IPPE. Altogether, by fiscal year 2002 the MPCA was projected to have spent $800 million. Though much of its work remains incomplete, the ultimate goal of the MPCA is to build a sturdy cooperation in the field of nuclear safety and to prevent the proliferation of fissile materials and related technology.

It is widely acknowledged that since 1995 there have been no confirmed thefts or diversions of significant quantities of weapons-grade fissile material. What is not clear, however, is whether this apparent hiatus in the illicit trafficking of nuclear materials is permanent or simply a passing phase. On an optimistic note, some nonproliferation experts believe that lack of demand, increased awareness, and international assistance to the newly independent states have all contributed to this ebb in the flow of smuggled nuclear substances. On the other hand, one could also argue that a failure to share information by the international intelligence community, and the increasing sophistication of nuclear smugglers, have created the false impression that nuclear thefts and diversions are a thing of the past.

NONPROLIFERATION REGIMES AND TREATIES

Treaties have existed in world politics since the times of the Greeks and Romans. An international treaty is usually negotiated between two (bilateral) or more (multilateral) states and typically deals with the rights and duties each party has in reference to the issue being addressed. They are usually signed by the legitimate ruling administration of a sovereign state, but signing the treaty is not usually the last step taken in its approval; it also needs to be ratified in order for it to take effect. Ratification essentially involves a majority approval by the legislative branch of the country. In the United States, a treaty is ratified by gaining the approval of two-thirds of the U.S. Senate. When the parties have achieved ratification, a treaty comes into effect.

International biological, chemical, nuclear, and missile capabilities are covered under several treaties and agreements, including the Biological and Toxin Weapons Convention (BTWC), Chemical Weapons Convention (CWC), Nuclear Nonproliferation Treaty (NPT), and the Missile Technology Control Regime (MTCR), among others.

The Biological and Toxin Weapons Convention (BTWC)

The BTWC, which prohibits the development, production, and stockpiling of biological and toxin weapons, was opened for signature in 1972. Today it has 162 signatories, 144 of which have ratified the treaty. Its biggest drawback, however, remains the lack of an overarching monitoring and/or verification body to make sure parties are abiding by the treaty. This shortcoming was especially evident when President Boris Yeltsin of Russia announced

in 1992 that the former Soviet Union had aggressively pursued an offensive biological capability despite having signed the BTWC. So far, all negotiations for the proposed verification protocol have proved fruitless, especially since it would only apply to those states that ratify the protocol, thereby creating a two-tiered regime of states subjected to verification procedures and those that are exempt. Also, there is no single way to distinguish which biological facilities fall under the BTWC. It must be noted, however, that unlike the NPT or the MTCR, the BTWC is a nondiscriminatory regime, where all parties involved are subject to the same procedures.

The Chemical Weapons Convention (CWC)

The CWC was developed and opened for signature in 1993; to date, it has 172 state signatories, 135 of which have ratified the convention. The CWC has very intrusive and strict measures written into its declaration. It calls for the prohibition of the development, production, stockpiling, and retention of chemical weapons. It also discourages states from assisting or inducing other parties to develop such capabilities. The organization responsible for overseeing the CWC is the Organization for the Prohibition of Chemical Weapons (OPCW), based in The Hague in the Netherlands. The OPCW has the responsibility to conduct routine inspections as well as challenge inspections of facilities believed to be in violation of the CWC. The annual OPCW report from 1999 stated that a total of 234 inspections have been conducted at 167 facilities worldwide.

The Australia Group

In addition to the BTWC and the CWC, an informal group of 30 counties came together in response to the use of chemical weapons during the Iran-Iraq war and formed the Australia Group. These states came up with a list of materials that could potentially be used in the development of biological and/or chemical weapons and restricted their export to known or suspected states of proliferation concern.

The Nuclear Nonproliferation Treaty (NPT)

The NPT, perhaps the most comprehensive agreement, entered into force in 1970 and has 187 member states. To date, the only states of concern that have refused to sign the NPT are Cuba, India, Pakistan, and Israel. The NPT is a two-tiered agreement, which means there are separate obligations for nuclear weapons states (including the United States, United Kingdom, Russia, China, and France) and nonnuclear weapons states. The nuclear weapons states are required not to transfer any weapons capabilities to nonnuclear weapons states and to work on eventual disarmament. Meanwhile, the nonnuclear weapons states resolve not to develop nuclear capabilities, in return for technological assistance (in the energy sector) from nuclear weapons states. The NPT has an escape clause that allows a country to withdraw upon three months notice.

The Missile Technology Control Regime (MTCR)

The MTCR is not a formal treaty like the ones mentioned above, but it is by far the most effective regime that covers the proliferation of missile technology. Formed in 1987, the MTCR is a group of 32 states that aim to limit or prohibit transfer of missile and dual-use nuclear/missile capabilities. In 1993 the MTCR extended its guidelines on export controls/restrictions to cover missiles delivering biological and chemical capabilities along with nuclear.

The Treaty on the Principles Governing the Activities of States in the Exploration and Use of Outer Space, Including the Moon and Other Celestial Bodies

The Treaty on the Principles Governing the Activities of States in the Exploration and Use of Outer Space, Including the Moon and Other Celestial Bodies, also called the Outer Space Treaty, was signed January 27, 1967, and has 115 parties, though it was negotiated predominantly by the United States and Soviet Union. Its intent is to limit the militarization of the moon, outer space, and celestial bodies. The treaty requires that countries use celestial bodies for peaceful purposes only—not for any military bases, fortifications, or weapons testing.

The Treaty Between the United States and the Soviet Union on the Limitation of Antiballistic Missile Systems (ABM Treaty)

The Treaty Between the United States and the Soviet Union on the Limitation of Antiballistic Missile Systems, also called the Antiballistic Missile (ABM) treaty, was signed May 26, 1972, and has only two parties: the United States and the Russian Federation (former Soviet Union). It prohibits deployment of an antiballistic missile (ABM) system, or one designed to counter missiles in flight, for the defense of territory or the building of bases for such a defense. In December 2001 President George W. Bush formally notified Russia of his intention to pull out of the ABM treaty by June 2002. He said he could not provide adequate national security to the American people if the United States were to uphold the treaty, which bars development and deployment of a national missile defense system, or one intended to knock incoming nuclear warheads out of the sky before they jeopardize any part of America. Both President Bush and Secretary of State Colin Powell have said they felt both sides were still committed to moving ahead with deep cuts in the numbers of strategic nuclear warheads.

The Interim Agreement Between the United States and the Union of Soviet Socialist Republics on Certain Measures with Respect to the Limitation of Strategic Offensive Arms (SALT I)

The Interim Agreement Between the United States and the Union of Soviet Socialist Republics on Certain Measures with Respect to the Limitation of Strategic Offensive Arms, also called the Strategic Arms Limitation Treaty I (SALT I), was signed May 26, 1972, and included as parties the United States and the Soviet Union. This agreement, like the ABM treaty, arose from the first series of Strategic Arms Limitation Talks (SALT), which ran from November 1969 through May 1972. The United States and the Soviet Union agreed in this treaty to freeze the number of ICBM launchers. This was done in order to prohibit the conversion of older launchers to accommodate newer, heavier, and more lethal ICBMs. Increased submarine-launched ballistic missiles (SLBMs) were allowed to each side if an equal number of land-based launchers were destroyed.

The Treaty Between the United States and the Union of Soviet Socialist Republics on the Limitation of Strategic Offensive Arms (SALT II)

The Treaty Between the United States and the Union of Soviet Socialist Republics on the Limitation of Strategic Offensive Arms, also called the Strategic Arms Limitation Treaty II (SALT II), was signed June 18, 1979, by the United States and the Soviet Union. It was negotiated as a result of the SALT II talks, which ran from 1972 to 1979, and put limits on the number of ballistic missiles and their launchers. Each country was limited to 2,250 launchers plus 1,320 launchers for multiple independently targetable reentry vehicles (MIRVed) missiles. A MIRVed missile is a nuclear delivery vehicle capable of carrying more than one warhead, where each warhead can be independently targeted toward different objectives. Newer ICBMs and air-to-surface ballistic missiles (ASBMs) were limited to 10 warheads per missile, while SLBMs were allowed 14 warheads per missile. Also under this treaty, space-based weapons were prohibited.

A protocol (less formal agreement) lasting two years was also signed at the same time as the treaty, and called for a prohibition on the deployment of ASBMs, mobile ICBMs, ground-launched cruise missiles, and sea-launched cruise missiles with a range of over 600 kilometers.

Although President Jimmy Carter submitted the treaty for ratification by the U.S. Senate immediately after signing, congressional concerns and the Soviet invasion of Afghanistan caused the treaty to be removed from consideration. For that reason, the treaty was never signed and never became a binding legal agreement, though for approximately seven years it had the force of a politically binding agreement. In May 1986 President Ronald Reagan, citing Soviet violations, declared that the United States would no longer honor the SALT II limits. The United States then exceeded those limits in November of that year.

The Treaty Between the United States of America and the Union of Soviet Socialist Republics on the Reduction and Limitation of Strategic Offensive Arms (START I)

The Treaty Between the United States of America and the Union of Soviet Socialist Republics on the Reduction and Limitation of Strategic Offensive Arms, also called the

TABLE 3.14

Systems deployed outside the Russian Federation at the time of signature of the START I treaty

State	ICBMs/warheads	Heavy bombers/warheads	Total: SOAs/warheads
Belarus	81/81		81/81
Kazakhstan	104/1,040	40/320	144/1,360
Ukraine	176/1,240	42/336	218/1,576

SOURCE: "Table 4. Systems Deployed Outside the Russian Federation at Signature," in *American Defense Policy,* 7th ed., Peter L. Hays et al., eds., Johns Hopkins University Press, Baltimore, MD, 1997

Strategic Arms Reduction Treaty I (START I), was signed July 31, 1991, by the United States and the Soviet Union. Currently, the following states of the former Soviet Union have acceded to the treaty limitations: Belarus, Kazakhstan, the Russian Federation, and Ukraine. The point of START I was to reduce the numbers of strategic offensive arms possessed by the United States and the Soviet Union, including ICBMs, SLBMs, and heavy bombers, and to limit the number of nuclear warheads for each party to 6,000. The parties agreed to limits of 4,900 warheads on deployed ballistic missiles and 1,100 on deployed mobile ICBMs. The treaty also limited the former Soviet Union to only 154 deployed heavy ICBMs, versus the 308 that were in place before the treaty (with each allegedly carrying 10 warheads). The parties agreed to exchange telemetric information, or data radioed from the missiles themselves, from all test flights of ICBMs and SLBMs and to exchange the equipment necessary to interpret the data.

Compliance with the START limits is achieved through verification measures. Verification is an obstacle to the ratification of many arms control agreements because of its inherent intrusiveness, and is often used as an excuse by politicians not to reach an arms control agreement. Verification includes both verification itself and monitoring. Monitoring involves intelligence gathering, analyses, and data exchanges. Verification is more of a legal formality and a policy process that either supports or questions the conclusions reached through monitoring. For START signatories, the chief body assigned to monitor compliance is the Joint Compliance and Inspection Commission, which has met in Geneva, Switzerland, since 1991.

The Russian Federation succeeded the Soviet Union as a party to the treaty after the latter's breakup, but many strategic offensive arms had been located in the former Soviet states of Belarus, Kazakhstan, and Ukraine. (See Table 3.14.) Consequently, a protocol was signed in Lisbon, Spain, on May 23, 1992, making START I a multi-party treaty of five nations (the United States, the Russian Federation, Belarus, Kazakhstan, and Ukraine) instead of a bilateral treaty (with the United States and the Russian Federation only).

TABLE 3.15

Strategic Arms Reduction Treaty (START) I and II weapon limits and completion dates

	Start I	Start II Phase 1	Start II Phase 2
Reduction completion date	Seven years after entry into force	2000	2003
Total attributed warheads	6,000	3,800–4,250	3,000–3,500
Ballistic missile warheads	4,900	3,800–4,250	3,000–3,500
MIRVed ICBMs	Not addressed	1,200	0
Heavy ICBMs	1,540	650	0
Mobile ICBMs	1,100	1,100	1,100
SLBMs	Not addressed	2,160	1,700–1,750

SOURCE: "Table 7. START I and II Limits and Completion Dates," in *American Defense Policy,* 7th ed., Peter L. Hays et al., eds., Johns Hopkins University Press, Baltimore, MD, 1997

The Treaty on Open Skies

The Treaty on Open Skies, signed March 24, 1992, in Helsinki, Finland, is made up of members of NATO and the former Warsaw Pact. Participating states have the right to conduct, and the obligation to receive, overhead flights by unarmed observation aircraft, excluding helicopters. These aircraft are authorized to carry certain accessories such as cameras (including panoramic, still-frame, and video) and infrared scanning devices. Host nations may require that a host aircraft be used during the flight; this is known as the "taxi option." Otherwise, the inspecting party provides the aircraft used in the flight. All aircraft and sensor suites, prior to use, must undergo certification inspections. Negotiated annual quotas limit the number of flights each country can conduct and must receive. Each country must accept as many flights as it is allowed to conduct. Countries with a larger land mass get to have a larger quota. For example, the U.S. and Russian quota is currently 42 flights per year whereas Portugal has only two. Data from any such flight may be acquired by any state.

The Treaty Between the United States and the Russian Federation on Further Reduction and Limitation of Strategic Offensive Arms (START II)

The Treaty Between the United States and the Russian Federation on Further Reduction and Limitation of Strategic Offensive Arms, also called the Strategic Arms Reduction Treaty II (START II), was signed January 3, 1993, by the United States (President George H. W. Bush) and the Russian Federation (President Boris Yeltsin). Forming the basis of the START II treaty were the mutually agreed-upon objectives of eliminating all MIRVed ICBMs (missiles carrying multiple warheads) and achieving deep cuts in SLBMs. START II takes nearly all of its definitions, procedures, and compliance schemes from START I. The missile eliminations take place in two phases. (See Table 3.15.) By 2003 each party must have decreased its deployed strategic weapons to 3,000–3,500 warheads. The treaty has special provisions concerning reuse of hardware from the eliminated heavy ICBMs. For example, the missiles and their launch canisters can be converted to space launch vehicles, and missile silos may be converted to launch single-warhead ICBMs. All non-converted equipment, however, must be destroyed.

Bombers, such as the B-2, are to be held up to more scrutiny. B-2s must be exhibited and inspectable and can no longer test with long-range nuclear air launched cruise missiles (ALCMs). Up to 100 nuclear heavy bombers would be reoriented to a conventional role. The treaty also requires that nuclear and conventional bombers be based apart, that their crews must be trained apart, and that the bombers must have observable differences that can be picked up through visible inspections (in order to easily discern their distinct conventional or nuclear role).

Additional compliance monitoring features were incorporated into START II. In particular, it increases the number of on-site inspections, especially of converted heavy ICBM silos and heavy bombers. Meeting in Geneva, Switzerland, the Bilateral Implementation Commission administers the compliance regime.

The Future of WMD Arms Control: Attempts at START III

President Bill Clinton of the United States and President Boris Yeltsin of Russia agreed upon a framework for START III negotiations during their March 1997 summit meeting in Helsinki, Finland. Clinton and Yeltsin reaffirmed their commitment to begin formal negotiations on START III as soon as Russia had ratified START II. The proposed START III agreement would have established a maximum of 2,000–2,500 strategic nuclear weapons for each of the parties by December 2007, or a 30–45 percent reduction in the number of total deployed strategic warheads permitted under START II. START III would have included new measures to ensure that warhead inventories were "visible" to National Technical Means (NTM or another word for satellites) and that the slated destruction of warheads actually proceeded. The Russian Federation later proposed a reduction of the overall threshold to 1,500 warheads, an even more substantial reduction.

As of early 2000 Russia still remained officially committed to the reduction of strategic nuclear warheads to 1,500 for each party. However, the administration of President George W. Bush maintains that a minimum of 2,000–2,500 warheads is required for adequate nuclear deterrence. Although Russian ratification of START II occurred in mid-2000, it now appears that START III will not be negotiated. On November 13, 2001, President Bush announced unilateral strategic reductions by the United States outside the previous START framework.

CHAPTER 4
PREPARING FOR BIOLOGICAL AND CHEMICAL ATTACKS

Given the late 2001 spate of mail laced with *Bacillus anthracis,* or the bacteria that causes anthrax, and concerns about terrorists using weapons of mass destruction, U.S. national security officials have significantly increased their preparations for terrorist attacks. Domestic preparedness has received great attention since the September 11, 2001, terrorist attacks on the United States and the subsequent creation of the U.S. Department of Homeland Security.

While conventional weapons, such as explosives and firearms, remain the most likely means by which terrorists will attempt to harm U.S. civilians, there is an increasing probability of an attack involving biological or chemical weapons. Many nations and terrorist groups have explored the use of such weapons on small and large scales, and many countries, including the United States, have existing chemical and/or biological weapons programs or possess materials used in these types of weapons. Though it is hard to determine exactly which countries possess which capabilities, the Monterey Institute of International Studies has compiled a list of countries known or suspected to possess chemical or biological weapons. (See Table 3.2 in Chapter 3.) Biological warfare–related technology, materials, information, and expertise—including information on potential U.S. vulnerabilities—are increasingly available.

Genetic engineering is only one of several technologies that might allow countries or groups to develop agents, such as modified viruses, that would be difficult to detect and diagnose, or that could defeat current procedures for protection and treatment. Further, all of the materials needed to produce such agents are dual-use in nature, meaning they have both military and civilian applications, so are readily available. Any country with the political will to do so and a competent scientific base can produce agents. Still, the preparation and effective use of these weapons is harder than it looks.

The threat from chemical warfare may also grow in coming years. Many states have chemical warfare programs, and it is likely that these capabilities will spread to additional states and terrorist groups.

Government officials consider smaller-scale bioterrorist events to be more likely than large-scale ones, since there is much less work involved in a small-scale attack. But federal public health agencies, such as the Centers for Disease Control and Prevention (CDC), have little choice but to prepare for a variety of attacks.

THE FEDERAL ROLE

The U.S. General Accounting Office (GAO) defines biological and chemical terrorism as the threatened or intentional release of viruses, bacteria, poisonous gases, liquids, or other toxic substances for the purpose of influencing the conduct of government, intimidating or coercing a population, or simply intending to cause widespread harm. Any such act that has the potential for, or the intention of, infecting, injuring, or killing hundreds, thousands, or even millions of people is considered terrorism.

In 2001 the GAO identified more than 40 federal departments and agencies with some role in combating terrorism, with 29 of those having some role in preparing for, or responding to, the public health and medical consequences of a biological or chemical attack. (See Table 4.1.) The cabinet-level departments involved include the U.S. Departments of Agriculture (USDA), Commerce, Defense (DOD), Energy (DOE), Health and Human Services, Justice, Transportation, Treasury, and Veterans' Affairs, along with two independent agencies, the Environmental Protection Agency (EPA) and the Federal Emergency Management Agency (FEMA). Within these larger divisions, departmental agencies take on various roles, as well.

These departments and agencies may work alone or with other agencies in emergency planning for averting or responding to attacks. Table 4.2 lists further details about four federal departments and agencies that provide assistance to state and local governments for emergency planning. These units participate in activities that include, but are not limited to: 1) detecting biological agents; 2) developing a national stockpile of pharmaceuticals (drugs) with which to treat victims of disasters; and 3) developing vaccines, such as the anthrax vaccine, for the widespread inoculation of U.S. citizens and residents. Figure 4.1 shows the federal teams trained to respond in the event of a chemical or biological attack.

TABLE 4.1

Federal departments and agencies having responsibilities related to the public health and medical consequences of a bioterrorist attack

- USDA – U.S. Department of Agriculture
  - APHIS – Animal and Plant Health Inspection Service
  - ARS – Agricultural Research Service
  - FSIS – Food Safety Inspection Service
  - OCPM – Office of Crisis Planning and Management
- DOC – Department of Commerce
  - NIST – National Institute of Standards and Technology
- DOD – Department of Defense
  - DARPA – Defense Advanced Research Projects Agency
  - JTFCS – Joint Task Force for Civil Support
  - National Guard
  - U.S. Army
- DOE – Department of Energy
- HHS – Department of Health and Human Services
  - AHRQ – Agency for Healthcare Research and Quality
  - CDC – Centers for Disease Control and Prevention
  - FDA – Food and Drug Administration
  - NIH – National Institutes of Health
  - OEP – Office of Emergency Preparedness
- DOJ – Department of Justice
  - FBI – Federal Bureau of Investigation
  - OJP – Office of Justice Programs
- DOT – Department of Transportation
  - USCG – U.S. Coast Guard
- Treasury – Department of the Treasury
  - USSS – U.S. Secret Service
- VA – Department of Veterans Affairs
- EPA – Environmental Protection Agency
- FEMA – Federal Emergency Management Agency

SOURCE: Janet Heinrich, *Bioterrorism: Public Health and Medical Preparedness,* U.S. General Accounting Office, Washington, DC, October 9, 2001

Funding for Research

As Table 4.3 shows, between fiscal years 2000 and 2001, federal departments and agencies reported that total funding for research on biological and chemical terrorism increased from $141.2 million to $156.8 million. Table 4.3 also provides examples of the activities funded by each agency's budget.

In this analysis of funding for bioterrorism research, one can discern the growing number of agencies involved in such research. At least five departments or agencies—the USDA Agricultural Research Service, Office of Emergency Preparedness, Federal Bureau of Investigation (FBI), Secret Service, and EPA—did not receive money for research on bioterrorism in fiscal year 2000, but were given a total of about $7.2 million for such research in fiscal year 2001. (See Table 4.3.)

Funding for Preparedness

Federal departments and agencies spent almost $650 million on bioterrorism- and terrorism-preparedness activities for fiscal years 2000 and 2001: $296 million in 2000 and $347 million in 2001. (See Table 4.4.) Funding for bioterrorism preparedness was more than double that for research in fiscal year 2001 ($156.8 million versus $347 million). (See Table 4.3.)

The largest federal spenders in the bioterrorism and terrorism arena were the CDC ($147.3 million) and the

TABLE 4.2

Selected federal activities providing assistance to state and local governments for emergency planning relevant to a bioterrorist attack

Department or agency	Activities	Target audience
Department of Health and Human Services, Centers for Disease Control (HHS–CDC)	Provides grants, technical support, and performance standards to support bioterrorism preparedness and response planning.	State and local health agencies
Department of Health and Human Services, Office of Emergency Preparedness (HHS–OEP)	Enters into contracts to enhance medical response capability. The program includes a focus on response to bioterrorism, including early recognition, mass postexposure treatment, mass casualty care, and mass fatality management.	Local jurisdictions (for fire, police, and emergency medical services; hospitals; public health agencies; and other services)
Department of Justice, Office of Justice Programs (DOJ–OJP)	Assists states in developing strategic plans. Includes funding for training, equipment acquisition, technical assistance, and exercise planning and execution to enhance state and local capabilities to respond to terrorist incidents.	States (for fire, law enforcement, emergency medical, and hazardous materials response services; hospitals; public health departments; and other services)
Federal Emergency Management Agency (FEMA)	Provides grant assistance to support state and local consequence management planning, training, and exercises for all types of terrorism, including bioterrorism.	State emergency management agencies

SOURCE: Janet Heinrich, "Table 1: Selected Federal Activities Providing Assistance to State and Local Governments for Emergency Planning Relevant to a Bioterrorist Attack," in *Bioterrorism: Public Health and Medical Preparedness,* U.S. General Accounting Office, Washington, DC, October 9, 2001

FIGURE 4.1

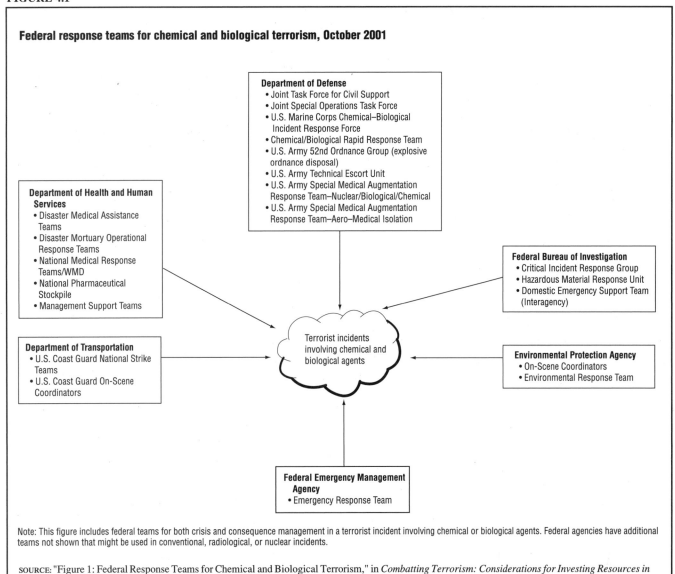

Federal response teams for chemical and biological terrorism, October 2001

Department of Defense
- Joint Task Force for Civil Support
- Joint Special Operations Task Force
- U.S. Marine Corps Chemical–Biological Incident Response Force
- Chemical/Biological Rapid Response Team
- U.S. Army 52nd Ordnance Group (explosive ordnance disposal)
- U.S. Army Technical Escort Unit
- U.S. Army Special Medical Augmentation Response Team–Nuclear/Biological/Chemical
- U.S. Army Special Medical Augmentation Response Team–Aero–Medical Isolation

Department of Health and Human Services
- Disaster Medical Assistance Teams
- Disaster Mortuary Operational Response Teams
- National Medical Response Teams/WMD
- National Pharmaceutical Stockpile
- Management Support Teams

Federal Bureau of Investigation
- Critical Incident Response Group
- Hazardous Material Response Unit
- Domestic Emergency Support Team (Interagency)

Department of Transportation
- U.S. Coast Guard National Strike Teams
- U.S. Coast Guard On-Scene Coordinators

Terrorist incidents involving chemical and biological agents

Environmental Protection Agency
- On-Scene Coordinators
- Environmental Response Team

Federal Emergency Management Agency
- Emergency Response Team

Note: This figure includes federal teams for both crisis and consequence management in a terrorist incident involving chemical or biological agents. Federal agencies have additional teams not shown that might be used in conventional, radiological, or nuclear incidents.

SOURCE: "Figure 1: Federal Response Teams for Chemical and Biological Terrorism," in *Combatting Terrorism: Considerations for Investing Resources in Chemical and Biological Preparedness,* GAO-01-162T, U.S. General Accounting Office, Washington, DC, October 17, 2001

National Guard ($93.3 million), part of the DOD. (See Table 4.4.) Between them, these two agencies controlled more than two-thirds of all federal preparedness funding in 2001. Table 4.4 gives examples of the types of programs funded by the CDC and National Guard, as well as other federal agencies with preparedness budgets.

THE CENTERS FOR DISEASE CONTROL AND PREVENTION (CDC)

Most investments in national defense increase national security, especially by acting as a deterrent against hostile acts. Similarly, investments in the public health system, most experts feel, will provide the best civil defense against biological and chemical terrorism. In the lead among federal agencies preparing for future homeland terrorism incidents is the CDC, headquartered in Atlanta, Georgia. The CDC's programs fighting terrorism—partic-

ularly bioterrorism—integrate planning and training to develop public health preparedness, and include surveillance (monitoring trends), epidemiology (studying the incidence, distribution, and control of disease), rapid laboratory diagnosis, emergency response, and information systems (computers and telecommunications).

The CDC is currently assisting state and local public health departments by:

1) Identifying the biological agents likely to be involved in a terrorist attack

2) Developing case definitions to assist in detecting and managing infection with these agents

3) Establishing a Rapid Response and Advanced Technology laboratory, which can provide fast identification of biological and chemical agents rarely seen in the United States

TABLE 4.3

Total reported funding for research on bioterrorism and terrorism by federal departments and agencies, fiscal years 2000–01

[Dollars in millions]

Department or agency	Fiscal year 2000 funding	Fiscal year 2001 funding	Sample activities
U.S. Department of Agriculture (USDA)— Agricultural Research Service	0	$0.5	Improving detection of biological agents
Department of Energy	$35.5	$39.6	Developing technologies for detecting and responding to a bioterrorist attack Developing models of the spread of and exposure to a biological agent after release
Department of Health and Human Services (HHS)—Agency for Healthcare Research and Quality	$5.0	0	Examining clinical training and ability of frontline medical staff to detect and respond to a bioterrorist threat Studying use of information systems and decision support systems to enhance preparedness for medical care in the event of a bioterrorist event
HHS—Centers for Disease Control and Prevention (CDC)	$48.2	$46.6	Developing equipment performance standards Conducting research on smallpox and anthrax viruses and therapeutics
HHS—Food and Drug Administration (FDA)	$8.8	$9.1	Licensing of vaccines for anthrax and smallpox Determining procedures for allowing use of not-yet-approved drugs and specifying data needed for approval and labeling
HHS—National Institutes of Health	$43.0	$49.7	Developing new therapies for smallpox virus Developing smallpox and bacterial antigen detection system
HHS—Office of Emergency Preparedness (OEP)	0	$4.6	Overseeing a study on response systems
Department of Justice (DOJ)—Office of Justice Programs (OJP)	$0.7	$4.6	Developing a biological agent detector
DOJ—Federal Bureau of Investigation	0	$1.1	Conducting work on detection and characterization of biological materials
Department of the Treasury— Secret Service	0	$0.5	Developing a biological agent detector
Environmental Protection Agency (EPA)	0	$0.5	Improving detection of biological agents

SOURCE: Janet Heinrich, "Total Reported Funding for Research on Bioterrorism and Terrorism by Federal Departments and Agencies, Fiscal Year 2000 and Fiscal Year 2001," in *Bioterrorism: Public Health and Medical Preparedness,* U.S. General Accounting Office, Washington, DC, October 9, 2001

4) Establishing a National Pharmaceutical Stockpile Program designed to make medical material available anywhere in the United States within 12 hours of a bioterrorist event

5) Developing a nationwide integrated information, communications, and training network with the Health Alert Network, the National Electronic Data Surveillance System, and Epidemic Information Exchange. The CDC defines the Health Alert Network (HAN) as: "...a nationwide program to establish the communications, information, distance-learning, and organizational infrastructure for a new level of defense against health threats, including the possibility of bioterrorism." Considered to be an improvement on the existing system of tracking diseases, the National Electronic Data Surveillance System (NEDSS) will create a nation–wide standard for the collection and analysis of all health related data. According to the CDC, the Epidemic Information Exchange (Epi-x) is a "...secure, web-based communications network that serves as a powerful communications exchange between CDC, state and local health departments, poison control centers, and other public health professionals. The system provides rapid reporting, immediate notification, editorial support, and coordination of health investigations for public health professionals."

In other programs, the CDC seeks to enhance the public health infrastructure and to expand response capacity, provides training in preparedness and response for public health employees, and continues to support and grow its networked information systems, along with its pharmaceutical stockpiles.

BIOATTACK: THE DALLES INCIDENT

Civilians are vulnerable to foodborne or waterborne bioterrorism, as demonstrated by the intentional salmonella contamination of restaurant salad bars in and around The Dalles, Oregon, in September and October 1984. A total of 751 persons came down with salmonella gastroenteritis from eating or working at those salad bars.

The outbreak occurred in two waves: September 9–September 18 and September 19–October 10. Most cases occurred in ten restaurants. Epidemiological studies of customers at four restaurants and of employees at all ten restaurants indicated that eating from salad bars was

TABLE 4.4

Total reported funding for preparedness activities on bioterrorism and terrorism by federal departments and agencies, fiscal years 2000–01

(Dollars in millions)

Department or agency	Fiscal year 2000 funding	Fiscal year 2001 funding	Sample activities
Department of Agriculture—Animal and Plant Health Inspection Service	0	$0.2	Developing educational materials and training programs specifically dealing with bioterrorism
Department of Defense (DOD)—Joint Task Force for Civil Support	$3.4	$8.7	Planning, and when directed, commanding and controlling DOD's weapons of mass destruction and high-yield explosive consequence management capabilities in support of FEMA
DOD—National Guard	$70.0	$93.3	Managing response teams that would enter a contaminated area to gather samples for on-site evaluation
DOD—U.S. Army	$29.5	$11.7	Maintaining a repository of information about chemical and biological weapons and agents, detectors, and protection and decontamination equipment
Department of Health and Human Services—Centers for Disease Control	$124.9	$147.3	Awarding planning grants to state and local health departments to prepare bioterrorism response plans Improving surveillance methods for detecting disease outbreaks Increasing communication capabilities in order to improve the gathering and exchanging of information related to bioterrorist incidents
Department of Health and Human Services—Food and Drug Administration	$0.1	$2.1	Improving capabilities to identify and characterize foodborne pathogens Identifying biological agents using animal studies and microbiological surveillance
Department of Health and Human Services—Office of Emergency Preparedness	$35.3	$46.1	Providing contracts to increase local emergency response capabilities Developing and managing response teams that can provide support at the site of a disaster
Department of Justice—Office of Justice Programs	$7.6	$5.3	Helping prepare state and local emergency responders through training, exercises, technical assistance, and equipment programs Developing a data collection tool to assist states in conducting their threat, risk, and needs assessments, and in developing their preparedness strategy for terrorism, including bioterrorism
Environmental Protection Agency	$0.1	$2.0	Providing technical assistance in identifying biological agents and decontaminating affected areas Conducting assessments of water supply vulnerability to terrorism, including contamination with biological agents
Federal Emergency Management Agency (FEMA)	$25.1	$30.3	Providing grant assistance and guidance to states for planning and training Maintaining databases of safety precautions for biological, chemical, and nuclear agents

SOURCE: Janet Heinrich, "Total Reported Funding for Preparedness Activities on Bioterrorism and Terrorism by Federal Departments and Agencies, Fiscal Year 2000 and Fiscal Year 2001," in *Bioterrorism: Public Health and Medical Preparedness,* U.S. General Accounting Office, Washington, DC, October 9, 2001

the major risk factor for infection. Eight of the ten affected restaurants (80 percent) operated a salad bar, compared with only three of the twenty-eight nonaffected restaurants (11 percent) in The Dalles.

The food items seemingly responsible differed somewhat from restaurant to restaurant. The investigation did not identify any water supply, food item, supplier, or distributor common to all affected restaurants, nor were the employees exposed to any single common source. Infected employees may have contributed to the spread of the illness but did not initiate the outbreak, nor did food-rotation errors or inadequate refrigeration of the salad bars (though they may have facilitated bacteria growth).

A criminal investigation revealed that members of a religious commune, the Rajneeshees had deliberately contaminated the salad bars with salmonella bacteria. The Rajneeshees wanted to sicken a good portion of the population in the town of The Dalles in order to keep residents from voting, so they could win a county election. According to most accounts, cult members decided to experiment with using salmonella and, if successful, to contaminate The Dalles's water system on election day. About a month before the election, the Rajneeshees poisoned two visiting county commissioners on a hot day by plying them with refreshing drinks of cold water laced with salmonella. Then, on a shopping trip to The Dalles, they sprinkled salmonella on produce in grocery stores. When that experiment did not produce adequate results, the Rajneeshees took vials of salmonella and clandestinely sprinkled the bacteria in and around the salad bars of the town's ten most popular restaurants. Within a few weeks, more than 700 people got sick. A salmonella bacteria strain found in a laboratory at the commune was indistinguishable from the strain involved in the outbreak of salmonellosis.

TABLE 4.5

Criteria and weighting[a] used to evaluate potential biological threat agents

Disease	Public health impact		Dissemination potential		Public perception	Special preparation	Category
	Disease	Death	P-D[b]	P-P[c]			
Smallpox	+	++	+	+++	+++	+++	A
Anthrax	++	+++	+++	0	+++	+++	A
Plague[d]	++	+++	++	++	++	+++	A
Botulism	++	+++	++	0	++	+++	A
Tularemia	++	++	++	0	+	+++	A
VHF[e]	++	+++	+	+	+++	++	A
VE[f]	++	+	+	0	++	++	B
Q Fever	+	+	++	0	+	++	B
Brucellosis	+	+	++	0	+	++	B
Glanders	++	+++	++	0	0	++	B
Melioidosis	+	+	++	0	0	++	B
Psittacosis	+	+	++	0	0	+	B
Ricin toxin	++	++	++	0	0	++	B
Typhus	+	+	++	0	0	+	B
Cholera[g]	+	+	++	+/-	+++	+	B
Shigellosis[g]	+	+	++	+	+	+	B

[a]Agents were ranked from highest threat (+++) to lowest (0).
[b]Potential for production and dissemination in quantities that would affect a large population, based on availability, BSL requirements, most effective route of infection, and environmental stability.
[c]Person-to-person transmissibility.
[d]Pneumonic plague.
[e]Viral hemorrhagic fevers due to Filoviruses (*Ebola, Marburg*) or Arenaviruses (e.g., *Lassa, Machupo*).
[f]Viral encephalitis.
[g]Examples of food- and waterborne diseases.

SOURCE: Lisa D. Rotz, Ali S. Kahn, Scott R. Lillibridge, Stephen M. Ostroff, and James M. Hughes, "Table 2. Criteria and weighting[a] used to evaluate potential biological threat agents," in "Public Health Assessment of Potential Biological Terrorism Agents," *Emerging Infectious Diseases,* vol. 8, num. 2, February 2002

U.S. food and water are probably the world's safest, but even without deliberate contamination, there are still unintentional nationwide outbreaks of contamination. These outbreaks demonstrate the need for ongoing vigilance. The federal government coordinates multiagency efforts to confront possible biological and chemical attacks against the U.S. population.

CRITICAL BIOLOGICAL AND CHEMICAL AGENTS

Biological Agents

THREAT DELINEATION. The first step in preparing for biological or chemical attacks is the detection of threats. The CDC has gone to great lengths to identify and prioritize biological and chemical weapons agents. Priorities are based less on the likelihood of an agent's use than on the probability that it can cause widespread catastrophe. Agents have traditionally been evaluated based on military concerns and troop protection, but civilian populations differ in many ways from military populations, having a wider age range and a wider range of health conditions. In general, civilian populations are more vulnerable, and consequences of an attack will be more severe. This means that military priority lists cannot simply be carried over and applied to civilian threats.

In 1999 Congress began an initiative to upgrade public health capabilities to respond to potential biological and chemical attacks, making the CDC the lead agency for overall public health planning. The CDC, in turn, formed a Bioterrorism Preparedness and Response Office to focus on several areas of preparedness, including planning, improved surveillance and epidemiologic capabilities, rapid laboratory diagnostics, enhanced communications, and medical therapeutics stockpiling.

To focus the preparedness efforts properly, the first step was to have critical biological and chemical agents formally identified and prioritized. Many biological agents affect human beings, but relatively few, authorities reasoned, have the potential to create public health catastrophes that would severely strain public health and medical infrastructures in the United States, so the CDC sought a new threat-assessment method that would provide a reviewable, reproducible, standardized means of threat assessment. This went beyond the military's assessment of threats on the battlefield. In addition, it went beyond the work of a previous civilian group, the Working Group in Civilian Biodefense, which had used an expert panel's consensus to identify several biological agents that would have a high impact if used aggressively against a civilian population.

On June 3–4, 1999, the CDC convened its own meeting of national experts to review the threat potential of various biological and chemical agents to civilian populations. The experts included academic infectious disease experts, national public health experts, CDC personnel, civilian and military intelligence experts, and law enforcement officials. The experts reviewed a number of unclassified documents regarding threat agents: 1) the Select Agent list (a CDC list of specific agents that have a potential bio-criminal use.); 2) the Australia Group List for Biological Agents for Export Control; 3) the Biological and Toxin Weapons Convention list; and 4) the World Health Organization Biological Weapons list. Participants with appropriate security clearances also reviewed intelligence information on classified suspected biological agent threats to civilians.

Genetically engineered (artificially manipulated DNA) or recombinant (DNA altered by combining genetic material from different sources) agents were considered but not included in the final lists, because too little was known about them. No attempt was made, either, to assess the public health system's current level of preparedness against the use of any specific agent, since the experts felt they could not judge that. They chose not to rely on outside information regarding the likelihood that one agent would be used over another in prioritizing the list of biological/chemical threat agents.

Instead, the participants identified agents they believed had the potential for great public health impact based on subjective assessments in four general categories: overall public health impact (the death or disease rates), dissemination potential (how much the disease could spread), public perception of its impact, and the special preparedness needed for each agent. These criteria were weighted on a scale from zero to three for each agent, in order to evaluate the potential threat from each. A factor given the most weight received a three (+++), and the factor given the least weight received a zero (0). (See Table 4.5.) Final category assignments—A, B, or C threat status—were based on the ratings the agents received in each of the four areas. (See Table 4.6.)

Category A agents have the greatest potential for causing disruption, disease, and mass casualties, and require the broadest public health preparedness, including improved surveillance, laboratory diagnosis, and medication stockpiling. Examples of Category A agents are those that cause smallpox, anthrax, plague, botulism, and tularaemia. (See Table 4.6.)

Category B agents have the potential for large-scale catastrophe but generally would cause fewer cases of severe illness and death than Category A agents. They would have a smaller public health and medical impact, have lower public awareness, and require fewer special preparedness measures. Although these, too, should receive heightened awareness from the medical and emergency communities, along with more surveillance and improved laboratory diagnostic capabilities, these are not needed for Category B agents on the order suggested for

TABLE 4.6

Critical biological agents that pose a risk to national security

Category A

The U.S. public health system and primary health-care providers must be prepared to address varied biological agents, including pathogens that are rarely seen in the United States. High-priority agents include organisms that pose a risk to national security because they

- can be easily disseminated or transmitted person-to-person;
- cause high mortality, with potential for major public health impact;
- might cause public panic and social disruption; and
- require special action for public health preparedness (Box 2).

Category A agents include

- variola major (smallpox);
- *Bacillus anthracis* (anthrax);
- *Yersinia pestis* (plague);
- *Clostridium botulinum* toxin (botulism);
- *Francisella tularensis* (tularaemia);
- filoviruses,
  — Ebola hemorrhagic fever,
  — Marburg hemorrhagic fever; and
- arenaviruses,
  — Lassa (Lassa fever),
  — Junin (Argentine hemorrhagic fever) and related viruses.

Category B

Second highest priority agents include those that

- are moderately easy to disseminate;
- cause moderate morbidity and low mortality; and
- require specific enhancements of CDC's diagnostic capacity and enhanced disease surveillance.

Category B agents include

- *Coxiella burnetti* (Q fever);
- *Brucella* species (brucellosis);
- *Burkholderia mallei* (glanders);
- alphaviruses,
  — Venezuelan encephalomyelitis,
  — eastern and western equine encephalomyelitis;
- ricin toxin from *Ricinus communis* (castor beans);
- epsilon toxin of *Clostridium perfringens;* and
- *Staphylococcus* enterotoxin B.
  A subset of List B agents includes pathogens that are food- or waterborne. These pathogens include but are not limited to
- *Salmonella* species,
- *Shigella dysenteriae,*
- *Escherichia coli* O157:H7,
- *Vibrio cholerae,* and
- *Cryptosporidium parvum.*

Category C

Third highest priority agents include emerging pathogens that could be engineered for mass dissemination in the future because of

- availability;
- ease of production and dissemination; and
- potential for high morbidity and mortality and major health impact.

Category C agents include

- Nipah virus,
- hantaviruses,
- tickborne hemorrhagic fever viruses,
- tickborne encephalitis viruses,
- yellow fever, and
- multidrug-resistant tuberculosis.

Preparedness for List C agents requires ongoing research to improve disease detection, diagnosis, treatment, and prevention. Knowing in advance which newly emergent pathogens might be employed by terrorists is not possible; therefore, linking bioterrorism preparedness efforts with ongoing disease surveillance and outbreak response activities as defined in CDC's emerging infectious disease strategy is imperative.

SOURCE: Ali S. Khan, Alexandra M. Levitt, and Michael J. Sage, "BOX 3. Critical biological agents," in "Biological and Chemical Terrorism: Strategic Plan for Preparedness and Response," *Morbidity and Mortality Weekly Report*, vol. 49, num. RR-4, April 21, 2000

TABLE 4.7

Steps in preparing public health agencies for biological attacks

- Enhance epidemiologic capacity to detect and respond to biological attacks.
- Supply diagnostic reagents to state and local public health agencies.
- Establish communication programs to ensure delivery of accurate information.
- Enhance bioterrorism-related education and training for health-care professionals.
- Prepare educational materials that will inform and reassure the public during and after a biological attack.
- Stockpile appropriate vaccines and drugs.
- Establish molecular surveillance for microbial strains, including unusual or drug-resistant strains.
- Support the development of diagnostic tests.
- Encourage research on antiviral drugs and vaccines.

SOURCE: Ali S. Khan, Alexandra M. Levitt, and Michael J. Sage, "BOX 2. Preparing public health agencies for biological attacks," in "Biological and Chemical Terrorism: Strategic Plan for Preparedness and Response," *Morbidity and Mortality Weekly Report*, vol. 49, num. RR-4, April 21, 2000

Category A agents. In Category B are some agents that the CDC and its experts know have undergone development as weapons but that otherwise do not meet Category A criteria, as well as some agents of concern for food and water safety. Examples of Category B agents include organisms that cause Q fever, brucellosis, and glanders, as well as food- or waterborne agents such as salmonella and *E. coli* pathogens. (See Table 4.6.)

Category C agents do not currently appear to present a high bioterrorism threat, but may emerge as future threats as scientific knowledge about them improves. These agents are addressed by the CDC's overall preparedness efforts—efforts intended to improve detection and treatment of unexplained illnesses and emerging infectious diseases. Category C agents include the Nipah virus, hantaviruses, yellow fever, and multidrug-resistant tuberculosis. (See Table 4.6.)

The agents were categorized based on the evaluation criteria applied to them, especially in Categories A and B. For example, the public health impact of smallpox (Category A) ranks higher than that of brucellosis (Category B), because the mortality for those untreated is higher for the former (about 30 percent) than the latter (about 2 percent). In addition, smallpox has a higher dissemination potential, because it can be transmitted person-to-person. It ranks higher for special public health preparedness, as well, because additional vaccine must be made and stockpiled, and improved surveillance, educational, and diagnostic efforts are necessary. Other Category A threats, such as inhalation anthrax and plague, also have higher public impact ratings than brucellosis, because of their higher morbidity (illness) and mortality (death) rates. Although mass production of Category B agents *Vibrio cholerae* (the organism causing cholera) and *Shigella spp* (the cause of shigellosis) would be easier than that of anthrax spores, these agents produce lower morbidity and mortality, so their public health impact, or dissemination threat, would be less. Though infectious doses of these bacteria are very

low, it also requires great effort to use them effectively. The total amount of bacteria required, and the advanced state of current water purification and food-processing techniques, would limit these agents' effectiveness for intentional, large-scale water or food contamination.

PREPAREDNESS ACTIVITIES. In addition to identifying major biological agents and threats, the CDC provides resources for the nine basic steps, listed in Table 4.7, involved in national biological attack preparation. Enhancing epidemiologic capacity means adding additional resources to trace the source and spread of disease. Supplying diagnostic reagents means providing chemical compounds to state and local public health agencies for a variety of medical purposes ranging from detection to prevention.

Chemical Agents

THREAT DELINEATION. Chemical agents can range from warfare agents to toxic substances in common commercial use. Like the threat of biological warfare, the likelihood of chemical warfare also is likely to grow in the next several years. Many states have chemical capabilities now, and it is likely those capabilities will spread to other states and possibly even terrorists. The fact that chemical warfare–related technologies are increasingly available, coupled with the relative ease with which chemical agents can be produced, increases the U.S. government's concern that terrorist states or groups may use them in the future.

The CDC takes a similar, if slightly different, approach to gauging chemical threats as biological ones. It provides much the same resources to state and local public health agencies and emergency services teams, in order for them to be prepared for chemical attacks. However, the CDC's identification and prioritization of critical chemical agents differs from that of biological agents. Because hundreds of new chemicals are introduced internationally each month, the categories of chemical agents are necessarily more generic than for biological agents.

As it does with biological threats and agents, the CDC has identified and prioritized chemical agents according to criteria such as: Are the agents already known to be used as weapons? Are they readily available to hostile states and terrorists? Are they likely to cause morbidity or mortality? Are they likely to cause panic or disruption? Do they require special actions for public health preparedness? (See Table 4.8.)

Table 4.8 lists all of the CDC's chemical agent categories, along with notable examples of each. The types of chemical agents most likely to be used are nerve agents (tabun, sarin, soman, GF, and VX), blood agents (hydrogen cyanide and cyanogen chloride), blister agents (lewisite, mustards, and phosgene oxime), and heavy metals (arsenic, lead, and mercury). Some common chemical agents and their effects are listed in Table 3.5 in Chapter 3.

TABLE 4.8

Chemical agents that might be used by terrorists

Chemical agents that might be used by terrorists range from warfare agents to toxic chemicals commonly used in industry. Criteria for determining priority chemical agents include

- chemical agents already known to be used as weaponry;
- availability of chemical agents to potential terrorists;
- chemical agents likely to cause major morbidity or mortality;
- potential of agents for causing public panic and social disruption; and
- agents that require special action for public health preparedness (Box 4).

Categories of chemical agents include
- nerve agents,
  — tabun (ethyl N,N-dimethylphosphoramidocyanidate),
  — sarin (isopropyl methylphosphanofluoridate),
  — soman (pinacolyl methyl phosphonofluoridate),
  — GF (cyclohexylmethylphosphonofluoridate),
  — VX (o-ethyl-[S]-[2-diisopropylaminoethyl]-methylphosphonothiolate);
- blood agents,
  — hydrogen cyanide,
  — cyanogen chloride;
- blister agents,
  — lewisite (an aliphatic arsenic compound, 2-chlorovinyldichloroarsine),
  — nitrogen and sulfur mustards,
  — phosgene oxime;
- heavy metals,
  — arsenic,
  — lead,
  — mercury;
- Volatile toxins,
  — benzene,
  — chloroform,
  — trihalomethanes;
- pulmonary agents,
  — phosgene,
  — chlorine,
  — vinyl chloride;
- incapacitating agents,
  — BZ (3-quinuclidinyl benzilate);
- pesticides, persistent and nonpersistent;
- dioxins, furans, and polychlorinated biphenyls (PCBs);
- explosive nitro compounds and oxidizers,
  — ammonium nitrate combined with fuel oil;
- flammable industrial gases and liquids,
  — gasoline,
  — propane;
- poison industrial gases, liquids, and solids,
  — cyanides,
  — nitriles; and
- corrosive industrial acids and bases,
  — nitric acid,
  — sulfuric acid.

SOURCE: Ali S. Khan, Alexandra M. Levitt, and Michael J. Sage, "BOX 5. Chemical agents," in "Biological and Chemical Terrorism: Strategic Plan for Preparedness and Response," *Morbidity and Mortality Weekly Report*, vol. 49, num. RR-4, April 21, 2000

PREPAREDNESS ACTIVITIES. The CDC also provides recommendations to help public health agencies prepare for potential chemical attacks. To begin with, agencies should take a generic approach to the treatment of chemical agent injuries, treating those exposed according to clinical syndrome, or the group of symptoms they have, rather than the specific agent. These syndromes include burns and trauma, cardiorespiratory failure, neurologic damage, and shock. Those who respond and treat affected individuals must also communicate with the authorities responsible for environmental sampling for, and decontamination of areas affected by, such chemical agents.

TABLE 4.9

Steps in preparing public health agencies for chemical attacks

- Enhance epidemiologic capacity for detecting and responding to chemical attacks.
- Enhance awareness of chemical terrorism among emergency medical service personnel, police officers, firefighters, physicians, and nurses.
- Stockpile chemical antidotes.
- Develop and provide bioassays for detection and diagnosis of chemical injuries.
- Prepare educational materials to inform the public during and after a chemical attack.

SOURCE: Ali S. Khan, Alexandra M. Levitt, and Michael J. Sage, "BOX 4. Preparing public health agencies for chemical attacks," in "Biological and Chemical Terrorism: Strategic Plan for Preparedness and Response," *Morbidity and Mortality Weekly Report*, vol. 49, num. RR-4, April 21, 2000

The CDC's five steps in preparing public health agencies for chemical attacks are listed in Table 4.9. (Enhancing epidemiological capacity refers to mapping the origin and spread of disease symptoms. Bioassays are intended to determine the relative strength of a chemical agent by comparing its effect on a test organism with that of a standard-strength preparation).

Laboratory Response Network

The CDC has described five key focus areas of state and local efforts to prepare for biological and chemical attacks:

1) Preparedness and prevention

2) Detection and surveillance

3) Diagnosis and characterization of biological and chemical agents

4) Response

5) Communication

Perhaps the most technically challenging of the five focus areas is the third area: diagnosis and characterization of biological and chemical agents. For that reason, the CDC and its partners created a multilevel laboratory response network for bioterrorism. (See Figure 4.2.) This network links state-of-the-art clinical labs to state and local public health agencies in all states, districts, territories, and selected cities and counties. The CDC has set up a four-level hierarchy of labs, according to their respective capabilities. Level D is the most sophisticated; level A is the least sophisticated. The more sophisticated labs provide both specimen testing for, and training/consultation to, their less sophisticated counterparts.

The four types of laboratories are described in detail in Figure 4.2 and summarized below:

- Level A labs are public health and hospital labs focusing on the early detection of intentionally disseminated biological agents.

FIGURE 4.2

Multilevel laboratory response network for bioterrorism that will link clinical labs to public health agencies

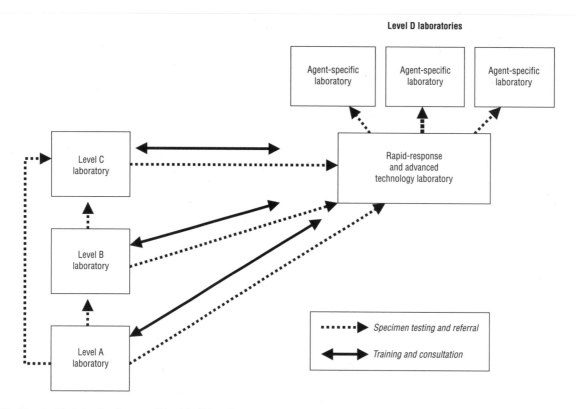

Functional Levels of the Laboratory Response Network for Bioterrorism

Level A: Early detection of intentional dissemination of biological agents — Level A laboratories will be public health and hospital laboratories with low-level biosafety facilities. Level A laboratories will use clinical data and standard microbiological tests to decide which specimens and isolates should be forwarded to higher level biocontainment laboratories. Level A laboratory staff will be trained in the safe collection, packaging, labeling, and shipping of samples that might contain dangerous pathogens.

Level B: Core capacity for agent isolation and presumptive-level testing of suspect specimens — Level B laboratories will be state and local public health agency laboratries that can test for specific agents and forward organisms or specimens to higher level biocontainment laboratories. Level B laboratories will minimize false positives and protect Level C laboratories from overload. Ultimately, Level B laboratories will maintain capacity to perform confirmatory testing and characterize drug susceptibility.

Level C: Advanced capacity for rapid identification — Level C laboratories, which could be located at state health agencies, academic research centers, or federal facilities, will perform advanced and specialized testing. Ultimately, Level C laboratories will have the capacity to perform toxicity testing and employ advanced diagnostic technologies (e.g., nucleic acid amplification and molecular fingerprinting). Level C laboratories will participate in the evaluation of new tests and reagents and determine which assays could be transferred to Level B laboratories.

Level D: Highest level containment and expertise in the diagnosis of rare and dangerous biological agents — Level D laboratories will be specialized federal laboratories with unique experience in diagnosis of rare diseases (e.g., smallpox and Ebola). Level D laboratories also will develop or evaluate new tests and methods and have the resources to maintain a strain bank of biological agents. Level D laboratories will maintain the highest biocontainment facilities and will be able to conduct all tests performed in Level A, B,and C laboratories, as well as additional confirmatory testing and characterization, as needed. They will also have the capacity to detect genetically engineered agents.

SOURCE: Ali S. Khan, Alexandra M. Levitt, and Michael J. Sage, "FIGURE 1. Multilevel laboratory response network for bioterrorism that will link clinical labs to public health agencies," in "Biological and Chemical Terrorism: Strategic Plan for Preparedness and Response," *Morbidity and Mortality Weekly Report,* vol. 49, num. RR-4, April 21, 2000

• Level B labs are state and local public agency labs mostly testing suspect specimens and forwarding organisms or specimens to higher-level biocontainment laboratories.

• Level C labs are labs at state health agencies, academic research centers, and federal facilities performing toxicity testing, molecular fingerprinting, and other advanced techniques.

• Level D labs are specialized federal laboratories with unique experience in diagnosing rare diseases. They represent the highest-level containment capability and diagnostic expertise for analysis of rare, dangerous agents.

A crucial part of the CDC laboratory response network is the in-house, rapid-response, advanced-technology laboratory it is creating. This laboratory provides 24-hour diagnostic "confirmatory and reference support" for terrorism-response teams. The network also includes regional chemical laboratories for diagnosing exposure to chemical agents and has links to other departments (for example, the EPA, which is responsible for environmental sampling).

PROTECTING ANIMALS AND PLANTS

The Animal and Plant Health Inspection Service (APHIS)

Animals and plants, especially those that human beings depend on for food, are also subject to attack. On the front line of this problem is the USDA's Animal and Plant Health Inspection Service (APHIS). APHIS is a largely unknown agency but an important one. It is one of many on the GAO list slated to be merged into the U.S. Department of Homeland Security supported by President George W. Bush, because it monitors the nation's borders for foreign agricultural diseases and pests. It protects farm animals from disease and pestilence and provides a host of services to cattle ranchers, milk producers, turkey farmers, and other agrarian groups.

One in eight American jobs and 13 percent of the U.S. gross national product (the value of all the goods and services produced in the country) are dependent on the agricultural productivity of the United States. The country's economic stability depends on a safe and readily available food supply system. U.S. crops and livestock could be tempting targets to terrorists because of the perceived ease of attack and the limited varieties of plant seeds in use. Livestock and plant pathogens could threaten U.S. agricultural productivity and cause economic damage. Disrupting supply lines for food stocks that would feed troops or threatening the safety of those items supplied may also erode military readiness.

Potential threats to U.S. agricultural products and livestock come from a number of pathogens and agents. Animals could contract many types of disease, including anthrax, Q fever, brucellosis, foot-and-mouth disease (FMD), Venezuelan equine encephalitis, hog cholera, African swine fever, avian influenza, Newcastle disease, Rift Valley fever, rinderpest, and others. (Table 4.10 lists some of the pathogens that the DOD believes may threaten U.S. plants and animals.) Many staple plants, such as corn, wheat, rice, and soybeans, are susceptible to disease. Soybean rust, for example, can be easily introduced and spreads quickly, causing U.S. soybean producers, processors, livestock producers (who feed soy products to their animals), and consumers to lose up to $8 billion annually, according to USDA estimates.

Some of these plant and animal agents can be found outside U.S. borders, and many can be readily transported, inadvertently or intentionally, into the United States, some with low risk of detection. APHIS is the agency responsible for diagnosis and management of all suspicious agricultural disease outbreaks. Binding international agreements force countries to immediately

TABLE 4.10

Foreign livestock and plant pathogens which threaten agricultural productivity

Animal Disease	Plant Disease
Foot and Mouth Disease	Soybean Rust (Soybean Plant)
Vesicular Stomatitis	Ear Rot (Corn)
Rinderpest Gibberella	Karnal Bunt (Wheat)
African Swine Fever	Ergot (Sorghum)
Highly Pathogenic Avian Influenza	Bacterial Blight (Rice)
Rift Valley Fever	Ring Rot (Potatoes)
Lumpy Skin Disease	Wirrega Blotch (Barley)
Bluetongue	
Sheep and Goat Pox	
Swine Vesicular Disease	
Contagious Bovine Pleuropneumonia	
Newcastle Disease	
African Horse Sickness	
Classical Swine Fever	

SOURCE: "Foreign Livestock and Plant Pathogens which Threaten U.S. Agricultural Productivity," in *Proliferation: Threat and Response*, U.S. Department of Defense, Office of the Secretary of Defense, Washington, DC, January 2001

disclose select plant and animal disease outbreaks, regardless of severity. Such disclosures can have an instant impact on export trade, as other countries prohibit potentially contaminated items from entering their borders. APHIS's authority, depending on the pathogen involved, extends as far as confiscation of property and eradication of all plant and animal hosts within certain zones of quarantine. National security and public trust can both be threatened in such cases, depending on the extent of disease transmission, the success of the government's response, and the amount of time it takes to get things back to normal.

Foot-and-Mouth Disease (FMD)

One example of how countries' livestock industries can be affected by disease has been the various outbreaks of foot-and-mouth (also called hoof-and-mouth) disease (FMD). During an outbreak in the United Kingdom in 1967 and 1968, for example, more than 430,000 animals were destroyed; a much more recent outbreak in 2000–01 in the United Kingdom and Ireland forced the destruction of more than 8 million animals at over 10,000 locations. The outbreak caused severe economic hardships throughout the United Kingdom and parts of Europe.

A member of the picornavirus family, FMD is endemic in many parts of the world, but the United States has not seen cases since the 1920s. Thus few American veterinarians are familiar with the early stages of FMD infection. An animal becomes infected shortly after exposure, but well before the onset of clinical symptoms. When symptoms do occur, they may include a sudden rise in temperature, followed by an eruption of blisters in the mouth, in the nostrils, on areas of tender skin, and on the feet. The blisters expand, then break, exposing raw, eroded skin surfaces.

Eating becomes difficult and painful. Because the soft tissue under the hooves is swollen, the animal starts limping. Livestock raised for meat lose weight, and dairy cattle and goats give far less milk. FMD kills very young animals and causes pregnant females to abort.

The mere transport of infected tissue can start an epidemic—a single infected cow or pig can generate sufficient viral particles to communicate the disease over vast geographic areas in weeks. An outbreak of the highly contagious disease could be easily introduced to the United States and might debilitate the U.S. livestock industry. An outbreak could cost as much as $20 billion over 15 years in increased consumer costs, reduced livestock productivity, and restricted trade, according to the USDA.

APHIS does not permit imports of FMD-positive animals. While the development of an effective vaccine is believed to be imminent, vaccinating all susceptible animals would cost about $1 billion annually, a prohibitive cost. In addition, the vaccine would not eradicate the disease. Currently the only effective countermeasure for FMD is the slaughter and incineration of all exposed and infected animals.

CHAPTER 5

INTERNATIONAL TERRORISM

On September 11, 2001, nineteen terrorists hijacked four U.S. commercial airliners and proceeded to fly two of the planes into the twin towers of the World Trade Center in New York City and one into the Pentagon in Washington, D.C. The fourth plane crashed in Pennsylvania. More than 3,000 people were killed and thousands more injured as a result of these devastating attacks that caught the United States and the rest of the world by surprise. After spending years on the backburner, the term "terrorism" captured the world's attention. It caused a media frenzy and spread fear and insecurity among the American public at a rate unparalleled since the early days of the Cold War (1945–89) between the United States and the Soviet Union. Before this attack on U.S. territory, "Osama bin Laden" and "al-Qaeda" were terms heard mostly among terrorism experts. Now these names, and many other terms associated with terrorism, are almost omnipresent in the media and in politics.

DEFINING TERRORISM

As with "national security," "terrorism" is a tricky term to define, particularly since it involves subjective social issues and relies on the unique perceptions of the definer. The saying "one man's terrorist is another man's freedom fighter" illustrates this difficulty. Most analysts find it much easier to define whether a specific act is terrorist in nature than to find a broad definition of the term itself.

Although many experts believe that there is generally an intuitive understanding of what constitutes terrorism, it is important for governments to define the term for the purposes of prevention and retaliation. Some definitions of "terrorism" offered by academic sources and government-policy analysts include:

- "The political use of violence or intimidation." — *American Heritage Dictionary*

- "...the threat of violence, individual acts of violence, or a campaign of violence designed primarily to instill

fear." —Brian Michael Jenkins, "International Terrorism: A New Mode of Conflict," in David Carlton and Carlo Schaerf (eds.), *International Terrorism and World Security*, Croom Helm, London, 1975

- "...the illegitimate use of force to achieve a political objective when innocent people are targeted." —Walter Laqueur, *The Age of Terrorism,* Little, Brown, Boston, 1987

- "...coercive intimidation, premeditated acts or threats of violence systemically aimed at instilling such fear in the target that it will force the target to alter its behavior in the way desired by the terrorists." —Paul Wilkinson, *Technology and Terrorism,* Frank Cass, London, 1993

- "...the recurrent use or threatened use of politically-motivated and clandestinely organized violence, by a group whose aim is to influence a psychological target in order to make it behave in a way which the group desires." —C. J. M. Drake, *Terrorist Target Selection,* St. Martin's Press, New York, 1998

- "...the unlawful use of force or violence against persons or property to intimidate or coerce a Government, the civilian population, or any segment thereof, in furtherance of political or social objectives." —Federal Bureau of Investigation (FBI)

- "...the unlawful use of—or threatened use of—force or violence against individuals or property to coerce or intimidate governments or societies, often to achieve political, religious, or ideological objectives." —U.S. Department of Defense

- "...premeditated, politically motivated violence perpetrated against noncombatant targets by subnational groups or clandestine agents, usually intended to influence an audience." —U.S. Department of State

Such definitions show that even experts cannot agree on one definition of "terrorism." Most of the time, it is the legitimate authority in power that decides whether a group or individual is terrorist in nature.

MOTIVATIONS AND TRENDS

Intelligence specialists call terrorism a "transnational" threat, because the people who make up terrorist groups may not come from, represent, or be sponsored by a particular country. Instead, they can operate across international boundaries and against any number of countries to further their cause or objectives. Though sometimes state-sponsored, terrorists are infrequently what American officials call "state actors," such as foreign governments; rather, they are generally doing their own work and pursuing their own goals.

Terrorism generally involves some political or religious message and is almost always violent in nature. Some of the actions that the U.S. State Department defines as terrorist activities include:

- The hijacking or sabotage of any conveyance (including an aircraft, vessel, or vehicle)

- Seizing or detaining, and threatening to kill, injure, or continue to detain, another individual in order to compel a third person (or governmental organization) to do or abstain from doing any act as an explicit or implicit condition for the release of the individual seized or detained

- A violent attack upon an internationally protected person (defined as 1) a chief of state, head of government, or foreign minister in a country other than his or her own and any accompanying family member; or 2) any other representative, officer, employee, or agent of the U.S. government, a foreign government, or international organization and any member of his or her family/household) or upon the liberty of such a person

- An assassination

- Using any biological agent, chemical agent, nuclear weapon or device, explosive, firearm, or other weapon or dangerous device with intent to endanger, directly or indirectly, the safety of one or more individuals or to cause substantial damage to property (other than for mere personal monetary gain)

- A threat, attempt, or conspiracy to do any of these activities

Violence and terrorism usually occur together, as the message delivered by the terrorists is intended to reach an audience beyond simply the targets or victims of an attack. As a result, most terrorist attacks are also quite symbolic in nature. In the September 11 attacks, the World Trade Center towers and the Pentagon represented the might of the U.S. economy and military. In the past, other symbolic terrorist targets have included temples, synagogues, government offices, military bases and barracks, and police personnel.

Terrorist tactics have varied over the years as well. They have ranged from single-person attacks to those involving mass destruction and casualties. Kidnappings, sabotage, assassinations, knifing campaigns, hijackings, murders, bombings, bank robberies, and cyberattacks are all tactics employed by terrorists.

Most terrorist attacks are motivated by political or religious conflict. Ethnonationalist or separatist attacks were prevalent during the Cold War, when state ideologies were more easily categorized. These terrorist groups desired their own sovereign territory in which to pursue a chosen political philosophy. When the collapse of the Soviet Union brought an end to the bipolar global order in the early 1990s, most separatist terrorist groups found themselves without prominent state funders and without defining political ideologies.

Separatist conflicts continue in many parts of the world, including Colombia, Chechnya, the former Yugoslavia, the Basque region of France and Spain, Ireland, and several African states, but most of these conflicts have taken the form of national civil wars rather than terrorist attacks. Yet the kidnappings of Western missionaries by Abu Sayyaf rebels in the Philippines and a November 2002 movie theater takeover by Chechen rebels in Moscow, Russia (in which more than 100 people—including at least two U.S. citizens—were killed when the Russian government used paralyzing gas to try to rescue them) are clear indications that separatist agendas around the world are far from resolved.

Terror groups motivated by religious obligations, however, have been on the rise since the 1980s. For centuries, religion and violence have occasionally gone hand in hand—the fervor inspired by religion is often felt to justify the violence undertaken in its name. Terrorists feel they are committing violent acts for the sake of divinity and religious sanctity.

Most separatist or secular (nonreligious) groups have a set political agenda in mind and must always strive to maintain the support of their constituency. This means they cannot commit heinous acts without risking alienating such support or facing widespread condemnation. Religious terrorists may not care about such support, as they believe God is their main audience. Or, they may believe that they are fighting for downtrodden people everywhere, whom they seek to defend against "infidels" in a holy war sanctioned by a divine power. Following this logic, it may be much easier for a religiously motivated terrorist group to perpetrate a mass-casualty attack. Examples include the 1995 Tokyo, Japan, nerve-gas attack orchestrated by the Aum Shinrikyo cult and the September 11 attacks undertaken by al-Qaeda members.

FIGURE 5.1

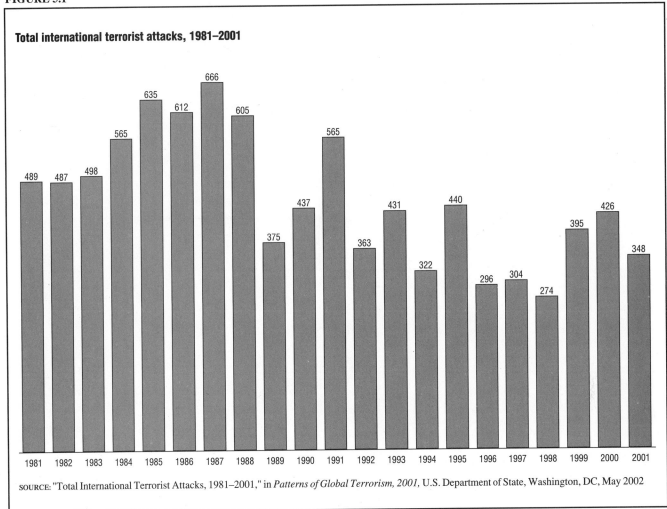

Total international terrorist attacks, 1981–2001

SOURCE: "Total International Terrorist Attacks, 1981–2001," in *Patterns of Global Terrorism, 2001,* U.S. Department of State, Washington, DC, May 2002

Religion and politics are not always easy to separate. In the case of cults or millenarian groups (those believing in the 1,000-year period of Christian triumph on Earth as predicted in the Bible) that shut themselves away from society, the single-minded religious agenda is not hard to identify. However, when one profiles certain Islamic groups operating out of the Middle East, it is clear that both religion and politics are involved in the groups' ideologies. Hizballah, for example, which has a defining Islamic philosophy, also serves as a strong political faction in Lebanon. This is the case as well with the group Hamas, which calls upon religion to recruit followers but is also a formidable political alternative to the Palestinian Authority in the West Bank and Gaza.

Another identifiable trend in the world of terrorism is the emergence of "cells," or ad-hoc groups that form to conduct a particular attack without a strong organizational structure, base, or leader. The danger in such small amorphous and ephemeral groups is that they are hard to track, because of their short-lived nature and lack of established patterns. Single-issue terrorist groups, such as those fighting against abortion or for various environmental purposes, can also fall into the "cell" pattern, though they may tend to focus more on urbanized areas and promote causes that are more restrictive than the broader goals of religious or nationalist/separatist terrorist organizations.

INTERNATIONAL TERRORISM STATISTICS

The average number of international terrorist attacks from 1981 to 2001 was about 450 per year. (See Figure 5.1.) This average was lower during the years 1996–2001—about 350 per year. The total number increased 8 percent from 1999 to 2000, from 392 to 423 attacks, but dropped 18 percent from 2000 to 2001, to 348 attacks in the latter year.

Of total anti-U.S. terror attacks as of 2000, those against businesses (almost 400) far outnumbered those against other types of targets (18 attacks against diplomatic targets, 13 against government targets, and 4 against military targets). (See Figure 5.2.) In 2000 there were 152 bombings of the Colombian pipeline, a multinational oil pipeline in Colombia, that accounted for 40 percent of international terrorist acts in that year. Of the 346 international terrorist attacks in 2001, 178 (51 percent) were bombings of the Colombian pipeline.

FIGURE 5.2

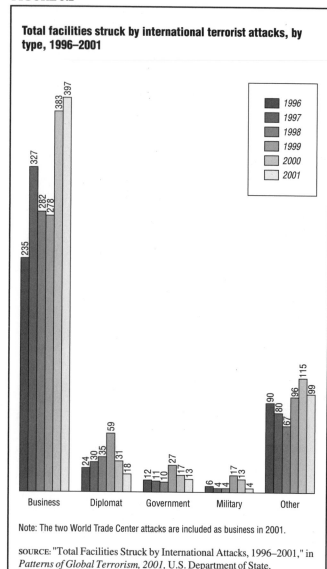

Total facilities struck by international terrorist attacks, by type, 1996–2001

Legend: 1996, 1997, 1998, 1999, 2000, 2001

Note: The two World Trade Center attacks are included as business in 2001.

SOURCE: "Total Facilities Struck by International Attacks, 1996–2001," in *Patterns of Global Terrorism, 2001*, U.S. Department of State, Washington, DC, May 2002

FIGURE 5.3

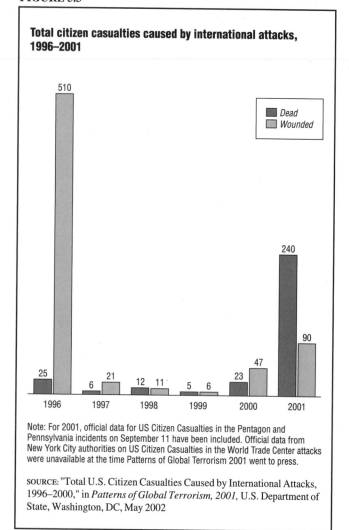

Total citizen casualties caused by international attacks, 1996–2001

Legend: Dead, Wounded

Note: For 2001, official data for US Citizen Casualties in the Pentagon and Pennsylvania incidents on September 11 have been included. Official data from New York City authorities on US Citizen Casualties in the World Trade Center attacks were unavailable at the time Patterns of Global Terrorism 2001 went to press.

SOURCE: "Total U.S. Citizen Casualties Caused by International Attacks, 1996–2000," in *Patterns of Global Terrorism, 2001*, U.S. Department of State, Washington, DC, May 2002

The decline in the total number of attacks does not represent a decline in the number of casualties inflicted in each attack. According to the U.S. State Department, in the 423 international terrorist attacks of 2000, 405 people were killed and 791 were wounded, compared with 233 killed and 706 wounded in 1999. Because more than 3,000 people were killed in the September 11, 2001, attacks by al-Qaeda, casualties in 2001 far outnumbered those of any previous year. Approximately 3,370 people were killed in international terrorist attacks in 2001, the highest annual death toll from terrorism ever recorded.

The number of U.S. fatalities from international terrorism from 1995 to 2000 averaged about 13 per year, with the highest number, 25, occurring in 1996. (See Figure 5.3.) According to CNN, the number of casualties from the four September 11 attacks totaled 3,012. In addition to those killed or injured in the September 11 attacks, 8 U.S. citizens were killed and 15 were wounded in separate international terrorist attacks in 2001.

STATE-SPONSORED TERRORISM

The Nature of State-Sponsored Terrorism

In the 2001 edition of the U.S. State Department's *Patterns of Global Terrorism* report, seven countries, including Iraq, were identified as sponsors of terrorism. But exactly what is state-sponsored terrorism? Characterizing the phenomenon briefly is almost as difficult as coming up with a succinct definition for the term "terrorism" itself. Nevertheless, a crucial part of the concept is a sovereign government's involvement (at varying levels) with individual actors or organizations that perpetrate acts of terror. Boaz Ganor, an expert at the International Policy Institute for Counterterrorism in Herzliya, Israel, claims there are a variety of reasons why states might choose to sponsor terrorism. One of the most obvious is the ability to "achieve strategic ends in circumstances where the use of conventional armed forces is deemed inappropriate, ineffective, too risky or too difficult."

State sponsorship of terrorism dates back centuries, as rulers and governments throughout history have aided subnational organizations to wreak havoc on their enemies. The Cold War of the 20th century witnessed abundant support for revolutionary and guerilla organizations by the Soviet and U.S. superpowers. (Guerilla groups are generally irregular forces that fight for revolutionary causes and employ tactics not usually employed by states' regular military forces, like hit-and-run operations and illicit fund-raising.) These groups were seen by the United States and the Soviet Union as conduits to establish more potential allies and fewer potential enemies without the larger threat of a global war. Such efforts occasionally even went so far as to establish "puppet" regimes—essentially, governments put into power through the efforts of a larger, more powerful sponsoring state, which would preach the sponsor's doctrine and promote its interests and philosophies in a given region.

One distinct characteristic of state-sponsored terrorism is its covert nature, including plausible deniability, or the ability of a state to credibly claim it has no knowledge of the terrorist activities occurring. State support for terrorist groups allows the violent expression of the state's unfulfilled goals without overtly pressuring other governments toward certain political ends. State sponsorship of terrorism aspires to promote domestic and foreign policy through clandestine means.

State-sponsored terrorism is also frequently employed to silence dissidents of a regime. Iran, Iraq, Libya, and Syria are a few of the countries identified by the U.S. Department of State as sponsoring such crimes.

State sponsors are often seen as quite desirable by terrorist entities, because of the resources they can provide that would otherwise be difficult and costly to acquire. According to a 1993 State Department report, "International terrorism would not have flourished as it has during the past few decades without the funding, training, safe haven, weapons, and logistic support provided to terrorists by sovereign states."

One of the most blatant acts of state-sponsored terrorism, and one that put the phenomenon on the center stage of international relations, was the 1979 taking of hostages by Iranian "revolutionists." For more than a year, Americans waited anxiously as a group of fundamentalist "students" held 52 Americans hostage in Iran for 444 days. Many of the so-called students were actually agents of the incoming radical Islamic regime headed by Ayatollah Khomeini. This fundamentalist regime had been implicated as a sponsor of several acts of terrorism in the region over the years.

Hossein Sheikhosleslam, a leading figure among the revolutionary students, went on to hold the prestigious post of assistant for political affairs in the Iranian Foreign Ministry after the coup. The Iranian hostage crisis was followed by more than a decade of violence by fundamentalist Islamic and nationalist groups in the Middle East, fueled by anti-Western sentiments, and supported by a handful of states sharing similar ideologies.

Levels of Support

Boaz Ganor has outlined the levels of culpability (blame or guilt) a state incurs based on its depth of involvement in the sponsorship of terrorist activities. According to Ganor, the escalating scale of state involvement begins with mere ideological support and ends with direct terrorist attacks by government agents. The six levels of state involvement outlined by Ganor are:

1) Ideological support. Communism, democracy, and Islamic fundamentalism are a few of the doctrines that a state might choose to support through a puppet regime or terrorist organization.

2) Financial support. This requires funding terrorist organizations with cash in order to carry out their operations.

3) Military support. Training and the supplying of weapons fall under this category. For example, many experts agree that the attack on the USS *Cole* in Aden, Yemen, would not have been possible without some form of military assistance from a state.

4) Operational support. This category involves the logistical support that is involved in carrying out any terrorist operation, such as providing falsified documents and safe havens.

5) Initiating/orchestrating terrorist attacks. It is at this level that states move from passive and indirect complicity to orchestrating terrorist attacks themselves.

6) Direct attacks by government agents. In such instances, agents of the state carry out the attacks themselves to further state agendas and interests.

State Sponsors of International Terrorism

Each year, the U.S. State Department identifies countries it considers terror sponsors, or countries that repeatedly support international terrorism, on a watch list. Countries on the list suffer four sets of U.S. government sanctions. First, a ban on arms-related exports and sales goes into effect. Second, a 30-day congressional notification is required for the export of dual-use items, or those with both civilian and military uses, that could increase military capability or the ability to support terrorism. Third, prohibitions are implemented on economic assistance. Finally, there are various financial and other restrictions, such as U.S. opposition of loans by international financial institutions to terror list countries and the lifting of diplomatic immunity to allow families of terrorist victims to file civil lawsuits in U.S. courts.

The State Department's 2001 list appeared in its annual publication *Patterns of Global Terrorism*. It included Iran, Iraq, Syria, Libya, Sudan, North Korea, and Cuba. Four additional countries—Afghanistan, Pakistan, Lebanon, and Yemen—are listed informally as safe harbors or training grounds for terrorists. In addition, transition states may lend terrorist sponsor states political and material support.

The State Department's list of state sponsors of terrorism is often debated among terrorism experts, many of whom believe it is outdated and merely a political tool the United States uses in order to impose sanctions. Critics of the list also claim that it intentionally does not include some countries, like Saudi Arabia, that are known to have terrorist links but are important to the United States for economic or other reasons.

After the attacks of September 11, 2001, President George W. Bush stated, "Every nation, in every region, now has a decision to make. Either you are with us, or you are with the terrorists. From this day forward, any nation that continues to harbor or support terrorism will be regarded by the United States as a hostile regime." Some state sponsors on the list, like Libya, Sudan, Iran, and Syria, made initial limited moves to cooperate with the international community's campaign against terrorism. Despite hostile relations with the United States, all four states offered deep condolences after the 9/11 attacks. Iran publicly stated that the United States had every right to seek retaliation for these attacks and even closed its boundaries with Afghanistan in order to prevent terrorists from escaping U.S. forces. The Sudan clamped down on extremists within its own boundaries and arrested several alleged members of the al-Qaeda organization.

Despite these moves, the State Department emphasizes that none of its seven state sponsors of terrorism has yet taken all necessary actions to divest itself fully of terrorist ties. For example, the State Department claims Iran and Syria have sought to have it both ways. They have clamped down on certain terrorist groups, such as al-Qaeda, but have maintained their support for others, like Hamas and Hizballah, insisting they are national liberation movements.

In 2002 the United States was carrying out military operations against terrorists in such countries as Afghanistan and Pakistan. This new global war on terrorism could: 1) cause many more U.S. casualties abroad in upcoming months and years; 2) incite further terrorist acts against the U.S. homeland and U.S. interests abroad; and 3) destabilize some of the regions to which the United States carries the war, notably the Middle East. The prospect of increased regional instability in the Middle East raises the possibility that the war on terrorism could become counterproductive over the long term. President Bush made it clear that the first military campaign of the war would only target terrorist organizations and any governments that provided them with safe havens. Many in the Arab world, however, looked upon the war in Afghanistan as anti-Islamic, or an affront to Islam, the religion to which the vast majority of Arabs belong.

Governments of some of the predominantly Islamic countries in the Middle East, including Kuwait, Jordan, and Saudi Arabia, have supported the United States in the past. Others, especially Pakistan, Saudi Arabia, and Egypt, were particularly helpful after the events of September 11, 2001. Still, many of these countries have faced some degree of opposition from domestic groups who believe that the West exploits the region and supports oppressive regimes.

Such perceptions of American support for illegitimate and tyrannical governments are one of the primary motivations for groups such as al-Qaeda, in which charismatic leaders exploit individual frustrations and channel them into a hatred for the West, particularly the United States. Understanding these motivations is very important to help policymakers counter the problem in the long run. Over the years, disaffected individuals from repressed societies have grown increasingly irate with American foreign policies, especially U.S. involvement in the Middle East. They consider U.S. actions in the region as evidence of collaboration with regimes that compromise pure Islamic values and consequently lead to global oppression of Muslims (followers of Islam).

Besides collaboration, other U.S. policies in the Middle East have also contributed to animosities that may present themselves through hostile acts like terrorism. Immediately following the 1991 Persian Gulf War, the United States established military bases in Saudi Arabia in order to have a forward-deployed force (a military force positioned in a region to reach a tactical advantage) in case tensions resumed. The United States has continued its presence in the country ever since. For many Muslims around the world, the notion of a foreign military "occupying" the soil that hosts two of the most sacred sites in Islam (Mecca and Medina) is a sacrilege. Strong American support, both political and military, for the Jewish state of Israel in a region that is predominantly Arab/Muslim also inflames anti-American sentiment.

Still, the United States is interested in the Middle East for a variety of reasons. The region is a major supplier of oil and natural gas and continues to hold large deposits of these vital resources. Western dependence on oil makes American strategic involvement in the region crucial to ensure that oil continues to flow out of the region at reasonable prices. Given Iraqi aggression in the early 1990s, the United States also feels that its presence provides some sense of security for its Persian Gulf allies and thus promotes regional stability.

MIDDLE EAST TENSIONS: THE ISRAELI/PALESTINIAN CONFLICT AND OTHER ISSUES. Tensions with many of the countries in the Middle East have been a problem for the United States for many years. There is much resentment of U.S. support for Israel, a Jewish nation located in the midst of mainly Muslim states. The dispute between Israel and its neighbors, particularly the Palestinians, goes back to 1948, when European Jews gained independence from Western powers occupying the Middle East (mainly Great Britain) and formed an independent Jewish state. The Jews felt the need for their own state in the area of the Middle East that three religions, Judaism, Islam, and Christianity, consider sacred ground. During World War II (1939–45), more than 6 million European Jews had been exterminated by the Nazis during the Holocaust. Many of those who survived had lost numerous relatives and loved ones. They not only felt uncomfortable remaining in Europe but yearned for a homeland in the Holy Land— the biblical "Promised Land" of their ancestors—and a place in which to arrange for their own protection.

However, the indigenous Palestinians and other Arabs in the area were pushed out of some regions by the creation of the new state. They resented that lands they believed were theirs had been taken over by Israel in the vacuum created by the departure of the British. Since that time, the Jews have fought several wars with their Arab neighbors, including the Six-Day War. In that conflict, in June 1967, Israel seized some of the most contested areas in the region: the Sinai Peninsula, the Golan Heights, the West Bank, the Gaza Strip, and East Jerusalem, while fighting Egypt, Jordan, and Syria. Iraq, Kuwait, Saudi Arabia, Sudan, and Algeria also offered aid against the Israeli attacks, but within six days Israel has taken control of the contested areas. Egypt lost the Sinai Peninsula and the Gaza Strip, Jordan lost East Jerusalem and the West Bank, and Syria lost the Golan Heights. Since that time, various peace agreements have forced Israel out of parts of those territories.

Many Palestinians, especially those in groups advocating violence (in order to reclaim land) like the Palestine Islamic Jihad and Hamas, feel Jews have taken a rigid and militant stance in favor of taking, holding, and defending Israel, a concept known as Zionism. To them, Zionism, the motivating force for Israel's original independence, continues more than half a century later in the occupied West Bank. There, a new generation of orthodox Jewish settlers has been residing and building homes and schools throughout the occupied territories. This perceived Zionism has bred Palestinian nationalist groups, which to Arab nations seem to be legitimate movements for national liberation, not terrorist groups. These Arab factions are also largely anti-American, because Ameri-can policy has generally favored Israel, which it sees as an outpost of Western-style democracy in the Middle East and a reliable ally.

The actions of the Israelis have exacerbated tensions, and the Palestinians and Arab nations in the region, including Lebanon, Syria, Iran, and Iraq, have pursued terrorism to try to force Israel out of certain areas. Some terrorist groups and nations in the Middle East advocate the elimination of Israel and the creation of a Palestinian state at any cost. Increasingly, suicide bombing is being used as a tool against Israeli civilians as well as the military. Such bombers give their lives for what they perceive as martyrdom. These methods have drawn criticism from various outsiders, more retaliatory measures from Israel, and praise from groups of Arabs who feel more and more desperate. The United States has tried to serve as a broker of peace, but this peace brokering is viewed with skepticism by countries that believe U.S. solutions have a bias in Israel's favor. Consequently, a more even-handed American approach to resolving the region's rivalries is the U.S. foreign-policy goal in the volatile region.

In general, the Middle East has seen a resurgence of terrorism in the early years of the 21st century, mostly due to intensifying Arab anger at Israel's refusal to remove settlers and forces from the West Bank and Gaza Strip and the U.S. and allied war on terrorism in Afghanistan and Pakistan. Though Yassir Arafat's Palestinian Authority had subdued terrorist groups like Hamas and the Islamic Jihad from their customary violence for about a year, such violence returned in the Palestinian Intifada (uprising) of 2000–02 and Israel's subsequent invasion of the occupied territories.

More than ever, previously peaceful Islamic charitable organizations are supporting harder-line political groups. Stronger, more organized, and more spontaneous Islamic political movements, many in the West believe, are providing both loyal support and conspiratorial cover for terrorist activities. As of 2002, many defense analysts believed the most palpable threat to U.S. national security was Islamic extremists in the Middle East, both in hostile countries and in terrorist groups supported by those countries. Terrorist sponsors and "informal" sponsors, though they might be located in the Middle East, can support terrorist organizations around the world. Neither the state sponsors nor the terrorist groups themselves respect international boundaries.

Given the difficulties noted earlier, how does the United States condemn and combat terrorist acts and the extreme, violent ideology of radical groups in the region without appearing anti-Islamic? Part of the answer lies in alliances. After the September 11, 2001, attacks, Pakistan, a Muslim country, began playing a major role in the worldwide antiterrorism coalition. Russia also largely supported the U.S. war on terrorism, though the United States had previously aided Islamic radicals in Afghanistan fighting Soviet occupation in the 1980s and 1990s.

IRAN. Iran is a state of concern for the United States. The country underwent a conversion from a society favorable to U.S. interests to one unfavorable to the United States in 1979, when the monarchy of Iran was deposed by a fundamentalist Islamic revolution. The U.S. government believes these fundamentalists support terrorism.

In the early 2000s, more moderate forces began to have some influence in the Iranian government. Iran's hostility toward the West, particularly in the form of aggressive comments about harming Israel or the United States, lessened. It renounced the fatwa (a formal legal statement researched by an Islamic cleric in Islamic holy texts and through consultation with other Islamic scholars and clerics) death sentence that its clerics had called for earlier against expatriate Indian author Salman Rushdie. They had originally claimed Rushdie deserved death because of what they considered his sacrilegious writings, and the author had gone into hiding. Reformist President Mohammad Khatami claimed that Iran would no longer support terrorism. In addition, Iran began to offer assistance to the United States by actively investigating members of al-Qaeda.

Despite these recent changes, according the State Department report *Patterns of Global Terrorism, 2001,* released in May 2002, Iran remained the most dangerous "rogue" state. The State Department justifies this designation by stating that even though Iran is seemingly assisting the United States in battling some terrorist groups, it is supporting others at the same time (such as Hizballah, Hamas, and the Palestine Islamic Jihad).

IRAQ. The State Department claims that, in general, state sponsorship of terrorism has decreased over the past several years, but it continues to list Iraq as a consistent state of concern in the field. In the past, Iraq has been linked to radical Palestinian terrorist organizations (such as the Arab Liberation Front and the Abu Nidal Organization). In addition, Iraqi Intelligence Service (IIS) agents were believed to be involved in a plot to assassinate then-President George H. W. Bush during a trip to Kuwait in April 1993. Abu Ibrahim, the former head of the now-disbanded 15 May Organization, which masterminded several bombings, has sought refuge in Iraq, as has Abdul Yassin, a suspect in the 1993 World Trade Center bomb plot. Iraq has also provided financial, military, and operational support to the Mujahedin-e Khalq Organization, an Iranian terrorist faction that opposes the existing Iranian government and has carried out several attacks and assassinations. Several terrorist attacks have been carried out against United Nations (UN) relief workers and others attempting to remove land mines from territory in Iraq since the mid-1990s.

Iraqi agents are also believed to be involved in several attacks against dissidents and "enemies of the state." An Iraqi scientist was assassinated in December 1992 as he was about to defect to Jordan. According to the U.S. State Department, the IIS has opened new posts in foreign capitals and dissidents are being warned to be wary of any newly established group for expatriates (those who have left their native country either by choice or through being forced out). Women, who traditionally have not fulfilled such roles in strict Islamic societies, are now being employed to infiltrate dissident groups and assassinate leading dissidents.

In early 1999, reports emerged from Eastern Europe of a deadly plot to bomb the Prague, Czech Republic headquarters of Radio Free Europe, which houses Radio Liberty. Radio Liberty had begun broadcasting its services to Iraq in 1998, much to the displeasure of Iraqi authorities. Although specific details of the case still remain classified, it is believed that the alleged bomb plot was being orchestrated by the IIS.

Iraq was the only Arab Muslim country that did not condemn the September 11, 2001, attacks on the United States, and it even expressed sympathy for Osama bin Laden following U.S. retaliatory strikes. In 2001 Iraq continued to provide training, bases, and political encouragement to numerous terrorist groups. In addition, it employs terrorism against rebel Iraqi groups that are opposed to Saddam Hussein's command, and has granted political asylum to several hijackers of a 2000 Saudi Arabian Airlines flight. Effective means of countering terrorism sponsored by Iraq were still being debated as of early 2003.

SYRIA. Although Syria has made a point of clamping down on certain terrorist groups, such as al-Qaeda, it continues to support other terrorist groups, such as Hamas and Hizballah, insisting that these are purely national liberation movements. In 2001 Syria continued to harbor and provide logistics support to a number of terrorist groups, allowing Hamas, the Palestine Islamic Jihad, and other Palestinian groups to maintain offices in Damascus. The United States considers Syria a state of concern.

LIBYA. In the 1980s Libya fired missiles at American aircraft doing maneuvers off the Libyan coast. Libyan agents were also involved in the April 1986 bombing of La Belle Discotheque, a popular Berlin, Germany, nightclub frequented by U.S. military personnel. A soldier and a civilian were killed in the attack and approximately 200 people were injured. In retaliation, President Ronald Reagan allowed U.S. aircraft to strike targets within Libya in an operation code-named "El Dorado Canyon." Ten days after the bombing at La Belle, U.S. planes simultaneously struck five military targets within Libyan territory. Libyan leader Muammar Qaddafi's daughter was killed in the attack. Even though Libya was anticipating some retaliation in response to the Berlin bombing, the magnitude and synchronization of the U.S. attacks caught their air defenses completely off-guard.

Two years later, on December 21, 1988, a bomb exploded on board Pan Am Flight 103 over Lockerbie, Scotland, and killed all 259 of the plane's passengers, plus 11 more people on the ground. Two Libyans were connected to the incident but could not be charged, as they took refuge in Libyan territory. Nearly 12 years after the attack, Libya agreed to hand over the two suspects, al-Amin Khalifa Fhimah and Abdel Basset Ali al-Megrahi, to a special Scottish court convened in the Netherlands. After a two-year trial, the court delivered its verdict in January 2002. Abdel Basset Ali al-Megrahi was convicted of murder and sentenced to life in prison; al-Amin Khalifa Fhimah was found not guilty of the crimes. Al-Megrahi appealed his conviction, but the verdict was upheld in March 2002.

The U.S. State Department noted in *Patterns of Global Terrorism, 2001* that Libya is one of two states (the other being Sudan) that seem closest to understanding what they must do to get out of the terrorism business, and each has taken steps in the that direction. For example, following the September 11, 2001, terrorist attacks, Qaddafi issued a statement condemning the attacks as horrific and gruesome. He urged Libyans to donate blood for the U.S. victims. On September 16, 2001, he declared that the United States was justified in retaliating for the attacks. After September 11, Qaddafi repeatedly denounced terrorism.

In general, Libya appears to have curtailed its support for international terrorism, although it may maintain residual contact with a few groups. Qaddafi's government has in recent years sought to recast itself as a peacemaker, offering to mediate a number of conflicts, such as the military standoff between India and Pakistan that began in December 2001. Still, Libya's past record of terrorist activity hinders Qaddafi's efforts to shed Libya's rogue state image, and U.S. sanctions remain in force.

SUDAN. The United States and Sudan have continued and enhanced the counterterrorism dialogue they began in mid-2000. Like Libya, Sudan condemned the September 11, 2001, attacks. It pledged itself to combating terrorism and cooperating with the United States. The Sudanese government has stepped up its counterterrorist cooperation with various U.S. agencies, and Sudanese authorities have investigated and apprehended extremists suspected of involvement in terrorist activities. In late September 2001, the UN recognized these positive steps by removing UN sanctions on the country.

However, the U.S. State Department still designates Sudan as a state sponsor of terrorism, and unilateral U.S. sanctions remain in place. The United States contends that a number of international terrorist groups, including al-Qaeda, the Egyptian Islamic Jihad, the Egyptian group al-Gama'a al-Islamiyya, the Palestine Islamic Jihad, and

Hamas, continue to use Sudan as a safe haven, primarily for conducting logistical and other support activities. Still, the State Department concedes that press coverage about Sudan's cooperation with the United States may have led some terrorist elements to leave the country.

NORTH KOREA. North Korea, also known as the Democratic People's Republic of Korea, has been on the list of designated state sponsors of terrorism since 1988, after it allegedly shot down a South Korean plane carrying civilians in 1987. Another reason North Korea is on the list is because the country offered sanctuary to four Japanese Communist League/Red Army Faction members after they hijacked a Japanese Airline flight to North Korea in 1970. In addition, the U.S. State Department reports evidence of recent sales of small arms to terrorist groups.

In a statement released shortly after the September 11, 2001, attacks, North Korea repeated its official policy of opposing and not supporting terrorism. It also signed the UN Convention for the Suppression of the Financing of Terrorism, agreed to be bound by the Convention Against the Taking of Hostages, and indicated its willingness to sign five related agreements.

CUBA AND TIES TO LATIN AMERICA. Cuban leader Fidel Castro continues to be ambiguous about the U.S.-declared "war on terrorism." In October 2001 he called the war "worse than the original attacks—militaristic and fascist." When that statement did not gain him the support he anticipated, Castro instead declared Cuba's support for the war on terrorism. He eventually signed all 12 UN counterterrorism conventions, as well as the Ibero-American declaration on terrorism at the 2001 Ibero-American summit. Cuba did not protest the detention of approximately 600 al-Qaeda members captured in Afghanistan at the U.S. Naval Base at Guantanamo Bay, Cuba.

In addition to such evidence, American officials believe that Castro still accepts terror as a political tactic. Twenty members of the Basque Homeland and Freedom (Euskadi Ta Askatasuna) guerrilla group, whose cause is the separation and independence of the Basque region from Spain, continue to reside in Cuba with the knowledge of the Cuban government. Cuba also provides a degree of safe haven and support to members of the Revolutionary Armed Forces of Colombia and National Liberation Army groups, both Colombian organizations that commit acts of terrorism against Colombian political, military, and economic targets, and kidnap and kill citizens of other countries, including the United States. In August 2001 a Cuban spokesman revealed that Sinn Fein's official representative for Cuba and Latin America, Niall Connolly, one of three Irish Republican Army members arrested in Colombia on suspicion of providing explosives training to the Revolutionary Armed Forces of Colombia, had been based in Cuba for five years.

The tri-border area of Latin America, where the boundaries of Argentina, Brazil, and Paraguay meet, is also considered to be a hotbed for terrorist and other illicit activities. The U.S. State Department has claimed that groups such as Hamas, Hizballah, and al-Qaeda use the region for various logistical and financial (mostly money-laundering) purposes. The three governments have pledged to fight terrorism and, since September 11, 2001, have made several arrests of individuals linked to terror groups.

SUBSTATE TERROR GROUPS

Beyond the countries named on the U.S. State Department's list of state sponsors of terrorism, there are a variety of terrorist groups that are essentially transnational (beyond national boundaries) and substate (under a state level) in nature. Table 5.1 lists the 35 groups designated by the U.S. Secretary of State as "foreign terrorist organizations." These designations are made pursuant to section 219 of the Immigration and Nationality Act, as amended by the Antiterrorism and Effective Death Penalty Act of 1996, and carry legal consequences. There are three specific criteria that such a group must fit: 1) it must be a foreign entity; 2) it must engage in terrorist activity; and 3) the terrorist activities undertaken by the group must pose a threat to American nationals and U.S. national security.

In addition to the groups named as foreign terrorist organizations, there are a variety of other terrorist groups that are not a part of the list, because they do not fit the strict legal criteria designated by the State Department. However, these groups are closely monitored by authorities, as their activities are considered essentially terrorist in nature. These organizations are detailed in Table 5.2.

Officially, it is the policy of the U.S. government not to negotiate with terrorists. In practice, however, the government has departed from that policy to negotiate at times with terrorist groups like the Palestinian Liberation Organization and the Irish Republican Army as a way of getting those groups to the bargaining table with their regional enemies.

TERRORISM AROUND THE WORLD

Terrorist attacks sometimes stem from specific regional conflicts. One example of this type of conflict is in Northern Ireland, where the Irish Republican Army has launched terrorist acts against the British government and Irish protestants in an attempt to gain independence for Northern Ireland. Another is in the Basque region of northern Spain and southern France, where the Basque separatist group Euskadi Ta Askatasuna seeks an independent Basque homeland. In addition, one of the most destructive and deadly regional conflicts is between the Palestinians and Israelis over disputed territory in the Middle East.

Though the greater part of terrorism across the globe is internal, this does not mean it is of less importance to the United States. Turmoil within even one nation can destabilize entire regions. In addition, there may be consequences to the United States from terrorist groups mainly interested in other countries. In Uzbekistan, the Islamic Movement of Uzbekistan kidnapped four U.S. citizens in August 2000 while they were mountain climbing (the four Americans later escaped). The Revolutionary Armed Forces of Colombia kidnapped three U.S. Indian rights activists in March 1999, later executing them in Venezuela. In February 2002 the Movement of Holy Warriors in Pakistan kidnapped and beheaded American journalist Daniel Pearl.

Also, since many terrorist groups use methods that indiscriminately kill civilians, Americans visiting certain areas that harbor internal terrorist groups may be at risk from random violence. The Tamil Tigers in Sri Lanka, the Revolutionary Armed Forces and National Liberation Army of Colombia, and the Irish Republican Army in Ireland and Great Britain have all used bombings that have killed scores of people. Such actions could unintentionally target American citizens if they happened to be in the wrong place at the wrong time.

Southeast Asia is increasingly becoming of major concern to the United States, because of terrorist organizations operating out of the region. Groups like the Abu Sayyaf Group in the Philippines choose methods of terrorism that include kidnapping foreign hostages to receive ransom money. An October 2002 nightclub bombing in Bali, Indonesia, by members of the Jemaah Islamiyah militant Muslim network, which is linked to al-Qaeda and seeks to set up an Islamic state in Southeast Asia, killed almost 200 people, mostly foreign tourists and several Americans. More than 300 were injured in the blast.

Also, because of the highly subjective nature of the term "terrorism," U.S. actions abroad have sometimes been called terrorist in character by other nations. Cuba is one of the most vociferous of the states including substate groups that accuse America of carrying out terrorist acts abroad. Some of the U.S. actions (mostly undertaken unilaterally) that are cited in support of such theories include:

- The U.S. blockade on Cuba since 1963

- Varied interventions in Latin America during the Cold War, including support for the Pinochet government in Chile, the Contras in Nicaragua, and various death squads in Honduras and El Salvador

- Support for the mujahideen, who fought the Soviets in Afghanistan during the 1980s

- The invasion of Grenada in 1983

- Support of Saddam Hussein's Iraq during the 1980 Iran/Iraq War

(Note): Text continues on page 100.)

TABLE 5.1

State Department-designated foreign terrorist organizations as of May 2002

Organization name	Description	Activities	Strength	Location/Area of Operation	External Aid
Abu Nidal organization (ANO) a.k.a. Fatah Revolutionary Council, Arab Revolutionary Brigades, Black September, and Revolutionary Organization of Socialist Muslims	International terrorist organization led by Sabri al-Banna. Split from PLO in 1974. Made up of various functional committees, including political, military, and financial.	Has carried out terrorist attacks in 20 countries, killing or injuring almost 900 persons. Targets include the United States, the United Kingdom, France, Israel, moderate Palestinians, the PLO, and various Arab countries. Major attacks included the Rome and Vienna airports in December 1985, the Neve Shalom synagogue in Istanbul and the Pan Am Flight 73 hijacking in Karachi in September 1986, and the City of Poros day-excursion ship attack in Greece in July 1988. Suspected of assassinating PLO deputy chief Abu Iyad and PLO security chief Abu Hul in Tunis in January 1991. ANO assassinated a Jordanian diplomat in Lebanon in January 1994 and has been linked to the killing of the PLO representative there. Has not attacked Western targets since the late 1980s.	Few hundred plus limited overseas support structure.	Al-Banna relocated to Iraq in December 1998, where the group maintains a presence. Has an operational presence in Lebanon including in several Palestinian refugee camps. Financial problems and internal disorganization have reduced the group's activities and capabilities. Authorities shut down the ANO's operations in Libya and Egypt in 1999. Has demonstrated ability to operate over wide area, including the Middle East, Asia, and Europe.	Has received considerable support, including safehaven, training, logistic assistance, and financial aid from Iraq, Libya, and Syria (until 1987), in addition to close support for selected operations.
Abu Sayyaf Group (ASG)	The ASG is the most violent of the Islamic separatist groups operating in the southern Philippines. Some ASG leaders have studied or worked in the Middle East and allegedly fought in Afghanistan during the Soviet war. The group split from the Moro National Liberation Front in the early 1990s under the leadership of Abdurajak Abubakar Janjalani, who was killed in a clash with Philippine police on 18 December 1998. His younger brother, Khadaffy Janjalani, has replaced him as the nominal leader of the group, which is composed of several semi-autonomous factions.	Engages in kidnappings for ransom, bombings, assassinations, and extortion. Although from time to time it claims that its motivation is to promote an independent Islamic state in western Mindanao and the Sulu Archipelago, areas in the southern Philippines heavily populated by Muslims, the ASG now appears to use terror mainly for financial profit. The group's first large-scale action was a raid on the town of Ipil in Mindanao in April 1995. In April of 2000, an ASG faction kidnapped 21 persons, including 10 foreign tourists, from a resort in Malaysia. Separately in 2000, the group abducted several foreign journalists, 3 Malaysians, and a US citizen. On 27 May 2001, the ASG kidnapped three US citizens and 17 Filipinos from a tourist resort in Palawan, Philippines. Several of the hostages, including one US citizen, were murdered.	Believed to have a few hundred core fighters, but at least 1000 individuals motivated by the prospect of receiving ransom payments for foreign hostages allegedly joined the group in 2000-2001.	The ASG was founded in Basilan Province, and mainly operates there and in the neighboring provinces of Sulu and Tawi-Tawi in the Sulu Archipelago. It also operates in the Zamboanga peninsula, and members occasionally travel to Manila and other parts of the country. The group expanded its operations to Malaysia in 2000 when it abducted foreigners from a tourist resort.	Largely self-financing through ransom and extortion; may receive support from Islamic extremists in the Middle East and South Asia. Libya publicly paid millions of dollars for the release of the foreign hostages seized from Malaysia in 2000.
Al-Aqsa Martyrs Brigade	The al-Aqsa Martyrs Brigade comprises an unknown number of small cells of Fatah-affiliated activists that emerged at the outset of the current *intifadah* to attack Israeli targets. It aims to drive the Israeli military and settlers from the West Bank, Gaza Strip, and Jerusalem and to establish a Palestinian state.	Al-Aqsa Martyrs Brigade has carried out shootings and suicide operations against Israeli military personnel and civilians and has killed Palestinians who it believed were collaborating with Israel. At least five US citizens, four of them dual Israeli-US citizens, were killed in these attacks. The group probably did not attack them because of their US citizenship. In January 2002, the group claimed responsibility for the first suicide bombing carried out by a female.	Unknown.	Al-Aqsa operates mainly in the West Bank and has claimed attacks inside Israel and the Gaza Strip.	Unknown.

TABLE 5.1

State Department-designated foreign terrorist organizations as of May 2002 [CONTINUED]

Organization name	Description	Activities	Strength	Location/Area of Operation	External Aid
Armed Islamic Group (GIA)	An Islamic extremist group, the GIA aims to overthrow the secular Algerian regime and replace it with an Islamic state. The GIA began its violent activity in 1992 after Algiers voided the victory of the Islamic Salvation Front (FIS)—the largest Islamic opposition party—in the first round of legislative elections in December 1991.	Frequent attacks against civilians and government workers. Between 1992 and 1998 the GIA conducted a terrorist campaign of civilian massacres, sometimes wiping out entire villages in its area of operation. Since announcing its campaign against foreigners living in Algeria in 1993, the GIA has killed more than 100 expatriate men and women—mostly Europeans—in the country. The group uses assassinations and bombings, including car bombs, and it is known to favor kidnapping victims and slitting their throats. The GIA hijacked an Air France flight to Algiers in December 1994. In late 1999 a French court convicted several GIA members for conducting a series of bombings in France in 1995.	Precise numbers unknown; probably around 200.	Algeria	Algerian expatriates, some of whom reside in Western Europe, provide some financial and logistic support. In addition, the Algerian Government has accused Iran and Sudan of supporting Algerian extremists.
'Asbat al-Ansar	'Asbat al-Ansar—the Partisans' League—is a Lebanon-based, Sunni extremist group, composed primarily of Palestinians, which is associated with Usama Bin Ladin. The group follows an extremist interpretation of Islam that justifies violence against civilian targets to achieve political ends. Some of those goals include overthrowing the Lebanese Government and thwarting perceived anti-Islamic influences in the country.	'Asbat al-Ansar has carried out several terrorist attacks in Lebanon since it first emerged in the early 1990s. The group carried out assassinations of Lebanese religious leaders and bombed several nightclubs, theaters, and liquor stores in the mid-1990s. The group raised its operational profile in 2000 with two dramatic attacks against Lebanese and international targets. The group was involved in clashes in northern Lebanon in late December 1999 and carried out a rocket-propelled grenade attack on the Russian Embassy in Beirut in January 2000.	The group commands about 300 fighters in Lebanon.	The group's primary base of operations is the 'Ayn al-Hilwah Palestinian refugee camp near Sidon in southern Lebanon.	Probably receives money through international Sunni extremist networks and Bin Ladin's al-Qaida network.
Aum Supreme Truth (Aum) a.k.a. Aum Shinrikyo, Aleph	A cult established in 1987 by Shoko Asahara, the Aum aimed to take over Japan and then the world. Approved as a religious entity in 1989 under Japanese law, the group ran candidates in a Japanese parliamentary election in 1990. Over time the cult began to emphasize the imminence of the end of the world and stated that the United States would initiate Armageddon by starting World War III with Japan. The Japanese Government revoked its recognition of the Aum as a religious organization in October 1995, but in 1997 a government panel decided not to invoke the Anti-Subversive Law against the group, which would have outlawed the cult. A 1999 law gave the Japanese Government author-	On 20 March 1995, Aum members simultaneously released the chemical nerve agent sarin on several Tokyo subway trains, killing 12 persons and injuring up to 6,000. The group was responsible for other mysterious chemical accidents in Japan in 1994. Its efforts to conduct attacks using biological agents have been unsuccessful. Japanese police arrested Asahara in May 1995, and he remained on trial facing charges in 13 crimes, including 7 counts of murder at the end of 2001. Legal analysts say it will take several more years to conclude the trial. Since 1997 the cult continued to recruit new members, engage in commercial enterprise, and acquire property, although it scaled back these activities significantly in 2001 in response to public outcry. The cult maintains an Internet home page. In July 2001, Russian authorities arrested a group of Russian Aum followers who had planned to set off bombs near the Imperial Palace in Tokyo as part of an operation to free Asahara from jail and then smuggle him to Russia.	The Aum's current membership is estimated at 1,500 to 2,000 persons. At the time of the Tokyo subway attack, the group claimed to have 9,000 members in Japan and up to 40,000 worldwide.	The Aum's principal membership is located only in Japan, but a residual branch comprising an unknown number of followers has surfaced in Russia.	None.

TABLE 5.1

State Department-designated foreign terrorist organizations as of May 2002 [CONTINUED]

Organization name	Description	Activities	Strength	Location/Area of Operation	External Aid
Aum Supreme Truth (Aum) a.k.a. Aum Shinrikyo, Aleph (cont'd)	ization to continue police surveillance of the group due to concerns that Aum might launch future terrorist attacks. Under the leadership of Fumihiro Joyu the Aum changed its name to Aleph in January 2000 and claimed to have rejected the violent and apocalyptic teachings of its founder. (Joyu took formal control of the organization early in 2002 and remains its leader.)				
Basque Fatherland and Liberty (ETA) a.k.a Euzkadi Ta Askatasuna	Founded in 1959 with the aim of establishing an independent homeland based on Marxist principles in the northern Spanish Provinces of Vizcaya, Guipuzcoa, Alava, and Navarra, and the southwestern French Departments of Labourd, Basse-Navarra, and Soule.	Primarily involved in bombings and assassinations of Spanish Government officials, security and military forces, politicians, and judicial figures. ETA finances its activities through kidnappings, robberies, and extortion. The group has killed more than 800 persons and injured hundreds of others since it began lethal attacks in the early 1960s. In November 1999, ETA broke its "unilateral and indefinite" cease-fire and began an assassination and bombing campaign that has killed 38 individuals and wounded scores more by the end of 2001.	Unknown; may have hundreds of members, plus supporters.	Operates primarily in the Basque autonomous regions of northern Spain and southwestern France, but also has bombed Spanish and French interests elsewhere.	Has received training at various times in the past in Libya, Lebanon, and Nicaragua. Some ETA members allegedly have received sanctuary in Cuba while others reside in South America.
Al-Gama'a al-Islamiyya (Islamic Group, IG)	Egypt's largest militant group, active since the late 1970s; appears to be loosely organized. Has an external wing with supporters in several countries worldwide. The group issued a cease-fire in March 1999, but its spiritual leader, Shaykh Umar Abd al-Rahman, sentenced to life in prison in January 1996 for his involvement in the 1993 World Trade Center bombing and incarcerated in the United States, rescinded his support for the cease-fire in June 2000. The Gama'a has not conducted an attack inside Egypt since August 1998. Senior member signed Usama Bin Ladin's *fatwa* in February 1998 calling for attacks against US. Unofficially split into two factions; one that supports the cease-fire led by Mustafa Hamza, and one led by Rifa'i Taha Musa, calling for a return to armed operations. Taha Musa in	Group conducted armed attacks against Egyptian security and other government officials, Coptic Christians, and Egyptian opponents of Islamic extremism before the cease-fire. From 1993 until the cease-fire, al-Gama'a launched attacks on tourists in Egypt, most notably in November 1997 at Luxor that killed 58 foreign tourists. Also claimed responsibility for the attempt in June 1995 to assassinate Egyptian President Hosni Mubarak in Addis Ababa, Ethiopia. The Gama'a has never specifically attacked a US citizen or facility but has threatened US interests.	Unknown. At its peak the IG probably commanded several thousand hard-core members and a like number of sympathizers. The 1999 cease-fire and security crackdowns following the attack in Luxor in 1997, and more recently security efforts following September 11, probably have resulted in a substantial decrease in the group's numbers.	Operates mainly in the Al-Minya, Asyu't, Qina, and Sohaj Governorates of southern Egypt. Also appears to have support in Cairo, Alexandria, and other urban locations, particularly among unemployed graduates and students. Has a worldwide presence, including the United Kingdom, Afghanistan, Yemen, and Austria.	Unknown. The Egyptian Government believes that Iran, Bin Ladin, and Afghan militant groups support the organization. Also may obtain some funding through various Islamic nongovernmental organizations.

TABLE 5.1

State Department-designated foreign terrorist organizations as of May 2002 [CONTINUED]

Organization name	Description	Activities	Strength	Location/Area of Operation	External Aid
Al-Gama'a al-Islamiyya (Islamic Group, IG) (cont'd)	early 2001 published a book in which he attempted to justify terrorist attacks that would cause mass casualties. Musa disappeared several months thereafter, and there are conflicting reports as to his current whereabouts. Primary goal is to overthrow the Egyptian Government and replace it with an Islamic state, but disaffected IG members, such as those potentially inspired by Taha Musa or Abd al-Rahman, may be interested in carrying out attacks against US and Israeli interests.				
HAMAS (Islamic Resistance Movement)	Formed in late 1987 as an outgrowth of the Palestinian branch of the Muslim Brotherhood. Various HAMAS elements have used both political and violent means, including terrorism, to pursue the goal of establishing an Islamic Palestinian state in place of Israel. Loosely structured, with some elements working clandestinely and others working openly through mosques and social service institutions to recruit members, raise money, organize activities, and distribute propaganda. HAMAS's strength is concentrated in the Gaza Strip and a few areas of the West Bank. Also has engaged in political activity, such as running candidates in West Bank Chamber of Commerce elections.	HAMAS activists, especially those in the Izz el-Din al-Qassam Brigades, have conducted many attacks— including large-scale suicide bombings— against Israeli civilian and military targets. In the early 1990s, they also targeted Fatah rivals and began a practice of targeting suspected Palestinian collaborators, which continues. Increased operational activity in 2001 during the *intifadah*, claiming numerous attacks against Israeli interests. Group has not targeted US interests and continues to confine its attacks to Israelis inside Israel and the territories.	Unknown number of hardcore members; tens of thousands of supporters and sympathizers.	Primarily the West Bank, Gaza Strip, and Israel. In August 1999, Jordanian authorities closed the group's Political Bureau offices in Amman, arrested its leaders, and prohibited the group from operating on Jordanian territory. HAMAS leaders also present in other parts of the Middle East, including Syria, Lebanon, and Iran.	Receives funding from Palestinian expatriates, Iran, and private benefactors in Saudi Arabia and other moderate Arab states. Some fundraising and propaganda activity take place in Western Europe and North America.
Harakat ul-Mujahidin (HUM) (Movement of Holy Warriors)	The HUM is an Islamic militant group based in Pakistan that operates primarily in Kashmir. It is politically aligned with the radical political party, Jamiat-i Ulema-i Islam Fazlur Rehman faction (JUI-F). Long-time leader of the group, Fazlur Rehman Khalil, in mid-February 2000 stepped down as HUM emir, turning the reins over to the	Has conducted a number of operations against Indian troops and civilian targets in Kashmir. Linked to the Kashmiri militant group al-Faran that kidnapped five Western tourists in Kashmir in July 1995; one was killed in August 1995 and the other four reportedly were killed in December of the same year. The HUM is responsible for the hijacking of an Indian airliner on 24 December 1999, which resulted in the release of Masood Azhar—an important leader in the former Harakat ul-Ansar imprisoned by the Indians in 1994—and Ahmad Omar Sheikh, who	Has several thousand armed supporters located in Azad Kashmir, Pakistan, and India's southern Kashmir and Doda regions. Supporters are mostly Pakistanis and Kashmiris and also include Afghans and Arab veterans of the Afghan war. Uses light and heavy machine-guns, assault rifles, mortars, explosives, and rockets. HUM	Based in Muzaffarabad, Rawalpindi, and several other towns in Pakistan, but members conduct insurgent and terrorist activities primarily in Kashmir. The HUM trained its militants in Afghanistan and Pakistan.	Collects donations from Saudi Arabia and other Gulf and Islamic states and from Pakistanis and Kashmiris. The HUM's financial collection methods also include soliciting donations from magazine ads and pamphlets. The sources and amount of HUM's military funding are unknown. In anticipation of asset seizures by the Pakistani Government, the HUM withdrew funds from bank accounts

TABLE 5.1

State Department-designated foreign terrorist organizations as of May 2002 [CONTINUED]

Organization name	Description	Activities	Strength	Location/Area of Operation	External Aid
Harakat ul-Mujahidin (HUM) (Movement of Holy Warriors) (cont'd)	popular Kashmiri commander and his second-in-command, Farooq Kashmiri. Khalil, who has been linked to Bin Ladin and signed his *fatwa* in February 1998 calling for attacks on US and Western interests, assumed the position of HUM Secretary General. HUM operated terrorist training camps in eastern Afghanistan until Coalition airstrikes destroyed them during fall, 2001.	was arrested for the abduction/murder in January-February 2001 of US journalist Daniel Pearl.	lost a significant share of its membership in defections to the Jaish-e-Mohammed (JEM) in 2000.		and invested in legal businesses, such as commodity trading, real estate, and production of consumer goods. Its fundraising in Pakistan has been constrained since the government clampdown on extremist groups and freezing of terrorist assets.
Hizballah (Party of God) a.k.a. Islamic Jihad, Revolutionary Justice Organization, Organization of the Oppressed on Earth, and Islamic Jihad for the Liberation of Palestine	Formed in 1982 in response to the Israeli invasion of Lebanon, this Lebanon-based radical Shi'a group takes its ideological inspiration from the Iranian revolution and the teachings of the Ayatollah Khomeini. The Majlis al-Shura, or Consultative Council, is the group's highest governing body and is led by Secretary General Hassan Nasrallah. Hizballah formally advocates ultimate establishment of Islamic rule in Lebanon and liberating all occupied Arab lands, including Jerusalem. It has expressed as a goal the elimination of Israel. Has expressed its unwillingness to work within the confines of Lebanon's established political system; however, this stance changed with the party's decision in 1992 to participate in parliamentary elections. Although closely allied with and often directed by Iran, the group may have conducted operations that were not approved by Tehran. While Hizballah does not share the Syrian regime's secular orientation, the group has been a strong tactical ally in helping Syria advance its political objectives in the region.	Known or suspected to have been involved in numerous anti-US terrorist attacks, including the suicide truck bombings of the US Embassy in Beirut in April 1983 and US Marine barracks in Beirut in October 1983 and the US Embassy annex in Beirut in September 1984. Three members of Hizballah, 'Imad Mughniyah, Hasan Izz-al-Din, and Ali Atwa, are on the FBI's list of 22 Most Wanted Terrorists for the hijacking in 1985 of TWA Flight 847 during which a US Navy diver was murdered. Elements of the group were responsible for the kidnapping and detention of US and other Western hostages in Lebanon. The group also attacked the Israeli Embassy in Argentina in 1992 and is a suspect in the 1994 bombing of the Israeli cultural center in Buenos Aires. In fall 2000, it captured three Israeli soldiers in the Shaba Farms and kidnapped an Israeli noncombatant whom it may have lured to Lebanon under false pretenses	Several thousand supporters and a few hundred terrorist operatives.	Operates in the Bekaa Valley, Hermil, the southern suburbs of Beirut, and southern Lebanon. Has established cells in Europe, Africa, South America, North America, and Asia.	Receives substantial amounts of financial, training, weapons, explosives, political, diplomatic, and organizational aid from Iran and received diplomatic, political, and logistical support from Syria.

TABLE 5.1

State Department-designated foreign terrorist organizations as of May 2002 [CONTINUED]

Organization name	Description	Activities	Strength	Location/Area of Operation	External Aid
Islamic Movement of Uzbekistan (IMU)	Coalition of Islamic militants from Uzbekistan and other Central Asian states opposed to Uzbekistani President Islom Karimov's secular regime. Before the counterterrorism coalition began operations in Afghanistan in October, the IMU's primary goal was the establishment of an Islamic state in Uzbekistan. If IMU political and ideological leader Tohir Yoldashev survives the counterterrorism campaign and can regroup the organization, however, he might widen the IMU's targets to include all those he perceives as fighting Islam. The group's propaganda has always included anti-Western and anti-Israeli rhetoric.	The IMU primarily targeted Uzbekistani interests before October 2001 and is believed to have been responsible for five car bombs in Tashkent in February 1999. Militants also took foreigners hostage in 1999 and 2000, including four US citizens who were mountain climbing in August 2000, and four Japanese geologists and eight Kyrgyzstani soldiers in August 1999. Since October, the Coalition has captured, killed, and dispersed many of the militants who remained in Afghanistan to fight with the Taliban and al-Qaida, severely degrading the IMU's ability to attack Uzbekistani or Coalition interests in the near term. IMU military leader Juma Namangani apparently was killed during an air strike in November. At year's end, Yoldashev remained at large.	Militants probably number under 2000.	Militants are scattered throughout South Asia and Tajikistan. Area of operations includes Afghanistan, Iran, Kyrgyzstan, Pakistan, Tajikistan, and Uzbekistan.	Support from other Islamic extremist groups and patrons in the Middle East and Central and South Asia. IMU leadership broadcasts statements over Iranian radio.
Jaish-e-Mohammed (JEM) (Army of Mohammed)	The Jaish-e-Mohammed (JEM) is an Islamic extremist group based in Pakistan that was formed by Masood Azhar upon his release from prison in India in early 2000. The group's aim is to unite Kashmir with Pakistan. It is politically aligned with the radical political party, Jamiat-i Ulema-i Islam Fazlur Rehman faction (JUI-F). The United States announced the addition of JEM to the US Treasury Department's Office of Foreign Asset Control's (OFAC) list—which includes organizations that are believed to support terrorist groups and have assets in US jurisdiction that can be frozen or controlled—in October and the Foreign Terrorist Organization list in December. The group was banned and its assets were frozen by the Pakistani Government in January 2002.	The JEM's leader, Masood Azhar, was released from Indian imprisonment in December 1999 in exchange for 155 hijacked Indian Airlines hostages. The 1994 HUA kidnappings by Omar Sheikh of US and British nationals in New Delhi and the July 1995 HUA/A1 Faran kidnappings of Westerners in Kashmir were two of several previous HUA efforts to free Azhar. The JEM on 1 October 2001 claimed responsibility for a suicide attack on the Jammu and Kashmir legislative assembly building in Srinagar that killed at least 31 persons, but later denied the claim. The Indian Government has publicly implicated the JEM, along with Lashkar-e-Tayyiba, for the 13 December attack on the Indian Parliament that killed 9 and injured 18.	Has several hundred armed supporters located in Azad Kashmir, Pakistan, and in India's southern Kashmir and Doda regions, including a large cadre of former HUM members. Supporters are mostly Pakistanis and Kashmiris and also include Afghans and Arab veterans of the Afghan war. Uses light and heavy machine-guns, assault rifles, mortars, improvised explosive devices, and rocket grenades.	Based in Peshawar and Muzaffarabad, but members conduct terrorist activities primarily in Kashmir. The JEM maintained training camps in Afghanistan until the fall of 2001.	Most of the JEM's cadre and material resources have been drawn from the militant groups Harakat ul-Jihad al-Islami (HUJI) and the Harakat ul-Mujahedin (HUM). The JEM had close ties to Afghan Arabs and the Taliban. Usama Bin Ladin is suspected of giving funding to the JEM. The JEM also collects funds through donation requests in magazines and pamphlets. In anticipation of asset seizures by the Pakistani Government, the JEM withdrew funds from bank accounts and invested in legal businesses, such as commodity trading, real estate, and production of consumer goods.

TABLE 5.1

State Department-designated foreign terrorist organizations as of May 2002 [CONTINUED]

Organization name	Description	Activities	Strength	Location/Area of Operation	External Aid
Al-Jihad a.k.a. Egyptian Islamic Jihad, Jihad Group, Islamic Jihad	Egyptian Islamic extremist group active since the late 1970s. Merged with Bin Ladin's al-Qaida organization in June 2001, but may retain some capability to conduct independent operations. Continues to suffer setbacks worldwide, especially after 11 September attacks. Primary goals are to overthrow the Egyptian Government and replace it with an Islamic state and attack US and Israeli interests in Egypt and abroad.	Specializes in armed attacks against high-level Egyptian Government personnel, including cabinet ministers, and car-bombings against official US and Egyptian facilities. The original Jihad was responsible for the assassination in 1981 of Egyptian President Anwar Sadat. Claimed responsibility for the attempted assassinations of Interior Minister Hassan al-Alfi in August 1993 and Prime Minister Atef Sedky in November 1993. Has not conducted an attack inside Egypt since 1993 and has never targeted foreign tourists there. Responsible for Egyptian Embassy bombing in Islamabad in 1995; in 1998 attack against US Embassy in Albania was thwarted.	Unknown, but probably has several hundred hardcore members.	Operates in the Cairo area, but most of its network is outside Egypt, including Yemen, Afghanistan, Pakistan, Lebanon, and the United Kingdom, and its activities have been centered outside Egypt for several years.	Unknown. The Egyptian Government claims that Iran supports the Jihad. Its merger with al-Qaida also boosts Bin Ladin's support for the group. Also may obtain some funding through various Islamic nongovernmental organizations, cover businesses, and criminal acts.
Kahane Chai (Kach)	Stated goal is to restore the biblical state of Israel. Kach (founded by radical Israeli-American rabbi Meir Kahane) and its offshoot Kahane Chai, which means "Kahane Lives," (founded by Meir Kahane's son Binyamin following his father's assassination in the United States) were declared to be terrorist organizations in March 1994 by the Israeli Cabinet under the 1948 Terrorism Law. This followed the groups' statements in support of Dr. Baruch Goldstein's attack in February 1994 on the al-Ibrahimi Mosque—Goldstein was affiliated with Kach—and their verbal attacks on the Israeli Government. Binyamin Kahane and his wife in a drive-by shooting in December 2000 in the West Bank.	Organize protests against the Israeli Government. Harass and threaten Palestinians in Hebron and the West Bank. Have threatened to attack Arabs, Palestinians, and Israeli Government officials. Have vowed revenge for the death of Binyamin Kahane and his wife.	Unknown.	Israel and West Bank settlements, particularly Qiryat Arba' in Hebron	Receives support from sympathizers in the United States and Europe.
Kurdistan Workers' Party (PKK)	Founded in 1974 as a Marxist-Leninist insurgent group primarily composed of Turkish Kurds. The group's goal has been to establish an independent Kurdish state in southeastern Turkey, where the population is predominantly Kurdish. In the early 1990s, the PKK moved beyond rural-based insurgent activities to include urban terrorism. Turkish authorities captured Chairman Abdullah Ocalan in Kenya in early 1999; the	Primary targets have been Turkish Government security forces in Turkey. Conducted attacks on Turkish diplomatic and commercial facilities in dozens of West European cities in 1993 and again in spring 1995. In an attempt to damage Turkey's tourist industry, the PKK bombed tourist sites and hotels and kidnapped foreign tourists in the early to mid-1990s.	Approximately 4,000 to 5,000, most of whom currently are located in northern Iraq. Has thousands of sympathizers in Turkey and Europe.	Operates in Turkey, Europe, and the Middle East.	Has received safehaven and modest aid from Syria, Iraq, and Iran. Damascus generally upheld its September 2000 antiterror agreement with Ankara, pledging not to support the PKK.

TABLE 5.1

State Department-designated foreign terrorist organizations as of May 2002 [CONTINUED]

Organization name	Description	Activities	Strength	Location/Area of Operation	External Aid
Kurdistan Workers' Party (PKK) (cont'd)	Turkish State Security Court subsequently sentenced him to death. In August 1999, Ocalan announced a "peace initiative," ordering members to refrain from violence and requesting dialogue with Ankara on Kurdish issues. At a PKK Congress in January 2000, members supported Ocalan's initiative and claimed the group now would use only political means to achieve its new goal, improved rights for Kurds in Turkey.				
Lashkar-e-Tayyiba (LT) (Army of the Righteous)	The LT is the armed wing of the Pakistani-based religious organization, Markaz-ud-Dawa-wal-Irshad (MDI)—a Sunni anti-US missionary organization formed in 1989. The LT is led by Abdul Wahid Kashmiri and is one of the three largest and best-trained groups fighting in Kashmir against India; it is not connected to a political party. The United States in October announced the addition of the LT to the US Treasury Department's Office of Foreign Asset Control's (OFAC) list—which includes organizations that are believed to support terrorist groups and have assets in US jurisdiction that can be frozen or controlled. The group was banned and its assets were frozen by the Pakistani Government in January 2002.	The LT has conducted a number of operations against Indian troops and civilian targets in Kashmir since 1993. The LT claimed responsibility for numerous attacks in 2001, including a January attack on Srinagar airport that killed five Indians along with six militants; an attack on a police station in Srinagar that killed at least eight officers and wounded several others; and an attack in April against Indian border security forces that left at least four dead. The Indian Government publicly implicated the LT along with JEM for the 13 December attack on the Indian Parliament building.	Has several hundred members in Azad Kashmir, Pakistan, and in India's southern Kashmir and Doda regions. Almost all LT cadres are non-Kashmiris mostly Pakistanis from madrassas across the country and Afghan veterans of the Afghan wars. Uses assault rifles, light and heavy machine-guns, mortars, explosives, and rocket propelled grenades.	Has been based in Muridke (near Lahore) and Muzaffarabad. The LT trains its militants in mobile training camps across Pakistan-administered Kashmir and had trained in Afghanistan until fall of 2001.	Collects donations from the Pakistani community in the Persian Gulf and United Kingdom, Islamic NGOs, and Pakistani and Kashmiri businessmen. The LT also maintains a website (under the name of its parent organization Jamaat ud-Daawa), through which it solicits funds and provides information on the group's activities. The amount of LT funding is unknown. The LT maintains ties to religious/military groups around the world, ranging from the Philippines to the Middle East and Chechnya through the MDI fraternal network. In anticipation of asset seizures by the Pakistani Government, the LT withdrew funds from bank accounts and invested in legal businesses, such as commodity trading, real estate, and production of consumer goods.
Liberation Tigers of Tamil Eelam (LTTE) Other known front organizations: World Tamil Association (WTA), World Tamil Movement (WTM), the Federation of Associations of Canadian Tamils (FACT), the Ellalan Force, and the Sangilian Force.	Founded in 1976, the LTTE is the most powerful Tamil group in Sri Lanka and uses overt and illegal methods to raise funds, acquire weapons, and publicize its cause of establishing an independent Tamil state. The LTTE began its armed conflict with the Sri Lankan Government in 1983 and relies on a guerrilla strategy that includes the use of terrorist tactics.	The Tigers have integrated a battlefield insurgent strategy with a terrorist program that targets not only key personnel in the countryside but also senior Sri Lankan political and military leaders in Colombo and other urban centers. The Tigers are most notorious for their cadre of suicide bombers, the Black Tigers. Political assassinations and bombings are commonplace. The LTTE has refrained from targeting foreign diplomatic and commercial establishments.	Exact strength is unknown, but the LTTE is estimated to have 8,000 to 10,000 armed combatants in Sri Lanka, with a core of trained fighters of approximately 3,000 to 6,000. The LTTE also has a significant overseas support structure for fundraising, weapons procurement, and propaganda activities.	The Tigers control most of the northern and eastern coastal areas of Sri Lanka but have conducted operations throughout the island. Headquartered in northern Sri Lanka, LTTE leader Velupillai Prabhakaran has established an extensive network of checkpoints and informants to keep track of outsiders who enter the group's area of control.	The LTTE's overt organizations support Tamil separatism by lobbying foreign governments and the United Nations. The LTTE also uses its international contacts to procure weapons, communications, and any other equipment and supplies it needs. The LTTE exploits large Tamil communities in North America, Europe, and Asia to obtain funds and supplies for its fighters in Sri Lanka often through false claims or even extortion.

TABLE 5.1

State Department-designated foreign terrorist organizations as of May 2002 [CONTINUED]

Organization name	Description	Activities	Strength	Location/Area of Operation	External Aid
Mujahedin-e Khalq Organization (MEK or MKO) a.k.a. The National Liberation Army of Iran (NLA, the militant wing of the MEK), the People's Mujahidin of Iran (PMOI), National Council of Resistance (NCR), Muslim Iranian Student's Society (front organization used to garner financial support)	The MEK philosophy mixes Marxism and Islam. Formed in the 1960s, the organization was expelled from Iran after the Islamic Revolution in 1979, and its primary support now comes from the Iraqi regime of Saddam Hussein. Its history is studded with anti-Western attacks as well as terrorist attacks on the interests of the clerical regime in Iran and abroad. The MEK now advocates a secular Iranian regime.	Worldwide campaign against the Iranian Government stresses propaganda and occasionally uses terrorist violence. During the 1970s the MEK killed several US military personnel and US civilians working on defense projects in Tehran. It supported the takeover in 1979 of the US Embassy in Tehran. In 1981 the MEK planted bombs in the head office of the Islamic Republic Party and the Premier's office, killing some 70 high-ranking Iranian officials, including chief Justice Ayatollah Mohammad Beheshti, President Mohammad-Ali Rajaei, and Premier Mohammad-Javad Bahonar. In 1991, it assisted the government of Iraq in suppressing the Shia and Kurdish uprisings in northern and southern Iraq. Since then, the MEK has continued to perform internal security services for the Government of Iraq. In April 1992, it conducted attacks on Iranian Embassies in 13 different countries, demonstrating the group's ability to mount large-scale operations overseas. In recent years the MEK has targeted key military officers and assassinated the deputy chief of the Armed Forces General Staff in April 1999. In April 2000, the MEK attempted to assassinate the commander of the Nasr Headquarters—the inter-agency board responsible for coordinating policies on Iraq. The normal pace of anti-Iranian operations increased during the "Operation Great Bahman" in February 2000, when the group launched a dozen attacks against Iran. In 2000 and 2001, the MEK was involved regularly in mortar attacks and hit-and-run raids on Iranian military and law enforcement units and government buildings near the Iran-Iraq border. Since the end of the Iran-Iraq War the tactics along the border have garnered few military gains and have become commonplace. MEK insurgent activities in Tehran constitute the biggest security concern for the Iranian leadership. In February 2000, for example, the MEK attacked the leadership complex in Tehran that houses the offices of the Supreme Leader and President.	Several thousand fighters located on bases scattered throughout Iraq and armed with tanks, infantry fighting vehicles, and artillery. The MEK also has an overseas support structure. Most of the fighters are organized in the MEK's National Liberation Army (NLA).	In the 1980s the MEK's leaders were forced by Iranian security forces to flee to France. Since resettling in Iraq in 1987, the group has conducted internal security operations in support of the Government of Iraq. In the mid-1980s the group did not mount terrorist operations in Iran at a level similar to its activities in the 1970s, but by the 1990s the MEK had claimed credit for an in-creasing number of operations in Iran.	Beyond support from Iraq, the MEK uses front organizations to solicit contributions from expatriate Iranian communities.
National Liberation Army (ELN)—Colombia	Marxist insurgent group formed in 1965 by urban intellectuals inspired by Fidel Castro and Che Guevara. Began a dialogue with Colombian officials in 1999 following a campaign of mass kidnappings—each involving at least one US citizen—to demonstrate its strength and continuing viability and force the Pastrana	Kidnapping, hijacking, bombing, extortion, and guerrilla war. Modest conventional military capability. Annually conducts hundreds of kidnappings for ransom, often targeting foreign employees of large corporations, especially in the petroleum industry. Frequently assaults energy infrastructure and has inflicted major damage on pipelines and the electric distribution network.	Approximately 3,000–5,000 armed combatants and an unknown number of active supporters.	Mostly in rural and mountainous areas of north, northeast, and southwest Colombia, and Venezuela border regions.	Cuba provides some medical care and political consultation.

TABLE 5.1

State Department-designated foreign terrorist organizations as of May 2002 [CONTINUED]

Organization name	Description	Activities	Strength	Location/Area of Operation	External Aid
National Liberation Army (ELN)—Colombia (cont'd)	administration to negotiate. Peace talks between Bogotá and the ELN, started in 1999, continued sporadically through 2001 until Bogota broke them off in August, but resumed in Havana, Cuba, by year's end.				
The Palestine Islamic Jihad (PIJ)	Originated among militant Palestinians in the Gaza Strip during the 1970s. PIJ-Shiqaqi faction, currently led by Ramadan Shallah in Damascus, is most active. Committed to the creation of an Islamic Palestinian state and the destruction of Israel through holy war. Also opposes moderate Arab governments that it believes have been tainted by Western secularism.	PIJ activists have conducted many attacks including large-scale suicide bombings against Israeli civilian and military targets. The group increased its operational activity in 2001 during the *Intifadah*, claiming numerous attacks against Israeli interests. The group has not targeted US interests and continues to confine its attacks to Israelis inside Israel and the territories.	Unknown.	Primarily Israel, the West Bank and Gaza Strip, and other parts of the Middle East, including Lebanon and Syria, where the leadership is based.	Receives financial assistance from Iran and limited logistic support assistance from Syria.
Palestine Liberation Front (PLF)	Broke away from the PFLP-GC in mid-1970s. Later split again into pro-PLO, pro-Syrian, and pro-Libyan factions. Pro-PLO faction led by Muhammad Abbas (Abu Abbas), who became member of PLO Executive Committee in 1984 but left it in 1991.	The Abu Abbas-led faction is known for aerial attacks against Israel. Abbas's group also was responsible for the attack in 1985 on the cruise ship Achille Lauro and the murder of US citizen Leon Klinghoffer. A warrant for Abu Abbas's arrest is outstanding in Italy.	Unknown.	PLO faction based in Tunisia until Achille Lauro attack. Now based in Iraq.	Receives support mainly from Iraq. Has received support from Libya in the past.
Popular Front for the Liberation of Palestine (PFLP)	Marxist-Leninist group founded in 1967 by George Habash as a member of the PLO. Joined the Alliance of Palestinian Forces (APF) to oppose the Declaration of Principles signed in 1993 and suspended participation in the PLO. Broke away from the APF, along with the DFLP, in 1996 over ideological differences. Took part in meetings with Arafat's Fatah party and PLO representatives in 1999 to discuss national unity and the reinvigoration of the PLO but continues to oppose current negotiations with Israel.	Committed numerous international terrorist attacks during the 1970s. Since 1978 has conducted attacks against Israeli or moderate Arab targets, including killing a settler and her son in December 1996. Stepped up operational activity in 2001, highlighted by the shooting death of Israeli Tourism Minister in October to retaliate for Israel's killing of PFLP leader in August.	Some 800.	Syria, Lebanon, Israel, West Bank, and Gaza.	Receives safehaven and some logistical assistance from Syria.
Popular Front for the Liberation of Palestine—General Command (PFLP-GC)	Split from the PFLP in 1968, claiming it wanted to focus more on fighting and less on politics. Opposed to Arafat's PLO. Led by Ahmad Jabril, a former captain in the Syrian Army. Closely tied to both Syria and Iran.	Carried out dozens of attacks in Europe and the Middle East during 1970s-80s. Known for cross-border terrorist attacks into Israel using unusual means, such as hot-air balloons and motorized hang gliders. Primary focus now on guerrilla operations in southern Lebanon, small-scale attacks in Israel, West Bank, and Gaza.	Several hundred.	Headquartered in Damascus with bases in Lebanon.	Receives support from Syria and financial support from Iran.

TABLE 5.1

State Department–designated foreign terrorist organizations as of May 2002 [CONTINUED]

Organization name	Description	Activities	Strength	Location/Area of Operation	External Aid
Al-Qaida	Established by Usama Bin Ladin in the late 1980s to bring together Arabs who fought in Afghanistan against the Soviet Union. Helped finance, recruit, transport, and train Sunni Islamic extremists for the Afghan resistance. Current goal is to establish a pan-Islamic Caliphate throughout the world by working with allied Islamic extremist groups to overthrow regimes it deems "non-Islamic" and expelling Westerners and non-Muslims from Muslim countries. Issued statement under banner of "The World Islamic Front for Jihad Against the Jews and Crusaders" in February 1998, saying it was the duty of all Muslims to kill US citizens—civilian or military—and their allies everywhere. Merged with Egyptian Islamic Jihad (Al-Jihad) in June 2001.	On 11 September, 19 al-Qaida suicide attackers hijacked and crashed four US commercial jets, two into the World Trade Center in New York City, one into the Pentagon near Washington, DC, and a fourth into a field in Shanksville, Pennsylvania, leaving about 3,000 individuals dead or missing. Directed the 12 October 2000 attack on the USS Cole in the port of Aden, Yemen, killing 17 US Navy members, and injuring another 39. Conducted the bombings in August 1998 of the US Embassies in Nairobi, Kenya, and Dar es Salaam, Tanzania, that killed at least 301 individuals and injured more than 5,000 others. Claims to have conducted three bombings that targeted US troops in Aden, Yemen, in December 1992. Al-Qaida is linked to the following plans that were not carried out: to assassinate Pope John Paul II during his visit to Manila in late 1994, to kill President Clinton during a visit to the Philippines in early 1995, the midair bombing of a dozen US trans-Pacific flights in 1995, and to set off a bomb at Los Angeles International Airport in 1999. Also plotted to carry out terrorist operations against US and Israeli tourists visiting Jordan for millennial celebra-tions in late 1999. (Jordanian authorities thwarted the planned attacks and put 28 suspects on trial.) In December 2001, suspected al-Qaida associate Richard Colvin Reid attempted to ignite a shoe bomb on a transatlantic flight from Paris to Miami.	Al-Qaida may have several thousand members and associates. Also serves as a focal point or umbrella organization for a worldwide network that includes many Sunni Islamic extremist groups, some members of al-Gama'a al-Islamiyya, the Islamic Move-ment of Uzbekistan, and the Harakat ul-Mujahidin.	Al-Qaida has cells worldwide and is reinforced by its ties to Sunni extremist networks. Coalition attacks on Afghanistan since October 2001 have dismantled the Taliban—al-Qaida's protectors—and led to the capture, death, or dis-persal of al-Qaida operatives. Some al-Qaida members at large probably will attempt to carry out future attacks against US interests.	Bin Ladin, member of a billionaire family that owns the Bin Ladin Group construction empire, is said to have inherited tens of millions of dollars that he uses to help finance the group. Al-Qaida also maintains moneymaking front businesses, solicits donations from like-minded supporters, and illicitly siphons funds from donations to Muslim charitable organizations. US efforts to block al-Qaida funding has hampered al-Qaida's ability to obtain money.
Real IRA (RIRA) a.k.a True IRA	Formed in early 1998 as clandestine armed wing of the 32-County Sovereignty Movement, a "political pressure group" dedi-cated to removing British forces from Northern Ireland and unifying Ireland. The 32-County Sovereignty Movement opposed Sinn Fein's adoption in September 1997 of the Mitchell principles of democracy and nonviolence and opposed the amendment in December 1999 of Articles 2 and 3 of the Irish Constitution, which laid claim to Northern Ireland. Michael "Mickey" McKevitt, who left the IRA to protest its cease-fire, leads the group; Bernadette Sands-McKevitt, his wife, is a founder-member of the 32-County Sovereignty Movement, the political wing of the RIRA.	Bombings, assassinations, and robberies. Many Real IRA members are former IRA members who left that organization following the IRA cease-fire and bring to RIRA a wealth of experience in terrorist tactics and bombmaking. Targets include British military and police in Northern Ireland and Northern Ireland Protestant communities. RIRA is linked to and understood to be responsible for the car bomb attack in Omagh, Northern Ireland on 15 August 1998 that killed 29 and injured 220 persons. The group began to observe a cease-fire following Omagh but in 2000 and 2001 resumed attacks in Northern Ireland and on the UK mainland against targets such as MI6 headquarters and the BBC.	100–200 activists plus possible limited support from IRA hard-liners dissatisfied with the IRA cease-fire and other republican sympathizers. British and Irish authorities arrested at least 40 members in the spring and summer of 2001, including leader McKevitt, who is cur-rently in prison in the Irish Republic awaiting trial for being a member of a terrorist organi-zation and directing terrorist attacks.	Northern Ireland, Irish Republic, Great Britain.	Suspected of receiving funds from sympathizers in the United States and of attempting to buy weapons from US gun dealers. RIRA also is reported to have purchased sophisticated weapons from the Balkans. Three Irish nationals associated with RIRA were extradited from Slovenia to the UK and are awaiting trial on weapons procurement charges.

TABLE 5.1

State Department-designated foreign terrorist organizations as of May 2002 (CONTINUED)

Organization name	Description	Activities	Strength	Location/Area of Operation	External Aid
Revolutionary Armed Forces of Colombia (FARC)	Established in 1964 as the military wing of the Colombian Communist Party, the FARC is Colombia's oldest, largest, most capable, and best-equipped Marxist insurgency. The FARC is governed by a secretariat, led by septuagenarian Manuel Marulanda, a.k.a. "Tirofijo," and six others, including senior military commander Jorge Briceno, a.k.a. "Mono Jojoy." Organized along military lines and includes several urban fronts. In 2001, the group continued a slow-moving peace negotiation process with the Pastrana Administration that has gained the group several concessions, including a de-militarized zone used as a venue for negotiations.	Bombings, murder, kidnapping, extortion, hijacking, as well as guerrilla and conventional military action against Colombian political, military, and economic targets. In March 1999 the FARC executed three US Indian rights activists on Venezuelan territory after it kidnapped them in Colombia. Foreign citizens often are targets of FARC kidnapping for ransom. Has well-documented ties to narcotics traffickers, principally through the provision of armed protection.	Approximately 9,000-12,000 armed combatants and an unknown number of supporters, mostly in rural areas.	Colombia with some activities—extortion, kidnapping, logistics, and R&R—in Venezuela, Panama, and Ecuador.	Cuba provides some medical care and political consultation.
Revolutionary Nuclei a.k.a. Revolutionary Cells	Revolutionary Nuclei (RN) emerged from a broad range of antiestablishment and anti-US/NATO/EU leftist groups active in Greece between 1995 and 1998. The group is believed to be the successor to or offshoot of Greece's most prolific terrorist group, Revolutionary People's Struggle (ELA), which has not claimed an attack since January 1995. Indeed, RN appeared to fill the void left by ELA, particularly as lesser groups faded from the scene. RN's few communiqués show strong similarities in rhetoric, tone, and theme to ELA proclamations. RN has not claimed an attack since November 2000.	Beginning operations in January 1995, the group has claimed responsibility for some two dozen arson attacks and explosive low-level bombings targeting a range of US, Greek, and other European targets in Greece. In its most infamous and lethal attack to date, the group claimed responsibility for a bomb it detonated at the Intercontinental Hotel in April 1999 that resulted in the death of a Greek woman and injured a Greek man. Its modus operandi includes warning calls of impending attacks, attacks targeting property vice individuals; use of rudimentary timing devices; and strikes during the late evening-early morning hours. RN last attacked US interests in Greece in November 2000 with two separate bombings against the Athens offices of Citigroup and the studio of a Greek/American sculptor. The group also detonated an explosive device outside the Athens offices of Texaco in December 1999. Greek targets have included court and other government office buildings, private vehicles, and the offices of Greek firms involved in NATO-related defense contracts in Greece. Similarly, the group has attacked European interests in Athens, including Barclays Bank in December 1998 and November 2000.	Group membership is believed to be small, probably drawing from the Greek militant leftist or anarchist milieu.	Primary area of operation is in the Athens metropolitan area.	Unknown, but believed to be self-sustaining.

TABLE 5.1

State Department-designated foreign terrorist organizations as of May 2002 [CONTINUED]

Organization name	Description	Activities	Strength	Location/Area of Operation	External Aid
Revolutionary Organization 17 November (17 November)	Radical leftist group established in 1975 and named for the student uprising in Greece in November 1973 that protested the military regime. Anti-Greek establishment, anti-US, anti-Turkey, anti-NATO, and committed to the ouster of US Bases, removal of Turkish military presence from Cyprus, and severing of Greece's ties to NATO and the European Union (EU).	Initial attacks were assassinations of senior US officials and Greek public figures. Added bombings in 1980s. Since 1990 has expanded targets to include EU facilities and foreign firms investing in Greece and has added improvised rocket attacks to its methods. Most recent attack claimed was the murder in June 2000 of British Defense Attaché Stephen Saunders.	Unknown, but presumed to be small.	Athens, Greece.	Unknown.
Revolutionary People's Liberation Party/Front (DHKP/C) a.k.a. Devrimci So, Revolutionary Left, Dev Sol	Originally formed in 1978 as Devrimci Sol, or Dev Sol, a splinter faction of the Turkish People's Liberation Party/Front. Renamed in 1994 after factional infighting, it espouses a Marxist ideology and is virulently anti-US and anti-NATO. Finances its activities chiefly through armed robberies and extortion.	Since the late 1980s has concentrated attacks against current and retired Turkish security and military officials. Began a new campaign against foreign interests in 1990. Assassinated two US military contractors and wounded a US Air Force officer to protest the Gulf War. Launched rockets at US Consulate in Istanbul in 1992. Assassinated prominent Turkish businessman and two others in early 1996, its first significant terrorist act as DHKP/C. Turkish authorities thwarted DHKP/C attempt in June 1999 to fire light antitank weapon at US Consulate in Istanbul. Conducted its first suicide bombings, targeting Turkish police, in January and September 2001. Series of safehouse raids and arrests by Turkish police over last three years have weakened group significantly.	Unknown.	Conducts attacks in Turkey, primarily in Istanbul. Raises funds in Western Europe.	Unknown.
The Salafist Group for Call and Combat (GSPC)	The Salafist Group for Call and Combat (GSPC) splinter faction that began in 1996 has eclipsed the GIA since approximately 1998, and currently is assessed to be the most effective remaining armed group inside Algeria. In contrast to the GIA, the GSPC has gained popular support through its pledge to avoid civilian attacks inside Algeria (although, in fact, civilians have been attacked). Its adherents abroad appear to have largely co-opted the external networks of the GIA, active particularly throughout Europe, Africa, and the Middle East	The GSPC continues to conduct operations aimed at government and military targets, primarily in rural areas. Such operations include false roadblocks and attacks against convoys transporting military, police, or other government personnel. According to press reporting, some GSPC members in Europe maintain contacts with other North African extremists sympathetic to al-Qaida, a number of whom were implicated in terrorist plots during 2001.	Unknown; probably several hundred to several thousand inside Algeria.	Algeria.	Algerian expatriates and GSPC members abroad, many residing in Western Europe, provide financial and logistics support. In addition, the Algerian Government has accused Iran and Sudan of supporting Algerian extremists in years past.

TABLE 5.1

State Department-designated foreign terrorist organizations as of May 2002 [CONTINUED]

Organization name	Description	Activities	Strength	Location/Area of Operation	External Aid
Sendero Luminoso (Shining Path, or SL)	Former university professor Abimael Guzman formed Sendero Luminoso in the late 1960s, and his teachings created the foundation of SL's militant Maoist doctrine. In the 1980s SL became one of the most ruthless terrorist groups in the Western Hemisphere; approximately 30,000 persons have died since Shining Path took up arms in 1980. Its stated goal is to destroy existing Peruvian institutions and replace them with a communist peasant revolutionary regime. It also opposes any influence by foreign governments, as well as by other Latin American guerrilla groups, especially the Tupac Amaru Revolutionary Movement (MRTA). In 2001, the Peruvian National Police thwarted an SL attack against "an American objective", possibly the US Embassy, when they arrested two Lima SL cell members. Additionally, Government authorities continued to arrest and prosecute active SL members, including Ruller Mazombite, a.k.a. "Camarada Cayo", chief of the protection team of SL leader Macario Ala, a.k.a. "Artemio", and Evorcio Ascencios, a.k.a. "Camarada Canale", logistics chief of the Huallaga Regional Committee. Counterterrorist operations targeted pockets of terrorist activity in the Upper Huallaga River Valley and the Apurimac/Ene River Valley, where SL columns continued to conduct periodic attacks.	Conducted indiscriminate bombing campaigns and selective assassinations. Detonated explosives at diplomatic missions of several countries in Peru in 1990, including an attempt to car bomb the US Embassy in December. Peruvian authorities continued operations against the SL in 2001 in the countryside, where the SL conducted periodic raids on villages.	Membership is unknown but estimated to be 200 armed militants. SL's strength has been vastly diminished by arrests and desertions.	Peru, with most activity in rural areas.	None.
United Self-Defense Forces/Group of Colombia (AUC– Autodefensas Unidas de Colombia)	The AUC--commonly referred to as the paramilitaries—is an umbrella organization formed in April 1997 to consolidate most local and regional paramilitary groups each with the mission to	AUC operations vary from assassinating suspected insurgent supporters to engaging guerrilla combat units. Colombian National Combat operations generally consist of raids and ambushes directed against suspected insurgents. The AUC generally avoids engagements with government security	Estimated 6,000 to 8,150, including former military and insurgent personnel.	AUC forces are strongest in the northwest in Antioquia, Córdoba, Sucre, and Bolivar Departments. Since 1999, the group demonstrated a growing presence in other northern and southwestern	None.

TABLE 5.1

State Department-designated foreign terrorist organizations as of May 2002 [CONTINUED]

Organization name	Description	Activities	Strength	Location/Area of Operation	External Aid
United Self-Defense Forces/Group of Colombia (AUC–Autodefensas Unidas de Colombia) (cont'd)	protect economic interests and combat insurgents locally. The AUC—supported by economic elites, drug traffickers, and local communities lacking effective government security—claims its primary objective is to protect its sponsors from insurgents. The AUC now asserts itself as a regional and national counter-insurgent force. It is adequately equipped and armed and reportedly pays its members a monthly salary. AUC political leader Carlos Castaño has claimed 70 percent of the AUC's operational costs are financed with drug-related earnings, the rest from "donations" from its sponsors.	forces and actions against US personnel or interests.		departments. Clashes between the AUC and the FARC insurgents in Putumayo in 2000 demonstrated the range of the AUC to contest insurgents throughout Colombia.	

SOURCE: Adapted from "Appendix B: Background Information on Designated Foreign Terrorist Organizations," U.S. Department of State, Office of the Coordinator for Counterterrorism, Washington, DC, May 2002 [Online] http://www.state.gov/s/ct/rls/pgtrpt/2001/html/10252.htm [accessed July 23, 2002]

TABLE 5.2

Other terrorist groups worldwide, December 2002

Organization Name	Description	Activities	Strength	Location/ Area of Operation	External Aid
Alex Boncayao Brigade (ABB)	The ABB, the breakaway urban hit squad of the Communist Party of the Philippines New People's Army, was formed in the mid-1980s. The ABB was added to the Terrorist Exclusion list in December 2001.	Responsible for more than 100 murders and believed to have been involved in the murder in 1989 of US Army Col. James Rowe in the Philippines. In March 1997 the group announced it had formed an alliance with another armed group, the Revolutionary Proletarian Army (RPA). In March 2000, the group claimed credit for a rifle grenade attack against the Department of Energy building in Manila and strafed Shell Oil offices in the central Philippines to protest rising oil prices	Approximately 500.	The largest RPA/ABB groups are on the Philippine islands of Luzon, Negros, and the Visayas.	Unknown.
Al-Ittihad al-Islami (AIAI) a.k.a. Islamic Union	Somalia's largest militant Islamic organization rose to power in the early 1990s following the collapse of the Siad Barre regime. Aims to establish an Islamic regime in Somalia and force the secession of the Ogeden region of Ethiopia.	Primarily insurgent-style attacks against Ethiopian forces and other Somali factions. The group is believed to be responsible for a series of bomb attacks in public places in Addis Ababa in 1996 and 1997 as well as the kidnapping of several relief workers in 1998. AIAI sponsors Islamic social programs, such as orphanages and schools, and provides pockets of security in Somalia.	Estimated at some 2,000 members, plus additional reserve militias.	Primarily in Somalia, with limited presence in Ethiopia and Kenya.	Receives funds from Middle East financiers and Western diaspora remittances, and suspected training in Afghanistan. Maintains ties to al-Qaida. Past weapons deliveries from Sudan.
Allied Democratic Forces (ADF)	A diverse coalition of former members of the National Army for the Liberation of Uganda (NALU), Islamists from the Salaf Tabliq group, Hutu militiamen, and fighters from ousted regimes in Congo. The conglomeration of fighters formed in 1995 in opposition to the government of Ugandan President Yoweri Museveni.	The ADF seeks to use the kidnapping and murder of civilians to create fear in the local population and undermine confidence in the Government. The group is suspected to be responsible for dozens of bombings in public areas. A Ugandan military offensive in 2000 destroyed several ADF camps, but ADF attacks continued in Kampala in 2001.	A few hundred fighters.	Western Uganda and eastern Congo.	Received past funding, supplies, and training from the Government of Sudan. Some funding suspected from sympathetic Hutu groups.
Anti-Imperialist Territorial Nuclei (NTA)	Clandestine leftist extremist group that appeared in the Friuli region in Italy in 1995. Adopted the class struggle ideology of the Red Brigades of the 1970s-80s and a similar logo—an encircled five-point star—for their	Criticized US/NATO presence in Italy and attacked property owned by US Air Force personnel at Aviano Air Base. Claimed responsibility for a bomb attack in September 2000 against the Central European	Approximately 20 members.	Mainly in northeastern Italy, including Friuli, Veneto, and Emilia.	None evident.

TABLE 5.2

Other terrorist groups worldwide, December 2002 [CONTINUED]

Organization Name	Description	Activities	Strength	Location/ Area of Operation	External Aid
Anti-Imperialist Territorial Nuclei (NTA) (cont.)	declarations. Opposes what it perceives as US and NATO imperialism and condemns Italy's foreign and labor polices.	Initiative office in Trieste and a bomb attack in August 2001 against the Venice Tribunal building. Threw gasoline bombs at the Venice and Rome headquarters of the then-ruling party, Democrats of the Left, during the NATO inter-vention in Kosovo.			
Army for the Liberation of Rwanda (ALIR) a.k.a. Interahamwe, Former Armed Forces (ex-FAR)	The FAR was the army of the Rwandan Hutu regime that carried out the genocide of 500,000 or more Tutsis and regime opponents in 1994. The Interahamwe was the civilian militia force that carried out much of the killing. The groups merged and recruited additional fighters after they were forced from Rwanda into the Democratic Republic of Congo (then Zaire) in 1994. They are now often known as the Army for the Liberation of Rwanda (ALIR), which is the armed branch of the PALIR or Party for the Liberation of Rwanda.	The group seeks to topple Rwanda's Tutsi-dominated government, reinstitute Hutu-control, and, possibly, complete the genocide. In 1996, a message allegedly from the ALIR threatened to kill the US Ambassador to Rwanda and other US citizens. In 1999, ALIR guerrillas critical of alleged US-UK sup-port for the Rwandan regime kidnapped and killed eight foreign tourists including two US citizens in a game park on the Congo-Uganda border. In the current Congolese war, the ALIR is allied with Kinshasa against the Rwandan invaders.	Several thousand ALIR regular forces operate alongside the Congo-lese army on the front lines of the Congo civil war, while a like number of ALIR guerrillas operate behind Rwanda lines in eastern Congo closer to the Rwandan border and sometimes within Rwanda.	Mostly Democratic Republic of the Congo and Rwanda, but some operations in Burundi.	The Democratic Republic of the Congo provides ALIR forces in Congo with training, arms, and supplies.
Cambodian Freedom Fighters (CFF) a.k.a. Cholana Kangtoap Serei Cheat Kampouchea	The Cambodian Freedom Fighters (CFF) emerged in November 1998 in the wake of political violence that saw many influential Cambodian leaders flee and the Cambodian People's Party assume power. With an avowed aim of overthrowing the Government, the group is led by a Cambodian-American, a former member of the opposition Sam Rainsy Party, and its member-ship includes Cambodian-Americans based in Thailand and the United States and former soldiers from the separatist Khmer Rouge, Royal Cambodian Armed Forces, and various political factions.	The CFF has on at least one occasion attacked government facilities and planned other bombing attacks. In late November 2000, the CFF staged an attack on several government installa-tions, during which at least eight persons died and more than a dozen were wounded, including civilians. The group's leaders claimed responsibility for the attack. Following a trial of 32 CFF members arrested for the attack, five received life sentences, 25 received lesser jail terms, and two were acquitted. In April 1999, five other members of the CFF were arrested for plotting to blow up a fuel depot outside Phnom Penh with antitank weapons.	Exact strength is unknown, but totals probably never have exceeded 100 armed fighters.	Northeastern Cambodia near the Thai border.	US-based leadership collects funds from the Cambodian-American community.

TABLE 5.2

Other terrorist groups worldwide, December 2002 [CONTINUED]

Organization Name	Description	Activities	Strength	Location/ Area of Operation	External Aid
Continuity Irish Republican Army (CIRA) a.k.a. Continuity Army Council	Radical terrorist splinter group formed in 1994 as the clandestine armed wing of Republican Sinn Fein (RSF), which split from Sinn Fein in the mid-1980s. "Continuity" refers to the group's belief that it is carrying on the original IRA goal of forcing the British out of Northern Ireland, and CIRA actively seeks to recruit IRA members.	CIRA has been active in the border areas of Northern Ireland where it has carried out bombings, assassinations, kidnappings, extortion, and robberies. Targets include British military and Northern Ireland security targets and Northern Ireland Loyalist paramilitary groups. Does not have an established presence on the UK mainland. CIRA is not observing a cease-fire and in October said decommissioning weapons would be "an act of treachery."	Fewer than 50 hardcore activists but is said to have recruited new members in Belfast.	Northern Ireland, Irish Republic.	Suspected of receiving funds and arms from sympathizers in the United States. May have acquired arms and materiel from the Balkans in cooperation with the Real IRA.
First of October Antifacist Resistance Group (GRAPO) a.k.a. Grupode Resistencia Anti-Fascista Primero de Octubre	Formed in 1975 as the armed wing of the illegal Communist Party of Spain during the Franco era. Advocating the overthrow of the Spanish Government and replacement with a Marxist-Leninist regime, GRAPO is vehemently anti-US, calls for the removal of all US military forces from Spanish territory, and has conducted and attempted several attacks against US targets since 1977. The group issued a communiqué following the 11 September attacks in the United States, expressing its satisfaction that "symbols of imperialist power" were decimated and affirming that "the war" has only just begun.	GRAPO has killed more than 90 persons and injured more than 200. The group's operations traditionally have been designed to cause material damage and gain publicity rather than inflict casualties, but the terrorists have conducted lethal bombings and close-range assassinations. In May 2000, the group killed two security guards during a botched armed robbery attempt of an armored truck carrying an estimated $2 million, and in November 2000, members assassinated a Spanish policeman in a possible reprisal for the arrest that month of several GRAPO leaders in France. The group also has bombed business and official sites, employment agencies and the Madrid headquarters of the ruling Popular Party, for example including the Barcelona office of the national daily El Mundo in October 2000, when two police officers were injured.	Unknown but likely fewer than a dozen hard-core activists. Spanish and French officials have made periodic large-scale arrests of GRAPO members, crippling the organization and forcing it into lengthy rebuilding periods. The French and Spanish arrested several key leaders in 2001.	Spain	None
Harakat ul-Jihad-I-Islami (HUJI) a.k.a. Movement of Islamic Holy War	HUJI, a Sunni extremist group that follows the Deobandi tradition of Islam, was founded in 1980 in Afghanistan to fight in the jihad	Has conducted a number of operations against Indian military targets in Kashmir. Linked to the Kashmiri militant group al-Faran	Exact numbers are unknown, but there may be several hundred members in Kashmir.	Pakistan and Kashmir. Trained members in Afghanistan until fall of 2001.	Specific sources of external aid are unknown.

TABLE 5.2

Other terrorist groups worldwide, December 2002 [CONTINUED]

Organization Name	Description	Activities	Strength	Location/ Area of Operation	External Aid
Harakat ul-Jihad-I-Islami (HUJI) (cont.)	against the Soviets. It is also affiliated with the Jamiat Ulema-I-Islam Fazlur Rehman faction (JUI-F) and the Deobandi school of Sunni Islam. The group, led by chief commander Amin Rabbani, is made up primarily of Pakistanis and foreign Islamists who are fighting for the liberation of Kashmir and its accession to Pakistan.	that kidnapped five Western tourists in Kashmir in July 1995; one was killed in August 1995 and the other four reportedly were killed in December of the same year.			
Harakat ul-Jihad-I-Islami/Bangladesh (HUJI-B) a.k.a. Movement of Islamic Holy War	The mission of HUJI-B, led by Shauqat Osman, is to establish Islamic rule in Bangladesh. HUJI-B has connections to the Pakistani militant groups Harakat ul-Jihad-i-Islami (HUJI) and Harak ul-Mujahidin (HUM), who advocate similar objectives in Pakistan and Kashmir.	HUJI-B was accused of stabbing a senior Bangladeshi journalist in November 2000 for making a documentary on the plight of Hindus in Bangladesh. HUJI-B was suspected in the July 2000 assassination attempt of Bangladeshi Prime Minister Sheikh Hasina.	HUJI-B has an estimated cadre strength of over several thousand members.	Operates and trains members in Bangladesh, where it maintains at least six camps.	Funding of the HUJI-B comes primarily from madrassas in Bangladesh. The group also has ties to militants in Pakistan that may provide another funding source.
Islamic Army of Aden (IAA) a.k.a. Aden-Abyan Islamic Army (AAIA)	The Islamic Army of Aden (IAA) emerged publicly in mid-1998 when the group released a series of communiqués that expressed support for Usama Bin Ladin, appealed for the overthrow of the Yemeni Government and the commencement of operations against US and other Western interests in Yemen.	Engages in bombings and kidnappings to promote its goals. Kidnapped 16 British, Australian, and US tourists in late December 1998 near Mudiyah in southern Yemen. Since the capture and trial of the Mudiyah kidnappers and the execution in October 1999 of the group's leader, Zein al-Abidine al-Mihdar (a.k.a. Abu Hassan), individuals associated with the IAA have remained involved in terrorist activities. In 2001 the Yemeni Government convicted an IAA member and three associates for their roles in the October 2000 bombing of the British Embassy in Sanaa.	Not known.	Operates in the southern governorates of Yemen—primarily Aden and Abyan.	Not known.
Irish Republican Army (IRA) a.k.a. Provisional Irish Republican Army (PIRA), the Provos (Now almost universally referred to as the PIRA to distinguish it from RIRA and CIRA.)	Terrorist group formed in 1969 as clandestine armed wing of Sinn Fein, a legal political movement dedicated to removing British forces from Northern Ireland and unifying Ireland. Has a Marxist orientation. Organized into small, tightly knit cells under the leadership of the Army Council.	The IRA has been observing a cease-fire since 1997 and in October 2001 took the historic step of putting an unspecified amount of arms and ammunition "completely beyond use." The International Commission on Decommissioning characterized the step as a significant	Several hundred members, plus several thousand sympathizers— despite the possible defection of some members to RIRA or CIRA.	Northern Ireland, Irish Republic, Great Britain, Europe.	Has in the past received aid from a variety of groups and countries and considerable training and arms from Libya and the PLO. Is suspected of receiving funds, arms, and other terrorist related materiel from sympathizers in the United States. Similarities in operations suggest links to ETA.

TABLE 5.2

Other terrorist groups worldwide, December 2002 [CONTINUED]

Organization Name	Description	Activities	Strength	Location/ Area of Operation	External Aid
Irish Republican Army (IRA) (cont.)		act of decommissioning. The IRA retains the ability to conduct operations. Its traditional activities have included bombings, assassinations, kidnappings, punishment beatings, extortion, smuggling, and robberies. Bombing campaigns were conducted against train and subway stations and shopping areas on mainland Britain. Targets included senior British Government officials, civilians, police, and British military targets in Northern Ireland. The IRA's current cease-fire (since July 1997) was preceded by a cease-fire from 1 September 1994 to February 1996.			
Al Jama'a al-Islamiyyah al-Muqatilah bi-Libya a.k.a. Libyan Islamic Fighting Group, Fighting Islamic Group, Libyan Fighting Group, Libyan Islamic Group	Emerged in 1995 among Libyans who had fought against Soviet forces in Afghanistan. Declared the Government of Libyan leader Muammar Qadhafi un-Islamic and pledged to overthrow it. Some members maintain a strictly anti-Qadhafi focus and organize against Libyan Government interests but others are aligned with Usama Bin Ladin's al-Qaida organization or are active in the international mujahidin network.	Claimed responsibility for a failed assassination attempt against Qadhafi in 1996 and engaged Libyan security forces in armed clashes during the mid to late 1990s. Currently engages in few armed attacks against Libyan interests either in Libya or abroad. Some members may be aligned with al-Qaida or involved in al-Qaida activities.	Not known but probably has several hundred active members.	Probably maintains a clandestine presence in Libya, but since late 1990s many members have fled to various Middle Eastern and European countries.	Not known. May obtain some funding through private donations, various Islamic non-governmental organizations, and criminal acts.
Japanese Red Army (JRA) a.k.a. Anti-Imperialist International Brigade (AIIB)	An international terrorist group formed around 1970 after breaking away from Japanese Communist League-Red Army Faction. Fusako Shigenobu led the JRA until her arrest in Japan in November 2000. The JRA's historical goal has been to overthrow the Japanese Government and monarchy and to help foment world revolution. After her arrest Shigenobu announced she intended to pursue her goals using a legitimate	During the 1970s, JRA carried out a series of attacks around the world, including the massacre in 1972 at Lod Airport in Israel, two Japanese airliner hijackings, and an attempted takeover of the US Embassy in Kuala Lumpur. In April 1988, JRA operative Yu Kikumura was arrested with explosives on the New Jersey Turnpike, apparently planning an attack to coincide with the bombing of a USO club	About six hardcore members; undetermined number of sympathizers. At its peak the group claimed to have 30 to 40 members.	Location unknown, but possibly in Asia and/or Syrian-controlled areas of Lebanon.	Unknown.

TABLE 5.2

Other terrorist groups worldwide, December 2002 [CONTINUED]

Organization Name	Description	Activities	Strength	Location/ Area of Operation	External Aid
Japanese Red Army (JRA) (cont.)	political party rather than revolutionary violence, and the group announced it would disband in April 2001. May control or at least have ties to Anti-Imperialist International Brigade (AIIB); also may have links to Antiwar Democratic Front—an overt leftist political organization—inside Japan. Details released following Shigenobu's arrest indicate that the JRA was organizing cells in Asian cities, such as Manila and Singapore. The group had a history of close relations with Palestinian terrorist groups—based and operating outside Japan—since its inception, primarily through Shigenobu. The current status of the connections is unknown.	in Naples, a suspected JRA operation that killed five, including a US servicewoman. He was convicted of the charges and is serving a lengthy prison sentence in the United States. Tsutomu Shirosaki, captured in 1996, is also jailed in the United States. In 2000, Lebanon deported to Japan four members it arrested in 1997 but granted a fifth operative, Kozo Okamoto, political asylum. Longtime leader Shigenobu was arrested in November 2000 and faces charges of terrorism and passport fraud.			
Kumpulan Mujahidin Malaysia (KMM)	Kumpulan Mujahidin Malaysia (KMM) favors the overthrow of the Mahathir government and the creation of an Islamic state comprising Malaysia, Indonesia, and the southern Philippines. Malaysian authorities believe that smaller, more violent, extremist groups have split from KMM. Zainon Ismail, a former mujahid in Afghanistan, established KMM in 1995. Nik Adli Nik Abdul Aziz, currently detained under Malaysia's Internal Security Act (ISA), assumed leadership in 1999. Malaysian police assert that three Indonesian extremists, one of whom is in custody, have disseminated militant ideology to the KMM.	Malaysia is currently holding 48 alleged members of the KMM and its more extremist wing under the ISA for activities deemed threatening to Malaysia's national security, including planning to wage a jihad, possession of weaponry, bombings and robberies, the murder of a former state assemblyman, and planning attacks on foreigners, including US citizens. Several of the arrested militants have reportedly undergone military training in Afghanistan, and some fought with the Afghan mujahidin during the war against the former Soviet Union. Others are alleged to have ties to Islamic extremist organizations in Indonesia and the Philippines.	Malaysian police assess the KMM to have 70 to 80 members. The Malaysian press reports that police are currently tracking 200 suspected Muslim militants.	The KMM is reported to have networks in the Malaysian states of Perak, Johor, Kedah, Selangor, Terengganu, and Kelantan. They also operate in Wilayah Persukutuan, the federal territory comprising Kuala Lumpur. According to press reports, the KMM has ties to radical Indonesian Islamic groups and has sent members to Ambon, Indonesia to fight against Christians.	Largely unknown, probably self-financing.
Lord's Resistance Army (LRA)	Founded in 1989 as the successor to the Holy Spirit Movement, the LRA seeks to overthrow the incumbent Ugandan Government and re-	The LRA frequently kills and kidnaps local Ugandan civilians in order to discourage foreign investment and precipitate a crisis in Uganda.	Estimated 2,000.	Northern Uganda and southern Sudan	The LRA has been supported by the Government of Sudan.

TABLE 5.2

Other terrorist groups worldwide, December 2002 [CONTINUED]

Organization Name	Description	Activities	Strength	Location/ Area of Operation	External Aid
Lord's Resistance Army (LRA) (cont.)	place it with a regime that will implement the group's brand of Christianity.				
Loyalist Volunteer Force (LVF)	An extreme loyalist group formed in 1996 as a faction of the mainstream loyalist Ulster Volunteer Force (UVF) but did not emerge publicly until February 1997. Composed largely of UVF hardliners who have sought to prevent a political settlement with Irish nationalists in Northern Ireland by attacking Catholic politicians, civilians, and Protestant politicians who endorse the Northern Ireland peace process. In October 2001 the British Government ruled that the LVF had broken the cease-fire it declared in 1998. The LVF decommissioned a small but significant amount of weapons in December 1998, but it has not repeated this gesture.	Bombings, kidnappings, and close-quarter shooting attacks. LVF bombs often have contained Powergel commercial explosives, typical of many loyalist groups. LVF attacks have been particularly vicious: The group has murdered numerous Catholic civilians with no political or terrorist affiliations, including an 18-year-old Catholic girl in July 1997 because she had a Protestant boyfriend. The terrorists also have conducted successful attacks against Irish targets in Irish border towns. In 2000 and 2001, the LVF also engaged in a violent feud with other loyalists in which several individuals were killed.	Approximately 150 activists.	Northern Ireland, Ireland.	None
Orange Volunteers (OV)	Terrorist group that appeared about 1998-99 and is comprised largely of disgruntled loyalist hardliners who split from groups observing the cease-fire. OV seeks to prevent a political settlement with Irish nationalists by attacking Catholic civilian interests in Northern Ireland.	The group has been linked to pipe-bomb attacks and sporadic assaults on Catholics. Following a successful security crackdown at the end of 1999, the OV declared a cease-fire in September 2000 and remained quiet in 2001.	Up to 20 hardcore members, some of whom are experienced in terrorist tactics and bombmaking.	Northern Ireland.	None.
People Against Gangsterism and Drugs (PAGAD)	PAGAD was formed in 1996 as a community anti-crime group fighting drugs and violence in the Cape Flats section of Cape Town but by early 1998 had also become antigovernment and anti-Western. PAGAD and its Islamic ally Qibla view the South African Government as a threat to Islamic values and consequently promote greater political voice for	PAGAD's activities were severely curtailed in 2001 by law enforcement and prosecutorial efforts against leading members of the organization. There were no urban terror incidents from September 2000 through 2001, compared to nine bombings in the Western Cape in 2000 that caused serious injuries and a total of	Estimated at several hundred members. PAGAD's G-Force probably contains fewer than 50 members.	Operates mainly in the Cape Town area, South Africa's foremost tourist venue.	Probably has ties to Islamic extremists in the Middle East.

TABLE 5.2

Other terrorist groups worldwide, December 2002 [CONTINUED]

Organization Name	Description	Activities	Strength	Location/ Area of Operation	External Aid
People Against Gangersterism and Drugs (PAGAD) (cont.)	South African Muslims. Abdus Salaam Ebrahim currently leads both groups. PAGAD's G-Force (Gun Force) operates in small cells and is believed responsible for carrying out acts of terrorism. PAGAD uses several front names including Muslims Against Global Oppression (MAGO) and Muslims Against Illegitimate Leaders (MAIL) when launching anti-Western protests and campaigns.	189 bomb attacks since 1996. PAGAD's previous bombing targets have included South African authorities, moderate Muslims, synagogues, gay nightclubs, tourist attractions, and Western-associated restaurants. PAGAD is believed to have masterminded the bombing on 25 August 1998 of the Cape Town Planet Hollywood.			
Red Hand Defenders (RHD)	Extremist terrorist group formed in 1998 composed largely of Protestant hardliners from loyalist groups observing a cease-fire. RHD seeks to prevent a political settlement with Irish nationalists by attacking Catholic civilian interests in Northern Ireland. In July 2001 the group issued a statement saying it considered all nationalists as "legitimate targets." RHD is a cover name often used by elements of the banned Ulster Defense Association and the Loyalist Volunteer Force.	In recent years, the group has carried out numerous pipe bombings and arson attacks against "soft" civilian targets such as homes, churches, and private businesses, including a bombing outside a Catholic girls school in North Belfast. RHD claimed responsibility for the car-bombing murder in March 1999 of Rosemary Nelson, a prominent Catholic nationalist lawyer and human rights campaigner in Northern Ireland, and for the murder of a Catholic journalist in September 2001.	Up to 20 members, some of whom have considerable experience in terrorist tactics and bombmaking.	Northern Ireland.	None
Revolutionary Proletarian Initiative Nuclei (NIPR)	Clandestine leftist extremist group that appeared in Rome in 2000. Adopted the logo of the Red Brigades of the 1970s and 1980s—an encircled five-point star—for their declarations. Opposes Italy's foreign and labor polices.	Claimed responsibility for a bomb attack in April 2001 on building housing a US-Italian relations association and an international affairs institute in Rome's historic center. Claimed to have carried out the May 2000 explosion in Rome at an oversight committee facility for implementation of the law on strikes in public services. Claimed responsibility for an explosion in February 2002 on Via Palermo adjacent to Interior Ministry in Rome.	Approximately 12 members.	Mainly in Rome, Milan, Lazio, and Tuscany.	None evident.
Revolutionary United Front (RUF)	The RUF is a loosely organized guerrilla force seeking to retain control of the lucrative diamond-producing regions of Sierra Leone. The group	During 2001, reports of serious abuses by the RUF declined significantly. The resumption of the Government's Disarm-	Estimated at several thousand supporters and sympathizers.	Sierra Leone, Liberia, Guinea	A UN experts panel report on Sierra Leone said President Charles Taylor of Liberia provides support and leadership to the RUF. The UN has

TABLE 5.2

Other terrorist groups worldwide, December 2002 [CONTINUED]

Organization Name	Description	Activities	Strength	Location/ Area of Operation	External Aid
Revolutionary United Front (RUF) (cont.)	funds itself largely through the extraction and sale of diamonds obtained in areas of Sierra Leone that it controls.	ament, Demobilization, and Reintegration program in May 2001 was largely responsible. From 1991-2000, the group used guerrilla, criminal, and terror tactics, such as murder, torture, and mutilation, to fight the government, intimidate civilians, and keep UN peacekeeping units in check. In 2000 they held hundreds of UN peacekeepers hostage until their release was negotiated, in part, by the RUF's chief sponsor, Liberian President Charles Taylor. The group also has been accused of attacks in Guinea at the behest of President Taylor.			identified Libya, Gambia, and Burkina Faso as conduits for weapons and other materiel for the RUF.
The Tunisian Combatant Group (TCG)	Also referred to as the Tunisian Islamic Fighting Group, the TCG's goals reportedly include establishing an Islamic government in Tunisia and targeting Tunisian and Western interests. Founded probably in 2000 by Tarek Maaroufi and Saifallah Ben Hassine, the group has come to be associated with al-Qa'ida and other North African Islamic extremists in Europe who have been implicated in anti-US terrorist plots there during 2001. In December, Belgian authorities arrested Maaroufi and charged him with providing stolen passports and fraudulent visas for those involved in the assassination of Ahmed Shah Massood, according to press reports.	Tunisians associated with the TCG are part of the support network of the international Salafist movement. According to Italian authorities, TCG members there engage in false document trafficking and recruitment for Afghan training camps. Some TCG associates are suspected of planning an attack against the US, Algerian, and Tunisian diplomatic interests in Rome in January 2001. Members reportedly maintain ties to the Algerian Salafist Group for Call and Combat (GSPC).	Unknown	Western Europe, Afghanistan.	Unknown
Tupac Amaru Revolutionary Movement (MRTA)	Traditional Marxist-Leninist revolutionary movement formed in 1983 from remnants of the Movement of the Revolutionary Left, a Peruvian insurgent group active in the 1960s. Aims to establish a Marxist regime and to rid Peru of all imperialist elements (primarily US and Japanese influence).	Previously conducted bombings, kidnappings, ambushes, and assassinations, but recent activity has fallen drastically. In December 1996, 14 MRTA members occupied the Japanese Ambassador's residence in Lima and held 72 hostages for more than four months. Peruvian forces	Believed to be no more than 100 members, consisting largely of young fighters who lack leadership skills and experience.	Peru with supporters throughout Latin America and Western Europe. Controls no territory.	None

TABLE 5.2

Other terrorist groups worldwide, December 2002 [CONTINUED]

Organization Name	Description	Activities	Strength	Location/ Area of Operation	External Aid
Tupac Amaru Revolutionary Movement (MRTA) (cont.)	Peru's counterterrorist program has diminished the group's ability to carry out terrorist attacks, and the MRTA has suffered from infighting, the imprisonment or deaths of senior leaders, and loss of leftist support. In 2001, several MRTA members remained imprisoned in Bolivia.	stormed the residence in April 1997 rescuing all but one of the remaining hostages and killing all 14 group members, including the remaining leaders. The group has not conducted a significant terrorist operation since and appears more focused on obtaining the release of imprisoned MRTA members.			
Turkish Hizballah	Turkish Hizballah is a Kurdish Islamic (Sunni) extremist organization that arose in the late 1980s in the Diyarbakir area in response to Kurdistan Workers' Party atrocities against Muslims in southeastern Turkey, where (Turkish) Hizballah seeks to establish an independent Islamic state. The group comprises loosely organized factions, the largest of which are Ilim, which advocates the use of violence to achieve the group's goals, and Menzil, which supports an intellectual approach.	Beginning in the mid-1990s, Turkish Hizballah, which is unrelated to Lebanese Hizballah, expanded its target base and modus operandi from killing PKK militants to conducting low-level bombings against liquor stores, bordellos, and other establishments that the organization considered "anti-Islamic." In January 2000, Turkish security forces killed Huseyin Velioglu, the leader of (Turkish) Hizballah's Ilim faction, in a shootout at a safehouse in Istanbul. The incident sparked a year-long series of operations against the group throughout Turkey that resulted in the detention of some 2,000 individuals; authorities arrested several hundred of those on criminal charges. At the same time, police recovered nearly 70 bodies of Turkish and Kurdish businessmen and journalists that (Turkish) Hizballah had tortured and brutally murdered during the mid to late-1990's. The group began targeting official Turkish interests in January 2001, when 10-20 operatives particpated in the assassination of the Diyarbakir police chief, the group's most sophisticated operation to date.	Possibly a few hundred members and several thousand supporters.	Primary area of operation is in southeastern Turkey, particularly the Diyarbakir region.	Turkish officials charge that Turkish Hizballah receives at least some assistance, including training, from Iran.
Ulster Defense Association/Ulster Freedom Fighters (UDA/UVF)	The UDA, the largest loyalist paramilitary group in Northern Ireland, was formed in 1971 as an umbrella organization	The group has been linked to pipe bombings and sporadic assaults on Catholics in Northern Ireland; it stepped up	Estimates vary from 2,000 to 5,000 members, with several hundred active in paramilitary operations.	Northern Ireland.	None

TABLE 5.2

Other terrorist groups worldwide, December 2002 [CONTINUED]

Organization Name	Description	Activities	Strength	Location/ Area of Operation	External Aid
Ulster Defense Association/Ulster Freedom Fighters (UDA/UVF) (cont.)	for loyalist paramilitary groups. It remained a legal organization until 1992, when the British Government proscribed it. Among its members are Johnny Adair, the only person ever convicted of directing terrorism in Northern Ireland, and Michael Stone, who killed three in a gun and grenade attack on an IRA funeral. The UDA joined the UVF in declaring a cease-fire in 1994; it broke down in January 1998 but was later restored. In October 2001, the British Government ruled that the UDA had broken its cease-fire. The organization's political wing, the Ulster Democratic Party, was dissolved in November 2001.	attacks in 2001. William Stobie, the group's former quartermaster who admitted to passing information about the UDA to the British Government, was murdered in December; the Red Hand Defenders claimed responsibility for the killing.			

SOURCE: Adapted from "Appendix C. Background Information on Other Terrorist Groups," in *Patterns of Global Terrriorism 2001*, U.S. Department of State, Washington, DC, May 2002

- The "accidental" shooting of an Iranian passenger airliner in 1988 that killed 290 civilians

- The 1989 invasion of Panama

- Intervention in the Middle East on behalf of Kuwait in 1991 and the ensuing bombing of Iraq

- The naval blockade of Serbia and Montenegro in 1993

- The 1994 intervention in Haiti

- A bombing of the Chinese embassy in Belgrade that killed three Chinese citizens

- Alleged support for numerous assassinations and attempted assassinations over the years of individuals such as Francois Duvalier (Haiti), Patrice Lumumba (Congo), Fidel Castro (Cuba), Raul Castro (Cuba), Ernesto Che Guevara (Cuba), Salvador Allende (Chile), Mobutu Sese Seko (Zaire), Muammar Qaddafi (Libya), Ayatollah Khomeini (Iran), and Saddam Hussein (Iraq)

INTERNATIONAL TERRORISM DIRECTED AGAINST THE UNITED STATES

Introduction: September 11, 2001, and Anti-American Terrorism

In 1993 the World Trade Center in New York City, a symbol of American financial wealth and power, was the target of international terrorists, who detonated a bomb in the underground parking garage, killing 6 people and injuring 1,000. On September 11, 2001, the World Trade Center once again became the target of a Muslim extremist terrorist group, along with other symbolic American targets, such as the Pentagon in Washington, D.C. During the attacks, 19 Middle Eastern men, 15 of whom were Saudi Arabian and all of whom were members of al-Qaeda, hijacked and then crashed four commercial jetliners.

Five of the terrorists hijacked American Airlines Flight 11, departing Boston, Massachusetts, for Los Angeles, California, at 7:45 A.M. At 8:45 A.M., they intentionally piloted the aircraft into the North Tower of the World Trade Center. Another five terrorists hijacked United Airlines Flight 175, which departed Boston for Los Angeles at 7:58 A.M. At 9:05 A.M. they flew the plane into the South Tower of the World Trade Center. The crashed planes, carrying tons of jet fuel in their full tanks for the long journey across the country, ignited upon impact, causing a fire with 4,000-degree temperatures that melted the internal structure of the 104-story World Trade Center office towers. Both towers eventually completely collapsed, destroying other buildings and property as they fell. More than 255 firefighters and 70 police officers died inside the towers as they tried to rescue the thousands of office workers and facility personnel trapped inside.

When the official cleanup and recovery efforts in New York City ended with a final ceremony on May 30, 2002, the New York City Office of Emergency Management gave final totals for the destruction caused by the attacks. Of the 2,823 people killed in New York, 1,102 victims had been identified. An estimated 3.1 million hours of labor were spent on cleanup, and more than 1.8 million tons of debris had been removed in 108,342 truckloads. The leveling of the World Trade Center towers also caused property damage in the billions of dollars. Tens of thousands of people had to be evacuated from their homes in Manhattan. Air pollution initially increased, and authorities suspected there might be lasting health effects from the shattered debris, air pollution, and rubble.

Terrorists using knives and box cutters also hijacked American Airlines Flight 77, a Boeing 757 commercial airliner with 64 persons aboard. The plane had departed at 8:10 A.M. from Dulles International Airport, in suburban Herndon, Virginia, outside Washington, D.C. At 9:39 A.M., the terrorists directed the plane into the west side of the Pentagon in Washington, D.C. The left side of the building was destroyed. The number of those killed included 64 passengers and crew members aboard the plane and 125 military and civilian personnel on the ground. Another 80 were injured.

Terrorists hijacked United Airlines Flight 93, also a Boeing 757, carrying 44 passengers and crew from Newark International Airport in New Jersey to San Francisco International Airport in California. The hijackers took over the plane's controls and headed the aircraft toward Washington, D.C. It is believed the intended goal of the plane was the White House. But the passengers, having heard about the World Trade Center attacks during their flight, attempted to retake control of the plane and stormed the cockpit. The plane crashed in the countryside near Shanksville, Pennsylvania, killing all aboard.

The September 11 attacks were the most destructive acts of war or terrorist violence against Americans on U.S. soil since the Japanese attack on the naval base at Pearl Harbor, Hawaii, in 1941. The total estimated death toll from the September 11 attacks was 3,056 people, including citizens of 78 countries.

The U.S. Justice Department quickly determined that the attacks were conducted by al-Qaeda, under the leadership of Osama bin Laden. From 1998 to 2001 al-Qaeda was suspected of being responsible for the majority of U.S. deaths from international terrorism. The attacks of September 11, 2001, followed the al-Qaeda-attributed bombing of the USS *Cole* in the port of Aden, Yemen, on October 12, 2000, which killed 17 U.S. sailors and injured 39 others. The U.S. government also found al-Qaeda responsible for the August 1998 bombings of U.S. embassies in Nairobi, Kenya, and Dar Es Salaam, Tanzania, in which 12 U.S. citizens were killed.

There are also other bombings that may not have been the work of al-Qaeda but of related Muslim extremist terrorists. These would include the first bombing of the World Trade Center in 1993. In addition, in June 1996 the Khobar Towers military barracks near Dahran, Saudi Arabia, were bombed, and in 1994 a U.S. military assistance headquarters in Jiddah, Saudi Arabia, was bombed.

These acts, occurring roughly over the decade 1992–2002, represent a resurgence of anti-American terrorism by Middle Eastern extremists. The first round of such attacks in the 1980s killed hundreds of U.S. military and diplomatic personnel. In 1983 an Arab terrorist organization bombed the American embassy in Beirut, Lebanon, beginning a sustained period of violence from Middle Eastern terrorist organizations against U.S. targets overseas—mainly embassies, barracks, and other facilities.

Attacks against diplomatic, military, and government personnel or facilities are significant, because they are symbols of U.S. strength. They are usually better protected than most businesses, but make more attractive targets. Military targets, in terms of U.S. troops, are found worldwide, with 255,065 U.S. military personnel stationed abroad as of December 31, 2001. (See Table 5.3.) About 118,000 were stationed in Europe and 91,000 were stationed in East Asia and the Pacific. Only about 26,000 troops, or about 1 percent of American troops, were stationed in North Africa, the Near East, and South Asia. This figure represented a jump in that region, which includes the Middle East, from only 14,000 U.S. troops there in June 2000.

Al-Qaeda—Understanding the Phenomenon

Many Americans were not familiar with the name Osama bin Laden and the group al-Qaeda prior to September 11, 2001, but the rise of this enigmatic terrorist leader and his organization can be traced back to the early 1980s. Many Muslim leaders around the world were outraged by the Soviet invasion of Afghanistan in December 1979, and rallied to declare a jihad ("holy war") against the invading superpower, which had an official platform of atheism. Many individuals, mainly Arabic, heeded the call and arrived in Afghanistan to fight as defenders of Islam. They came to be known as the "mujahideen," holy warriors who strove to protect their religion at all costs. One of these holy warriors was Osama bin Laden.

Bin Laden came from a wealthy Yemeni family in Saudi Arabia. Driven by the religious obligation he felt, he arrived in Afghanistan in order to defend his faith. Many scholars claim that bin Laden was more of a financier for the mujahideen than an actual fighter on the frontlines. Still, it was in Afghanistan that bin Laden met prominent militants, such as Muhammed Atef and Ayman al-Zawahiri, who would later become a vital part of the al-Qaeda network.

TABLE 5.3

Active duty military personnel strengths by regional area and country, December 31, 2001

Regional Area/ Country	Total	Army	Navy	Marine Corps	Air Force
United States and Territories					
Continental United States (CONUS)	947,955	340,883	199,694	134,248	273,130
Alaska	15,926	6,593	55	27	9,251
Hawaii	33,191	16,100	6,929	5,719	4,443
Guam	3,398	32	1,583	129	1,654
Johnston Atoll	29	3	0	0	26
Puerto Rico	2,525	804	1,642	23	56
Trust Territory of the Pacific Islands	25	25	0	0	0
U. S. Virgin Islands	5	1	3	0	1
Transients	27,208	10,408	12,385	2,638	1,777
Afloat	99,485	0	99,485	0	0
Total - United States and Territories	**1,129,747**	**374,849**	**321,776**	**142,784**	**290,338**
Europe					
Albania	5	2	2	0	1
Austria	21	4	0	12	5
Belgium*	1,554	871	106	28	549
Bosnia and Herzegovina	3,109	3,090	2	16	1
Bulgaria	11	3	1	5	2
Croatia	1	0	0	0	1
Cyprus	27	3	0	19	5
Czech Republic*	15	2	0	8	5
Denmark*	28	2	5	7	14
Estonia	7	0	2	5	0
Finland	16	2	1	10	3
France*	70	13	11	24	22
Germany*	71,434	55,565	319	302	15,248
Gibraltar	4	0	4	0	0
Greece*	526	80	312	66	68
Greenland*	153	0	0	0	153
Hungary*	26	4	0	13	9
Iceland*	1,713	3	993	47	670
Ireland	10	2	0	8	0
Italy*	11,854	2,606	5,051	142	4,055
Latvia	3	2	0	0	1
Lithuania	4	2	1	1	0
Luxembourg*	10	10	0	0	0
Macedonia, The Former Yugoslav Republic of	346	345	0	0	1
Malta	7	0	0	7	0
Netherlands*	696	376	26	13	281
Norway*	187	12	12	118	45
Poland*	20	6	0	11	3
Portugal*	992	14	46	7	925
Romania	20	6	1	11	2
Serbia (includes Kosovo)	5,200	5,196	1	1	2
Slovakia	1	0	0	0	1
Slovenia	12	5	0	6	1
Spain*	1,778	45	1,329	147	257
Sweden	11	1	1	5	4
Switzerland	19	1	3	11	4
Turkey*	2,170	179	25	207	1,759
United Kingdom*	11,361	431	1,247	157	9,526
Afloat	4,728	0	2,657	2,071	0
Total - Europe	**118,149**	**68,883**	**12,158**	**3,485**	**33,623**
Former Soviet Union					
Armenia	2	1	0	0	1
Azerbaijan	9	0	0	8	1
Belarus	1	1	0	0	0
Georgia	10	2	0	7	1
Kazakhstan	11	2	0	7	2

TABLE 5.3

Active duty military personnel strengths by regional area and country, December 31, 2001 [CONTINUED]

Regional Area/ Country	Total	Army	Navy	Marine Corps	Air Force
Former Soviet Union (cont'd)					
Kyrgyzstan	7	1	0	5	1
Moldova	3	2	0	0	1
Russia	88	21	4	50	13
Tajikistan	1	1	0	0	0
Turkmenistan	7	1	0	6	0
Ukraine	9	5	1	0	3
Uzbekistan	3	1	0	0	2
Total - Former Soviet Union	**151**	**38**	**5**	**83**	**25**
East Asia and Pacific					
Australia	188	10	55	52	71
Burma	9	3	0	5	1
Cambodia	7	6	0	1	0
China (Includes Hong Kong)	54	10	13	25	6
Fiji	3	0	1	2	0
Indonesia (Includes Timor)	48	9	26	10	3
Japan	39,691	1,850	5,448	19,265	13,128
Korea, Republic of	37,972	28,989	319	150	8,514
Laos	3	2	0	0	1
Malaysia	18	3	2	6	7
New Zealand	7	2	2	0	3
Philippines	31	8	7	9	7
Singapore	160	6	93	17	44
Thailand	114	42	10	30	32
Vietnam	14	6	0	6	2
Afloat	12,503	0	12,307	196	0
Total - East Asia and Pacific	**90,822**	**30,946**	**18,283**	**19,774**	**21,819**
North Africa, Near East, and South Asia					
Afghanistan	9	0	0	9	0
Algeria	11	1	2	7	1
Bahrain	1,280	21	984	248	27
Bangladesh	8	2	0	6	0
Diego Garcia	537	3	505	0	29
Egypt	665	353	34	206	72
India	16	4	3	5	4
Iraq	1	0	0	1	0
Israel	38	5	3	18	12
Jordan	22	8	0	8	6
Kuwait	4,300	2,125	4	161	2,010
Lebanon	4	4	0	0	0
Morocco	18	5	4	6	3
Nepal	6	0	0	6	0
Oman	560	3	1	12	544
Pakistan	23	3	1	13	6
Qatar	72	41	3	14	14
Saudi Arabia	4,802	291	27	40	4,444
Sri Lanka	9	0	2	7	0
Syria	6	2	0	4	0
Tunisia	16	5	2	7	2
United Arab Emirates	207	3	7	7	190
Yemen	3	3	0	0	0
Afloat	13,559	0	13,559	0	0
Total - North Africa, Near East, and South Asia	**26,172**	**2,882**	**15,141**	**785**	**7,364**
Sub-Saharan Africa					
Angola	0	0	0	0	0
Botswana	7	0	0	7	0
Burundi	6	0	0	6	0
Cameroon	9	2	0	6	1

TABLE 5.3

Active duty military personnel strengths by regional area and country, December 31, 2001 [CONTINUED]

Regional Area/ Country	Total	Army	Navy	Marine Corps	Air Force
Sub-Saharan Africa					
(cont'd)					
Chad	10	4	0	6	0
Congo (Kinshasa)	9	2	0	6	1
Cote D'Ivoire	23	5	1	15	2
Djibouti	1	1	0	0	0
Ethiopia	10	4	0	6	0
Gabon	0	0	0	0	0
Ghana	9	2	0	7	0
Guinea	7	1	0	6	0
Kenya	50	10	1	36	3
Liberia	8	1	0	6	1
Madagascar	1	0	1	0	0
Mali	6	0	0	6	0
Mozambique	5	0	0	5	0
Niger	7	1	0	6	0
Nigeria	11	3	0	6	2
Rwanda	0	0	0	0	0
Senegal	10	1	2	7	0
Sierra Leone	2	0	0	1	1
Somalia	0	0	0	0	0
South Africa	30	3	1	21	5
St. Helena (Includes Ascension Island)	2	0	0	0	2
Tanzania, United Republic of	10	0	1	9	0
Togo	4	0	0	4	0
Uganda	8	1	0	7	0
Zambia	5	0	0	5	0
Zimbabwe	9	4	0	5	0
Total - Sub-Saharan Africa	**259**	**45**	**7**	**189**	**18**
Western Hemisphere					
Antigua	3	0	0	1	2
Argentina	29	4	4	15	6
Bahamas, The	21	0	16	5	0
Barbados	7	0	2	5	0
Belize	3	2	1	0	0
Bolivia	22	8	0	8	6
Brazil	40	6	7	23	4
Canada	165	17	50	10	88
Chile	30	5	7	10	8
Colombia	59	14	2	12	31
Costa Rica	8	2	0	6	0
Cuba (Guantanamo)	461	7	415	39	0
Dominican Republic	14	2	1	10	1
Ecuador	19	6	2	6	5
El Salvador	22	8	0	12	2
Grenada	2	0	0	2	0
Guatemala	15	8	0	6	1
Guyana	1	1	0	0	0
Haiti	13	6	0	7	0
Honduras	426	173	2	45	206
Jamaica	11	1	3	7	0
Mexico	28	8	2	13	5
Nicaragua	12	4	0	7	1
Panama	15	7	4	4	0
Paraguay	27	4	0	22	1
Peru	40	4	11	20	5
Suriname	2	2	0	0	0
Trinidad and Tobago	7	0	0	7	0
Uruguay	11	2	2	5	2
Venezuela	30	9	2	9	10
Afloat	12,013	0	12,013	0	0
Total - Western Hemisphere	**13,556**	**310**	**12,546**	**316**	**384**

TABLE 5.3

Active duty military personnel strengths by regional area and country, December 31, 2001 [CONTINUED]

Regional Area/ Country	Total	Army	Navy	Marine Corps	Air Force
Undistributed					
Ashore	5,956	0	0	5,956	0
Total - Undistributed	**5,956**	**0**	**0**	**5,956**	**0**
Total - Foreign Countries	**255,065**	**103,104**	**58,140**	**30,588**	**63,233**
Ashore	212,262	103,104	17,604	28,321	63,233
Afloat	42,803	0	40,536	2,267	0
*NATO Countries	104,587	60,219	9,482	1,297	33,589
Forward Deployment Pacific Theater	94,849	30,993	20,378	19,940	23,538
Total - Worldwide	**1,384,812**	**477,953**	**379,916**	**173,372**	**353,571**
Ashore	1,242,524	477,953	239,895	171,105	353,571
Afloat	142,288	0	140,021	2,267	0

SOURCE: "Active Duty Military Personnel Strengths by Regional Area and by Country (309A), December 31, 2001," U.S. Department of Defense, Washington Headquarters Services, Directorate for Information Operations and Reports, Washington, DC [Online] http://www.dior.whs.mil/mmid/m05/hst1201.pdf [accessed July 24, 2002]

After the Soviets left Afghanistan, bin Laden called for a worldwide jihad. He preached radical views of Islam and endorsed violent tactics, which led the Saudi government to strip away his citizenship. He then moved to the Sudan, where he set up a network of organizations and businesses to raise money for his cause. After receiving pressure from the United States, the Sudanese government asked bin Laden to leave. He relocated to war-torn Afghanistan, established a special relationship with the ruling Taliban authorities, and eventually was considered above the law in the country. Bin Laden set up various military camps to train young men from around the world in skills like assassination and espionage.

The name al-Qaeda ("the base") is not a term used by bin Laden himself. Western experts coined the phrase in order to label the unique loose-knit structure of the organization. There is not one cohesive group known as al-Qaeda. Instead, it is primarily a network of various individuals, cells, and other organizations that come together for a main common cause, the defense of Islam. They receive military training and financial support from top al-Qaeda leaders such as bin Laden.

Although the defense of Islam can be interpreted very broadly, bin Laden holds specific grievances against the United States. He specifically cites the U.S. military presence in Saudi Arabia, U.S.-led sanctions against Iraq, U.S. support for Israel, and other historical U.S. "terrorist" acts, such as the dropping of atomic bombs on Japan during World War II. Bin Laden calls for the creation of an Islamic nation, something along the lines of the Ottoman Empire. (The Ottoman Empire was a powerful Islamic kingdom that spread across Europe and parts of the Middle East from the early 14th century to the end of World War I.)

After the attacks of September 11, 2001, the U.S. military attacked Afghanistan, the one central location that could be associated with al-Qaeda. The organization has now taken on even greater decentralization and operates as a host of cells around the globe. Though bin Laden has eluded capture, he remains a high-priority target for counterterrorism agencies everywhere and continues to boost the morale of his followers through video- and audiotaped recordings he has secretly delivered to news agencies. The destruction of the al-Qaeda network has become a top priority for the United States in its efforts to combat terrorism.

FINANCING TERRORISM

Any terrorist organization, no matter its size or type, requires substantial amounts of money and resources to be able to carry out attacks and maintain some form of cohesion. Funding for such organizations can come from state sponsors, individual contributors, legitimate "front" organizations, and criminal activities:

- State sponsorship was a common phenomenon during the Cold War, when both the United States and the Soviet Union supported various groups whose ideologies matched theirs or challenged the ideology of the other side. Afghanistan, Angola, South Africa, and parts of Latin America all served as battlegrounds in the war fought between the two major blocs. Iran and Libya have often been accused of supporting fundamental Islamic groups in order to export the 1979 Islamic revolution and encourage anti-Western sentiments.

- Individual contributors come from a wide spectrum of society. Fundraisers target individuals' emotions to elicit money and other resources. Millionaires, expatriate nationals, and members of wealthy families are frequent fundraising targets of terrorist groups.

- Laundering money through front organizations provides a way for groups to transfer cash funds from legitimate causes to terrorist ones.

- Criminal activities, such as narcotics smuggling, bank robberies, and kidnappings, can also raise a great deal of money. For example, a right-wing group called the Order stole about $3.6 million dollars from an armored truck in 1984. The Turkish Kurdistan Workers' Party, the Revolutionary Armed Forces of Colombia, Peru's Shining Path, al-Qaeda, and Lebanon's Hizballah have all been linked to drug-related activities.

International efforts to curb the financing of terrorism have been weak and underdeveloped. The 9/11 terrorist attacks jumpstarted domestic and international initiatives to destroy the financial infrastructure of various terrorist groups, but such a goal is far from complete. Immediately following the attacks, President George W. Bush signed the Executive Order on Terrorist Financing, giving the U.S. Treasury Department the authority to block the assets of individuals and organizations associated with terrorist organizations. In April 2002 UN Resolution 1373 called for the suppression of all terrorism financing. Whether the cooperation and communication between governments needed to make these efforts effective will be forthcoming remains to be seen.

U.S. REACTION TO SEPTEMBER 11, 2001

Homeland Security

As authors Ashton B. Carter and William J. Perry observe in their book *Preventive Defense: A New Security Strategy for America* (Brookings Institution Press, Washington, DC, 1999), "Catastrophic terrorism is a military-scale threat divorced from the traditional context of foreign military conflict. This is entirely new in the American experience. Catastrophic terrorism challenges the U.S. government to reinvent a new national security structure from the ground up."

After the September 11, 2001, attacks, the U.S. government and public placed a new emphasis on "homeland security" and efforts to protect against homeland terrorism. Anthrax attacks in late 2001 encouraged a new examination of bioterrorism as well. The country was nervous and wanted to put new structures in place to prevent against future attacks.

In the wake of 9/11, the U.S. Congress, the president, and the intelligence community all knew a new terrorist attack could come at any time. Consequently, they felt that there should be more government efforts to protect against terrorism, and that these efforts should be directed by the White House. The federal government also bolstered the intelligence community—those parts of the government, including federal law enforcement, that cooperate with the U.S. Department of Defense to maintain national security.

President George W. Bush set up a new Office of Homeland Security (OHS) in the White House and appointed then–Pennsylvania governor Tom Ridge to head it. The OHS coordinates the work of law enforcement officials, the military, and the intelligence community. Its major responsibilities include 1) supporting "first responders," those first on the scene of a homeland terrorist incident or catastrophe; 2) defending against bioterrorism; 3) securing America's borders; and 4) using up-to-date technology to secure the United States in the future.

The first role of the OHS is acting to coordinate first responders to a terrorist or bioterrorist attack. First responders consist of the country's more than 1 million firefighters (approximately 750,000 of whom are volunteers); 556,000 full-time local police personnel, including approximately 436,000 sworn law enforcement officers; and 291,000 sheriff's office personnel, including 186,000 sworn officers. Another group of first responders is the country's 155,000 emergency medical technicians.

On March 12, 2002, the OHS implemented a system of threat conditions as a way of providing uniform advisories of possible terrorist threats. The five threat conditions range from "low" to "severe." Severe risk may necessitate the closing of government offices and the deployment of emergency personnel. Intermediate threat conditions are "guarded" (a general risk of terrorist attacks), "elevated" (a significant risk of terrorist attacks), and "high" (a high risk of terrorist attacks). Colors were assigned to each threat level: low is indicated by green; guarded by blue; elevated by yellow; high by orange; and severe by red.

The jokes that this confusing, color-coded system inspired were the least of the problems Tom Ridge faced. With too much responsibility, little authority, and no budget, the OHS came to be perceived by many as ineffective. After revelations of intelligence failures and new terrorist plots (including one to set off a "dirty bomb"), President Bush dropped his initial reluctance to make the OHS into a cabinet-level agency.

On June 6, 2002, President Bush proposed a major reorganization of the federal government that, when approved by Congress, would create a permanent cabinet-level Department of Homeland Security. Drawing on various ideas put forward by Ridge, Congress, and outside studies and commissions, President Bush's plan sought to unify responsibility for protecting against terrorist attacks on American soil. Prominent among the 22 federal entities that may be included in the new department are the Coast Guard, Immigration and Naturalization Service, Border Patrol, Customs Service, Transportation Security Administration, and the Federal Emergency Management Agency. Four divisions within the new department, reflecting its four major responsibilities, would be:

- Border and Transportation Security

- Emergency Preparedness and Response

- Chemical, Biological, Radiological, and Nuclear Countermeasures

- Information Analysis and Infrastructure Protection

H.R. 5710, which was approved by the U.S. Senate and signed into law by President Bush on November 26, 2002, officially established the Department of Homeland Security. The primary highlights of this 484-page document include: reorganization and tighter control of immigration within the United States; a shift of the Bureau of Alcohol, Tobacco, and Firearms from the Treasury Department to the Department of Justice; a call for greater research and development into possible increases in the Homeland Security infrastructure; and a provision of separate funds for the Homeland Security Advanced Research Projects Agency that would help identify cutting-edge technology to aid the department. The bill also calls for greater coordination between the government and private sector to increase various critical infrastructures (such as power grids and telecommunication lines) across the country. Security measures strengthening the Coast Guard and airport security, along with the allocation of greater funds for domestic preparedness, are also written into the bill.

Some critics of the new department fear that, with 170,000 employees and a $37 billion budget, it will lack simplicity and flexibility. Others contend that the work of assembling this huge superagency might take away from more urgent actions needed to combat terrorism. That the intended new agency might not pay enough attention to the roles of state and local governments and the private sector causes some concern, as do its potentially insufficient enforcement powers and limited access to raw data from the FBI, Central Intelligence Agency, and National Security Agency. Counterproposals include appointing high-level liaisons to force cooperation among units of the federal government and changing existing agencies to improve their effectiveness at fighting terrorism (for example, establishing a special domestic security group within the FBI like Great Britain's MI5).

Airport/Port Security

Within a few weeks of September 11, 2001, terrorism had become the nation's top priority. At home, the president and Congress immediately began devising extensive new long-term aviation security measures, but these would take at least several months to implement. To help ensure that every airport immediately received a strong security presence, the president asked the governors of the 50 states to call up the National Guard at the federal government's expense to augment existing security staff at every commercial airport nationwide.

Prior to their deployment, National Guard personnel received training in airport security techniques from the Federal Aviation Administration (FAA). Some National Guard units were also sent to reinforce security at train stations and harbors. After approximately seven months, once new airport security officers and screening procedures were in place, the National Guard units left their posts.

Meanwhile, airline travelers became accustomed to waiting in longer lines at airport ticket counters, baggage check-ins, and other preflight security checkpoints as more strict attention was paid to checking passenger identification and to other security measures. The methods used to detect threats at airports and elsewhere included more metal detectors, surveillance cameras, and even infrared sensors, applied to some or all passengers.

Congress took the responsibility for airport preflight and security screening away from the airlines and placed it with a new Transportation Security Administration (TSA). The TSA, with an expected workforce of 35,000 to 40,000 employees (including 28,000 passenger and baggage screeners), was predicted to become the largest U.S. government agency initiated since the 1960s. However, Congress also provided for a process through which airlines might be permitted to go back to previous methods of contracting out screening/security services within three years of the new TSA security inspectors' commencement of their duties.

Beginning in the mid-1960s, the United States had experienced a rash of airplane hijackings to Cuba. Consequently, in 1968 the FAA initiated a highly secret federal "sky marshal" program. Sky marshals are certified law enforcement officers who ride anonymously on certain air flights. They are allowed to carry firearms. Their primary responsibility is to maintain law and order during the flight. At the time of the September 11, 2001, terrorist attacks, specialists estimate about 40 sky marshals were working within the air transport system, mostly on international flights to and from the United States. Analysts expect the TSA will take over the sky marshal program and hire as many as 4,000 sky marshals.

In addition, there were security changes to airplanes themselves implemented after the 9/11 hijackings. The FAA ordered temporary reinforcement of cockpit doors. This strengthened doors not only against intrusion but also against penetration by small-arms fire and grenades. The FAA required airlines to install permanent cockpit door improvements by 2003. Airlines have also offered special personal defense training to their pilots and flight attendants.

Much debate ensued over whether pilots should be allowed to carry guns. Many people, including many of the pilots themselves, supported the idea of armed pilots, while others preferred nonlethal weapons such as stun guns, tazer guns, or mace. Still others believed reinforced cockpit doors and specially trained air marshals should be enough to stave off any attack. After weighing the pros and cons of the issue, H.R. 4635, the Arming Pilots Against Terrorism Act, was passed on July 10, 2002. It allows airline pilots to undergo weapons training and carry arms in the cockpit.

Other measures were also implemented to enhance overall transportation security. One of these was the scanning of a small percentage of the thousands of cargo containers that arrive at U.S. seaports each day. The scanning is done to search for explosives, radioactive materials, and biohazards.

The Patriot Act of 2001

The September 11 attacks caused the government to round up suspects vigorously, attempting to increase security at the possible expense of civil liberties. The U.S.

Department of Justice, the U.S. Department of the Treasury, the FBI, and other law enforcement agencies proceeded to detain, hold, or deport approximately 1,000 people on immigration and other violations. Law enforcement agencies obtained more leeway to wire-tap and detain suspects as well.

These authorizations came primarily through the Patriot Act, which was passed by Congress, signed by the president, and enacted on October 26, 2001. The act, which is 342 pages long, made changes, some large and some small, to more than 15 statutes. The government was given the authority to monitor the online search engine requests of almost any American, obtain a wire-tap of a suspected individual's cell or regular phone via one request to a judge; and add DNA samples to a federal DNA database of almost anyone convicted of "any crime of violence."

The Patriot Act also gave the FBI more access to the medical, financial, mental health, and educational records of individuals without having to show evidence of a crime and without a court order. The bill expanded the government's ability to conduct secret searches, and also permitted the attorney general to detain and incarcerate noncitizens based on suspicion of any act or behavior that might be construed as a threat to national security and to deny readmission to the United States of noncitizens (including lawful permanent residents) under certain conditions. Yet other steps were designed to tighten U.S. immigration practices and keep terrorists out of the country in the first place.

Many Americans are alarmed that as the federal government moved to deal decisively with terrorist threats, civil liberties were taken away. For example, critics of the Patriot Act claim the Justice Department's detention of thousands of people after September 11 and its refusal to identify them or formally accuse them of anything amounted to illegal detention. Still, determining the appropriate balance between security precautions and personal freedom is a matter of great debate. As the National Commission on Terrorism wrote in its 2001 report to Congress (*Countering the Changing Threat of International Terrorism,* U.S. Government Printing Office, Washington, DC), "U.S. leaders must find the appropriate balance by adopting counterterrorism policies which are effective but also respect the democratic traditions which are the bedrock of America's strength."

War on Terrorism

After the terrorist attacks of September 11, 2001, President George W. Bush declared a "war on terrorism" with four basic principles. First, no concessions or deals will be made to individuals or groups holding any U.S. citizen hostage. Second, terrorists will be tracked down and brought to justice for their crimes, no matter how long it takes. Third, any state that sponsors terrorism will be forced to change its behavior through isolation and applied pressure. Finally, training will be provided under the Antiterrorism Assistance program to strengthen the counterterrorist capabilities of countries that are working with the United States.

The war on terrorism has been unlike any other. In this war, the U.S. government and its citizens ceased to look upon the Atlantic and Pacific Oceans as shields from attack. For the first time, an American war was being conducted not against a foreign nation but against transnational enemies—al-Qaeda and other terrorist groups operating across international boundaries. These enemies had managed to bring major destruction and devastation, if not conventional war, to America's doorstep.

Even with knowledge of existing terrorist groups and cells, the government must pin down who, what, or where the enemy may be. Abroad, the president and Congress targeted al-Qaeda, the radical Muslim extremist group linked with the 9/11 attacks. Al-Qaeda's leader, exiled Saudi Arabian Osama bin Laden, was known to be operating terrorist training camps in Afghanistan. In the aftermath of the September 11 attacks, the president sent thousands of U.S. troops, hundreds of ships and planes, and many bombs and other weapons to Afghanistan. U.S. forces attacked the ruling Taliban party that had harbored bin Laden and other al-Qaeda terrorists.

Within a few months, the United States captured taped evidence that they believed proved bin Laden was the mastermind of the September 11 attacks. The tapes showed him gloating over the unexpected degree of his "success"—that is, getting the World Trade Center's twin towers to collapse. In earlier videos released by al-Qaeda shortly after the attacks, bin Laden praised the attacks and taunted the American people. Intelligence officials believe he had hoped to foster rebellions in Muslim countries in order to become a folk hero.

The military actions ordered by President Bush in Afghanistan were generally considered successful. The war, code-named Operation Enduring Freedom, included U.S. use of 12,000 bombs and missiles, the killing of at least 3,000 enemy troops, and the capture of 7,000 or more hostile combatants. Although most of the al-Qaeda forces killed or captured in the military effort were only indirectly related to al-Qaeda's global terrorist activities, the action succeeded in breaking the Taliban's hold on power in Afghanistan and in eliminating Afghanistan as an official safe haven for al-Qaeda.

AMERICA'S NEW RESOLVE: HOW AMERICANS FELT AFTER SEPTEMBER 11, 2001

Until the September 11, 2001, events in New York City, Washington, D.C., and Pennsylvania, America had

suffered relatively few total terrorist acts, compared with all those committed against both developed and developing nations. Indeed, in the last several decades, terrorism has become a weapon of choice in domestic, regional, and international disputes. Despite their prevalence in other areas of the world, the number of international terrorist attacks in 2000, or those involving the citizens or territory of more than one country, was lower for North America (0) than any other global region. (See Figure 5.4.) In that year, Latin America suffered the most attacks (194), mainly because of the constant fighting between rebel factions, drug lords, and governments. Even in 2001, though casualties were high, the total number of terrorist attacks on North America was still relatively low.

In the early 1990s, after the fall of the Soviet Union, U.S. defense planners believed that the principal threats to U.S. personnel and interests would still occur remotely—mostly in Europe, the Persian Gulf, or the Korean Peninsula. After September 11, 2001, however, the planners know all too well that major threats can enter the country almost as easily as people, goods, and money.

The breakup of the Soviet Union in 1989 had not, as a fringe benefit, weakened terrorism. Although it is likely that the Soviet bloc had provided much aid to terrorist organizations and nations supporting them, after the end of the Cold War, terrorists simply found other sources of funding. Those sources reportedly include underground banking systems, money acquired through drug trafficking, and laundered money. Osama bin Laden himself, as a former Saudi prince, is thought by intelligence specialists to have great personal wealth (hundreds of millions of dollars). The fall of the Soviet Union also did not limit the breeding grounds of terrorism to the Middle East—there have been increasingly frequent and violent acts of terrorism in many other parts of the world, such as Sri Lanka, South Asia, and the Pacific Rim.

Since the September 2001 attacks, Americans have concluded that threats to the homeland are larger, more complex, more difficult, and more urgent than ever. They understand that it is much harder than they thought to confront terrorist threats and at the same time maintain their values, civil liberties, economic pursuits, and way of life. Still, the citizens and the government of the United States are resolved to do so. Although public opinion has changed over time since September 11, 2001, one thing that has remained constant is the U.S. determination to protect itself from other such catastrophes.

Public Reaction to the September 11, 2001, Terrorist Attacks

IMMEDIATE REACTION: PUBLIC OPINION FROM SEPTEMBER 2001. As might be expected, the initial response of the American public to the terrorist attacks was fear, shock, and outrage. A Wirthlin Worldwide National Quorum

FIGURE 5.4

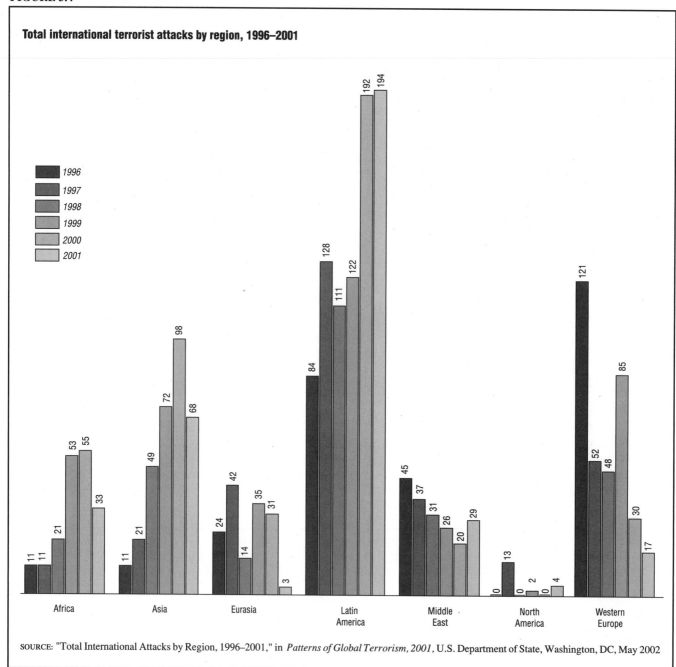

Total international terrorist attacks by region, 1996–2001

1996
1997
1998
1999
2000
2001

SOURCE: "Total International Attacks by Region, 1996–2001," in *Patterns of Global Terrorism, 2001*, U.S. Department of State, Washington, DC, May 2002

telephone survey was conducted September 15–17, and the results were reported in *The Wirthlin Report: Current Trends in Public Opinion from Wirthlin Worldwide* (vol. 11, no. 8, September 2001) and its research supplement. The survey found that about three of five Americans (63 percent) felt the terrorist attacks had "shaken [their] own personal sense of safety and security" either "a great deal" or "a good amount." Only 10 percent responded that the attacks had not shaken them at all. When asked "What do you believe is the greatest fear of most Americans?," the item most frequently mentioned was terrorist attack. Also mentioned as fears were death/dying (6 percent), losing freedom (5 percent), a nuclear strike (3 percent), and the unknown (2 percent). Three out of five people surveyed felt

they would have to implement changes in their everyday lives in the next five years because of the terrorist threat.

The "greatest fear of most Americans" mentioned second most frequently in the September 15–17 Wirthlin Worldwide survey was involvement in war, but more than 80 percent of Americans supported the use of military force against those responsible for the attacks. A Harris Poll from September 19–24, 2001, gave similar results: 66 percent of Americans felt that it would be worse to "fail to take very strong action against those who planned and supported these attacks" than to "take action that kills many innocent [sic] and loses the support of many of those who support us." Many (48 percent) thought it was

TABLE 5.4

Public opinion on why the 9/11 terrorists and their supporters hate the United States, September 2001

QUESTION: "WHICH ONE OF THE FOLLOWING DO YOU THINK IS THE MAIN REASON WHY THOSE WHO ATTACKED US AND THEIR SUPPORTERS HATE THE UNITED STATES?"

Base: All respondents

	Total %
Our democracy and freedom	26
Our support for Israel	22
Our values and way of life	20
Our influence on the economy and lives of Middle Eastern countries	17
Our economic and military power	11
Not sure/Refused	4

Notes: Results of a nationwide telephone survey of 1,012 adults conducted September 19–24, 2001.

SOURCE: "Table 2: Why, Americans Believe, Terrorists Attacked and Hate Us," in *The Harris Poll #48,* Harris Interactive, Inc., Rochester, NY, September 27, 2001

FIGURE 5.5

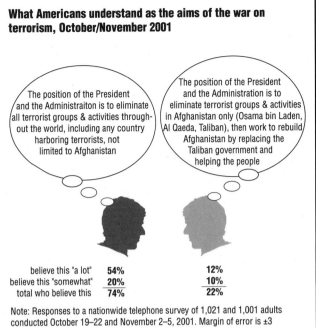

What Americans understand as the aims of the war on terrorism, October/November 2001

The position of the President and the Administraiton is to eliminate all terrorist groups & activities throughout the world, including any country harboring terrorists, not limited to Afghanistan

The position of the President and the Administration is to eliminate terrorist groups & activities in Afghanistan only (Osama bin Laden, Al Qaeda, Taliban), then work to rebuild Afghanistan by replacing the Taliban government and helping the people

believe this "a lot"	54%	12%
believe this "somewhat"	20%	10%
total who believe this	74%	22%

Note: Responses to a nationwide telephone survey of 1,021 and 1,001 adults conducted October 19–22 and November 2–5, 2001. Margin of error is ±3 percentage points.

SOURCE: "Most Understand Broad War Aims," in *The Wirthlin Report,* vol. 11, no. 10, Wirthlin Worldwide, McLean, VA, November 2001

impossible to take strong action against the terrorists without killing innocent people (*The Harris Poll #47,* September 26, 2001). In the same survey, 88 percent of respondents expressed the belief that "many other countries" would provide support to the United States in military action against the terrorists.

In Wirthlin Worldwide's September 15–17 poll, an overwhelming 96 percent of Americans felt that America would go to war against Afghanistan, but nearly half (45 percent) felt that military action would lead to more terrorist acts. The support of military action also remained strong in a survey conducted a week later (September 21–26) by Wirthlin Worldwide (*The Wirthlin Report,* vol. 11, no. 9, October 2001, and its research supplement), with 59 percent of respondents feeling that the death of American troops would not be too high a price to pay in order to respond to the attacks.

Fifty-seven percent of respondents felt President George W. Bush was dealing with the aftermath of September 11 well, according to the Wirthlin Worldwide poll of September 15–17; this figure jumped to 87 percent in the Wirthlin Worldwide survey conducted September 21–26. The September 19–24 Harris Poll (*The Harris Poll #48,* September 27, 2001) provided slightly higher numbers: 90 percent of the poll respondents said President Bush was doing either an excellent or a pretty good job.

Asked in a September 19–24 Harris Poll why America was attacked and why terrorists hate the United States, about one-quarter of respondents (26 percent) felt the most important reason was American democracy and freedom; only slightly smaller percentages thought the main reasons were U.S. support for Israel (22 percent) and "our values and way of life" (20 percent). (See Table 5.4.)

ONE TO THREE MONTHS LATER: PUBLIC OPINION FROM OCTOBER, NOVEMBER, AND DECEMBER 2001. Wirthlin Worldwide conducted telephone surveys over the periods October 19–22, 2001, and November 2–5, 2001, and asked respondents about some of the same issues they had covered in their September surveys (*The Wirthlin Report,* vol. 12, no. 2, March–April 2002). In these later surveys, support for military action to help stem terrorist activity remained strong. About three-quarters (74 percent) of Americans felt that the war on terrorism would be long and tough, with ramifications extending beyond Afghanistan. (See Figure 5.5.) Respondents also provided answers to the question, "What must be accomplished for you to conclude that the war on terrorism has been won?" (See Figure 5.6.) The most frequent responses to that question, given by 31 percent of those polled, fell into the general category of capturing/eliminating terrorists. Other respondents felt that the war on terrorism would never end (17 percent), or that it would not be over until there was peace or no more terrorism (14 percent).

The Harris Poll conducted its own research on Americans' feelings about, and understanding of, the war on terrorism in a November 14–20, 2001, poll, and reported its findings in *The Harris Poll #58* (November 24, 2001) and *The Harris Poll #60* (December 5, 2001). According to the mid-November Harris survey, 86 percent of Americans felt very confident or somewhat confident that the United States had "a clear plan for winning the war on terrorism." Only 14 percent of respondents felt "not very" or

FIGURE 5.6

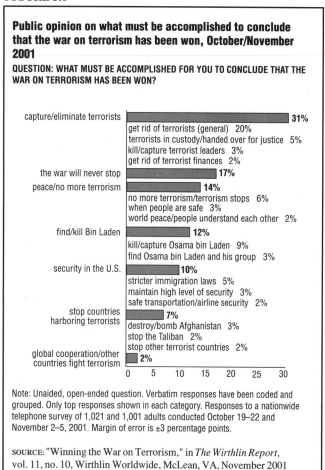

Public opinion on what must be accomplished to conclude that the war on terrorism has been won, October/November 2001

QUESTION: WHAT MUST BE ACCOMPLISHED FOR YOU TO CONCLUDE THAT THE WAR ON TERRORISM HAS BEEN WON?

capture/eliminate terrorists **31%**
get rid of terrorists (general) 20%
terrorists in custody/handed over for justice 5%
kill/capture terrorist leaders 3%
get rid of terrorist finances 2%
the war will never stop **17%**
peace/no more terrorism **14%**
no more terrorism/terrorism stops 6%
when people are safe 3%
world peace/people understand each other 2%
find/kill Bin Laden **12%**
kill/capture Osama bin Laden 9%
find Osama bin Laden and his group 3%
security in the U.S. **10%**
stricter immigration laws 5%
maintain high level of security 3%
safe transportation/airline security 2%
stop countries harboring terrorists **7%**
destroy/bomb Afghanistan 3%
stop the Taliban 2%
stop other terrorist countries 2%
global cooperation/other countries fight terrorism **2%**

0   5   10   15   20   25   30

Note: Unaided, open-ended question. Verbatim responses have been coded and grouped. Only top responses shown in each category. Responses to a nationwide telephone survey of 1,021 and 1,001 adults conducted October 19–22 and November 2–5, 2001. Margin of error is ±3 percentage points.

SOURCE: "Winning the War on Terrorism," in *The Wirthlin Report,* vol. 11, no. 10, Wirthlin Worldwide, McLean, VA, November 2001

FIGURE 5.7

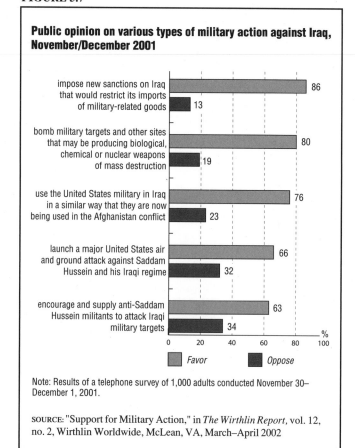

Public opinion on various types of military action against Iraq, November/December 2001

impose new sanctions on Iraq that would restrict its imports of military-related goods — Favor 86, Oppose 13

bomb military targets and other sites that may be producing biological, chemical or nuclear weapons of mass destruction — Favor 80, Oppose 19

use the United States military in Iraq in a similar way that they are now being used in the Afghanistan conflict — Favor 76, Oppose 23

launch a major United States air and ground attack against Saddam Hussein and his Iraqi regime — Favor 66, Oppose 32

encourage and supply anti-Saddam Hussein militants to attack Iraqi military targets — Favor 63, Oppose 34

0   20   40   60   80   100 %

▨ Favor   ▪ Oppose

Note: Results of a telephone survey of 1,000 adults conducted November 30– December 1, 2001.

SOURCE: "Support for Military Action," in *The Wirthlin Report,* vol. 12, no. 2, Wirthlin Worldwide, McLean, VA, March–April 2002

"not at all" confident about the U.S. strategy. About three of five respondents (61 percent) felt that the American government had clearly defined what it would mean to win the war on terrorism.

The same November Harris Poll found that while nearly half of all Americans (47 percent) remained at least somewhat anxious about their personal safety, slightly more than half (52 percent) were either not very anxious or not at all anxious. Two of five respondents (42 percent) said they were more concerned about their safety than before September 11.

A November 30–December 1 Wirthlin Worldwide poll (*The Wirthlin Report,* vol. 12, no. 2, March–April 2002) noted that Americans were in favor of action against Iraq. (See Figure 5.7.) The most popular option was sanctions (86 percent), but also mentioned were the bombing of military targets (80 percent) and approaching Iraq with measures similar to those being used in Afghanistan (76 percent). Even the least popular response, encouraging anti–Saddam Hussein militants to revolt from within the country, was favored by more than three of five respondents (63 percent).

AMERICANS' LATER FEELINGS ABOUT SEPTEMBER 11 AND NATIONAL SECURITY: POLLS FROM 2002. American

feelings remained strong about the national security ramifications of the September 11 attacks through mid-2002. In a Harris Poll from January 24–30, an overwhelming majority of Americans (93 percent) supported continuing the war on terrorism (*The Harris Poll #7,* February 6, 2002). A February 4–6, 2002 Gallup Poll found that 44 percent of Americans believed terrorism or international issues was America's largest problem. This number had dropped since October 2001 but remained relatively constant in December 2001, January 2002, and February 2002. Only 35 percent of respondents to the same Gallup Poll said they were at least somewhat worried that they or a family member would fall prey to a terrorist act.

Data from 2002 also defined who America felt its enemies were and how prepared the country was to deal with them. Gallup Polls from March 1–3, 2002, demonstrated that a large majority of Americans (78 percent) believed Muslim countries were generally unfavorable to the United States, as opposed to only 29 percent of respondents who felt the non-Muslim world was unfavorable to the United States. A February 4–6 Gallup Poll revealed that half of Americans (50 percent) felt that the strength of "the national defense is . . . about right at the present time," while a similar percentage (48 percent) felt the right amount of money was being spent for military purposes.

TABLE 5.5

Public opinion on various increases in law enforcement powers, September 2001 and March 2002

QUESTION: "HERE ARE SOME INCREASED POWERS OF INVESTIGATION THAT LAW ENFORCEMENT AGENCIES MIGHT USE WHEN DEALING WITH PEOPLE SUSPECTED OF TERRORIST ACTIVITY, WHICH WOULD ALSO AFFECT OUR CIVIL LIBERTIES. FOR EACH, PLEASE SAY IF YOU WOULD FAVOR OR OPPOSE IT."

Base: All respondents

		%	Favor	Oppose	Not sure/ Decline to answer
Expanded under-cover activites to penetrate groups under suspicion	Mar. 2002	%	88	10	2
	Sept. 2001	%	93	5	1
Stronger document and physical security checks for travelers	Mar. 2002	%	89	9	2
	Sept. 2001	%	93	6	1
Stronger document and physical security checks for access to government and private office buildings	Mar. 2002	%	89	10	1
	Sept. 2001	%	92	7	1
Use of facial–recognition technology to scan for suspected terrorists at various locations and public events	Mar. 2002	%	81	17	2
	Sept. 2001	%	86	11	2
Issuance of a secure I.D. technique for persons to access government and business computer systems, to avoid disruptions	Mar. 2002	%	78	16	6
	Sept. 2001	%	84	11	4
Closer monitoring of banking and credit card transactions, to trace funding sources	Mar. 2002	%	72	25	2
	Sept. 2001	%	81	17	2
Adoption of a national I.D. system for all U.S. citizens	Mar. 2002	%	59	37	5
	Sept. 2001	%	68	28	4
Expanded camera surveillance on streets and in public places	Mar. 2002	%	58	40	2
	Sept. 2001	%	63	35	2
Law enforcement monitoring of Internet discussions in chat rooms and other forums	Mar. 2002	%	55	41	4
	Sept. 2001	%	63	32	5
Expanded government monitoring of cell phones and email, to intercept communications	Mar. 2002	%	44	51	4
	Sept. 2001	%	54	41	4

Note: March data represent the results of a nationwide telephone survey of 1,017 adults conducted March 13–19, 2002.

SOURCE: "Table 1: Favor/Oppose Ten Proposals for Increased Law Enforcement Powers," in *The Harris Poll #16,* Harris Interactive, Inc., Rochester, NY, April 3, 2002

Data from *The Harris Poll #16* (April 3, 2002) compared the feelings of Americans on various increases in

TABLE 5.6

Public opinion on President Bush, February 2001–July 2002

QUESTION: "HOW WOULD YOU RATE THE JOB PRESIDENT GEORGE W. BUSH IS DOING AS A PRESIDENT—EXCELLENT, PRETTY GOOD, ONLY FAIR, OR POOR?"

Base: All adults

			Positive[1]	Negative[2]	Not Sure
2002	July	%	62	37	1
	June	%	70	28	2
	May	%	74	25	1
	April	%	75	23	3
	March	%	77	22	1
	February	%	79	20	1
	January	%	79	19	2
2001	December	%	82	17	1
	November	%	86	12	1
	October	%	88	11	1
	August	%	52	43	4
	July	%	56	39	5
	June	%	50	46	4
	May	%	59	35	6
	March	%	49	38	13
	February	%	56	26	18

[1]Positive = excellent or good.
[2]Negative = only fair or poor.

Note: July results from a nationwide telephone survey of 1,010 adults conducted July 18–22, 2002.

SOURCE: "Table 1: President Bush's Overall Job Rating," in *The Harris Poll #34,* Harris Interactive, Inc., Rochester, NY, July 24, 2002

law enforcement powers from September 2001 and March 2002. (See Table 5.5.) While support for all of the proposals mentioned dropped slightly over that period, support for items such as expanded undercover activities and stronger security checks for travelers remained high, at 88 percent and 89 percent respectively. The least popular option, opposed by 51 percent of the March 2002 respondents, was expanded cell phone and e-mail monitoring by the U.S. government.

Gallup found that approval ratings of President Bush's handling of foreign affairs remained high in polls conducted January 25–27, 2002 (83 percent) and February 4–6, 2002 (79 percent). In an April 5, 2002, Wirthlin Worldwide poll, more than three-fourths of Americans (78 percent) thought that President Bush was doing a good job as president. A July 18–22, 2002 Harris Poll found the percentage was slightly lower—only 62 percent of Americans felt positive about the job President Bush was doing, while 37 percent had negative feelings (*The Harris Poll #34,* July 24, 2002). Table 5.6 shows President Bush's popularity ratings as tracked by the Harris Poll from February 2001 to July 2002.

CHAPTER 6
DOMESTIC TERRORISM

The Federal Bureau of Investigation (FBI) divides terrorism into two distinct types: international terrorism and domestic terrorism. International terrorism is defined by the FBI as "the unlawful use of force or violence committed by a group or individual, who has some connection to a foreign power or whose activities transcend national boundaries, against persons or property to intimidate or coerce a government, the civilian population, or any segment thereof, in furtherance of political or social objectives." These incidents may take place within the United States or may involve U.S. citizens or interests overseas. Domestic terrorism, however, is defined by the FBI as terrorism that "involves groups or individuals who are based and operate entirely within the United States and Puerto Rico without foreign direction and whose acts are directed at elements of the U.S. government or population."

NOTABLE INCIDENTS OF DOMESTIC TERRORISM

Domestic terrorism is not new to the United States. In 1920 the financial district of New York City was a terrorist target—a massive bomb killed 30 people. An investigation centered on Sicilian, Romanian, and Russian terror groups, but the case was never solved. More than 80 years later, scars from the bombs can still be seen on some of the older buildings in New York's financial district.

In 1954 four armed, pro-independence Puerto Rican terrorists started shooting guns from the visitors' gallery of the U.S. House of Representatives. Five Congressmen were wounded.

In 1963 the bombing of the 16th Street Baptist Church in Birmingham, Alabama, killed four female African American victims; three were 14 years old and one was 11 years old. Almost 30 years later, the case was finally closed when, on May 22, 2002, Bobby Frank Cherry, 71, a former Ku Klux Klan member, was convicted of four counts of murder. Cherry, who was trained in demolition in the U.S. Army, claimed during the trial that he could not have planted the bomb the night before the attack because he was at home watching wrestling on television with his cancer-stricken wife. Prosecutors were able to show that not only was there no wrestling on television that night, but Cherry's wife was not diagnosed with cancer until two years after the bombing. Thomas E. Blanton, an accomplice in the bombing, was convicted in 2001 and sentenced to life in prison. A third accomplice, Robert Chambliss, was convicted in 1977 and later died in prison.

On April 19, 1995, a two-ton truck bomb exploded just outside the Alfred P. Murrah federal building in Oklahoma City, Oklahoma, killing 168 people and injuring 518. Because a daycare center was in the building very near the site of the explosion, many of the victims were children. There was a remarkable outpouring of grief for, and assistance to, bombing victims and their families. Rescue workers searched for bodies in the rubble for almost two weeks after the blast. Oklahoma City residents and others aided the rescue workers and made monetary donations to assist the victims and their families. The Oklahoma Baptist College Choir sang for the rescuers and victims. A local restaurant owner prepared nearly $12,000 worth of steaks to feed the workers. Several years later, a huge memorial was erected at the site of the bombing in honor of the victims.

Timothy McVeigh was arrested by federal authorities for the crime. McVeigh, a disgruntled former Army member who was rumored to be associated with an antigovernment militia group, evidently set the bomb in retaliation for the FBI's routing of the Branch Davidian cult in Waco, Texas, in 1994. McVeigh was convicted and then was executed by lethal injection on June 9, 2001. The government allowed the families of the victims to watch McVeigh's execution on closed-circuit television in the federal prison in which he died.

While the toll in lives and property damage was much lower than in the Oklahoma City bombing, a bombing at the 1996 Olympic Games in Atlanta, Georgia, created international alarm. During the Olympic summer games in July of that year, a nail-packed pipe bomb exploded in a large common area. One person was killed and more than 100 were injured. Authorities believed the perpetrator might have been affiliated with a Christian Identity group, many of which see the Olympic Games as satanic.

Shortly after the attack, suspicion centered on a security guard at Centennial Park, where the blast occurred, but he was later cleared and given an official apology. In May 1998 the FBI added Eric Robert Rudolph to its Top Ten Most Wanted list, seeking him for questioning about the Olympics bombing and two other incidents that followed. Rudolph was also charged with bombing the New Woman All Women Health Care Center in Birmingham, Alabama, in January 1998. In that blast, an off-duty police officer was killed and a nurse was seriously injured. A $1 million reward was offered by the FBI, the Bureau of Alcohol, Tobacco, and Firearms, and the Birmingham Police Department, but Rudolph remained on the run as of December 2002.

Over a 17-year period, an individual nicknamed the "Unabomber" committed 16 bombings in several states. Three people were killed and twenty-three injured in the attacks. After reading a 56-page manuscript supposedly written by the Unabomber and published in the *New York Times* and the *Washington Post* newspapers in 1995, David Kaczynski contacted the FBI and shared his fears that his brother, Theodore, might be the Unabomber. The manhunt for Theodore Kaczynski was one of the longest and most difficult in U.S. history, involving hundreds of federal and state law enforcement agents. Kaczynski was later captured and pled guilty at his trial. Although he claimed the bombings (usually letter bombs) were directed against the U.S. federal government, the victims were generally not directly related to the government. In January 1998 Kaczynski was sentenced to life imprisonment, with no possibility of parole, for his actions as the Unabomber.

Beginning on Friday, May 3, 2002, 18 pipe bombs were placed in rural mailboxes in Illinois, Iowa, Nebraska, Colorado, and Texas, injuring five people. On Tuesday, May 7, 2002, the FBI arrested 21-year-old college student Luke J. Helder in connection with the bombings. Helder was charged by federal prosecutors in Iowa with the use of an explosive device to maliciously destroy property affecting interstate commerce and with the use of a destructive device to commit a crime of violence, punishable by up to life imprisonment. The pipe bombs, some of which did not detonate, were accompanied by letters warning of excessive government control over individual behavior. As of February 2003 Helder's trial was pending while psychological testing was performed on the accused.

Anthrax Attacks, 2001

Anthrax, classified by the U.S. government as a potential weapon of mass destruction, is a bacterial disease spread through spores. The spores can live in soil or the wool or hair of diseased animals. Humans acquire the disease when the spores are inhaled or ingested. Ulcerous sores on the skin and lesions on the lungs are symptomatic of the disease. While potentially deadly if it spreads to the lungs, anthrax is treatable if identified early.

Terrorist attacks using anthrax occurred in the autumn of 2001. Anthrax-tainted letters were sent through the U.S. postal system in the first major bioterrorist attack against the U.S. homeland. There has been no demonstrable link between the terrorist attacks of September 11, 2001, and the anthrax attacks, but the anthrax attacks did prove that terrorists could use the U.S. Postal Service (USPS) to unleash germ warfare against American citizens, news organizations, and congressional representatives.

Lethal anthrax bacilli infected the skin or the lungs of personnel at various offices, all of which had received letters containing a suspicious white powder: the *Sun* tabloid newspaper in Boca Raton, Florida; the headquarters of NBC News in New York's Rockefeller Center; the New York headquarters of CBS News; the offices of the *New York Post* in New York; the congressional offices in Washington, D.C., of Senator Tom Daschle of South Dakota and Senator Patrick Leahy of Vermont; and facilities of the Microsoft Corporation in Nevada. The anthrax also appeared at several USPS processing facilities and at several outlying mail-sorting centers for federal government agencies such as the State Department and the Department of Defense.

Twenty-two persons developed anthrax. Five died from it: two postal workers in Washington, D.C., a Florida newspaper editor, an elderly Connecticut woman, and a New York hospital worker. The government ordered thousands more people, mostly postal workers, to take the antibiotic Cipro as a precautionary inoculation. Nine months later, health specialists estimated that the tainted letters may have cross-infected as many as 5,000 other pieces of mail.

The anthrax arrived in letters that contained a message referring to Allah (the name for God in Islam), and the message seemed to imply an association with Islamic terrorism. However, it became increasingly clear that a single person located within the United States could have packed the letters with anthrax spores. The attacks were not necessarily the work of a group, much less an Islamic terrorist group. The spores used had been highly "weaponized," or finely milled to diameters of between one and three microns. This technical feat ensured their maximum dispersal when the envelopes were opened or even as they shuttled from post office to post office. The level of sophistication in this refinement of the anthrax implied that a highly skilled scientist or technician within the U.S. military's own bioweapons research and testing program could have been responsible. As a result, though the perpetrators were still unknown as of early 2003, the anthrax attacks are generally considered domestic terrorism.

Another effect of the anthrax attacks was the slew of threats and hoaxes that followed. In late October 2001 a USPS employee, Sharon Ann Watson of Stafford, Virginia, was arrested on charges of perpetrating an anthrax hoax at the Falmouth, Virginia, post office where she worked. She was charged with knowingly mailing threatening communications and unlawful delay or destruction of mail. Each offense carried penalties of up to 20 years in prison.

By November 2001 a total of 353 postal facilities had been evacuated for varying amounts of time as a result of 8,674 hoaxes, threats, and suspicious mailing incidents, which averaged 578 per day. Postal inspectors had arrested 20 individuals for anthrax-related hoaxes, threats, and suspicious mailing incidents and were continuing to investigate 18 additional incidents. A reward of up to $2.5 million for information leading to the arrest and conviction of anyone mailing anthrax resulted in 165 investigative leads. The attacks caused an expensive, difficult logjam in mail delivery that forced the U.S. government to buy multimillion-dollar machines to begin irradiating all mail in an attempt to kill any dangerous bacteria it might contain.

THE INCIDENCE OF DOMESTIC TERRORIST ATTACKS AND CASUALTIES IN THE UNITED STATES

From 1980 to 1999 the FBI recorded 327 incidents or suspected incidents of terrorism within the United States, which killed 205 people and injured 2,037. Of the 327 incidents, 239 were attributed to domestic terrorists and 88 were international. During the same time period, 130 planned acts of terrorism were averted by U.S. law enforcement agencies. Of those, 88 were planned by domestic groups or individuals and 47 by international groups or individuals. In 2000 there were 8 incidents or suspected incidents within the United States.

According to the FBI, while the overall number of terrorist incidents declined from 1990 to 1999, the attacks resulted in greater destruction and more casualties than those of the previous ten years. In the 60 terrorist attacks in the United States between 1990 and 1999, 182 people were killed and nearly 2,000 were injured. By comparison, from 1980 to 1989, there were more than four times as many attacks (267), but the death toll was only 23, with 105 injuries. While totals for the year 2001 had not been calculated by the FBI as of January 2003, one incident, the terrorist attacks of September 11, 2001, produced higher casualty figures (more than 3,000 fatalities) than all previous terrorist incidents in the United States combined.

MOTIVATIONS AND TRENDS

Over the years, domestic terrorism has been driven by a variety of motivations, ranging from extreme leftist ideology to extreme right-wing doctrines. There are also special-interest groups that have undertaken terrorist attacks on U.S. soil, as well.

Left-Wing Organizations

According to the FBI's *Terrorism in the United States 1999,* terrorist groups on the extreme left tend to "profess a revolutionary socialist doctrine and view themselves as protectors of the people against dehumanizing effects of capitalism and imperialism." These groups were more prominent during the days of the Cold War between the United States and the Soviet Union, and they carried out several bombings from the 1960s to the 1980s. Between 1980 and 1985, 86 of the 184 recorded terrorist attacks were attributed to left-wing extremists by the FBI. The fall of the Soviet Union and a global shift away from Communist ideologies has greatly affected the motivations and capabilities of such groups.

In recent years, some left-wing groups have been fighting for the independence of Puerto Rico. Groups such as the Popular Puerto Rican Army often employ violent means in their attempts to secure full Puerto Rican independence from the United States. In 1998 three of the five recorded acts of terrorism within the United States and its territories occurred in Puerto Rico and were attributed by the FBI to the Popular Puerto Rican Army. Groups fighting for Puerto Rican independence were more active during the 1980s and carried out several bombings and violent attacks.

Other types of left-wing groups include anarchists and social extremists, whose causes generally vary but remain political and antiestablishment. They operate in groups or as individuals. Such groups were responsible for extensive damage during riots in Seattle, Washington, in 1999, during demonstrations against the World Trade Organization ministerial meeting.

Right-Wing Extremists

Right-wing groups, however, tend to be more anti–U.S. government in nature. Often, such groups believe in racial supremacy and refuse to follow any rules and regulations set forth by the government. The origins of such groups can be traced back to the birth of America. The widespread poverty and destitution that existed in the Southern states after their defeat in the Civil War (1861–65), combined with attitudes of racial superiority, created an atmosphere that gave birth to organizations like the Ku Klux Klan.

Contemporary right-wing extremists have toned down their rhetoric in order to attract a larger audience.

Members of the extreme right group often adhere to one or more of the following beliefs:

- Christian Identity adherents believe that Americans of white European descent are descendants of the ten lost tribes of Israel, that the Aryan race is God's chosen race, and that whites will defeat Jews and nonwhites during the Second Coming of Christ.

- White supremacists call for the supremacy of the white race above all others; extreme members of such organizations also believe that a special homeland should be established in order to maintain the purity of the white race.

- Militias are armed paramilitary groups that strongly believe the U.S. government is out to destroy them. They preach elaborate conspiracy theories—for example, that the U.S. government is merely a cog in a "new world order" run by the United Nations (UN).

- Patriot Movement members consider themselves to be true patriots who disagree with how the government currently functions and refuse to adhere to any federal, state, or local laws. Many have racist ideologies. According to the Intelligence Project of the Southern Poverty Law Center (SPLC), there are 158 Patriot groups operating within the United States, 73 of them militia groups (though not all of these groups advocate violence). (See Table 6.1.)

- Tax Protest Movement members believe that tax laws are incorrectly interpreted and that paying federal income tax should only occur on a voluntary basis.

The FBI claims that over the past decade or so there has been a rise in grass-roots patriot and militia movements that profess antigovernment sentiments and global conspiracy theories. This is due to the increasing prominence of the UN, growing U.S. involvement around the world, the passage of various gun-control legislation, and recent confrontations between militias and the law enforcement community. These groups present a unique threat to the federal government in that they often stockpile various types of weapons and refuse to acknowledge any law enforcement above the level of the county sheriff's office. Many also lack a cohesive organizational structure and an overall leader or headquarters. This makes these small, tightly knit groups hard to infiltrate or monitor.

An interesting tactic employed by some of these organizations is the use of "paper terrorism." Members of right-wing groups file a multitude of bogus claims and legal actions in the court system in order to inundate the judicial bureaucracy.

Special-Interest/Single-Issue Terrorism

Besides the left-wing and right-wing groups outlined earlier, there are a variety of special-interest groups, such as animal liberation groups, environmentalists, and antiabortion activists, that have committed acts of terror to draw attention to one specific cause. They have carried out destructive acts like arson, bombings, and even anthrax hoaxes in the past. These groups frequently use media outlets such as the Internet to disseminate their ideologies and recruit members.

ECOTERRORISM. The Earth Liberation Front (ELF) and the Animal Liberation Front (ALF) are the leading groups that have engaged in ecoterrorism over the past decade. They are composed of radical environmentalists and are primarily active across North America. ELF, for example, describes itself as "an international underground organization that uses direct action in the form of economic sabotage to stop the exploitation and destruction of the natural environment." Most ELF members believe in a form of deep ecology, or the theory that all nonhuman life has an intrinsic value and must be protected from the wickedness of humanity. Both ALF and ELF were created without a hierarchical and centralized structure, so that various subgroups and individuals are able to carry out actions under the umbrella of a larger group.

Ecoterrorists have taken action against a variety of targets that they believe endanger the Earth's environment in some way. Their targets primarily include golf clubs, ski resorts, oil companies, multinational corporations, research institutes involved in genetic modification, animal laboratories, and various U.S. government agencies. Their tactics have ranged from tree-spiking (inserting spikes in trees in order to damage any saws that might be used on them) and sabotage to arson and firebombing. In October 1998, during a single attack on a ski resort in Vail, Colorado, members of the ELF caused approximately $12 million worth of damage. On October 30, 2001, several members of ELF firebombed a wild-horse corral in California that belonged to the U.S. Bureau of Land Management. Group members are also suspected of causing damage to sport utility vehicles (SUVs) in various locations across the country. SUVs, they allege, kill the environment.

ANTIABORTION ACTIVISTS. Another cause that falls in the special-interest category is the antiabortion movement in the United States. Acts of violence against, and murders of, health care professionals involved in providing abortion rose rapidly in the 1980s and 1990s. Individuals and groups pursuing such activities belong to a larger pro-life movement in the United States that believes the rights of unborn children must be protected. Though many members of the pro-life movement do not support killing medical professionals, a fundamentalist segment of the group strongly believes that killing abortion providers is the only way to protect the unborn.

There is no overall structural organization to these groups. Individuals sharing similar beliefs primarily

TABLE 6.1

"Patriot" groups, 2002

TABLE 6.1

"Patriot" groups, 2002 [CONTINUED]

Alabama	Alabama Committee to Get US Out of the United Nations (Birmingham)
Alaska	Jefferson Party (Anchorage)
Arizona	American Patriot Friends Network (Glendale)
	Arizona Free Citizen's Militia (Tucson)
	Sovereign Citizen Resource Center (Thatcher)
Arkansas	Arkansas State Militia (Franklin County)
	Constitution Party (North Little Rock)
	Militia of Washington County (Fayetteville)
California	California Militia (Brea)
	Free Enterprise Society (Fresno)
	Freedom Law School (Tustin)
	John Birch Society (Brea)
	John Birch Society (Fountain Valley)
	John Birch Society (Laguna Hills)
	John Birch Society (Mission Viejo)
	John Birch Society (Newport Beach)
	John Birch Society (Oceanside)
	John Birch Society (Orange)
	John Birch Society (Riverside)
	John Birch Society (Santa Ana)
	Second Amendment Committee (Hanford)
	Southern California High Desert Militia (Oceanside)
	State Citizens Service Center Research Headquarters (Canoga Park)
	Truth In Taxation (Studio City)
	Truth Radio (Delano)
Colorado	American Freedom Network (Johnstown)
Connecticut	Connecticut 51st Militia (Terryville)
District of Columbia	American Free Press (Washington)
Florida	Citizens for Better Government (Gainesville)
	Constitution Party (Jupiter)
	Constitutional Guardians of America (Boca Raton)
Georgia	Constitution Party (Woodstock)
	Militia of Georgia (Lawrenceville)
Idaho	Police Against the New World Order (Kamiah)
	Sons of Liberty (Boise)
Illinois	Constitution Party (Springfield)
	Illinois State Militia (Addison)
	Southern Illinois Patriots League (Benton)
Indiana	Constitution Party (Shoals)
	Indiana Militia Corps 1st Brigade (Northwest Indiana)
	Indiana Militia Corps 2nd Brigade (Northeast Indiana)
	Indiana Militia Corps 3rd Brigade (Southwest Indiana)
	Indiana Militia Corps 4th Brigade (Southeast Indiana)
	Indiana Militia Corps 5th Brigade (Pendleton)
	Indiana State Militia 14th Regiment (Owen County)
	Indianapolis Baptist Temple (Indianapolis)
	NORFED (Evansville)
	Old Paths Baptist Church (Campbellsburg)
Iowa	Constitution Party (Randall)
Kansas	Constitution Party (Wichita)
Kentucky	Constitution Party (Louisville)
	Free Kentucky (Lebanon)
	Kentucky Mountain Rangers (Smilax)
	Kentucky State Militia (Nicholasville)
	Kentucky State Militia 9th Battalion (Western Kentucky)
	Take Back Kentucky (Clarkson)
Louisiana	Common Law Defense Fund (Lafayette)
Maine	Constitution Party (Spruce Head)
	Maine Militia (Belfast)
Maryland	Citizens Militia of Maryland (Baltimore)
	Constitution Party (Taneytown)
	Save A Patriot Fellowship (Westminster)
	Southern Sons of Liberty (Baltimore)
Michigan	Justice Pro Se (Dearborn)
	Lawful Path (Tustin)
	Michigan Militia (Detroit)

Michigan (cont.)	Michigan Militia Corps Wolverines (Kalamazoo)
	Michigan Militia Corps Wolverines, 3rd Division (Benzonia)
	Michigan Militia, Inc. (Redford)
	Proclaim Liberty Ministry (Adrian)
	Southern Michigan Regional Militia (Burton)
	Southern Michigan Regional Militia (Capac)
	Southern Michigan Regional Militia (Fowlerville)
	Southern Michigan Regional Militia (Monroe County)
	Southern Michigan Regional Militia (St. Clair)
	St. Clair County Militia (Capac)
Minnesota	Constitution Party (St. Paul)
	Minnesota Militia (St. Cloud)
Missouri	2nd Missouri Militia (Tuscumbia)
	7th Missouri Militia (Granby)
	Missouri 51st Militia (Grain Valley)
Montana	Militia of Montana (Noxon)
	Project 7 (Kalispell)
Nevada	Center for Action (Sandy Valley)
New Jersey	Constitution Party (Palmyra)
	New Jersey Committee of Safety (Shamong)
	New Jersey Militia (Trenton)
New Mexico	New Mexico Liberty Corps (Albuquerque)
New York	New York Patriot Militia (Slate Hill)
North Carolina	United America Party (Zebulon)
North Dakota	Constitution Party (Casselton)
Ohio	Central Ohio Unorganized Militia (Columbus County)
	Central Ohio Unorganized Militia (Franklin County)
	Central Ohio Unorganized Militia (Madison County)
	E Pluribus Unum (Grove City)
	Ohio Unorganized Militia (Columbiana County)
	Ohio Unorganized Militia Assistance Advisory Committee (Darke County)
	Ohio Unorganized Militia Assistance and Advisory Committee (Ashtabula County)
	Ohio Unorganized Militia Assistance and Advisory Committee (Champaign County)
	Ohio Unorganized Militia Assistance and Advisory Committee (Delaware County)
	Ohio Unorganized Militia Assistance and Advisory Committee (Lebanon)
	Ohio Unorganized Militia Assistance and Advisory Committee (Montgomery)
	Ohio Unorganized Militia Assistance and Advisory Committee (Portage County)
	Ohio Unorganized Militia Assistance and Advisory Committee (Westerville)
	Right Way L.A.W. (Akron)
	True Blue Freedom (Cincinnati)
Oklahoma	Present Truth Ministry (Panama)
Oregon	Constitution Party (Portland)
	Embassy of Heaven (Stayton)
	Emissary Publications (Clackamas)
	Freedom Bound International (Klamath Falls)
	Southern Oregon Militia (Eagle Point)
Pennsylvania	American Nationalist Union (Allison Park)
	Constitution Party National Office (Lancaster)
	Pennsylvania 1st Unorganized Militia (Harrisburg)
South Carolina	AWARE Group (Greenville)
	Constitution Party (Greenville)
Tennessee	Constitution Party (Germantown)
	Militia of East Tennessee (Knox County)
Texas	13th Texas Infantry Regiment (Austin)
	13th Texas Infantry Regiment (Bryan)
	13th Texas Infantry Regiment (Conroe)
	13th Texas Infantry Regiment (San Antonio)
	American Opinion Bookstore (San Antonio)
	Buffalo Creek Press (Cleburne)
	Church of God Evangelistic Association (Waxahachie)
	Citizens for Legal Reform (Dallas)

TABLE 6.1

"Patriot" groups, 2002 [CONTINUED]

Texas (cont.)	Constitution Party (Brenham)
	Constitution Society (Austin)
	John Birch Society (Austin)
	Living Truth Ministries (Austin)
	People's Court of Common Law (Arlington)
	Republic of Texas (Dallas)
	Republic of Texas (Fort Worth)
	Republic of Texas (Houston)
	Republic of Texas (Victoria)
	Republic of Texas (White Oak)
	Texas Unified Field Forces (Alto)
	Texas Unified Field Forces (Duncanville)
	Texas Unified Field Forces (Grimes County)
	Texas Unified Field Forces (Harleton)
	Texas Unified Field Forces (Harris County)
	Texas Unified Field Forces (Hill County)
	Texas Unified Field Forces (Hunt County)
	Texas Unified Field Forces (Huntington)
	Texas Unified Field Forces (Jackson County)
	Texas Unified Field Forces (Neches)
	Texas Unified Field Forces (Potter County)
	Texas Unified Field Forces (Red Rock)
	Texas Unified Field Forces (Tom Green County)
Vermont	Constitution Party (Quechee)
Virginia	Constitution Party (Vienna)
	Virginia Citizens Militia (Roanoke)
Washington	Constitution Party (Tacoma)
	Jural Society (Ellensburg)
	Yakima County Militia (Yakima County)
Wisconsin	Constitution Party (Watertowns)
	John Birch Society (Appleton)

SOURCE: Compiled by Information Plus staff

network through pamphlets and the Internet. Some Web sites even list names of abortion providers in the United States. Law enforcement officials believe these lists may provide "hit lists" for individuals who wish to kill those involved in abortions. Individuals who commit anti-abortion killings are hailed as heroes by the most conservative elements of the pro-life community. Besides targeting medical professionals, antiabortion groups also perform arson, bombings, blockades (so that workers and patients cannot get into clinics), and even anthrax hoaxes.

In response to increasing acts of violence committed against abortion providers and their clinics, Congress enacted the Freedom of Access to Clinical Entrances Act (FACT) in 1994. The legislation called for federal criminal penalties against any individual obstructing, harassing, or acting violently against abortion providers or recipients. Furthermore, in response to the 1998 murder of Dr. Bernard Slepian, a reproductive health care provider in New York, then–Attorney General Janet Reno established a Task Force on Violence Against Health Care Providers. Falling under the auspices of the U.S. Department of Justice, the task force is headed by the assistant attorney general for the Civil Rights Division. It is staffed by lawyers and other personnel from the Civil Rights and Criminal Divisions of the Department of Justice, as well as investigators from the FBI, Bureau of Alcohol, Tobacco, and Firearms, U.S. Postal Inspection Service, and U.S. Marshals Service.

WATCHDOG GROUPS: WHO MONITORS DOMESTIC TERRORISTS?

Besides the U.S. government, a number of watchdog groups, such as the Anti-Defamation League (ADL) and the Southern Poverty Law Center (SPLC), maintain a database of current domestic terrorist and militia groups. Besides keeping abreast of the activities of these groups, the ADL and SPLC also provide education and training to reduce hate crimes, or attacks perpetrated against an individual or a group based on ethnicity, religion, or sexual preference. Groups specifically preaching hateful ideologies against homosexuals and individuals of different races include various Ku Klux Klan, neo-Nazi, Black Separatist, and Racist Skinhead organizations.

The Anti-Defamation League (ADL)

The ADL was founded in Chicago in 1913 by Sigmund Livingston, with the mission "to stop the defamation of the Jewish people and to secure justice and fair treatment to all." Today, the ADL is one of the nation's premier civil rights/human relations agencies, dedicated to fighting anti-Semitism and all forms of bigotry, defending democratic ideals, and protecting civil rights for all. The ADL develops materials, programs, and services to build communication, understanding, and respect among diverse groups. It has conducted and published four national surveys and analyses of far-right extremism in the United States. The ADL Web site provides articles on a wide range of issues, including extremist groups, hate crimes, security awareness, and terrorism. The ADL's Web site had more than 3 million visitors in 2001.

Since it was founded, the ADL has acted against groups such as the Ku Klux Klan (by circulating pamphlets and calling on Presidents William Howard Taft and Theodore Roosevelt to denounce automaker Henry Ford's anti-Semitic books) and U.S. fascist groups (by accumulating a storehouse of information on extremist groups and individuals in the United States).

In 2002 the ADL took several measures to aid the fight against terrorism. It established a partnership with the Israel-based International Policy Institute for Counterterrorism (ICT) to facilitate meetings between ICT terrorism experts and American law enforcement, government officials, media, and community groups, and to distribute ICT publications in the United States. The ADL monitored the response of extremist groups to the attacks of September 11, 2001, by posting their statements on the ADL's Web site. The ADL also issues a periodic report on international and domestic terrorism called *Terrorism Update,* which is distributed to the media, members of Congress, the presidential administration, state and local legislators, academics, and Jewish organizations.

The Southern Poverty Law Center (SPLC)

The SPLC was founded as a small civil rights law firm in 1971 by Morris Dees and Joe Levin, two local lawyers who shared a commitment to racial equality. Today, the SPLC is a nonprofit organization that combats hate, intolerance, and discrimination through education and litigation. The center is internationally known for its tolerance education programs, its legal victories against white supremacist groups, its tracking of hate groups, and its sponsorship of the Civil Rights Memorial.

In 1981, in response to the resurgence of the Ku Klux Klan, the SPLC began to monitor hate activity. Today, the SPLC's Intelligence Project tracks the activities of more than 600 racist and neo-Nazi groups. In 1994, after uncovering links between white supremacist organizations and elements of the emerging antigovernment "Patriot" movement, the SPLC expanded its monitoring operation to include the activities of militias and other extremist antigovernment groups. Six months before the Oklahoma City bombing, the SPLC warned the U.S. attorney general that the new mixture of armed militia groups and those who hate was a recipe for disaster.

At the peak of the Patriot movement in the mid-1990s, the SPLC tracked more than 800 militia-like Patriot groups. Today, that number has dwindled to fewer than 200. Using information collected by the Intelligence Project during its monitoring and investigative activities, the SPLC provides comprehensive updates to law enforcement agencies, the media, and the general public through its quarterly publication, *Intelligence Report*.

Several of the SPLC's lawsuits have reached the U.S. Supreme Court, and many have resulted in landmark rulings. Most recently, the SPLC has developed novel legal strategies to shut down extremist activity and to help victims of hate crimes extract monetary damages from groups such as the Ku Klux Klan.

RESPONDING TO DOMESTIC TERRORISM

With increased attention being given to international terrorism groups such as al-Qaeda, issues of domestic terrorism may seem be on the backburner. On the contrary, though, many U.S. legislators are recognizing the problem of home-grown terror groups. On November 2, 2001, several members of Congress wrote to various environmental groups, urging them to abandon tactics of ecoterrorism. The Agroterrorism Act of 2001 fights domestic terrorism by increasing penalties against perpetrators, and the Hands Off Our Kids Act of 2001 calls for measures to stop groups like the ALF and ELF from recruiting young people for illegal activities.

Through interagency efforts, the U.S. government has also developed the Concept of Operations Plan (CONPLAN), which says it is designed to "prevent, deter, defeat, and respond decisively to terrorist attacks." Primary agencies involved in this plan are the Department of Justice (led by the FBI), Federal Emergency Management Agency, Department of Defense, Department of Energy, Environmental Protection Agency, and Department of Health and Human Services. These six agencies are responsible for coming up with tactical and strategic options to deal effectively with terrorist attacks in a coordinated fashion.

CHAPTER 7

CIVILIAN NATIONAL SECURITY INFRASTRUCTURE

At the apex of the U.S. federal government is the Constitution. (See Figure 7.1.) The Constitution gives the job of providing for America's national security to the president and the executive branch of the government, as well as to the legislative branch (the U.S. House of Representatives and the U.S. Senate). It designates the president the commander in chief of the American armed forces. Executive branch organs involved in national security can be found at the White House level—for example, the White House Office, the National Security Council (NSC), and the Office of Management and Budget (OMB)—and all the way down to the subcabinet/department, independent-agency level—for example, the Central Intelligence Agency (CIA), the Defense Nuclear Facilities Safety Board, and the Nuclear Regulatory Commission. Most national security responsibility falls under the executive branch of government.

This is not to say that the legislative branch plays a passive role in national security affairs. The U.S. Congress has several powers relating to foreign affairs and national security that are granted by the Constitution. But key powers requiring strong central direction, such as treaty-making, the appointing of ambassadors, and committing armed forces to conflicts, remain with the executive branch. There is a symbiotic relationship between the White House and Capitol Hill, as these powers are subject to approval by the Senate. Also, Congress has its own powers related to defense and national security. These include the rights to declare war; to raise armies, navies, and militias; to provide money for those forces; to authorize a draft (the pressing of individuals into mandatory military service); to make rules regulating the armed forces; to make all laws "necessary and proper" for carrying out the foregoing powers; and to provide advice and consent to the executive branch in foreign affairs—for example, approval of treaties that the executive branch has negotiated and its appointments of ambassadors, ministers, and other key officers of government.

Presidential prerogatives, especially those relating to unilaterally declaring wars, were greatly questioned during the Vietnam era. As the American public grew increasingly disenchanted with its extended military adventure in the Southeast Asian nation, they decided to limit the "imperial" war-making powers of the president. Despite President Richard M. Nixon's veto, Congress passed the War Powers Act in 1973. The legislative measure called for a 60-day waiting period before engaging in an undeclared war.

Some political scientists claim that the War Powers Act is nothing more than a mere "paper tiger"—something that looks effective on paper but that does not work in reality. Since the act's passage, U.S. presidents have violated the measure and invaded several countries (such as Lebanon, Grenada, and Panama) without congressional approval. Though Congress had not, as of January 2003, declared war on Iraq, under joint Resolution 114 the U.S. legislature granted President George W. Bush full authority to use any "necessary and appropriate" force against Iraq in order to protect America and its citizens without returning to Congress for approval.

Typically, the U.S. national security infrastructure leaves the executive branch in the position of "proposing" national security or foreign policy initiatives, such as treaties and agreements. It leaves the Congress, especially the Senate, in the position of "disposing" of them, as in ratifying treaties, approving foreign-aid budgets and defense appropriations, approving the appointment of ambassadors, and providing some oversight of intelligence and covert operations.

The roles of Congress and the executive branch are occasionally reversed. But the experience of the Constitution's framers was generally that the Congress, a "deliberative body" (a group that must debate and vote on issues before acting on them) acts slowly compared with the executive branch. Therefore, it would not be appropriate

FIGURE 7.1

Organization of the government of the United States, 2002

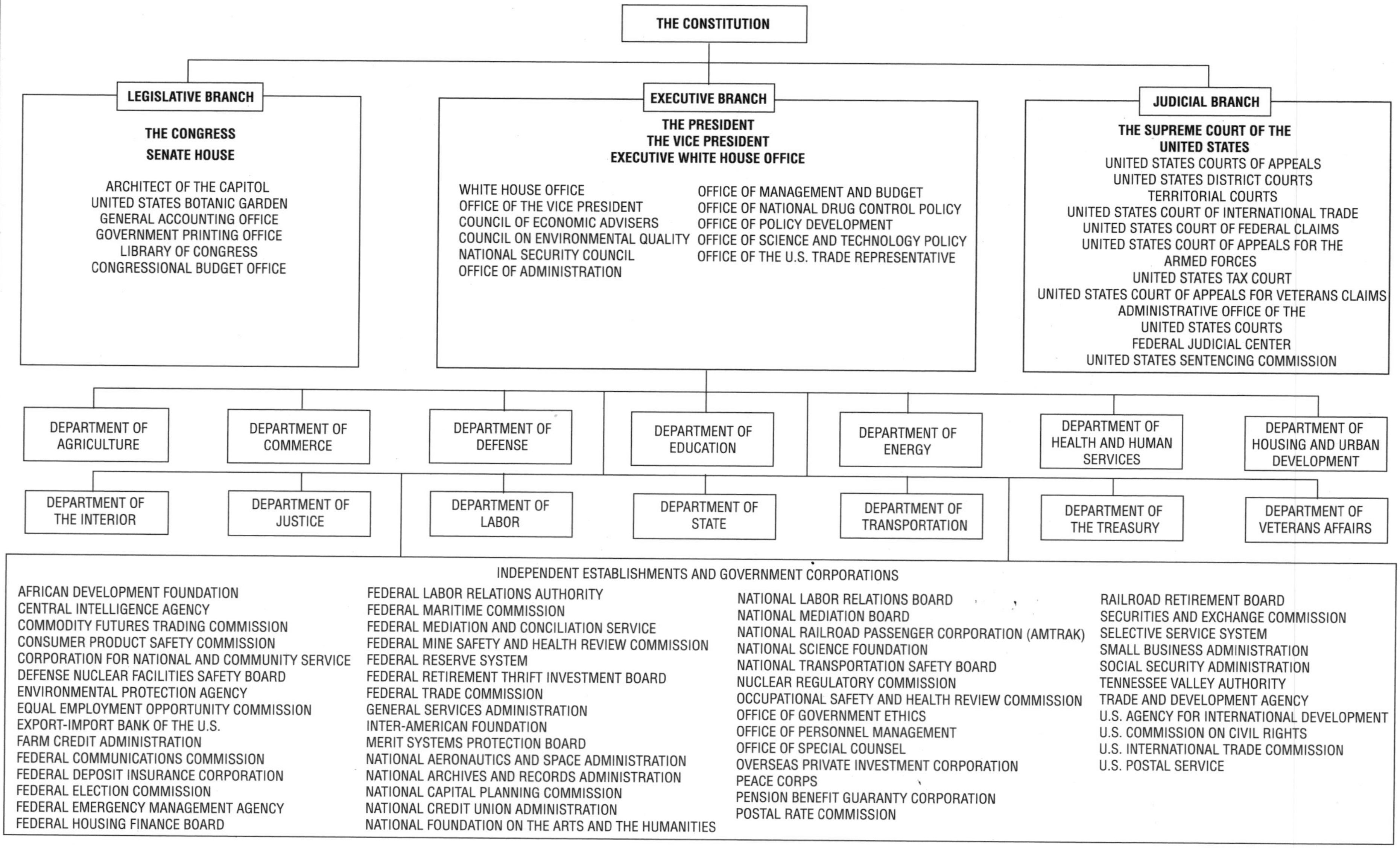

THE CONSTITUTION

LEGISLATIVE BRANCH

THE CONGRESS
SENATE HOUSE

ARCHITECT OF THE CAPITOL
UNITED STATES BOTANIC GARDEN
GENERAL ACCOUNTING OFFICE
GOVERNMENT PRINTING OFFICE
LIBRARY OF CONGRESS
CONGRESSIONAL BUDGET OFFICE

EXECUTIVE BRANCH

THE PRESIDENT
THE VICE PRESIDENT
EXECUTIVE WHITE HOUSE OFFICE

WHITE HOUSE OFFICE
OFFICE OF THE VICE PRESIDENT
COUNCIL OF ECONOMIC ADVISERS
COUNCIL ON ENVIRONMENTAL QUALITY
NATIONAL SECURITY COUNCIL
OFFICE OF ADMINISTRATION

OFFICE OF MANAGEMENT AND BUDGET
OFFICE OF NATIONAL DRUG CONTROL POLICY
OFFICE OF POLICY DEVELOPMENT
OFFICE OF SCIENCE AND TECHNOLOGY POLICY
OFFICE OF THE U.S. TRADE REPRESENTATIVE

JUDICIAL BRANCH

THE SUPREME COURT OF THE UNITED STATES
UNITED STATES COURTS OF APPEALS
UNITED STATES DISTRICT COURTS
TERRITORIAL COURTS
UNITED STATES COURT OF INTERNATIONAL TRADE
UNITED STATES COURT OF FEDERAL CLAIMS
UNITED STATES COURT OF APPEALS FOR THE ARMED FORCES
UNITED STATES TAX COURT
UNITED STATES COURT OF APPEALS FOR VETERANS CLAIMS
ADMINISTRATIVE OFFICE OF THE UNITED STATES COURTS
FEDERAL JUDICIAL CENTER
UNITED STATES SENTENCING COMMISSION

DEPARTMENT OF AGRICULTURE
DEPARTMENT OF COMMERCE
DEPARTMENT OF DEFENSE
DEPARTMENT OF EDUCATION
DEPARTMENT OF ENERGY
DEPARTMENT OF HEALTH AND HUMAN SERVICES
DEPARTMENT OF HOUSING AND URBAN DEVELOPMENT

DEPARTMENT OF THE INTERIOR
DEPARTMENT OF JUSTICE
DEPARTMENT OF LABOR
DEPARTMENT OF STATE
DEPARTMENT OF TRANSPORTATION
DEPARTMENT OF THE TREASURY
DEPARTMENT OF VETERANS AFFAIRS

INDEPENDENT ESTABLISHMENTS AND GOVERNMENT CORPORATIONS

AFRICAN DEVELOPMENT FOUNDATION
CENTRAL INTELLIGENCE AGENCY
COMMODITY FUTURES TRADING COMMISSION
CONSUMER PRODUCT SAFETY COMMISSION
CORPORATION FOR NATIONAL AND COMMUNITY SERVICE
DEFENSE NUCLEAR FACILITIES SAFETY BOARD
ENVIRONMENTAL PROTECTION AGENCY
EQUAL EMPLOYMENT OPPORTUNITY COMMISSION
EXPORT-IMPORT BANK OF THE U.S.
FARM CREDIT ADMINISTRATION
FEDERAL COMMUNICATIONS COMMISSION
FEDERAL DEPOSIT INSURANCE CORPORATION
FEDERAL ELECTION COMMISSION
FEDERAL EMERGENCY MANAGEMENT AGENCY
FEDERAL HOUSING FINANCE BOARD

FEDERAL LABOR RELATIONS AUTHORITY
FEDERAL MARITIME COMMISSION
FEDERAL MEDIATION AND CONCILIATION SERVICE
FEDERAL MINE SAFETY AND HEALTH REVIEW COMMISSION
FEDERAL RESERVE SYSTEM
FEDERAL RETIREMENT THRIFT INVESTMENT BOARD
FEDERAL TRADE COMMISSION
GENERAL SERVICES ADMINISTRATION
INTER-AMERICAN FOUNDATION
MERIT SYSTEMS PROTECTION BOARD
NATIONAL AERONAUTICS AND SPACE ADMINISTRATION
NATIONAL ARCHIVES AND RECORDS ADMINISTRATION
NATIONAL CAPITAL PLANNING COMMISSION
NATIONAL CREDIT UNION ADMINISTRATION
NATIONAL FOUNDATION ON THE ARTS AND THE HUMANITIES

NATIONAL LABOR RELATIONS BOARD
NATIONAL MEDIATION BOARD
NATIONAL RAILROAD PASSENGER CORPORATION (AMTRAK)
NATIONAL SCIENCE FOUNDATION
NATIONAL TRANSPORTATION SAFETY BOARD
NUCLEAR REGULATORY COMMISSION
OCCUPATIONAL SAFETY AND HEALTH REVIEW COMMISSION
OFFICE OF GOVERNMENT ETHICS
OFFICE OF PERSONNEL MANAGEMENT
OFFICE OF SPECIAL COUNSEL
OVERSEAS PRIVATE INVESTMENT CORPORATION
PEACE CORPS
PENSION BENEFIT GUARANTY CORPORATION
POSTAL RATE COMMISSION

RAILROAD RETIREMENT BOARD
SECURITIES AND EXCHANGE COMMISSION
SELECTIVE SERVICE SYSTEM
SMALL BUSINESS ADMINISTRATION
SOCIAL SECURITY ADMINISTRATION
TENNESSEE VALLEY AUTHORITY
TRADE AND DEVELOPMENT AGENCY
U.S. AGENCY FOR INTERNATIONAL DEVELOPMENT
U.S. COMMISSION ON CIVIL RIGHTS
U.S. INTERNATIONAL TRADE COMMISSION
U.S. POSTAL SERVICE

SOURCE: Adapted from "The Government of the United States," in *United States Government Manual 2002-2003*, National Archives and Records Administration, Office of the Federal Register, Washington, DC, 2002

for Congress to control functions requiring strong, immediate control, such as commanding the armed forces or negotiating treaties. If Congress was responsible for these types of functions, it could potentially act incompetently, or it might not act at all.

On national security matters, the president first works with executive staff, then with certain executive departments. The executive staffs and departments involved in national security include the White House staff; the NSC and its staff; the State Department; the Department of Defense (DOD), including the secretary of defense and the Joint Chiefs of Staff (JCS); the CIA; and the OMB. This chapter will specifically deal with the civilian branches of U.S. government that deal with national security. The military and its various aspects will be addressed in the following chapter.

WHITE HOUSE STAFF

The office of the White House consists of personal and political assistants to the president who serve at his request. They act as the president's eyes, ears, and manpower. The White House staff has seen tremendous growth in the last several decades. In the administration of President Herbert Hoover (1929–33), there were three secretaries, a military and a naval aide, and 20 clerks in the office. In 1997 the White House office of President Bill Clinton had a permanent staff of more than 400 people.

Growth has not been the only trend evident in the White House staff's structure over the years. Another has been the evolving and expanding role of the president's national security assistant, who heads the NSC staff. Since the early days of the Cold War between the United States and the Soviet Union during the Dwight D. Eisenhower administration (1953–61), the post of national security assistant (then called special assistant to the president for national security affairs) has become increasingly important. In each administration, the assistant's personal relationship with the president, and the president's wishes as to how the assistant should function, have modified the role. The national security assistant's role has also evolved as the NSC staff, which the assistant heads, has changed.

NATIONAL SECURITY COUNCIL (NSC)

The president's principal cabinet officers also serve as his closest national security advisers. The president, the vice-president, the secretary of state, and the secretary of defense make up the NSC, which was established by the National Security Act of 1947. That act mandated that the CIA director, also known as the director of central intelligence (DCI), and the chairman of the JCS also be advisers to the NSC. Their positions are advisory but mandatory. Present during most NSC meetings are the president, the vice-president, the secretary of state, the secretary of defense, the president's national security assistant, and others.

For example, on August 4, 1990, former President George H. W. Bush held an NSC meeting at Camp David to review military options after Iraq's invasion of Kuwait. The attendees were the president, the vice-president, and the secretaries of state and defense (NSC members); the national security assistant, the chairman of the JCS, and the DCI (NSC advisers); the White House chief of staff/spokesman; the commanders of the three armed forces; an undersecretary of defense; and an NSC staff director.

President Bill Clinton enlarged the membership of the NSC. The Clinton administration emphasized economic issues in forming national security policy, so the chairman of the new White House Economic Council was also made part of the NSC.

U.S. DEPARTMENT OF STATE

The Department of State was created in 1789. Its first secretary was Thomas Jefferson, who went on to become the third president of the United States. The State Department mainly represents the interests of the United States and its citizens in relations with foreign countries and also serves as a principal source of advice to the president on aspects of national security and foreign affairs.

The secretary of state is the president's principal adviser on foreign policy, but history shows that the secretary's power has been weaker or stronger depending on a particular president's own interests and activities in foreign affairs. President Nixon appointed William Rogers as secretary of state in 1969, but bypassed him systematically, humiliating him, according to some sources. Other presidents, like Ronald Reagan, had stronger secretaries. Reagan made Alexander Haig, former White House chief of staff and NATO commander, his secretary of state. Later, in 1983, Reagan tapped George Shultz for the post. Shultz had earlier been secretary of labor, secretary of the treasury, and director of the OMB, giving him useful experience and knowledge.

President George H. W. Bush focused closely on certain foreign policy areas, as if he was his own secretary of state. He appointed a longtime friend, James Baker, as secretary of state to handle the foreign policy areas President Bush was less concerned about. For example, the president personally oversaw the deployment of troops and other aspects of the Persian Gulf War of 1991. Baker crowned the U.S. victory in the Gulf War by arranging a Mideast peace conference.

During President Bill Clinton's first term, Warren Christopher served as a formidable secretary of state, allowing President Clinton to focus on domestic programs. This situation produced foreign policy successes attributable to key subordinates, like Richard Holbrooke, who negotiated the Dayton Peace Accords, and Dennis Ross, a special envoy who dominated the Middle East peace process.

The secretary of state faces the task of managing a huge bureaucracy. (See Figure 7.2.) For the most part, the U.S. Department of State is organized functionally—that is, according to the functions it performs, like counterterrorism, intelligence and research, protocol, and public affairs. However, under the undersecretary for political affairs, it is organized regionally, by foreign "desks," a classic structure that is found in many departments and agencies involved in foreign affairs, including the CIA. Throughout the department, there are distinct areas of functional or regional responsibility. Functional units naturally cut across regional lines, and within the foreign bureaus are special functional "desks." Sometimes analysis of an issue or problem by a foreign desk contradicts analysis from a functional bureau.

One of the State Department's challenges is to show that it can plan and achieve national security objectives, not just execute day-to-day American policy in foreign countries. The State Department's primary role is to project U.S. foreign policy abroad, and its primary function is to serve as the first interface that foreign people, in their own land, have with the American government. In a way, it is the one government department that has the job of putting other countries' needs on a par with those of the U.S. government. For this reason, it is sometimes said that the Department of State cannot be expected to plan and achieve national security objectives.

James Baker, secretary of state under President George H. W. Bush, expressed his frustration with this situation. He had served as undersecretary of commerce, White House chief of staff, and secretary of the treasury. In those positions, the needs of the American people and the U.S. government came first. To modify the Department of State's emphasis, Baker brought in many outsiders to perform key functions, relieving career foreign service officers, who had run the department traditionally and had gained many years of experience.

During his second term in 1996, President Bill Clinton appointed Madeline Albright the first female secretary of state. She was a specialist on Russian and Eastern European issues and spoke fluent Czech and French. After her unanimous confirmation by the U.S. Senate, she became the 64th secretary of state and the highest-ranking woman in the history of the executive branch. She tried to cure the State Department's reputation as not very dynamic with regard to national security and was an articulate exponent of the administration's views on the Chemical Weapons Convention, NATO expansion, and the Middle East peace process between Israel, Palestine, and other Middle Eastern nations.

President George W. Bush's secretary of state, General Colin Powell, had a long and distinguished Army career that culminated in his service as chairman of the JCS during the presidency of Bush's father. President George H. W. Bush and General Powell led the nation's successful prosecution of the Gulf War in 1991. Powell was the first African American JCS chairman and the first African American secretary of state.

In addition to its national security objectives, the State Department remains responsible for the official day-to-day presence of the U.S. government in foreign countries. The department follows the "country team" concept. The American ambassador, who is a representative of the American government, oversees all U.S. programs and personnel within a country, with the exception of American military forces in the country that may be in the field or in combat roles.

OFFICE OF MANAGEMENT AND BUDGET (OMB)

The president and his advisers control the most powerful armed forces and intelligence systems in history. These are employed to defend and secure the vital interests and security of the most powerful nation on Earth. Yet, their slightest move can cost millions of dollars. The president has little choice but to structure the priorities of national defense constantly within the defense budget.

The director of the OMB assists the president in preparing the federal budget and supervising its administration in executive branch agencies, such as those dedicated to defense and national security. OMB helps formulate the president's spending plans, which means that it assesses the cost-effectiveness of agency programs, policies, and procedures. The OMB also resolves the competing demands of defense and national security agencies to set funding priorities, and ensures that federal agency reports, rules, testimony, and proposed legislation are consistent with the president's budgetary policies.

In addition, OMB oversees and coordinates the administration's procurement, financial management, information, and regulatory policies. In each of these areas, OMB's role is to help improve administrative management, to develop better performance measures and coordinating mechanisms, and to reduce any unnecessary burdens on the taxpayer. The largest items in the national budget are defense and national security, so the president relies heavily on the OMB to set funding priorities.

THE INTELLIGENCE COMMUNITY: WHAT INFORMATION IS GATHERED, AND BY WHOM?

Organization

Below the level of cabinet members and presidential advisers is the next component of the national security apparatus: the intelligence community. The intelligence

FIGURE 7.2

Organization of the State Department, 2003

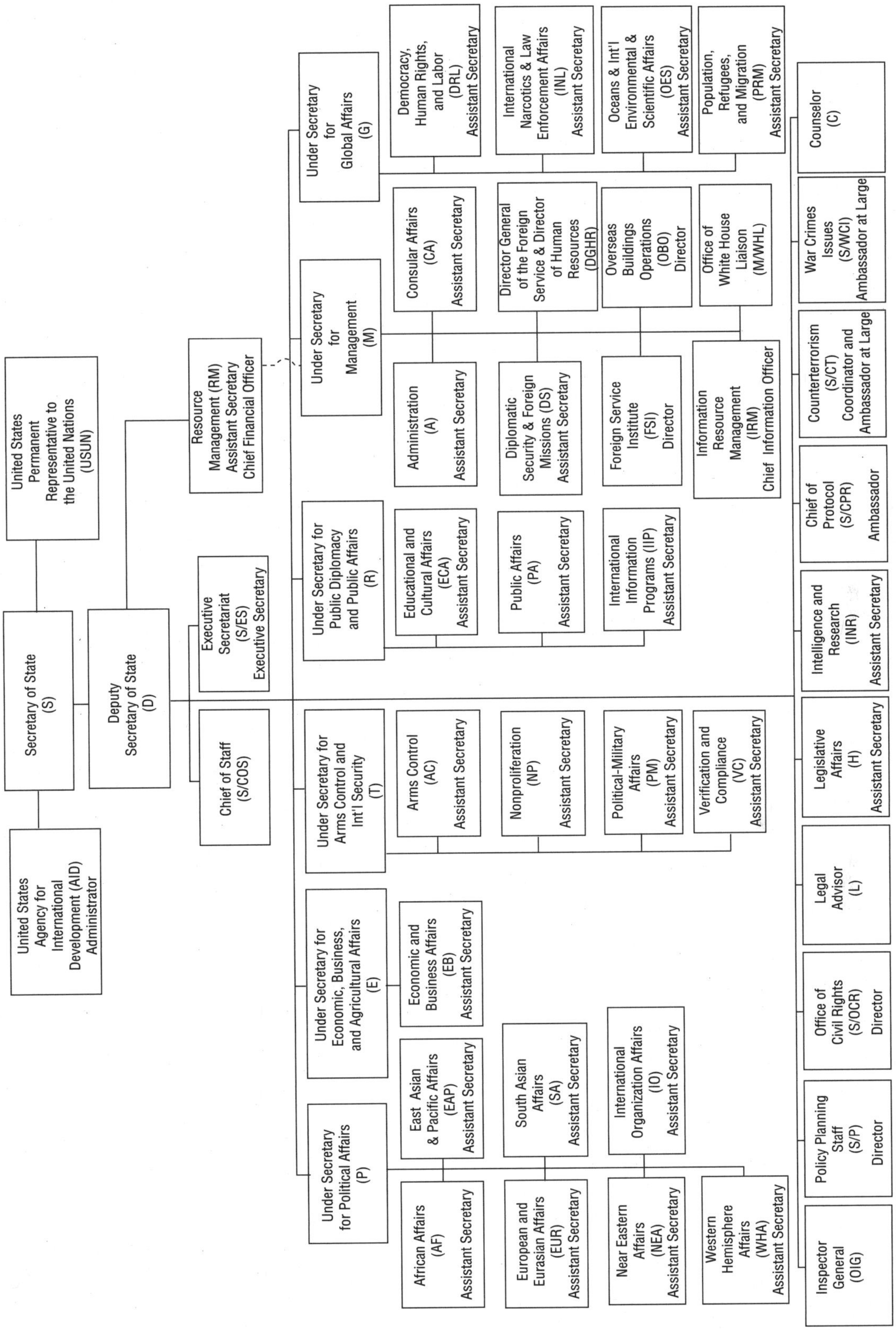

SOURCE: "Department of State Organization Chart," U.S. State Department, Washington, DC [Online] http://www.state.gov/r/pa/ei/rls/dos/7926.htm [accessed January 23, 2003]

FIGURE 7.3

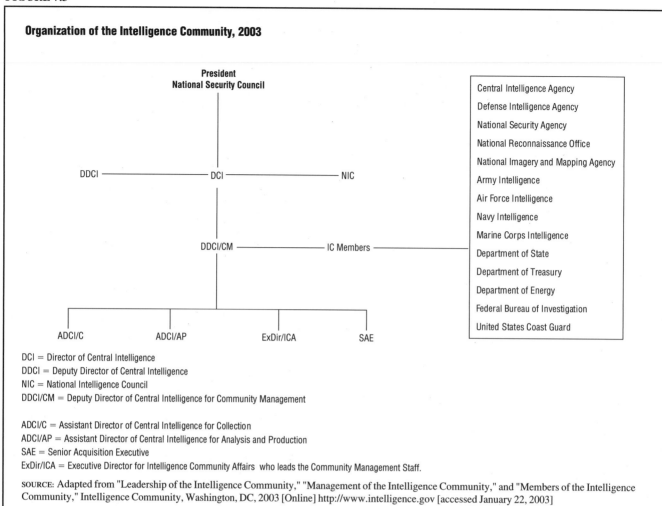

Organization of the Intelligence Community, 2003

President
National Security Council

DDCI ———————— DCI ———————— NIC

DDCI/CM ———————— IC Members ————————

ADCI/C   ADCI/AP   ExDir/ICA   SAE

Central Intelligence Agency

Defense Intelligence Agency

National Security Agency

National Reconnaissance Office

National Imagery and Mapping Agency

Army Intelligence

Air Force Intelligence

Navy Intelligence

Marine Corps Intelligence

Department of State

Department of Treasury

Department of Energy

Federal Bureau of Investigation

United States Coast Guard

DCI = Director of Central Intelligence
DDCI = Deputy Director of Central Intelligence
NIC = National Intelligence Council
DDCI/CM = Deputy Director of Central Intelligence for Community Management

ADCI/C = Assistant Director of Central Intelligence for Collection
ADCI/AP = Assistant Director of Central Intelligence for Analysis and Production
SAE = Senior Acquisition Executive
ExDir/ICA = Executive Director for Intelligence Community Affairs who leads the Community Management Staff.

SOURCE: Adapted from "Leadership of the Intelligence Community," "Management of the Intelligence Community," and "Members of the Intelligence Community," Intelligence Community, Washington, DC, 2003 [Online] http://www.intelligence.gov [accessed January 22, 2003]

community is a 14-piece collection of executive branch agencies and units conducting a variety of intelligence activities in furtherance of national security. These agencies are listed in the box ("IC Members") in Figure 7.3.

The National Security Act of 1947 established the CIA and made the DCI an adviser to the NSC. The DCI directs not just the CIA but the intelligence community—the complete set of 14 entities and agencies. Members of the intelligence community related to the DOD include the Defense Intelligence Agency (DIA), the National Security Agency (NSA), the National Reconnaissance Office (NRO), the National Imagery and Mapping Agency (NIMA), and intelligence agencies of the Army, Air Force, Navy, and the Marine Corps. Non-DOD agencies include the CIA, State Department, Energy Department, Treasury Department, Federal Bureau of Investigation (FBI), and the Coast Guard. The CIA, DIA, NSA, NRO, and NIMA are solely tasked with intelligence responsibilities, while the others are primarily concerned with other duties (such as law enforcement, border security, etc.) but deal with intelligence as a part of their mandate.

Information as Intelligence

What makes information intelligence? Intelligence is information that has a strategic value—information whose collection is deemed to be instrumental in making important national security decisions by the president, the DOD, or others in government. What also makes information intelligence is that it has been gathered at a more or less central location, where it can be integrated with other data, including secret data, and carefully analyzed.

TECHNICAL INTELLIGENCE. The intelligence community refers to the collection of technical data on opposing forces' weapons systems, personnel capabilities, and other technical information as "techint." A surprising amount of relevant techint comes from open (unclassified) sources, such as foreign and domestic newspapers, magazines, government reports, technical and professional journals, news media, academic studies, and popular literature. A much smaller amount of relevant techint comes from obscure, classified, and secret sources, such as lost or stolen weapons systems and government documents, stolen classified documents, stolen weapons or classified facility blueprints, and classified maps.

HUMAN INTELLIGENCE. Intelligence starts with spying, which was certainly the most common method of intelligence gathering prior to World War II (1939–45). In general, the community refers to the cultivation of human sources, whether open or secret, as "humint," short for human intelligence. Often, humint is the best (or only) way for U.S. defense planners to find out what another country's leadership thinks of its own capabilities. It is likely that humint will become more and more useful against threats like rogue states, transnational actors, terrorists, and organized crime, whose assets are smaller and thus less susceptible than sovereign states' forces to observation or surveillance via satellite-imaging from space or by other processes.

CIA field agents are one source of humint. They collect information from open sources like the media and recruit foreign citizens, either "defectors in place" (who volunteer their services) or "turned" informants (who are bribed or blackmailed into service). The latter can include foreign government officials or business people, paid informants in terrorist cells, and members of organized crime groups, among others. Soviet Lieutenant Colonel Pyotr Semyonovich Popov, for example, contributed invaluable data on his country's missile systems during the 1950s.

Once CIA field agents have collected information, they turn it over to their superiors, the station chiefs, who send it to CIA headquarters. Unlike their counterparts in the State and Defense Departments, CIA agents in the field and analysts in the home offices do not rotate their focus on foreign areas. Rather, they are given long-term assignments to allow them to focus on specific areas.

SIGNALS INTELLIGENCE. Signals intelligence consists of the interception and processing of electronic signals—for example, missile and satellite telemetry, shortwave radio transmissions, and cell-phone exchanges intercepted via ground-, air-, or space-based eavesdropping or monitoring equipment. The government devotes extremely large sums of money to this activity. Most estimates put the budget of the agency mainly responsible for this function, the NSA, at least on a par with that of the CIA, in the billions of dollars.

The federal government also funds In-Q-Tel, a not-for-profit venture capital project allied with the CIA, which, among other endeavors, has pursued technology to facilitate monitoring of the World Wide Web through custom information retrieval and multiple-language and anonymous search services.

IMAGERY INTELLIGENCE. Imagery intelligence is collected using photography from reconnaissance satellites and aircraft, as well as other types of photographic and image-producing processes. The satellites and aircraft used are known as "overhead platforms," one famous example of which was the U-2, a high-altitude plane with sophisticated cameras that was promoted by CIA Director Allen Dulles in the 1950s.

Intelligence provided by photo reconnaissance proved indispensable in defusing and managing the Cuban Missile Crisis of 1962, during which the Soviet Union placed ballistic missiles in Cuba and the administration of President John F. Kennedy had to decide how to respond. The images gave Kennedy an idea of the precise nature and extent of the new missile batteries, which he used in fashioning an appropriately measured U.S. military response. After a tense standoff, the Soviets eventually withdrew all their ballistic missiles from Cuba.

MEASUREMENT AND SIGNATURE INTELLIGENCE. Measurement and signature intelligence (often called "masint") is produced by collecting, storing, and analyzing atmospheric and environmental emissions, including radar, infrared, chemical, acoustic, and seismic data, usually as detected by specialized sensors. The CIA Science and Technology Directorate, for instance, employs seismic sensors to keep tabs on global military activity and has researched methods of detecting poisonous gases. Masint, according to specialists, came into being as the result of the SCUD missile hunts of the Persian Gulf War. Masint techniques are used to identify and locate specific weapons platforms by collecting information from a variety of sensors and specialized sensing equipment.

Covert Action

Only the president can direct the CIA to undertake a covert action. Such actions are usually recommended by the NSC. U.S. foreign policy objectives may not be fully realized by normal diplomatic means, but military action would be too extreme. In these cases, the president may direct the CIA to conduct a special activity abroad in support of foreign policy in which the role of the U.S. government is neither readily apparent nor publicly acknowledged. However, once ordered to undertake the activity, the DCI must notify congressional oversight committees.

In the past few decades, covert actions have often taken the form of assistance (money, equipment, and/or advice) to operatives in foreign lands, as those forces attempt to resolve situations in ways that are favorable to the interests of the United States. Most of these operations, being low-level and involving only a few people, have remained secret. Others, being larger-scale and involving many more participants, have found their way into the news.

Paramilitary operations are an extreme form of covert action. In these cases, CIA operatives go beyond giving advice to opposition groups and other elements, but may actually lead the charge and direct them. Such activities can be very controversial, because they fall within a gray area. Even though they do not involve uniformed U.S. military officers, and so do not come under the presidential restrictions on war-making of the War Powers Act, many people think such actions amount to undeclared war.

Indeed, when military personnel engage in CIA projects, they often resign their military posts. The military, however, holds their places to allow for reactivation once their missions as advisers have been accomplished. Many people feel that kind of behavior, however strategic its aims and objectives, is questionable and not in the best interests of the United States.

Among the more controversial covert actions undertaken by the CIA in the past four decades have been the Bay of Pigs invasion and the Phoenix Program. The former was notorious for its failure, while the latter drew fire for targeting civilians. Underestimating popular support for Cuban leader Fidel Castro, in 1961 the CIA sent a force of 1,500 men to Cuba, where they were decisively defeated. DCI Allen Dulles resigned after the disaster. The Phoenix Program, which started in 1968, was designed to lessen support for the Communist Viet Cong in South Vietnam but resulted in the deaths of at least 20,000 noncombatants.

THE CENTRAL INTELLIGENCE AGENCY (CIA)

The CIA's Role

Although all of the departments, agencies, and subunits of the intelligence community have specialties, the CIA sits atop them all. It was entrusted by Congress with the role of a central depository for intelligence and espionage functions, with "central" mostly meaning nondepartmental. This leaves the CIA, per Congress's intent, better able to focus directly on the overall community's three functions: 1) collecting vital intelligence; 2) disseminating it within the executive branch; and 3) conducting and coordinating spying, covert actions, and counterintelligence as effectively as possible.

The CIA's modern-day role derives from that of its World War II predecessor, the Office of Strategic Services (OSS), which had two main wartime functions: 1) for the first time in the nation's history, centrally gathering and analyzing intelligence; and 2) conducting covert operations, such as active aid to resistance movements in Europe, as authorized by the president.

The CIA is the only agency within the intelligence community authorized (and even then, only on a case-by-case basis) to conduct spying and covert actions abroad (though the president could conceivably order other agencies to be involved). However, both the National Security Act of 1947 and Executive Order 12333—United States Intelligence Activities (1981) prohibit the CIA from spying on or acting against U.S. citizens domestically. Executive Order 12333 specifically forbids "physical surveillance of a United States person in the United States

by agencies other than the FBI." Counterintelligence—monitoring and thwarting spying and intelligence activities against the United States, mostly within the United States—is a function assigned to the FBI domestically, with the CIA and the intelligence units of the armed services also assisting abroad.

There has been renewed interest in and debate over this particular subject since the passage of H.R. 3162, commonly known as the Patriot Act, in October 2002. This legislative measure calls for, among other things, fewer restrictions on information sharing among intelligence agencies and law enforcement authorities on suspected terrorists, as well as greater authority for law enforcement to monitor the phone conversations and e-mail activities of such individuals.

Secret vs. Public Information about the CIA

Legislation, passed in 1949, provided statutory authority for the CIA's undisclosed budget and staffing levels. The Central Intelligence Agency Act of 1949 exempted CIA funding from most of the usual appropriations procedures. Further, it allowed the agency not to divulge its "organization, functions, names, officials, titles, salaries, or numbers of personnel employed." The defense budget cleverly disguised funds intended for intelligence within the budgets of nonsecret defense agencies. Under the Central Intelligence Agency Act of 1949, CIA funds listed in the budgets of other agencies could be moved back to the agency free of limitations placed on the original appropriations. In this way, intelligence community programs were shielded from outside evaluation, making it impossible for congressional overseers to get an idea of their cost-effectiveness, much less their propriety.

As the Cold War flourished from 1947 to 1977, the intelligence community experienced unusual autonomy. Through 1977, 30 years after it was founded, the CIA was exempt from exposing and defending its budget. However, the gradual replacement of the Cold War by détente (a period of new U.S.-Soviet understanding, especially about arms control, that developed in the early 1970s) and other developments led Congress to weaken the intelligence community's power in the mid-1970s. During the mid- to late 1970s, although the intelligence community's budget was not made public, congressional oversight committees were given more authority over the CIA's behavior, especially its espionage and covert actions.

Little official information about the CIA's size or appropriations is publicly available even now, because almost all of its activities are secret. The overall extent of the headquarters complex located in Langley, Virginia, suggests that the usual estimate of about 20,000 employees at that location is accurate. But the number of agents, operatives, and others in various countries is unknown.

Estimates of current CIA budgets vary widely because CIA funds continue to be hidden in the annual budgets of other agencies. In 1997 the Federation of American Scientists sued for the intelligence community's budget data under the federal Freedom of Information Act. It was revealed that the fiscal year 1996 budget was $26.6 billion for all government agencies engaged in intelligence. Experts analyzing the data have estimated the CIA's portion of the budget at $3.1 billion, the NSA's at $3.7 billion, and the NRO's (higher due to a larger number of employees and greater technology usage) at $6.3 billion. In 1998 the total intelligence budget was estimated at $26.7 billion. The 1999 budget has not been publicly released as of January 2003.

Organizational Structure

A modern intelligence organization such as the CIA has a distinctive organizational chart, shown in Figure 7.4. There is a balance between functional and regional divisions as well as analytic and administrative divisions. Each of the CIA's three divisions, or "directorates," has its own deputy director. The Operations Directorate is responsible for covert actions and counterintelligence; the Science and Technology Directorate specializes in data interpretation; and the Intelligence Directorate generates reports based on analyses of raw data for the president and other members of the executive branch.

The DCI is distinct from other agency heads in that he or she serves as 1) head of the CIA; 2) head of the intelligence community; and 3) principal adviser on foreign intelligence to the NSC. Directors of other intelligence community agencies advise the DCI, in turn, by sitting on a number of specialized committees dealing with intelligence matters. Chief among these groups is the National Foreign Intelligence Board.

The DCI, in advising the NSC and the president, must be objective and resist political pressures that would influence his or her counsel. One way the CIA attempts to remain independent is by giving stable, lifelong careers to people who are not just competent technicians and accomplished specialists but who also pass a rigid background check, swear an oath of secrecy, and appear to possess such traits as loyalty, discretion, ingenuity, and a commitment to protecting and promoting American values. For this reason, the CIA places a high premium on trust and is often referred to by its employees as "the family." When the CIA's trust in its employees is misplaced, the consequences can be very serious, as illustrated by the case of Aldrich Ames, a high-ranking CIA official who sold secrets to the Soviet Union (and later Russia) from 1985 to 1994. Not only did Ames's treachery as head of the CIA's Soviet counterintelligence unit result in flawed American policy, but it also cost several agents their lives.

The Often Controversial History of the CIA

THE FIRST THREE DECADES. During its first 30 years, the CIA became known as a producer and disseminator of the highest-quality intelligence. It developed economic forecasting methods that helped gauge the Soviet Union's strength; disproved the "missile gap," which assumed that American weaponry was insufficient to counter the Soviet threat; and provided useful information during the Vietnam War. However, the agency also fell short of expectations on some occasions. It failed to warn of the Suez Crisis in 1956, the Yom Kippur War in 1973, Mikhail Gorbachev's ouster as president of the Soviet Union in 1991, and the September 11 terrorist attacks in 2001.

THE 1970s: INTELLIGENCE PROBLEMS AND CONGRESSIONAL CURBS. Congressional hearings during 1975 brought to light the CIA's role in several assassination plots against leaders of countries, including Chile, the Congo, Cuba, the Dominican Republic, Haiti, and Indonesia. There were also charges that CIA surveillance programs had been aimed at innocent foreign students, visitors to the United States, and Americans traveling abroad. Domestic practices of the CIA were attacked as illegal extensions of the CIA's foreign duties: domestic wiretaps, break-ins, and mail intercepts; infiltration of religious groups; surveillance of national political figures; training of local law enforcement in espionage techniques; and involvement in the academic world through subsidies and research contracts.

Concerned about possible domestic spying and public anger regarding the Watergate break-in of 1972, President Gerald Ford appointed a commission to report on CIA activities within U.S. borders. Before long, a number of congressional and executive actions had defined and limited the CIA's activities. In 1974 the first major restriction on the CIA's activities passed: the Hughes-Ryan amendments. They required the CIA to submit plans for covert activities to the president, who in turn had to justify them to appropriate committees of Congress as critical to national security.

The House and Senate Armed Services committees, up until this time, had loosely supervised the CIA, but stricter supervision began with the establishment of the Intelligence Oversight Board (IOB) by President Ford in 1976. The IOB is authorized to investigate the legality and appropriateness of intelligence activities and directs its reports to the attorney general if necessary. Also in 1976 the Senate Select Committee on Intelligence (SSCI) was set up, and the following year the House Permanent Select Committee on Intelligence (HPSCI) came into being.

Though the number of employees and size of the CIA's recent budgets have not been publicly disclosed, they are scrutinized by several other government agencies. Along with the SSCI and the HPSCI, the OMB and

FIGURE 7.4

The organization of the Central Intelligence Agency

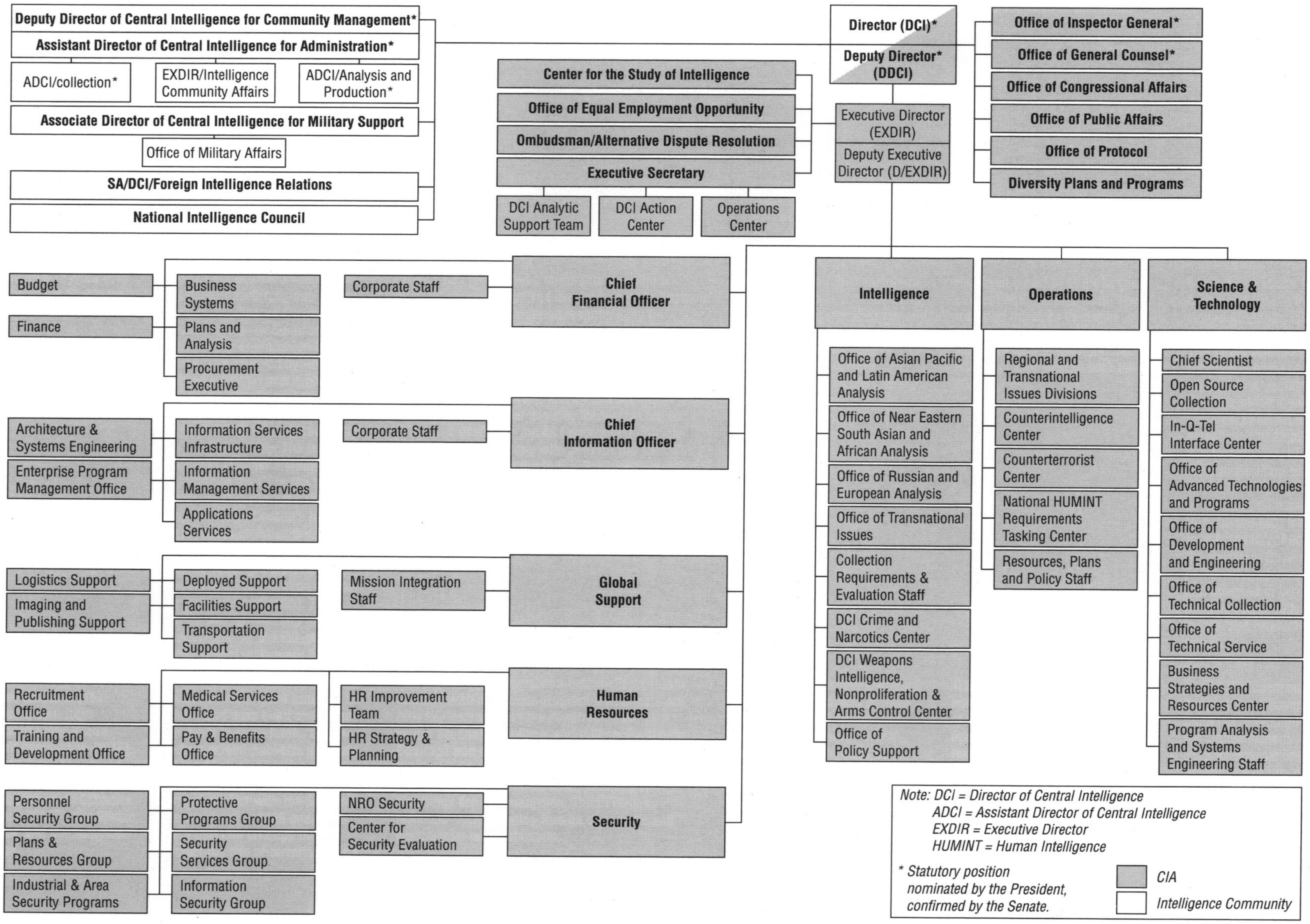

SOURCE: "Central Intelligence Agency," in *Factbook on Intelligence, 2001*, Central Intelligence Agency, Washington, DC, 2001

the Defense Subcommittees of the Appropriations Committees in both houses of Congress must review these details. As with all other government organizations, there is an examination and approval process that applies to the CIA's functions.

THE 1980s: IRAN-CONTRA. The infamous Iran-Contra affair of the 1980s is one of the largest scandals to have plagued the intelligence community. The Reagan administration was determined to contain what it felt was a threat by the Sandinista government of Nicaragua to export communism to nearby countries. In April 1984, when word leaked out that CIA agents had helped place mines in three Nicaraguan harbors, several congressional representatives claimed that the CIA had not informed them properly, and some were convinced that they had been deceived. As a result, Congress passed a law in 1986, known some months later as the Boland Amendment to the War Powers Act of 1973, that prohibited any military aid to the Nicaraguan government's opponents, called the Contras.

Still, Reagan's NSC was eager to continue such aid. The national security adviser and his staff, taking the view that the Boland Amendment did not apply to the NSC, continued the aid to the Contras by other means—for example, via private funds and contributions from other nations. The administration's efforts to skirt congressional appropriations (the only legitimate funds for national security) included efforts by members of the NSC to divert funds from sales of arms to Iran (although the sales of the arms were also done in an attempt to secure the release of American hostages).

Before long, Congress became extremely disenchanted with the CIA and the NSC. It investigated the Iran-Contra connection, finding that CIA personnel in Central America had rendered logistical and tactical support and assistance even after passage of the Boland Amendment. Congressional committees investigating the affair also concluded that senior officials of the CIA had misled Congress, withheld information, or failed to contradict others who they knew were giving incorrect testimony.

THE 1990s: ADDITIONAL SCRUTINY OF THE CIA. The Commission on Roles and Capabilities of the U.S. Intelligence Community was chartered by Congress in 1994 to play an advisory role on the use of intelligence in national security. In the years thereafter, it made a number of novel recommendations. For example, each year the government should disclose then-secret information, such as the current fiscal year's budget for the intelligence community and the total amount requested for the next fiscal year. As the commission noted, intelligence agencies "are institutions within a democracy, responsible to the president, the Congress, and ultimately, the people. Where accountability can be strengthened without damaging national security . . . it should be."

The 1996 report of a commission appointed by the Clinton administration to investigate the intelligence community also urged the CIA to pursue its mission with less secrecy and more accountability. The report suggested that the country take a middle-ground approach to the CIA's future by neither abolishing it nor giving it more powers.

The CIA Now and in the Future

Since the end of the Cold War and the Iran-Contra hearings, the intelligence community has tried to consolidate itself, foster cooperation among its members, better manage itself, and focus on more up-to-date, relevant activities like fighting global terrorism, assisting law enforcement in fighting narcotics producers and traffickers, and collecting economic intelligence. Budget pressures and post-Cold War realities have only given more "business" to the intelligence community. Some of these realities include transnational threats; proliferating nuclear, biological, and chemical weapons; regional instability and conflict; strategic nuclear and ballistic missile threats; global arms control monitoring and support; global U.S. peacekeeping missions; international organized crime; faster and more precise weapons; and the choice between coalition warfare and unilateral action.

To address the threat of terrorism against American interests abroad, for example, the CIA created the Counter-Terrorism Center (CTC) in 1986, three years after the U.S. embassy and Marine barracks bombings in Beirut, Lebanon. This interagency group includes members representing the Pentagon and FBI, as well as the CIA. Though the CTC has been criticized for failing to prevent the September 11, 2001, terrorist attacks masterminded by Osama bin Laden, it did succeed in capturing Abu Zubaydah, bin Laden's chief of operations and recruiting, on March 27, 2002.

Still, some Americans do not trust the CIA, and the intelligence community as a whole, and are wary of the national security agencies' sweeping new powers, provided through the Patriot Act, to conduct surveillance against U.S. residents. Other Americans state that there has to be some entity protecting the country and that, pursuant to its mission, the tasks and abilities of the intelligence community need be potentially unlimited in technical and geopolitical scope. For better or worse, an intelligence system is indispensable to protecting national security, yet a balance between security and civil rights must be maintained.

THE FEDERAL BUREAU OF INVESTIGATION (FBI)

The FBI is the part of the U.S. Department of Justice (DOJ) charged with investigating crimes and working with law enforcement agencies. According to the FBI's official mission, its duties are (given in the FBI's own words):

• To uphold the law through the investigation of violations of federal criminal law;

- To protect the United States from foreign intelligence and terrorist activities;

- To provide leadership and law enforcement assistance to federal, state, local, and international agencies; and

- To perform these responsibilities in a manner that is responsive to the needs of the public and is faithful to the Constitution of the United States.

(The FBI's duties as cited here come from the FBI's Web site, http://www.fbi.gov, as does much of the other information in this section.)

How the FBI Is Organized

The FBI is located in Washington, D.C., and is headed by a director, who holds a maximum term of 10 years. The director is appointed by the president but has to be approved by the Senate. The FBI director and the Washington, D.C., office coordinate the work of 56 field offices, about 400 satellite offices (called resident agencies), and more than 40 foreign posts (called legal attaché offices, or legats). As of January 31, 2002, there were nearly 28,000 FBI employees. About 11,400 of these were special agents, while 16,400 held support positions. Approximately one-third of FBI employees (9,800) work out of the Washington, D.C., headquarters, and the other two-thirds (18,000) work in field offices.

The FBI's goals are often confused with those of several other government agencies, notably the CIA, the Drug Enforcement Agency (DEA), and the Bureau of Alcohol, Tobacco, and Firearms (ATF). The FBI is distinct from the CIA in two major ways: (1) the CIA is specifically forbidden from collecting information on U.S. citizens or corporations (it is allowed to collect information only on foreign citizens and other countries); and (2) the CIA is not a law enforcement agency, but rather collects and analyzes data pertinent to national security. The FBI differs from both the DEA and the ATF in that those agencies have very specific missions (the enforcement of drug laws and the enforcement of firearms statutes, including the investigation of nonterrorist arsons and bombing incidents, respectively), while the FBI is the "primary law enforcement agency for the U.S. government" (FBI's Frequently Asked Questions [on-line], http://www.fbi.gov/aboutus/faqs/faqsone.htm).

The FBI's activities are monitored by a variety of government agencies. The FBI director reports directly to the U.S. attorney general. The FBI reports investigative findings to the attorney general and U.S. attorneys nationwide, and these findings are also often examined by judicial agencies. The U.S. Congress supervises FBI budget requests (which usually run about $3 billion per year), as well as its day-to-day operations and investigations.

The History of the FBI

THE EARLY YEARS: FOUNDING TO WORLD WAR II. The FBI came into being on July 26, 1908, when President Theodore Roosevelt's attorney general, Charles Bonaparte, ordered a group of special agents to report to Chief Examiner Stanley Finch. In 1909 this force was designated the Bureau of Investigation. At first, the bureau mainly investigated crimes like antitrust or naturalization violations. After the outbreak of World War I (1914–18), its mandate expanded, with the bureau gaining some responsibility in areas like espionage, sabotage, and selective service. It monitored individuals such as anarchists, communists, trade union activists, civil rights activists, and foreign resident agitators. However, after the war, as the *Microsoft Encarta Online Encyclopedia 2002* notes, "the bureau came under sharp criticism, when an independent review uncovered a range of abuses during . . . raids, including illegal searches and seizures, warrantless arrests, denial of legal counsel, and poor detainment conditions."

Throughout the 1920s and 1930s the bureau expanded. In 1924 perhaps the bureau's most famous director took office—J. Edgar Hoover, who would remain bureau/FBI director for almost half a century, until his death in 1972. Hoover immediately began to reform and "professionalize" the organization. The fingerprint database, which would come to be the largest repository of fingerprints in the world, was created in 1924. The FBI Laboratory was established in 1932 to analyze physical evidence. In 1934 agents gained the legal right to make arrests themselves, rather than having to rely on local law enforcement officials, and in 1935 the bureau became known by its current name, the Federal Bureau of Investigation.

As World War II (1939–45) started in Europe, the FBI began focusing significant energies on such wartime issues as sabotage, and as the United States entered the war in 1941, the bureau's responsibilities increased again. This time, it was responsible for enforcing the internment of American citizens of Japanese descent, something that was done, supporters argued, for reasons of national security, despite J. Edgar Hoover's protests that it was an unnecessary measure.

CONTROVERSIAL DECADES: THE 1950s TO 1970s. In the post–World War II period, the Soviet Union gained in power and became a major rival of the United States. The combined specters of communism and atomic weaponry made the American public nervous. The FBI began undertaking thorough background checks of applicants for government jobs—particularly those requiring access to nuclear data or materials.

Yet during the 1950s and 1960s, the FBI overstepped its bounds, providing secret assistance to the House Committee on Un-American Activities (HCUAA) and Senator Joseph McCarthy. The HCUAA and Senator McCarthy promoted communist "witch hunts" in an attempt to expose communist sympathizers, whom they felt had infiltrated all parts of American culture and government and who threatened national security. The FBI provided the HCUAA with information from confidential files.

The 1960s were a turbulent decade, during which the FBI tried to disrupt groups and supporters of various causes, including socialist groups, civil rights groups, and antiwar protesters, that the government felt affected national security.

In the 1970s there were attacks on the FBI's domestic information gathering after news damaging to the FBI emerged—notably, that many of the FBI investigations of the 1950s and 1960s were not always legal. At the time, public scrutiny went beyond the FBI's information activities to its program of domestic covert actions, called COINTELPRO—shorthand for "counterintelligence program." COINTELPRO was evidently intended to disrupt and discredit the leaders of certain domestic dissident groups, such as "New Left" groups (who opposed the Vietnam War), the U.S. Communist Party, the Socialist Workers Party, the Ku Klux Klan, black nationalists, the Black Panthers, and other extremist groups. It became clear that these secret disruptive activities, which dated back to the 1950s, went well beyond the law in most instances.

According to Kenneth O'Reilly (in "Federal Bureau of Investigation," *Dictionary of American History, Supplement,* Charles Scribner's Sons, 1996) "After Hoover's death in 1972, many of the FBI's files were opened under the Freedom of Information Act. They revealed that the bureau had done much more than compile intelligence on such 'dissidents' as civil rights leader Martin Luther King, Jr. Special agents committed thousands of burglaries to gather information and ran counterintelligence programs to 'neutralize' communists and anti-Vietnam protestors." The FBI also ran illegal wiretaps and collected and distributed information for political reasons. Special committees from the Senate and House investigated these abuses, and a 1977 DOJ task force referred to these types of actions as felonious conduct. It also became known that Hoover also used the power of the FBI to more or less blackmail politicians into keeping him in office, by using FBI staff to conduct research on prominent congressional representatives and senators, then using any negative information that was found as leverage against them.

The 1970s were also made turbulent by the Watergate scandal, which forced President Richard M. Nixon to resign. It also forced the acting FBI director, L. Patrick Gray, to resign because he had destroyed Watergate evidence and had leaked information on the FBI investigation to White House staff. Watergate hearings revealed that President Nixon had used the FBI to conduct illegal investigations of his political enemies.

COINTELPRO was terminated by the attorney general in 1971. Later, in the early 1990s, the FBI would pull back on its domestic counterintelligence activities, limiting its focus to domestic terrorist and antigovernment militia groups. In a way, this new-found restraint would be rewarded: the 1996 Anti-Terrorism Law, passed by Congress in response to the Oklahoma City, Oklahoma, and Atlanta, Georgia (Olympics), bombings, gave freer rein to the FBI to conduct surveillance and counterintelligence against truly violent groups.

RECENT HISTORY: THE 1980s THROUGH TODAY. In the early 1980s the prevalence of terrorism soared, and counterterrorism became an important part of the FBI's mission. At the same time, the FBI worked with the DEA to combat drug activity. In 1991 the Soviet Union disbanded, leaving the United States the one major superpower in the world. The FBI took this opportunity to concentrate more of its resources on domestic issues while still taking a large part in national security efforts. Not all of the FBI's domestic efforts were successful, and the deaths in 1992 of several people in Ruby Ridge, Idaho, and the 80 deaths resulting from a standoff at the Branch Davidian religious sect's compound in Waco, Texas, in 1993 turned some public opinion against the FBI. Many American politicians and citizens considered the Ruby Ridge and Waco incidents evidence that the FBI could not adequately handle "crisis situations."

In addition, then–FBI director William S. Sessions was accused of numerous ethical violations, including personal use of FBI resources. A DOJ investigation later confirmed these violations, but Sessions refused to resign, so he was fired by then-President Bill Clinton. Louis J. Freeh, who became FBI director in 1993, attempted to revitalize the beleaguered bureau, streamlining and overhauling various FBI procedures. An International Law Enforcement Academy was founded in 1995.

Terrorism continued to be a major issue throughout the 1990s, and the FBI participated in investigations of the 1993 World Trade Center bombing (New York City), the 1995 Alfred P. Murrah Federal Building bombing (Oklahoma City, Oklahoma), the "Unabomber" bombings of Theodore Kaczynski, and U.S. embassy bombings in Kenya and Tanzania.

The late 1990s saw more controversy, related to supposedly sloppy work at the FBI Laboratory and the investigation of Richard Jewell, who was questioned in connection with a bombing at the 1996 Olympic Games in Atlanta, Georgia. Jewell, a security guard who was working at the Olympics, was originally the FBI's prime suspect. Jewell was never charged and his name was ultimately cleared, but the FBI was suspected of leaking his name to the media and "conducting initial questioning of the security guard under false pretenses." The FBI Laboratories were cleared by a 1997 DOJ investigation of the most heinous charges, but the DOJ still found evidence of "substandard work, scientifically flawed reports, and misleading trial testimony" (*Microsoft Encarta Online Encyclopedia 2002*).

Most recently, the FBI has taken a lead role in investigations relating to the September 11, 2001, terrorist attacks, including the perpetrators of the attacks, the anthrax-laced letters that followed, and the prevention of future attacks. In the immediate aftermath of the attacks, more than half of the FBI's special agents, or 6,000 of 11,000 agents, were working on issues directly related to the attacks or prevention of future attacks.

FBI Investigations

The FBI defines its "investigative functions" as "applicant matters; civil rights; counterterrorism; foreign counterintelligence; organized crime/drugs; violent crimes and major offenders; and financial crime" (FBI's Frequently Asked Questions [online] http://www.fbi.gov/aboutus/faqs/faqsone.htm). It can take on any investigation that Congress has not expressly given to another federal agency. (Examples of investigations handled by other agencies include postal investigations, which are handled by the U.S. Postal Service; customs investigations, handled by the U.S. Customs Service; and counterfeiting investigations, handled by the Secret Service.) The mandate of the FBI includes gathering information and evidence and making arrests (at least on U.S. soil—special agents generally do not have the power to make arrests abroad). However, the FBI has no power to prosecute or recommend prosecution for specific individuals; those decisions must come from federal prosecutors working for the DOJ.

SPECIAL AGENTS. The FBI staff who carry out investigations are called special agents. They have numerous powers to help them fulfill their duties, including the rights to carry weapons (even on airplanes), to arrest suspects, and to subpoena witnesses of grand jury investigations. With judicial backing, they can tap telephone lines, read mail, and obtain personal documents such as tax returns and telephone bills.

There are numerous restrictions on exactly who can become a special agent. Applicants must be between the ages of 23 and 36, in good physical shape, and U.S. citizens. They must generally have a four-year college or university degree and a valid driver's license. The battery of testing candidates are subjected to includes vision and hearing checks, a drug test, a polygraph test, and a very thorough background check. All new agents have to undergo four months of training at the FBI Academy in Quantico, Virginia.

SHARING AUTHORITY WITH LOCAL LAW ENFORCEMENT. In investigations with "concurrent jurisdiction"

(for example, where a crime is a local, state, and federal violation at the same time), the FBI does not "outrank" the other agencies. Law enforcement agencies representing all levels of government, including the FBI, often work cooperatively on investigations. Some of the ways in which the FBI can assist local investigations include:

- Monitoring and identifying fugitives' fingerprints. According to *Microsoft Encarta Online Encyclopedia 2002,* the FBI maintains a database of more than 234 million fingerprints, or those of about 81 million people.

- Entering data on local fugitives into its national database, the National Crime Information Center. The center receives about 2 million inquiries a day from law enforcement agencies across the nation.

- Providing laboratory analysis of evidence.

- Pursuing and attempting to arrest fugitives who cross state lines or leave the country. According to information available on the FBI's Web site in August 2002, at any given time the FBI is searching for about 12,000 fugitives.

Local law enforcement agencies assist the FBI by providing it with crime statistics, which are then collected in the Uniform Crime Reporting Program. These statistics are provided by about 17,000 agencies, and the data represent 94 percent of the U.S. population. The FBI works with federal law enforcement agencies as well, both on specific investigations and in ongoing task forces, and also shares information with some foreign law enforcement organizations. Training of law enforcement officers is provided by the FBI to both domestic and foreign law enforcement staff.

INTERNATIONAL AND TERRORIST THREATS. The FBI has various duties in regard to terrorism and espionage. It investigates bombings both on U.S. soil and abroad, when the suspected target of the bombing is a U.S. citizen or a U.S. interest (such as an embassy). It works with other domestic and foreign agencies to share information that might be useful in combating terrorism. Hate groups and potential terrorist groups are monitored by the FBI in accordance with guidelines set by the attorney general. Only those groups showing strong evidence of a predilection toward unlawful behavior are monitored.

Beyond terrorism, the FBI also has other duties to protect the country from international threats, including counterintelligence. According to information available on the FBI's Web site in August 2002, "the FBI is responsible for detecting and lawfully countering actions of foreign intelligence services and organizations that employ human and technical means to gather information about the United States which adversely affects U.S. national interests" (FBI's Frequently Asked Questions [online] http://www.fbi.gov/aboutus/faqs/faqsone.htm). This espionage can consist of "the acquisition of classified, sensitive, or proprietary information from the U.S. government or U.S. companies." The FBI estimates that espionage costs the United States $100 billion each year.

A Changing FBI in the Wake of 9/11

After the September 11, 2001, terrorist attacks against America, a new wave of criticisms were leveled at the FBI. Several different incidents provided detractors with ammunition. For one, a group of FBI counterterrorism special agents based in Minneapolis, Minnesota, learned of a new student at a Minnesota flight school—one Zacarias Moussaoui. Moussaoui piqued the agents' interest because he paid $6,200 in cash for flight training and only wanted to learn to fly, not land, Boeing 747s. When Moussaoui's visa expired in August 2001 and he continued to remain in the country, the Minneapolis agents arrested him and did a thorough background check, only to discover that his background included ties to followers of Osama bin Laden. The agents requested a special search warrant to check a computer disk owned by Moussaoui, but their request was denied. Less than a week later, the September 11, 2001, terrorist attacks rocked the nation. As of early 2003, Moussaoui was being prosecuted as the alleged 20th hijacker, who would supposedly have participated in the attacks had he not been in FBI custody. In February 2003 his trial was postponed by a judge in Virginia so that Moussaoui's lawyers could interview a senior-level al-Qaeda operative whom Moussaoui claims was a co-conspirator.

A "whistle-blowing" letter from Minneapolis FBI Chief Counsel Colleen Rowley accused the FBI of deliberately obstructing the Minneapolis agents. Another FBI special agent, Kenneth Williams, wrote a memo in July 2001 warning of suspicious activity by Middle Eastern men in Arizona flight schools. The Phoenix, Arizona, agent suggested that FBI headquarters take a nationwide survey of Arab-American flight school students, but the memo was not passed along to the appropriate people and was never acted upon. The FBI director was not aware it existed until a few days after September 11, 2001. A 1998 memo out of the Oklahoma City, Oklahoma, FBI office warned of a similar phenomenon but did not receive much attention either.

As part of the wave of reforms undertaken after the 9/11 terrorist attacks, FBI Director Robert S. Mueller III suggested a major reorganization of the FBI to deal with such complaints. Director Mueller did not see this reorganization as a concrete plan, but rather as an "evolving road map" that can and must be adjusted to meet the needs of American security. According to a June 6, 2002, statement for the record before the Senate Committee on the Judiciary ("A New FBI Focus"), Director Mueller adapted previous strategic plans to come up with the following 10 priorities for the FBI (listed here in his own words):

1) Protect the United States from terrorist attack.

2) Protect the United States against foreign intelligence operations and espionage.

3) Protect the United States against cyber-based attacks and high-technology crimes.

4) Combat public corruption at all levels.

5) Protect civil rights.

6) Combat transnational and national criminal organizations and enterprises.

7) Combat major white-collar crime.

8) Combat significant violent crime.

9) Support federal, state, municipal, and international partners.

10) Upgrade technology to successfully perform the FBI's mission.

In the same statement, Director Mueller noted that the changes to the FBI to facilitate these priorities would be "built upon three key interrelated elements: (1) refocusing FBI mission and priorities; (2) realigning the FBI workforce to address these priorities; and (3) shifting FBI management and operational cultures to enhance flexibility, agility, effectiveness, and accountability."

The priority reorganization has led to important changes to the FBI's Counterterrorism, Counterintelligence, and Laboratory divisions, and the establishment of a Cyber Division, as well as a Security Division, Records Management Division, and Office of Law Enforcement Coordination. Other adaptations in the FBI include personnel changes and shifts, general coordination and information sharing, and changes in the way the FBI conducts criminal investigations.

PERSONNEL CHANGES. In addition to the movement of personnel from some divisions to other divisions, the personnel reorganization has led to four new executive assistant directors, who report directly to the FBI director. These assistant directors oversee the areas of counterterrorism and counterintelligence, criminal investigations, law enforcement services, and administration. This relieves some of the burden formerly shouldered by the FBI's deputy director, and also increases accountability and oversight.

The restructuring plan also calls for the nature of the FBI's workforce to change. Previously, most special agents have been generalists. In the future, Director Mueller would like to see many agents become subject experts, with knowledge in such fields as information technology, foreign languages, engineering, and so forth.

INFORMATION SHARING AND THE OFFICE OF LAW ENFORCEMENT COORDINATION. In a May 8, 2002, statement for the record before the Senate Committee on the Judiciary ("FBI Reorganization"), Director Mueller admitted that "information sharing," or FBI coordination with state and local law enforcement authorities, left something to be desired: "[Our] history of solid, personal relationships alone was not addressing the basic information needs of our counterparts. . . . Adding 650,000 state and local officers to our efforts is the only way to make this truly a national effort, not just a federal effort." Many of the proposed changes to specific FBI divisions integrate an increase in information sharing with state and local law enforcement agencies.

The FBI's plan also creates a new Office of Law Enforcement Coordination, whose purpose is to "improve relationships and information sharing with state and local police professionals and others. . . . [it] will also help the FBI tap into the strengths and capabilities of our partners" ("FBI Reorganization"). The new emphasis on information sharing has its genesis in local law enforcement complaints that the FBI has sometimes kept local agencies "out of the loop" and that FBI personnel turnover has had a damaging effect on cooperation efforts.

STRONGER FBI/CIA COOPERATION. The FBI is also strengthening its ties with the CIA to facilitate information sharing. In a June 27, 2002, statement for the record before the Senate Committee on Governmental Affairs ("Homeland Security"), Director Mueller noted that "[the FBI/CIA] relationship has a long history, and is the subject of much contemporary comment, most of it critical. But for those commentators, I would counsel caution. The relationship has changed, and is still changing, all for the better." As of June 2002 both CIA Director George Tenet and FBI Director Mueller participated in daily briefings with President Bush. FBI staff worked at CIA headquarters, and vice versa. Information about important security issues was exchanged between the two agencies on a daily basis.

SECURITY DIVISION ESTABLISHMENT. The FBI reorganization plan includes the creation of a Security Division, the purpose of which is to raise the level of FBI security practices and standards. This measure was in many ways a response to the 2001 arrest of Robert P. Hanssen, a veteran FBI special agent who was charged with selling national security secrets to the Soviet Union/Russia during a 15-year time span. As Director Mueller's May 8, 2002, statement declared, "We need to remedy the weaknesses that the Hanssen investigation made painfully obvious."

RECORDS MANAGEMENT DIVISION ESTABLISHMENT. Director Mueller's reorganization plan establishes a new Records Management Division. This division will be charged with modernizing FBI record-keeping systems, policies, and procedures in order to prevent important records from becoming lost or misplaced.

COUNTERTERRORISM DIVISION CHANGES. Much of Director Mueller's plan is focused on improvement of the FBI's counterterrorism investigations and programs. It calls for permanently moving 518 agents from criminal investigations to the areas of counterterrorism investigations (480), security improvements (13), and training of new special agents (25). These agents were previously assigned to drug investigations (400), white-collar crime investigations (59), and violent crime investigations (59).

Other changes to the Counterterrorism Division are meant to give the division a more central role in terrorism investigations and a more "robust" analytical capacity. In his June 6, 2002, statement before the Senate Committee on the Judiciary, Director Mueller outlined the "significant features and capabilities" of the revamped Counterterrorism Department as the following (in Director Mueller's own words):

- Establishment of a new, expansive multi-agency National Joint Terrorism Task Force at FBI Headquarters to complement task forces established in local FBI field offices and to improve collaboration and information sharing with other agencies;

- Establishment of "flying squads" at Headquarters and specialized regional assets to better support field investigative operations, deployments of FBI Rapid Deployment Teams, and provide [sic] a surge capacity for quickly responding to and resolving unfolding situations and developments in locations where there is not an FBI presence or there is a need to augment local FBI resources with specialized personnel;

- Augmentation of FBI capabilities to perform financial, communications, and strategic analyses of terrorist groups and networks; and

- Support for the DOJ's Foreign Terrorist Tracking Task Force and terrorism prevention outreach efforts.

COUNTERINTELLIGENCE DIVISION CHANGES. The restructuring plan for the FBI's Counterintelligence Division calls for a new espionage section, focusing on investigations. This will allow operations staff to concentrate their energies on detecting and thwarting intelligence threats. The division will work more closely than previously with other government agencies and the private sector to protect U.S. secrets. More highly trained personnel will be sought, and a "career path" will be established for these personnel to encourage retention. An Office of Intelligence was created in December 2001 to provide a "tactical intelligence analytical capacity" ("A New FBI Focus")—in other words, to try to create a "big picture" from what may be many seemingly unrelated pieces of data.

CYBER DIVISION ESTABLISHMENT. As of December 2001 the FBI introduced a Cyber Division. This group, according to Director Mueller's June 6, 2002, statement for the record, "will coordinate, oversee, and facilitate FBI investigations in which the Internet, on-line services, and computer systems and networks are the principal instruments or targets of foreign intelligence or terrorists and for criminal violations where the use of such systems is essential to the illegal activity." The FBI will work with private businesses, academia, and governmental agencies to procure the technology skills needed to conduct these high-tech investigations.

LABORATORY DIVISION CHANGES. According to Director Mueller's FBI reorganization plan, the Laboratory Division would be split into two separate divisions, Laboratory and Investigative Technologies, to address questions of "mission, staffing, and funding" ("A New FBI Focus"). The new Laboratory Division would collect, process, and analyze evidence. It would also provide training and conduct forensic research and development. The new Investigative Technologies Division would focus on more technical support to investigators, including electronic or physical surveillance and wireless or radio communications. Like the Laboratory Division, the Investigative Technologies Division would also have training and research and development functions.

CRIMINAL INVESTIGATION CHANGES. With the recent emphasis on improvements to the FBI's counterterrorism efforts, Director Mueller has been quick to point out that plans should be put into place to avoid a long-term detrimental effect on the FBI's "day-to-day" criminal investigation priorities, which are public corruption, civil rights, transnational and national criminal organizations, major white-collar crime, and significant violent crime. While staff are being transferred from criminal investigation areas like drug investigations, white-collar-crime investigations, and violent-crime investigations, these areas are still going strong. Drug investigations, which will lose 400 investigators, will still be staffed by more than 1,000 agents. White-collar-crime and violent-crime investigations will lose only 59 investigators each—about 2.5 percent of the total force for the former and 3 percent for the latter.

However, in the short run, according to one of Director Mueller's statements before the Senate Committee on the Judiciary, the FBI

> must be prepared . . . to defer criminal cases to others, even in significant cases, if other agencies possess the expertise to handle the matter adequately. In situations where other . . . capabilities are not sufficient to handle a case or situation, SACs [Special Agents in Charge] should be prepared to step in and provide FBI resources as needed. However, once the immediate situation is under control or resolved I expect SACs to reevaluate the level of FBI commitment and make necessary adjustments.

Director Mueller points out that it is also crucial for FBI agents working on seemingly mundane cases to be watchful for any evidence of terrorism. In his June 2002 statement he notes, "Other terrorist investigations have revealed patterns of low-level criminal activity by terrorists. It is the duty of every FBI employee to remain vigilant for suspicious activity or informant information that could be a tip-off to a future terrorist attack." That way, even FBI agents not involved in the FBI's Counterterrorism or Counterintelligence Divisions can become useful tools in the battle against terrorism.

THE DEPARTMENT OF HOMELAND SECURITY

In late November 2002 President George W. Bush signed the Department of Homeland Security (DHS) bill, thereby officially creating one of the most important domestic security agencies. The new department is the result of reorganizing 22 federal agencies into the DHS, which is headed by the director of homeland security. Former Pennsylvania Governor Tom Ridge was named the first secretary of the DHS. Efforts for establishing the DHS were spearheaded primarily in response to the September 11th terrorist attacks of 2001. For many, the term "homeland security" itself remains somewhat ambiguous. According to the National Strategy for Homeland Security, homeland security is "a concerted national effort to prevent terrorist attacks within the United States, reduce America's vulnerability to terrorism, and minimize the damage and recover from attacks that do occur." Six aspects of the department are: 1) intelligence and warning; 2) border and transportation security; 3) domestic counterterrorism; 4) protecting critical infrastructure and key assets; 5) defending against catastrophic threats; and 6) emergency preparedness and response.

The president keeps abreast of issues relating to homeland security through the director of the DHS, as well as an Advisory Council on Homeland Security. This council is primarily divided into counterterrorism and cyberspace security divisions, and features policy coordination committees that oversee plans between state and local governments. The budget for the new department is estimated at around $38 million, but this number is somewhat ambiguous as the DHS was created after the budget for fiscal year 2003 was already allocated. Concerns about the new agency revolve around defining the roles of the various subagencies that have undergone reorganization, issues related to information sharing among these agencies, and privacy concerns brought forth by various citizens' groups. As of January 2003, the DHS still had not established any official headquarters.

THE IMMIGRATION AND NATURALIZATION SERVICE (INS)

Immigrants have made the United States the strongest and most diverse country in the world, and the vast majority of legal immigrants work together to maintain the

TABLE 7.1

Principal activities and accomplishments of the border patrol, fiscal years 1994–2000

Activities and accomplishments	1994	1995	1996	1997	1998	1999	2000
Persons processed by the Border Patrol [1]	**1,046,576**	**1,336,518**	**1,561,234**	**1,422,829**	**1,566,984**	**1,591,969**	**1,689,195**
Deportable aliens located by the Border Patrol	**1,031,668**	**1,324,202**	**1,549,876**	**1,412,953**	**1,555,776**	**1,579,010**	**1,676,438**
Mexican aliens	999,890	1,293,508	1,523,141	1,387,650	1,522,918	1,534,515	1,636,883
Working in agriculture	5,162	4,487	2,684	3,521	3,270	1,599	1,330
Working in trades, crafts, industry, and service	8,068	12,552	9,413	10,146	6,616	2,383	2,167
Welfare/seeking employment	901,826	1,185,761	1,405,314	1,279,923	1,398,892	1,422,970	1,525,422
Canadian aliens	3,401	3,463	2,746	2,935	2,329	2,724	2,211
All others	28,377	27,231	23,989	22,368	30,529	41,771	37,344
Smugglers of aliens located	14,143	12,796	13,458	12,523	13,908	15,755	14,406
Aliens located who were smuggled into the United States	92,934	102,591	122,233	124,605	174,514	221,522	236,782
Seizures (conveyances)	9,134	9,327	11,129	11,792	14,401	16,803	17,269
Value of seizures (millions of dollars)	**1,622**	**2,012**	**1,256**	**1,095**	**1,405**	**2,004**	**1,945**
Narcotics	1,580	1,965	1,209	1,046	1,340	1,919	1,848
Other	43	46	47	49	64	86	97

[1] Includes deportable aliens located and non-deportable (*e.g.*, U.S. citizens and legal permanent resident aliens).

SOURCE: "Table 62. Principal Activities and Accomplishments of the Border Patrol Fiscal Years 1994–2000," in *Enforcement, Fiscal Year 2000*, U.S. Department of Justice, Immigration and Naturalization Service, Washington, DC [Online] http://www.ins.usdoj.gov/graphics/aboutins/statistics/ENF00yrbk/ENF2000.pdf [accessed August 5, 2002]

principles on which the United States was founded and make their adopted country a better place for everyone living within it. Even many illegal immigrants have a sincere loyalty to the United States and a desire to stay in the country because they believe the United States allows them to make better lives for themselves. Still, there are some people who enter the country without the best interests of the United States in mind. They may actively seek to do harm to the nation's citizens and values. These people, many of whom are living in the country illegally, can present national security threats to the United States.

The terrorist attacks of September 11, 2001, present a good example of how illegal immigration or illegal entrance into the United States threatens national security. Of the 19 alien airplane hijackers who participated in the 9/11 attacks, several had no immigration documents at all, and others had overstayed their visas (papers granted by the U.S. State Department, giving permission to travel within the United States). Authorities and the public are still not certain how some of the hijackers, of whom the FBI and Immigration and Naturalization Service (INS) had no record at all, actually entered the country. As a result, after the September 11 attacks, reforming the U.S. immigration system became an important issue.

What Is the INS?

The INS in its present form began in 1933, after the immigration and naturalization functions of two different agencies of the federal government were consolidated by

executive order within the Labor Department. It is headed by a commissioner who reports to the attorney general. During a period of increased international tensions prior to World War II, the INS was moved into the DOJ in 1940.

Since the INS determines who may enter the United States and enforces immigration laws with respect to those who remain, many people placed some of the blame for the September 11, 2001, terrorist events on the INS. The agency conducts immigration inspections of travelers entering (or seeking entry to) the United States; regulates permanent and temporary immigration to the United States, providing services such as granting legal permanent status, temporary status, and naturalization (the process of obtaining U.S. citizenship); controls U.S. borders; and works with other agencies to remove illegal aliens. The INS Web site (http://www.ins.gov/graphics/aboutins/insmission/dojplan.htm) lists under its "Strategic Plan" several goals, including to:

• Secure America's borders, especially to reduce the incidence of alien smuggling;

• Promote public safety by combating immigration-related crimes and removing individuals, especially criminals, who are unlawfully present in the United States;

• Provide timely and consistent services and achieve a substantial reduction in the benefits-processing backlog;

- Improve operational efficiency and organizational effectiveness of the INS workforce;

- Provide accurate, easy-to-use, readily accessible, and up-to-date information to meet planning and operational needs;

- Improve the efficiency of the inspections process for lawful entry of persons and goods;

- Adjudicate all immigration cases promptly and impartially in accordance with due process;

- Provide for the safe, secure, and humane confinement of detained persons awaiting trial, sentencing, or immigration proceedings.

The agency also shares the responsibility for inspection of all applicants seeking admission to the United States with the U.S. Customs Service at about 250 U.S. ports of entry at land, air, and sea locations. The INS and the Customs Service mainly prevent the entry of illegal aliens by detecting fraudulent documents, including claims of U.S. citizenship or permanent resident status. Inspectors from the two agencies also seize conveyances used for illegal entry, such as cars, trucks, and boats.

THE U.S. BORDER PATROL. It is the task of the U.S. Border Patrol, a subagency of the INS, to secure the 8,000 miles of U.S. borders—clearly a difficult and dangerous task. The Border Patrol must stop the influx of illegal aliens, the smuggling of aliens, and also seize illegal imports, like narcotics. Table 7.1 provides statistics on the Border Patrol's success in these areas. From 1994 to 2000 the number of deportable aliens stopped by the Border Patrol generally increased, particularly with regard to aliens smuggled into the United States.

The INS has been attempting to increase the total number of Border Patrol officers. (See Figure 7.5.) In 2000 the INS greatly augmented and enhanced its recruitment efforts. The Bush administration's 2002 budget called for adding a total of 1,140 Border Patrol agents during 2002 and 2003.

Restructuring the INS

In the wake of the events of September 11, 2001, Attorney General John Ashcroft announced in November 2001 the Bush administration's plans to reorganize the INS by 2003 if approved by Congress. The reorganization would divide the INS into two branches: one would handle enforcement of immigration laws, and the other would handle immigration services like naturalization. The positions

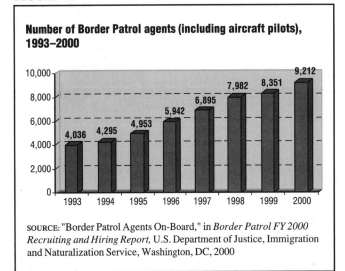

FIGURE 7.5

Number of Border Patrol agents (including aircraft pilots), 1993–2000

SOURCE: "Border Patrol Agents On-Board," in *Border Patrol FY 2000 Recruiting and Hiring Report*, U.S. Department of Justice, Immigration and Naturalization Service, Washington, DC, 2000

of regional director and district director would be eliminated in order to give command to officers with specific expertise. Other proposed changes included forming a more integrated law enforcement agency to deal with terrorism and illegal immigrant smuggling and creating an office of juvenile affairs to deal with unaccompanied minors. On December 7, 2001, INS Commissioner James W. Ziglar named Richard Cravener the INS director of restructuring. In April 2002 he testified before a U.S. House Committee that other changes, such as updating information technology and increasing the efficiency of processing immigration benefits programs, were also necessary.

In April 2002, with the Bush administration's support, Congress passed a bill that would break apart the immigration enforcement and services components of the INS into separate agencies. However, under the new Homeland Security bill signed by President Bush in November 2002, INS functions have instead been incorporated into the new DHS, where a more slow reformation is planned. The INS's immigration enforcement functions will be transferred to the Directorate of Border and Transportation Security under DHS and the immigration service functions will be placed under DHS' Bureau of Citizenship and Immigration Services. Until such changes and reorganizations are finalized, the INS remains authorized to locate and arrest aliens illegally attempting to enter the United States, those who have entered illegally, and those admitted legally but who have since lost their legal status. Once all INS functions are transferred to DHS, the INS itself will cease to exist as a separate entity.

CHAPTER 8

THE MILITARY, PEACEKEEPING, AND NATIONAL SECURITY

Within the executive branch of the U.S. government, the Department of Defense (DOD) works directly to deal with national security threats and keep the president's military options open. For fiscal year 2003, the DOD had a budget of almost $369 billion, with an additional $10 billion allocated, if needed, for the war on terrorism. This is a significant increase over the $328.9 billion allocated to the department in fiscal year 2002. Of the total 2003 budget, the Army receives $90.9 billion, the Navy/Marine Corps gets $108.3 billion, and the Air Force gets $107 billion, with the remainder going to various other DOD departments. The DOD employs more than 3.3 million employees, including an active-duty force of approximately 1.44 million, and maintains high-tech information systems, expertise, and weapons with which the president and others can make informed decisions that lead to decisive actions.

MILITARY ADMINISTRATION

Department of Defense (DOD) Organization

The secretary of defense is the president's principal defense adviser and oversees the DOD. The secretary advises the president on military strategy and policy, sets defense budgets, and administers the department. The Office of the Secretary of Defense is the secretary's staff, assisting him in directing the undersecretaries, assistant secretaries, and lower-ranking officials who populate the department, which is organized along both functional and regional lines. (See Figure 8.1.)

The DOD below the secretary and the secretary's office is made up of the Joint Chiefs of Staff (JCS; a council consisting of the highest-ranking member of each service) and their staff, called the joint staff; the three military departments (Army, Navy, Air Force); the nine unified combatant commands (the multiservice groups that directly control U.S. combat forces); and several defense agencies that provide services across the entire DOD, such as the Defense Intelligence Agency. (See Figure 8.2.)

The Secretary of Defense and the Goldwater-Nichols Act

Originally created in 1947, the position of secretary of defense was meant to be that of a basic coordinator of the armed services, which at that time were much more independent organizations. However, the Goldwater-Nichols Department of Defense Reorganization Act of 1986 (PL 99-433), sponsored by Senator Barry Goldwater (R-Arizona) and House Representative Bill Nichols (D-Alabama), attempted to reduce interservice rivalries and the services' independent organization, promoting "jointness" within the DOD. The act specified the chairman of the JCS as the "principal military advisor to the President, the National Security Council, and the Secretary of Defense." In addition to reporting JCS positions on issues and problems, the JCS chairman could now give any advice he or she thought appropriate. The act also created the new position of vice-chairman of the JCS.

To bridge differences within the separate services' personnel systems, the Goldwater-Nichols Act called for the creation of a "joint specialty," requiring the Army, Navy, and Air Force to send a share of their most outstanding officers to both the joint staff in Washington and the unified commands in the field. These officers also had to receive a specified share of available promotions. Goldwater and Nichols, the bill's congressional sponsors, had relied chiefly on analysis and policy recommendations drawn from a study on developing "jointness" and interservice cooperation, by the well-known Washington think-tank the Center for Strategic and International Studies.

The new measures yielded a defense secretary who, far more than a coordinator, could actively consult the president on defense policy. The military as a whole, according to specialists, became more flexible and responsive; the DOD became more centralized; and the role of defense secretary became more prominent and proactive.

FIGURE 8.1

Organization of the Office of the Secretary of Defense, March 2001

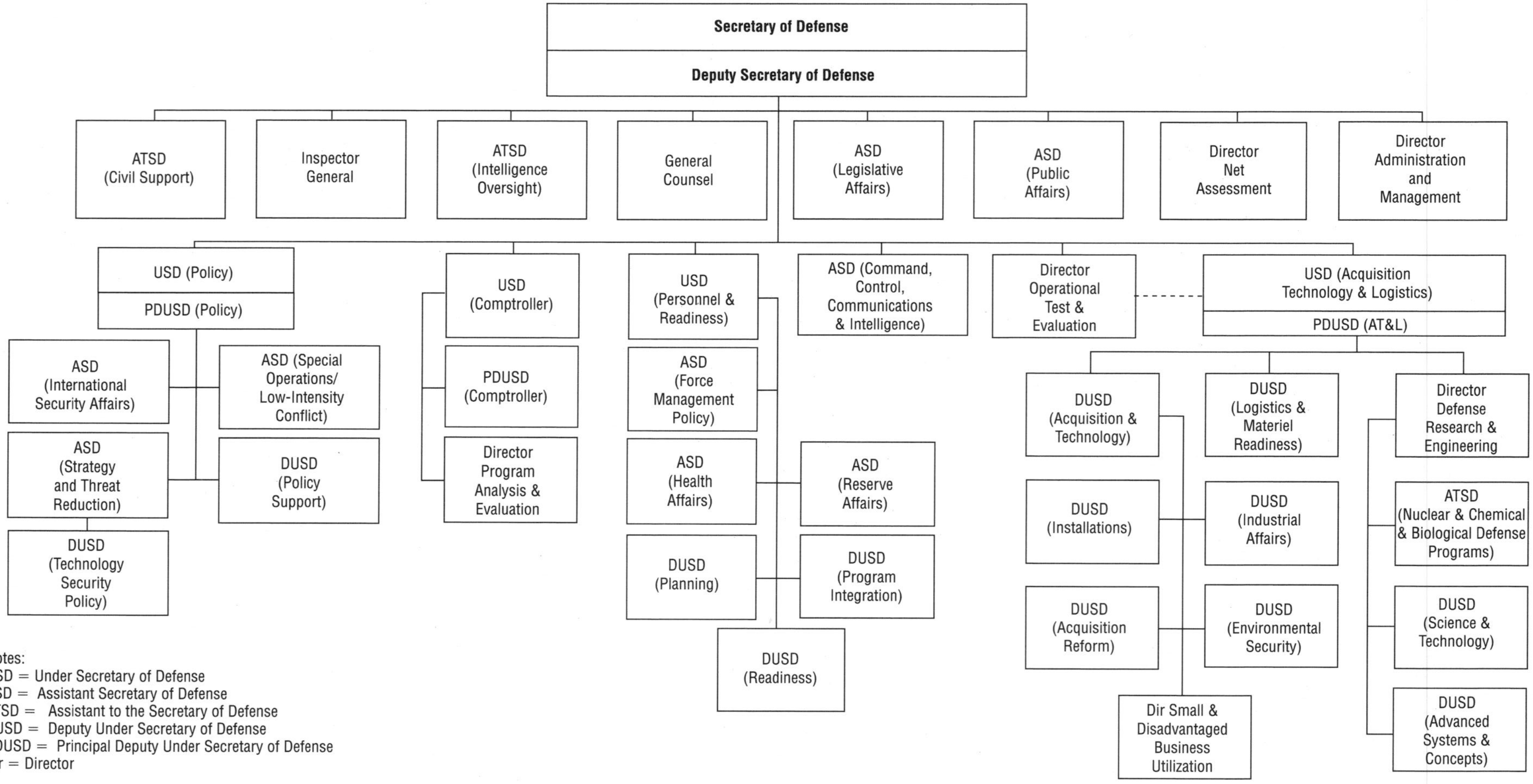

Notes:
USD = Under Secretary of Defense
ASD = Assistant Secretary of Defense
ATSD = Assistant to the Secretary of Defense
DUSD = Deputy Under Secretary of Defense
PDUSD = Principal Deputy Under Secretary of Defense
Dir = Director

SOURCE: "Office of the Secretary of Defense," in *DoD Organization and Functions Guidebook*, U.S. Department of Defense, Washington, DC, March 2001

FIGURE 8.2

Organization of the Department of Defense, March 2000

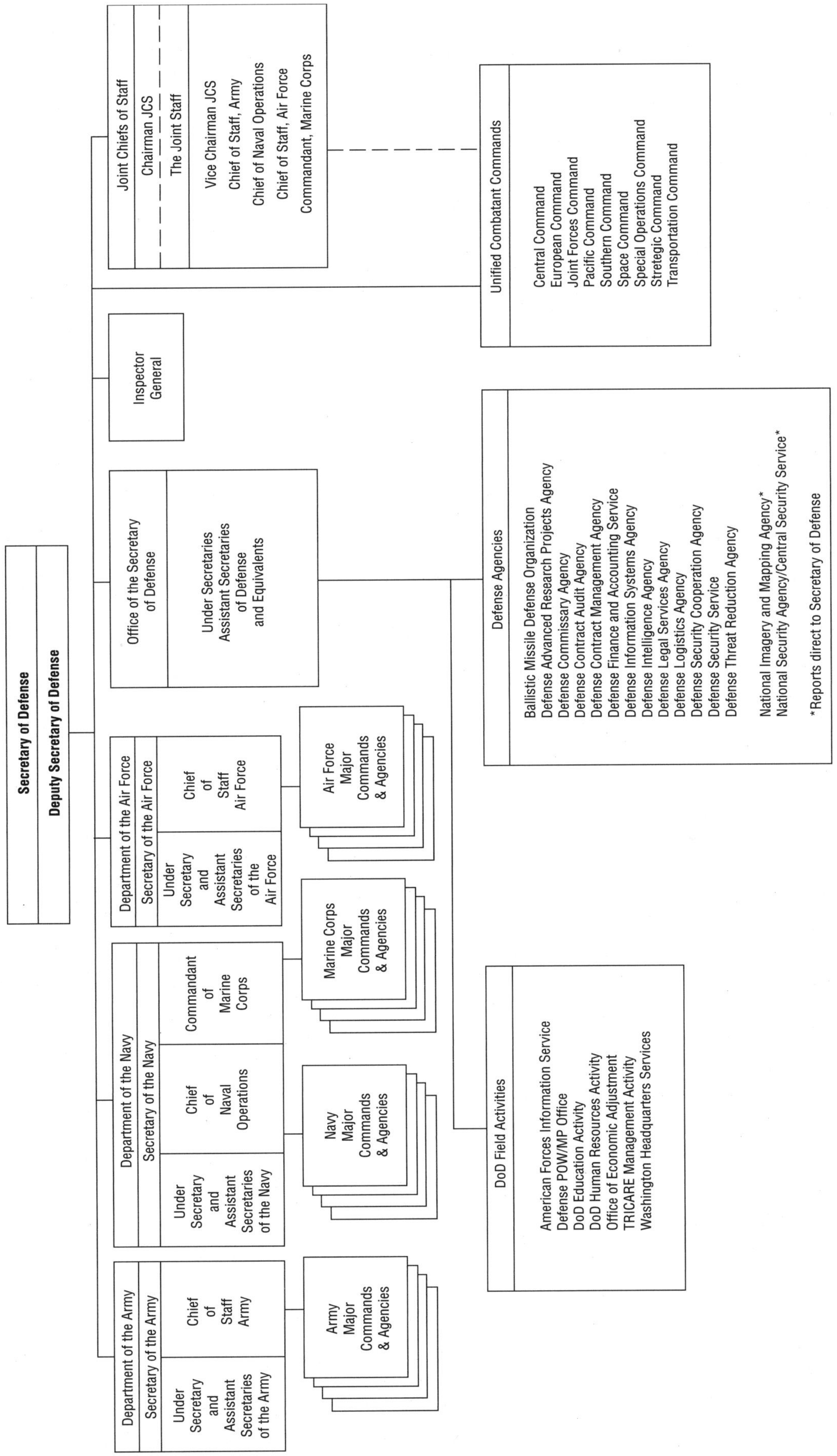

SOURCE: "Department of Defense," in *DoD Organization and Functions Guidebook*, U.S. Department of Defense, Washington, DC, March 2001

FIGURE 8.3

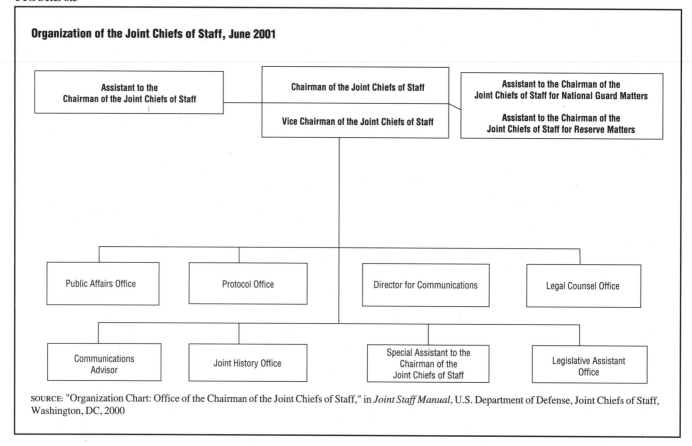

Organization of the Joint Chiefs of Staff, June 2001

SOURCE: "Organization Chart: Office of the Chairman of the Joint Chiefs of Staff," in *Joint Staff Manual*, U.S. Department of Defense, Joint Chiefs of Staff, Washington, DC, 2000

The Joint Chiefs of Staff (JCS)

The members of the JCS have been called the "hinge" between the highest U.S. civilian authorities and the uniformed services. Individually, they are the chiefs of their respective services—the Army, Navy, and Air Force. Collectively, they are the senior military advisers to the president, the National Security Council (NSC), and the defense secretary. As such, they include not only the Army and Air Force chiefs of staff, the chief of naval operations, and the Marine Corps commandant, but also generals, who act as chairman and vice-chairman of the JCS. (See Figure 8.3.)

One or both of these individuals represents the JCS as a whole at meetings of the NSC and other interagency forums. The Goldwater-Nichols Act included a significant attempt to improve the relationship of the JCS to the executive branch. It enhanced the JCS role by increasing the JCS chairman's power and conferring on individual JCS members the right to go directly to the president.

JCS chiefs and generals are important to a president seeking the support of the U.S. populace and Congress for a controversial national security initiative. For example, the JCS supported the president's resolve to achieve ratification of the Panama Canal Treaty in 1977–78. It also supported President Ronald Reagan's decision to discard the Strategic Arms Limitation Treaty II limits on nuclear weapons in 1986 and President George H. W. Bush's reduction of combat forces in Europe by half in 1990. However, some critics feel this record shows that the JCS too often succumbs to presidential pressure instead of staking out its own position on strategic issues.

U.S. Armed Services

The DOD provides the military forces needed to avoid war and to protect national security. The military departments are separate entities, with their own secretaries and service chiefs, which all report to the secretary of defense. (See Figure 8.4.) They are charged with organizing, training, equipping, and providing forces that will defend the nation and protect national security.

Three military departments, each with its own armed services, report directly to the DOD—the Army, Navy, and Air Force. The Marine Corps is a second armed service in the Department of the Navy. Also, the Coast Guard, generally under the control of the Department of Transportation, reports to the DOD during times of war.

THE ARMY. The U.S. Army was created during the American Revolution by the Continental Congress on June 14, 1775, and for more than two centuries it has worked at home and abroad to protect and maintain American interests. As of 2002 the Army maintained a standing force of just under 500,000 soldiers. Its main jurisdiction

FIGURE 8.4

Organization of military departments, July 1999

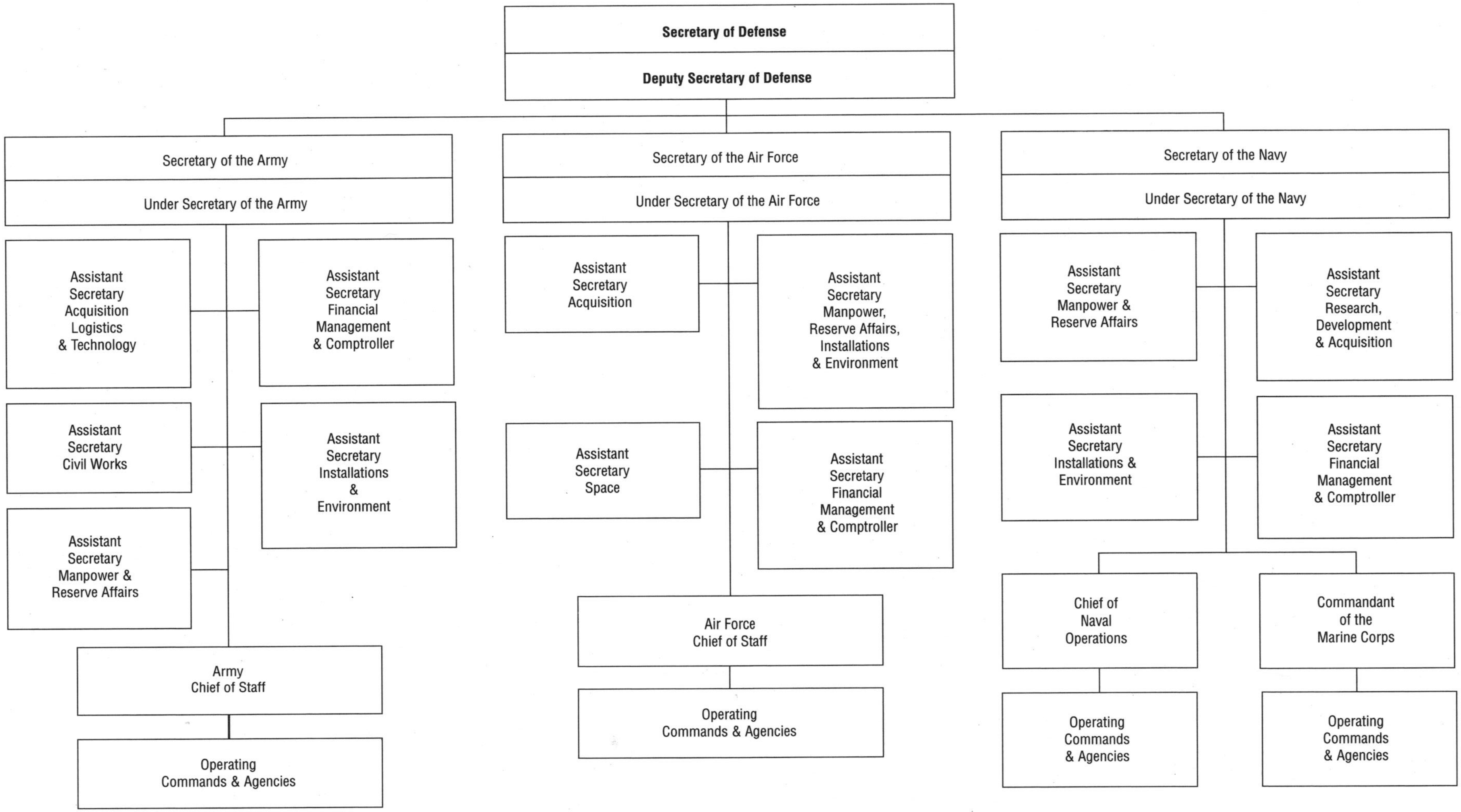

SOURCE: "Military Departments," in *DoD Organization and Functions Guidebook*, U.S. Department of Defense, Washington, DC, March 2001

is land combat, and it is often the decisive force in conflicts because of its ability to attack and control large geographic areas. Although the U.S. Army ranks behind many other countries in the number of active-duty soldiers, its advantages in equipment, technology, training, and mobility make it the world's most formidable ground force. It boasts advanced heavy weaponry, such as the M1 Abrams tank, which uses computer-firing controls and is able to fire accurately on targets even while moving. Other examples of Army weaponry include the AH-64 Apache attack helicopter, artillery multiple launch rocket systems, Patriot and Stinger antiaircraft missiles, grenade launchers, and machine guns.

THE NAVY. In a move to protect the freedom of the seas, the U.S. Congress created the U.S. Navy on April 30, 1798. The Navy's primary objectives have been to guard American shores from foreign attack, preserve freedom of the seas for commerce, protect American interests overseas, support U.S. allies, and serve as an instrument of American foreign policy. The U.S. Navy is by far the most capable navy in the world because of its advantages in technology, training, and readiness, along with more than 380,000 active-duty sailors. It controls a wide variety of military equipment, including ballistic-missile submarines, aircraft carriers, surface warships, attack submarines, land-based aircraft, and amphibious vessels.

THE AIR FORCE. Created by President Harry Truman in 1947, the U.S. Air Force plays a crucial role in national security through its control of air and space. It deploys aircraft to fight enemy aircraft, bomb enemy targets, provide reconnaissance, and transport soldiers for the other armed services. In addition, the Air Force maintains the greatest portion of the country's nuclear forces and military satellites. In 2002 the Air Force consisted of more than 364,000 active-duty members. The backbone of the Air Force fleet is its two types of fighter planes—the F-15 Eagle and the F-16 Fighting Falcon. More than 175 types of bombers, including the B-52 Stratofortress and B-2 stealth bomber, along with other planes for strategic airlift, complete the Air Force fleet of some 3,700 aircraft.

THE MARINES. The first battalions of the U.S. Marine Corps were formed in November 1775 to fight in the American Revolution. Today it is a military service operating within the Department of the Navy. In May 2002 the Marine Corps was made up of 172,192 active-duty soldiers. Marines are trained to fight in a combination of land, sea, and air operations and are a key element in U.S. rapid-response capability. The United States is the only country to have a Marine Corps as a truly independent fighting force.

THE COAST GUARD. Commissioned in 1790 to collect taxes from ships carrying imported goods, the U.S. Coast Guard is known today as a worldwide leader in maritime safety, search and rescue, and law enforcement operations. During peacetime, the Coast Guard operates under the Department of Transportation; during times of war or under presidential order, the Coast Guard serves as part of the U.S. Navy and operates in any maritime area to defend American national security. As of May 2002 almost 37,000 active-duty men and women served in the Coast Guard. It maintains a fleet of approximately 200 cutters (vessels 65 feet or longer), 1,400 smaller vessels, and more than 200 aircraft.

While all of the services were heavily influenced by the terrorist events of September 11, 2001, the Coast Guard in particular has gained new responsibilities for homeland security. Prior to the attacks, its vital missions included counternarcotics/drug interdiction, migrant interdiction, fisheries enforcement, marine safety, environmental protection, and, to some degree, port security. Now, however, port security has begun to dwarf other Coast Guard roles, which have been sharply reduced.

ATTEMPTS AT "JOINTNESS." Military specialists have long granted that the Army, Navy, Air Force, Marines, and Coast Guard have distinct service identities, "personalities," and cultures; that they suffer from interservice rivalries; and that these factors have as much impact on molding the armed services as national security threats. To mitigate these conditions, the Goldwater-Nichols Department of Defense Reorganization Act of 1986 required that officers serve in joint assignments before they can rise to the rank of general or admiral. The law broke down the services' cultural barriers in other ways, as well, promoting greater "jointness" and teamwork.

Unified Combatant Commands

The president applies his constitutional authority as commander in chief of the armed forces by filtering orders and other communications down through the secretary of defense, the JCS chairman, the JCS, the heads of the military agencies and the nine unified combatant commands. (See Figure 8.5.) Together the president and the secretary of defense are known as the National Command Authority. The JCS chairman is not formally part of the operational chain of command but still transmits orders from the National Command Authority to the nine unified combatant commands. In this chain of command, the secretary of defense is tantamount to a deputy commander in chief, who relies on the individual chiefs' advice and assistance to implement national commands.

The unified combatant commands directly control U.S. combat forces. Each command is composed of forces from two or more services; has a broad and continuing mission; and is normally organized on a geographical basis. The number of unified combatant commands is not fixed by law or regulation and may vary from time to time. The nine commands as of January 2003, and their

FIGURE 8.5

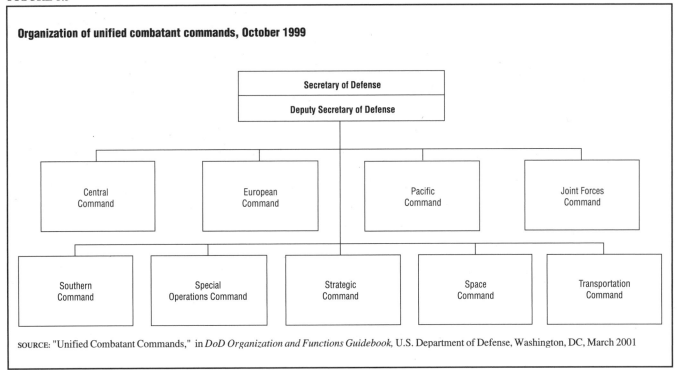

Organization of unified combatant commands, October 1999

SOURCE: "Unified Combatant Commands," in *DoD Organization and Functions Guidebook,* U.S. Department of Defense, Washington, DC, March 2001

locations, are as follows: U.S. European Command, Stuttgart-Vaihingen, Germany; U.S. Pacific Command, Honolulu, Hawaii; U.S. Joint Forces Command, Norfolk, Virginia; U.S. Southern Command, Miami, Florida; U.S. Central Command, MacDill Air Force Base, Florida; U.S. Space Command, Peterson Air Force Base, Colorado; U.S. Special Operations Command, MacDill Air Force Base, Florida; U.S. Transportation Command, Scott Air Force Base, Illinois; and the U.S. Strategic Command, Offutt Air Force Base, Nebraska.

Defense Agencies

Besides the various branches of the military, there are a number of agencies related to the DOD that perform a host of tasks ranging from advanced defense modeling to logistical support. Some of the primary defense-related organizations are detailed below.

DEFENSE ADVANCED RESEARCH PROJECTS AGENCY. The primary mission of the Defense Advanced Research Projects Agency is research and development within the realm of science and technology. It takes innovative, cutting-edge research ideas and tries to develop potential military applications by creating prototypes.

DEFENSE CONTRACT MANAGEMENT AGENCY. The Defense Contract Management Agency is the main contact point for most defense contractors/suppliers working for the U.S. military. It helps to ensure that military and allied government supplies are delivered on time and meet quality standards.

DEFENSE INFORMATION SYSTEMS AGENCY. The Defense Information Systems Agency is primarily a combat support organization that helps to plan, develop, operate, and support the DOD's C4I (command, control, communications, computers, and information) elements during times of both conflict and peace. The agency makes sure that the military's C4I systems are interoperable (able to operate between different branches and locations) and secure at all times.

DEFENSE INTELLIGENCE AGENCY. Also a combat support group, the Defense Intelligence Agency is a vital component of the U.S. intelligence infrastructure. Its personnel primarily gather information on foreign military intelligence. The agency is headquartered at the Pentagon in Washington, D.C., but has a significant operational presence at the Defense Intelligence Analysis Center, the Armed Forces Medical Intelligence Center, and the Missile and Space Intelligence Center.

DEFENSE LEGAL SERVICES AGENCY. The Defense Legal Services Agency is the main organization providing legal advice and services to DOD agencies and personnel. It is headed by the general counsel of the DOD, who is appointed by the president (with the advice and consent of the Senate). The general counsel also leads the DOD in all international negotiations and treaty commitments.

DEFENSE LOGISTICS AGENCY. As its name implies, the Defense Logistics Agency is responsible for providing logistical support (supplies and services) to military personnel around the world. As of April 2001 the agency was working out of 28 countries, while serving about 500 sites with its services.

DEFENSE SECURITY COOPERATION AGENCY. The Defense Security Cooperation Agency helps create and maintain ties between the U.S. and foreign militaries in order to achieve common defense goals. It runs a group of programs (authorized under the 1961 Foreign Assistance Act and the Arms Export Control Act) by which the DOD and military contractors sell materials and services abroad.

DEFENSE SECURITY SERVICE. Formerly known as the Defense Investigative Service, the Defense Security Service plays an integral part in the country's security infrastructure. It conducts personnel security investigations, provides industrial security products, and holds several comprehensive security trainings for DOD personnel.

DEFENSE THREAT REDUCTION AGENCY. The Defense Threat Reduction Agency has a crucial role in ensuring American preparedness for attacks involving weapons of mass destruction (WMD). Under the agency, all DOD resources are combined to ensure that the country is prepared for any potential WMD threat.

MISSILE DEFENSE AGENCY. Formerly known as the Ballistic Missile Defense Organization, the Missile Defense Agency has the primary mission of developing, testing, and preparing for the deployment of a missile defense system.

NATIONAL IMAGERY AND MAPPING AGENCY. The National Imagery and Mapping Agency provides geospatial intelligence, or geographic data gathered from satellite imagery (including imagery, imagery intelligence, and geospatial data and intelligence) from across the globe. Organizationally, it is divided into the Analysis and Production Directorate (intelligence analysis for policymakers), Acquisition Directorate (acquires and produces business solutions that help it advance the agency's mission), and Innovision Directorate (forecasts future environments and trends in the science and technology industry).

NATIONAL SECURITY AGENCY. The National Security Agency is the U.S. government's foremost intelligence organization in terms of gathering and analyzing electronic intelligence. Two primary missions of the agency, as outlined by its Web site (http://www.nsa.gov), are "designing cipher systems that will protect the integrity of U.S. information systems and searching for weaknesses in adversaries' systems and codes." The agency is headquartered in Fort Meade, Maryland, and employs a range of cryptographers, computer programmers, analysts, engineers, and researchers.

PENTAGON FORCE PROTECTION AGENCY. Established primarily in response to the terrorist attacks of September 11, 2001, the Pentagon Force Protection Agency is basically a police force for the Pentagon. The newly created agency incorporated the former security force for the Pentagon (Defense Protective Service) and provides law enforcement and security for the Pentagon.

PEACEKEEPING AS A DEFENSE STRATEGY

Military responses and treaties are not the only ways the United States and the world community as a whole attempt to defend themselves. In many ways, it is more desirable to prevent military problems before they start than to wait until tensions boil over. To this end, since the early 1990s the world community has placed more and more emphasis on peacekeeping efforts.

What Is Peacekeeping?

The term "peacekeeping" encompasses many different types of actions. In the landmark report *An Agenda for Peace: Preventive Diplomacy, Peacemaking, and Peacekeeping* (June 17, 1992), the secretary-general of the United Nations (UN) delineated four main "areas of action" for the UN in peace activities: preventive diplomacy, peacemaking, peacekeeping, and post-conflict peacebuilding. Preventive diplomacy aims to keep any sort of dispute or violence from arising. Peacemaking negotiates between states or other bodies that are already in an adversarial relationship, while peacekeeping consists of UN forces (which may not necessarily be military) actually positioned and active in a given location. Post-conflict peacebuilding acts as a follow-up to peacemaking and peacekeeping to strengthen institutions such as law enforcement and judicial systems, in order to ensure a lasting peace. In addition, the U.S. executive branch uses the term "peace operations," and in DOD terminology, peacekeeping falls under "operations other than war." For the sake of simplicity, this section will generally refer to all of these activities as "peacekeeping."

According to a December 2001 U.S. General Accounting Office (GAO) report (*United Nations Peacekeeping: Issues for Congress*), there is a "second generation" of peacekeeping missions coming into existence. These missions include "disarming or seizing weapons, aggressively protecting humanitarian assistance, and clearing land mines," along with "maintaining law and order (police), election monitoring, and human rights monitoring." This second generation of peacekeeping has overtaken first-generation peacekeeping missions, which involved monitoring cease-fires, reporting on situations, and, in some cases, intervention with limited means and resources.

Organizations Coordinating Peacekeeping Missions

UNITED NATIONS (UN). The UN is a multinational body that is most often associated with peacekeeping missions. As the GAO report *U.N. Peacekeeping: Status of Long-Standing Operations and U.S. Interests in Supporting Them* (April 1997) explains, under the auspices of the UN Security

TABLE 8.1

Ongoing United Nations peacekeeping missions as of June 30, 2002

Operation Name	Acronym	Location	Number of UN personnel	Number of U.S. personnel	Start date of action
United Nations Trace Supervision Organization	UNTSO	Middle East	143	2	June 1948
United Nations Military Observer Group in India and Pakistan	UNMOGIP	India-Pakistan (Asia)	44	0	January 1949
United Nations Peacekeeping Force in Cyprus	UNFICYP	Cyprus (Europe)	1,242	0	March 1964
United Nations Disengagement Observer Force	UNDOF	Golan Heights (Middle East)	1,003	0	June 1974
United Nations Interim Force in Lebanon	UNIFIL	Lebanon (Middle East)	3,629	0	March 1978
United Nations Iraq-Kuwait Observation Mission	UNIKOM	Iraq/Kuwait (Middle East)	1,098	12	April 1991
United Nations Mission for the Referendum in Western Sahara	MINURSO	Western Sahara (Africa)	243	7	April 1991
United Nations Observer Mission in Georgia	UNOMIG	Georgia (Europe)	106	2	August 1993
United Nations Mission in Bosnia and Herzegovina	UNMIBH	Bosnia and Herzegovina (Europe)	1,530	46	December 1995
United Nations Mission of Observers in Prevlaka	UNMOP	Prevlaka Peninsula (Europe)	27	0	February 1996
United Nations Interim Administration Mission in Kosovo	UNMIK	Kosovo (Europe)	4,548	537	June 1999
United Nations Mission in Sierra Leone	UNAMSIL	Sierra Leone (Africa)	17,484	0	October 1999
United Nations Organization Mission in the Democratic Republic of Congo	MONUC	Democratic Republic of the Congo (Africa)	4,233	0	December 1999
United Nations Mission in Ethiopia and Eritrea	UNMEE	Ethiopia and Eritrea (Africa)	4,152	7	July 2000
United Nations Mission of Support in East Timor	UNMISET	East Timor (Asia)	5,847	67	May 2002

SOURCE: Prepared by Information Plus staff from United Nations data

Council (led by permanent members the United States, China, France, Russia, and the United Kingdom),

the United Nations undertakes peacekeeping operations to help maintain or restore peace and security in areas of conflict. Such operations have been employed most commonly to supervise and maintain cease-fires, assist in troop withdrawals, and provide buffer zones between opposing forces. The main objective of peacekeeping operations, according to UN and U.S. policies, is to reduce tensions and provide a limited period of time for diplomatic efforts to achieve just and lasting settlements of the underlying conflicts.

Conditions of UN peacekeeping missions are generally set by the Security Council. Missions must have the consent of the parties in conflict and the host government, which also must provide complete freedom of movement to UN personnel. UN members provide the voluntary peacekeeping personnel, usually consisting of personnel from some or all of the nations in the UN. The missions do not interfere in the host government's internal affairs and try to avoid the use of force to carry out their objectives.

Between 1948 and June 1, 2002, the UN had been involved in 55 peacekeeping efforts around the globe, 15 of which were still ongoing (see Table 8.1 for statistics about the ongoing missions). Through April 1997 the UN had spent a total of $17 billion on peacekeeping operations, while individual year totals were $907 million in 1998 and $1.1 billion in 1999. Examples of the types of actions taken during UN peacekeeping missions include enforcing cease-fires, improving living conditions for minority groups, observing and verifying national elections, disarming warring factions, assisting in the formation of unified national governments, assisting legitimate governments in reestablishing their authority, working for the release of political prisoners and detainees, and assisting with refugee repatriation.

The total number of UN contributors to the 15 ongoing missions as of June 2002 was 45,329, but only 680 of these (about 1.5 percent) were Americans (see Table 8.1); the United States ranked 16th in the total number of participating UN peacekeeping forces among countries worldwide. In contrast, the five largest suppliers of contributors were Bangladesh (with 5,450 participants), Pakistan (4,817), Nigeria (3,451), India (3,022), and Ghana (2,489). Between them, these five countries comprised over 40 percent of the total UN peacekeeping force worldwide in mid-2002.

THE NORTH ATLANTIC TREATY ORGANIZATION (NATO) IN THE BALKANS. The North Atlantic Treaty Organization (NATO) is another organization that has been taking on peacekeeping operations around the world. This is an expansion of NATO's original mandate, which was much more defense-oriented. A September 2000 NATO fact sheet ("What Is NATO?") explains the change in focus: "following the momentous changes which occurred in Europe in the 1990s, [NATO] has become a catalyst for extending security and stability throughout Europe." Two of its most high-profile peacekeeping missions have been the Stabilization Force in Bosnia and Herzegovina (SFOR) and the Kosovo Force (KFOR).

SFOR, which began in December 1995, marked the first time NATO had really played a leading role in peacekeeping. The current SFOR mission, according to the NATO factsheet "Bosnia and Herzegovina—Facts and Figures" (March 8, 2001), "is related to the maintenance of a secure environment conducive to civil and political reconstruction." Some of the programs SFOR is implementing or assisting with include the collection and destruction of unregistered weapons, the investigation and apprehension of war criminals, assisting in the processing of property claims of returning refugees and displaced persons, maintaining and repairing roads to ensure freedom of movement, and both participating in the removal of mines and training others to do so.

According to a GAO report called *Balkans Security: Current and Projected Factors Affecting Regional Stability,* in January 2000 there were a total of 24,300 NATO-led forces in SFOR, 5,400 of whom were American. The number of personnel in the SFOR operation has been steadily dropping: a May 10, 2002, NATO press release listed the total number of participating troops at about 19,000, and explained that by the end of 2002, there were expected to be only 12,000 total personnel in the operation. In line with President George W. Bush's desire to reduce the U.S. presence in the Balkans, the number of U.S. troops has also dropped from the 5,400 there in January 2000; it stood at 3,132 as of November 1, 2001 (*Peacekeeping: Issues of U.S. Military Involvement,* GAO, Washington, DC, November 1, 2001).

The KFOR operation began after NATO air strikes designed to end the conflict between Serbian forces and Kosovar ethnic Albanians. In January 2000, according to *Balkans Security,* KFOR had a total of 45,700 military personnel, 7,000 of whom represented the United States. As with SFOR, the number of participants in KFOR has been steadily dropping: As of May 2002 KFOR consisted of about 38,000 military personnel from 39 countries, and by the end of 2002 the total number of KFOR personnel was projected to be 33,200. As with SFOR, U.S. personnel numbers have fallen to a November 1, 2001, estimate in *Peacekeeping: Issues of U.S. Military Involvement* of 6,515. More than half of KFOR's manpower is dedicated to the protection of Serbs and other ethnic minorities, many of whom are refugees now returning to their homes. The KFOR force is also collecting and destroying weapons and helping establish a local civil emergency force, among other activities.

The Debate About U.S. Involvement in Peacekeeping Missions

Peacekeeping is a topic of frequent and vehement debate among American politicians, military leaders, and citizens. Some people believe that the United States should maintain a policy of noninvolvement and refuse to get drawn into conflicts that do not directly involve U.S. interests. Others argue that the stability of the entire world does, in fact, directly relate to U.S. national security, so peacekeeping in distant nations is in our own best interests.

Other arguments center around the role of the United States in the community of nations. Some people suggest that since the United States is the leading superpower in the world, it should set an example for other nations by taking a leading role in peacekeeping operations. In addition, participating in peacekeeping operations with other nations can give the United States an idea, before a conflict breaks out, as to how its allies will perform in battlefield situations. According to former Secretary of Defense William S. Cohen (in "Creating an Environment for Peace, Stability, Confidence," *U.S. Foreign Policy Agenda,* December 1999), peacetime military cooperation can also "yield increased levels of trust, confidence-building, and rapport that far outlive any operation. . . . In the Department of Defense, we refer to them as 'force multipliers,' and they can make substantial contributions to success during times of war."

Others argue, as John Hillen, a former Army officer, does in an article in *NATO Review* (Summer 2001), that "superpowers don't do windows." In other words, America's strength is "large-scale war-fighting," and it should take a leadership role in that capacity, allowing other nations to take larger roles in peacekeeping operations.

A February 2002 report from the Peace Through Law Education Fund (*A Force for Peace and Security: U.S. and Allied Commanders' Views of the Military's Role in Peace Operations and the Impact on Terrorism of States in Conflict*) reports the results of interviews with more than 30 American and allied generals about peacekeeping. They found that, generally, the commanders agreed that participation in peacekeeping is "in our national interests and will be a key ingredient in the war against terrorism." (Terrorists often thrive in countries without strong police and judicial systems, feeding off of organized crime networks to distribute materials and cash. As peacekeeping missions strengthen law enforcement institutions, those areas become less and less appealing to terrorists.) The United States needs to be heavily involved in peacekeeping, as does the UN. The military leaders generally agreed that peacekeeping missions teach leadership and other valuable skills—including skills useful in the war against terrorism—to participating troops.

U.S. INTERESTS IN UN PEACEKEEPING MISSIONS. The 1997 GAO report *U.N. Peacekeeping: Status of Long-Standing Operations and U.S. Interests in Supporting Them* closely analyzed U.S. participation in the eight UN peacekeeping missions that were then ongoing and more than five years old. Two of these dated back to the 1940s. Summarizing the results of its analysis, the report states:

> Despite the long-standing operations' cost and mixed performance in carrying out their mandates, U.S. policymakers support continuing these operations because, in their view, they help to stabilize conflicts that could threaten U.S. foreign policy objectives. In their judgment, ending these operations—or even modifying them substantially—would risk renewed conflict and damage future peacemaking efforts.

The report goes on to explain that the costs of potential conflicts in strategically important areas, including the Middle East, the Persian Gulf, southern Europe, southern Africa, and southwest Asia, would be greater than the costs of maintaining the peacekeeping missions. Operations in the Middle East reduce tensions and keep Israel secure, both of which help keep the possibility of a peace settlement between Israel and the Palestinians alive. The Persian Gulf operations safeguard oil reserves and impede aggression from Iraq. Southern European operations maintain peace and stability in all of Europe. Therefore, the report concludes, while UN peacekeeping operations are by no means ideal, there are no better substitutes.

Yet debates surrounding peacekeeping missions are always present. Whether a current presidential administration is more focused on engaging the international community or maintaining an isolationist stance, U.S. relations with the outside world are directly pertinent to any peacekeeping involvement. Many in the American public question the necessity of sending their troops abroad and getting soldiers killed in battles that have no importance (or consequence) to national security interests. In recent years, such sentiments were especially noticeable after 18 U.S. soldiers were killed and 84 more wounded while enforcing Operation Restore Hope in Mogadishu, Somalia, in 1993. The losses suffered in Somalia led the American public to question the importance of fighting wars for others and continued support for UN operations. It was also a significant factor in American lack of intervention while ethnic massacres were being carried out in Rwanda in the mid-1990s.

In 1994, President Bill Clinton signed Presidential Decision Directive 25, which reviewed the U.S. relationship with international peacekeeping operations. The directive specifically focused on six main issues:

1) Thoroughly analyzing and making concise and coherent decisions about which peacekeeping missions American troops will be committed to;

2) Reducing U.S. costs for all UN peacekeeping operations;

3) Clearly identifying the command and control of U.S. troops in such a multinational situation;

4) Improving the UN's ability to manage peacekeeping operations;

5) Improving American management of peacekeeping operations (including leaving the State Department as the lead agency to fund and manage such endeavors;

6) Ensuring better cooperation between the White House, Capitol Hill, and the American public when dealing with such issues.

THE NATIONAL SECURITY STRATEGY AND PEACE-KEEPING IN THE BALKANS. *A National Security Strategy for a New Century* (White House, Washington, DC, December 1999) outlines some of the reasons the United States participates in peacekeeping missions. The GAO's *Balkans Security* applies these reasons specifically to SFOR and KFOR. According to the National Security Strategy, national interests can either be classified as vital, important, or humanitarian. Vital interests are those that are "of broad, overriding importance to the survival, safety, and vitality of the United States," while important interests are those that "do not affect the survival of the United States but do affect national well-being and the character of the world in which Americans live." Humanitarian interests that might merit U.S. military involvement include "(1) natural and manmade disasters; (2) promoting human rights and seeking to halt gross violations of those rights; and (3) supporting democratization, adherence to the rule of law, and civilian control of the military."

Peacekeeping missions can fall into any of these three categories. Vital interests include such things as the security of Europe, which might be threatened by instability in Bosnia/Herzegovina and Kosovo. Thus, the United States has an interest in participating in NATO's KFOR and SFOR operations. Vital interests, as listed in the National Security Strategy, specifically include NATO's operations in the Balkans. Humanitarian interests may be less specific and harder to pin down. They are not specifically listed in the National Security Strategy as reasons for participating in peacekeeping in the Balkans, but many U.S. government officials have informally mentioned humanitarian interests as a reason for involvement in SFOR and KFOR.

The Costs of Peacekeeping

MONETARY COST OF MISSIONS. One factor that plays a large role in the debate about peacekeeping missions is their cost. According to *Allied Contributions to the Common Defense: A Report to the United States Congress by the Secretary of Defense* (March 2001), the United States spent $220.1 billion on UN peace operations in 1999. This represented a 2.9 percent increase from 1998 spending, but an 80 percent drop from 1994's funding level of $1.1 trillion. Table 8.2 breaks down direct and indirect costs by mission for the fiscal years 1996–2001.

According to DOD estimates, the United States provided 30 percent of all funding for UN peace operations in 1999 (this does not count NATO operations such as SFOR and KFOR). But when international contributions are analyzed as a percentage of the various participating nations' gross domestic product (GDP), the United States ranks 16th in the world, donating 0.0022 percent of its GDP to peace operations. The countries that rank highest are Japan (0.0055 percent), Qatar (0.0041 percent), Italy (0.0037 percent), Spain (0.0036 percent), and Belgium (0.0033 percent).

Another issue with UN peacekeeping missions and finances is that the United States is in arrears in its

TABLE 8.2

Direct and indirect contributions to U.N. peacekeeping operations by mission, 1996–2001

U.N. peacekeeping operation	Duration	Indirect U.S. contributions by U.S. agencies (if any)	U.S. contributions (Constant fiscal year 2001 dollars in thousands)		
			Direct	Indirect	Total
Traditional peacekeeping operations					
U.N. Truce Supervision Organization in Palestine (Israel, Egypt, Lebanon, Syria, Jordan) (UNTSO)	June 1948 -	DOD: Military observer cost-of-living allowances	$ 37,990	$82	**$38,072**
U.N. Military Observer Group in India and Pakistan (UNMOGIP)	Jan. 1949 -	None	10,834	0	**10,834**
U.N. Disengagement Observer Force (Syrian Golan Heights) (UNDOF)	June 1974 -	None	47,753	0	**47,753**
U.N. Peacekeeping Force in Cyprus (UNFICYP)	Mar. 1964 -	USAID: Bicommunal humanitarian programs	35,034	46,935	**81,969**
U.N. Interim Force in Lebanon (UNIFIL)	Mar. 1978 -	State: Support for Israel-Lebanon border monitoring group DOD: Demining training	213,379	8,961	**222,340**
U.N. Mission of Observers in Prevlaka (Croatia)[1] (UNMOP)	Jan. 1996 -	None	[2]	0	**0**
U.N. Iraq-Kuwait Observation Mission (UNIKOM)	Apr. 1991-	DOD: Military exercises and operations to deter Iraqi aggression	25,891	5,807,153	**5,833,044**
U.N. Observer Mission in Georgia (UNOMIG)	Aug. 1993 -	USAID: Food aid State: Military education and training DOD: Demining training	31,028	91,085	**122,113**
U.N. Mission in Ethiopia and Eritrea (UNMEE)	July 2000 -	USAID: Border development program State: Military education and training, demining	71,300	3,705	**75,005**
U.N. Confidence Restoration Operation (Croatia) (UNCRO)	Mar. 1995- Jan. 1996	None	[3]	[3]	**0**
U.N. Preventive Deployment Force (Macedonia) (UNPREDEP)	Mar. 1995- Feb. 1999	DOD: Support for U.S. forces serving with U.N. peacekeeping operation	41,002	91,055	**132,057**
U.N. Verification Mission in Guatemala (MINUGUA)[4]	Jan.-May 1997	None	1,073	0	**1,073**
U.N. Observer Mission in Sierra Leone (UNOMSIL)	July 1998- Oct. 1999	DOD and State: Equipment and services for African peacekeeping forces	4,258	21,457	**25,715**
U.N. Mission of Observers in Tajikistan (UNMOT)	Dec. 1994- May 2000	State: Refugee assistance USAID: Food aid for refugees	14,828	33,433	**48,261**
Subtotal for traditional operations			**$534,370**	**$6,103,866**	**$6,638,236**
Multidimensional peacekeeping operations					
U.N. Mission for the Referendum in Western Sahara[5] (Morocco) (MINURSO)	Apr. 1991 -	None	25,429	0	**25,429**
U.N. Mission in Bosnia and Herzegovina (UNMIBH)	Dec. 1995 -	DOD: Troops for NATO-led coalition enforcing military provisions of the peace agreement State: Police and judicial training, demining Justice: Police and judicial training	323,516	11,680,585	**12,004,101**

TABLE 8.2

Direct and indirect contributions to U.N. peacekeeping operations by mission, 1996–2001 [CONTINUED]

U.N. peacekeeping operation	Duration	Indirect U.S. contributions by U.S. agencies (if any)	U.S. contributions (Constant fiscal year 2001 dollars in thousands)		
			Direct	Indirect	Total
Multidimensional peacekeeping operations					
U.N. Mission in Sierra Leone (UNAMSIL)	Oct. 1999 -	DOD and State: Support and training for African peacekeeping forces USAID: Food aid	278,698	221,692	**500,390**
U.N. Organization Mission in the Democratic Republic of the Congo (MONUC)	Dec. 1999 -	USAID: Emergency assistance and food aid Agriculture: Food donations	117,262	129,071	**246,333**
U.N. Protection Force (Bosnia, Croatia, Macedonia) (UNPROFOR)	Feb. 1992- Jan. 1996	DOD: Aircraft maintain no-fly zone over Bosnia	78,932	6	**78,932**
U.N. Transitional Administration for E. Slavonia, Baranja, and W. Sirmium (Croatia) (UNTAES)	Jan. 1996- Jan.1998	State: Refugee assistance and police training	66,706	15,983	**82,689**
U.N. Civilian Police Support Group (Croatia) (UNPSG)	Jan.-Oct. 1998				
U.N. Observer Mission in Liberia (UNOMIL)	Sep. 1993- Sep. 1997	USAID: Food aid and disaster relief DOD and State: Support for African peacekeeping forces	12,259	276,657	**288,916**
U.N. Assistance Mission for Rwanda (UNAMIR)	Oct. 1993- Mar. 1997	USAID: Food aid DOD: Support for demining State: Refugee assistance	15,507	140,838	**156,345**
U.N. Angola Verification Mission III (UNAVEM III)	Feb. 1995- Jun. 1997	USAID: Food aid, combatant retraining,	184,949	307,068	**492,017**
U.N. Observer Mission in Angola (MONUA)	June 1997- Feb. 1999	State: Refugee assistance and demining			
U.N. Mission in the Central African Republic (MINURCA)	Apr. 1998- Feb. 2000	State: Military education and training USAID: Food aid	0	968	**968**
U.N. Mission in Haiti (UNMIH)	Sep. 1993- Feb. 1996	DOD: Support for U.S. forces serving with U.N. peacekeepers State and DOD: Support for the national police	75,488	216,490	**291,978**
U.N. Support Mission in Haiti (UNSMIH)	July 1996- July 1997				
U.N. Transition Mission in Haiti (UNTMIH)	Aug.-Nov. 1997				
U.N. Civilian Police Mission in Haiti (MIPONUH)	Dec.1997- Mar. 2000				
U.N. Mission in East Timor (UNAMET)	June–Oct. 1999	DOD: support for international coalition forces State: Support for civilian police monitors USAID: transition assistance	2,141	19,575	**21,716**
Subtotal for multidimensional operations			**$1,180,887**	**$13,008,927**	**$14,189,814**

payments to the UN's peacekeeping accounts. As of December 31, 2000, the United States owed the UN more than $1.1 billion. This is due in large part to the fact that throughout the 1990s and early 21st century, the United States has paid less to the UN than the UN has assessed it owed. The United States actively sought a reduction in the level of fees it owed, which was finally granted by the UN in December 2000. Congress is currently involved in debates on exactly how, and how much of, the arrearage

will be paid. Table 8.3 shows the amount allocated by the United States for each UN peacekeeping operation for 2000, along with estimates for 2001 and 2002.

In regards to the NATO missions in Kosovo and Bosnia/Herzegovina, Table 8.4 shows estimates of U.S. funding for stabilization measures (including air strikes) in Bosnia and Kosovo. While not all this funding may be directly related to SFOR and KFOR, the numbers do

TABLE 8.2

Direct and indirect contributions to U.N. peacekeeping operations by mission, 1996–2001 [CONTINUED]

U.N. peacekeeping operation	Duration	Indirect U.S. contributions by U.S. agencies (if any)	U.S. contributions (Constant fiscal year 2001 dollars in thousands)		
			Direct	Indirect	Total
Nation-Building peacekeeping operations					
U.N. Interim Administration Mission in Kosovo (UNMIK)	June 1999 -	U.S. Agencies DOD: Troops for NATO-led coalition enforcing provisions of cease-fire and withdrawal agreements, public security, and assistance for local civilian protection units State: Refugee and economic assistance Agriculture: Food donations USAID: Refugee and development assistance Justice: Police and judicial training Treasury/Commerce: Technical assistance	446,175	4,833,670	**5,279,845**
U.N. Transitional Administration in East Timor (UNTAET)	Oct.1999 -	U.S. Agencies DOD: Humanitarian and civic assistance State: Support for U.N. administration and law enforcement USAID: Food aid, refugee assistance, and democracy building Justice: Police and judicial training	316,659	208,586	**525,245**
Subtotal for nation-building operations			**$762,834**	**$5,042,256**	**$5,805,090**
Total contributions for operations			**$2,478,091**	**$24,155,049**	**$26,633,140**
Assessments appropriated by the Congress for U.N. peacekeeping operations but not sent to the United Nations as of January 31, 2002			126,620	0	126,620
U.N. arrearage payments			847,830	0	847,830
Support for U.N. Rapidly Deployable Mission Headquarters			215	0	215
U.S. Military Observer Group overhead			0	7,105	7,105
Grand total[7]			**$3,452,755**	**$24,162,166**	**$27,614,921**

[1]This operation is located in an area of disputed ownership between Croatia and the Federal Republic of Yugoslavia (Serbia and Montenegro).
[2]Direct costs are included in UNMIBH.
[3]Direct and indirect costs for UNCRO are combined with costs for UNTAES.
[4]The U.N. mission was part of a larger non-U.N. regional peace operation with the same acronym.
[5]Morocco, Mauritania, and a local independence group dispute the ownership of this territory.
[6]Indirect costs are included in UNMIBH.
[7]Totals are adjusted to account for rounding errors.

SOURCE: "Table 2: U.S. Direct and Indirect Contributions to U.N. Peacekeeping Operations by Mission, Fiscal Years 1996–2001," in *U.N. Peacekeeping: Estimated U.S. Contributions, Fiscal Years 1996–2001,* GAO-02-294, U.S. General Accounting Office, Washington, DC, February 2002

demonstrate the importance the United States has placed on regional stability in this region of Europe over the last decade.

CONTRIBUTING PERSONNEL. Manpower is another of the concerns surrounding peacekeeping missions. Peacekeeping missions, despite their name, often take place in volatile locations, with the personal safety of the peacekeeping force often as at risk as that of actual combat troops. In UN peacekeeping operations, for example, 1,769 people have died since 1948. The total number of deaths of UN peacekeeping forces for recent years are: 50 fatalities in 2000; 64 in 2001; and 31 in the first six months of 2002 (January 1 through June 30).

According to *Allied Contributions to the Common Defense,* the United States contributed 11,138 people to UN and major non-UN peace operations in 2000. This

TABLE 8.3

U.N. peacekeeping assessed contributions, fiscal year 2000 allocations and fiscal years 2001–02 requests

(In millions of dollars)

Operation	FY2000 Allocations	FY2001 Request	FY2001 Estimates	FY2002 Request
U.N. Disengagement Observer Force (UNDOF)	7.567	17.800	10.221	10.435
U.N. Interim Force in Lebanon (UNIFIL)	31.803	37.000	63.521	24.963
U.N. Iraq-Kuwait Observation Mission (UNIKOM)	4.274	4.500	5.584	5.336
U.N. Angola Verification Mission III (UNAVEM III)/ U.N. Observer Mission in Angola (MONUA)	1.902	1.000	–	–
U.N. Mission for the Referendum in Western Sahara (MINURSO)	–	13.000	13.526	13.472
U.N. Mission in Bosnia and Herzegovina (Includes Intl. Police Task Force (IPTF)) (UNMIBH)/ U.N. Mission of Observers in the Prevlaka (UNMOP)	16.042	45.000	64.241	29.572
U.N. Interim Administration Mission in Kosovo (UNMIK)	95.131	138.000	186.545	122.850
U.N. Peacekeeping Force in Cyprus (UNFICYP)	5.874	6.500	6.416	6.709
U.N. Observer Mission in Georgia (UNOMIG)	7.327	7.800	9.036	8.203
U.N. Mission of Observers in Tajikistan (UNMOT)	2.339	4.600	–	–
U.N. Observer Mission in Sierra Leone (UNOMSIL)/ U.N. Mission in Sierra Leone (UNAMSIL)	128.083	118.000	180.367	318.000
United Nations Mission in East Timor (UNAMET)/ U.N. Transitional Administration in East Timor (UNTAET)	145.099	186.000	189.676	130.415
U.N. Observer Mission in the Democratic Republic of the Congo (MONUC)	30.240	94.466	5.286	83.550
U.N. Mission in Ethiopia and Eritrea (UNMEE)	–	29.000	84.241	57.269
Subtotals	**475.681**	**702.000**	**818.660**	**810.774**
War crimes tribunals	22.419	36.000	25.479	33.365
TOTALS	**498.100**	**738.666**	**844.139**	**844.139**

SOURCE: Adapted from Marjorie Ann Browne, "Table 2. U.N. Peacekeeping-Assessed Contributions FY2000 Allocations and FY2001 and FY2002 Requests," in *United Nations Peacekeeping: Issues for Congress,* Congressional Research Service, Washington, DC, December 4, 2001

TABLE 8.4

Estimated costs of U.S. operations in Bosnia and Kosovo, fiscal years 1992–2000

Dollars in millions

Country	1992	1993	1994	1995	1996	1997	1998	1999	2000	Total
Bosnia										
DOD[1]	$6	$139	$292	$347	$2,520	$2,283	$1,963	$1,538[2]	$1,603	**$10,691**
Civilian agencies	[3]	[3]	[3]	[3]	560[4]	500[4]	301	295	211	**1,867**
Subtotal	6	139	292	347	3,080	2,783	2,264	1,833	1,814	**12,558**
Kosovo										
DOD	0	0	0	0	0	0	0	3,000[5]	2,025	**5,025**
Civilian agencies	[3]	[3]	[3]	[3]	[6]	[6]	34[7]	256	302	**592**
Subtotal	0	0	0	0	0	0	34	3,256	2,327	**5,617**
Total	$6	$139	$292	$347	$3080	$2,783	$2,298	$5,089	$4,141	**$18,175**

[1]DOD costs from 1992 to 1995 include support for humanitarian airdrops over Bosnia, operation of a hospital in Croatia, the airlift of food and supplies to Sarajevo, enforcing a no-fly zone over Bosnia, and airstrikes in Bosnia but do not include munitions expended in these operations. DOD costs from 1996 to 1998 include over $40 million spent on U.S. participation in a U.N. peacekeeping operation in Macedonia.
[2]DOD's cumulative incremental costs as of September 1999 include Operation Joint Forge and Operation Deliberate Forge.
[3]Civilian costs from 1992 to 1995 include funding from the State Department, the U.S. Agency for International Development, and the Departments of Transportation and Treasury for the former Yugoslavia as a whole and are not delineated by country.
[4]This figure represents the State Department's cost estimate as of 1996. It includes costs for the U.S. Agency for International Development, the U.S. Information Agency, and the Departments of State, Agriculture, Commerce, Justice, and the Treasury.
[5]DOD's cumulative incremental costs as of September 1999 include Operations Balkan Calm, Joint Guardian, Allied Force, Eagle Eye, and Sustain Hope.
[6]Assistance in fiscal year 1996 and fiscal year 1997 is included in a U.S. Agency for International Development estimate of total assistance to the Balkans.
[7]Figure includes civilian agency costs for all of the Federal Republic of Yugoslavia, the bulk of which was dedicated to U.S. programs in Kosovo.

SOURCE: "Table 1: Estimated Costs of U.S. Operations in Bosnia and Kosovo, Fiscal Years 1992 Through 2000," in *Balkans Security: Current and Projected Factors Affecting Regional Stability,* U.S. General Accounting Office, Washington, DC, April 2000

was 6.8 percent fewer than were contributed in 1999, but it was still by far the largest number contributed by any country and made up about 18 percent of the total worldwide peace operation force. U.S. peacekeepers totaled 0.0001 percent of the U.S. labor force. When this peacekeepers-to-labor-force ratio is compared with that of other countries around the world, the United States ranks 19th. The nations providing the highest percentages of their labor force to peace operations in 2000 were United Arab Emirates (with 0.0008 percent), Norway (with 0.0005 percent), Greece (with 0.0005 percent), Denmark (with 0.0004 percent), and Italy (with 0.0004 percent).

POSSIBLE DETERIORATION OF COMBAT READINESS. According to *Peacekeeping: Issues of U.S. Military Involvement,* "The [George W.] Bush Administration's desire to reduce the commitment of U.S. troops to international peacekeeping stems largely from the major concerns of recent Congresses: that peacekeeping duties are detrimental to military 'readiness'; i.e., the ability of U.S. troops to defend the nations." Proponents of this argument note that military training teaches troops to be fighters, while peacekeeping skills are better learned through a law enforcement background. In addition, some argue, military action requires quick, decisive force, while peacekeeping generally calls for restraint. Can a soldier be both a good fighter and a good peacemaker?

Increasingly, many answer yes. As noted earlier, peacekeeping missions inherently require military skills to allow a quick and appropriate response to unforeseen risks. In addition, peacekeeping proponents argue, if the purpose of peacekeeping is to prevent conflict, who better to deter conflicts from starting than well-trained soldiers?

The demands of peacekeeping, though, definitely differ from those of actual combat participation. While troops engaged in peacekeeping activities may be able to expand their skills in such areas as intelligence, leadership, logistics, transportation, and engineering, according to some critics their skills in more combat-oriented arenas, such as shooting, combined arms skills, and unit maneuverability, may degrade. *Peacekeeping: Issues of U.S. Military Involvement* points out that many efforts are now being made to provide peacekeepers with ongoing combat training to reduce this deterioration. According to Christopher Bellamy, professor of military science and doctrine at Cranfield University in the United Kingdom, local populations respond best to peacekeeping troops who are "also unmistakably professional soldiers," but not too "heavy-handed" (*NATO Review,* Summer 2001).

CHAPTER 9

GLOBAL DYNAMICS OF NATIONAL SECURITY: ALLIANCES AND RESOURCES

Interdependence is one of the key words of foreign policy in the post–Cold War era. States are increasingly relying on each other, as well as nongovernmental and multinational entities, to accomplish their stated political and economic goals. Interdependence is a complicated phenomenon, because it does not rely on ideological loyalties, as the Communist and Democratic blocs each did during the Cold War. Ideologies are now being replaced by motivations like money and regional dominance in interstate alliances.

ALLIANCES

The United States faces a unique set of threats from different parts of the globe and continues to make alliances to suit its tactical and strategic national security goals. Such alliances are usually formal agreements that two or more entities enter into in order to defend their collective security goals. Some of the key allies for the United States in the new world order include the European nations (primarily the United Kingdom), Israel, and certain Persian Gulf states in the Middle East.

Since World War II (1939–45), the United States has signed a number of treaties assuring protection to states that needed military assistance, often to fight the Communist threat. However, members of the U.S. legislature have always been hesitant about committing U.S. resources for long periods of time. Besides formal alliances that have to be ratified by the U.S. Senate, the president can also enter into executive agreements that commit U.S. resources internationally but do not have to be ratified by the Senate, which gives the president greater flexibility in foreign affairs. Such agreements are usually initiated at the executive level of government, and terms are negotiated by a representative. The secretary of state authorizes the negotiator to sign the agreement. The Senate needs to be notified by the executive branch within 60 days of signing an executive agreement, and to be implemented it requires a

simple majority vote of the House and Senate. Many agreements require implementing bills to be passed by both chambers before they can take force. Congress can express its opposition to any particular executive agreement by withholding the necessary implementing legislation. The president's authority to negotiate executive agreements flows from two sources: the power granted to him or her in the Constitution as chief executive, and/or specific powers delegated to him or her by earlier acts of Congress. Instances of presidential initiatives involve the 1991 Persian Gulf War coalition, support for anti-Vietnam forces in Kampuchea, and aiding the Mujahideen in Afghanistan during the 1980s.

It is worth noting that often U.S. policymakers have to deal with states that are not necessarily considered close allies in any ideological sense. This would include authoritarian regimes and dictatorships that are not democratic in nature and that may even (intentionally or unintentionally) support anti-U.S. entities. However, support from countries like these (for example, Saudi Arabia and Kuwait) might be useful for America in terms of strategic regional goals or commercial interests (for example, oil). The United States also supported various substate groups opposing their respective governing bodies in Central America and the Caribbean (such as El Salvador, Chile, Nicaragua, and Haiti) and Africa during the 1980s. Mixed public reaction to actions such as these clearly demonstrates that national security is pursued through a variety of channels and that security agendas are not necessarily always clear-cut.

Currently, the United States pursues its national security agenda through international organizations, as well as state-level ties with allies and other countries. It must be kept in mind that any alliance entered into by a state or states requires certain commitments on behalf of all parties involved. These obligations can potentially constrain the American ability to shift policies and make some decisions. Thus it is extremely important for the United States to consider the flexibility of any commitment it makes, as the national security environment is constantly changing. Also worth noting is that most security commitments are designed to be honored by each succeeding U.S. administration, unless major changes in the security environment have occurred.

UNITED NATIONS (UN)

The United Nations (UN) is one of the leading players in the international arena and deals with a host of subjects, ranging from human rights to weapons of mass destruction (WMD) nonproliferation. The multinational organization can trace its roots back to the days immediately following World War II. At a conference in Yalta, in the Crimea (then part of the Soviet Union), in 1945, the leaders of the United Kingdom, the United States, and the Soviet Union decided that the UN was to be an international entity, with five permanent powers in its Security Council: China, France, the Soviet Union, the United States, and the United Kingdom. Each of these countries had the authority to veto a resolution from the General Assembly.

Creation of the UN was finalized at the San Francisco conference that same year, when the charter of the organization was signed and ratified by several countries. The UN charter sets forth the organization's rights and obligations and establishes its procedures. According to the UN Web site (http://www.un.org), the primary functions of the UN "are to maintain international peace and security; to develop friendly relations among nations; to cooperate in solving international economic, social, cultural and humanitarian problems and in promoting respect for human rights and fundamental freedoms; and to be a centre for harmonizing the actions of nations in attaining these ends."

For 2000–01 the budget for the UN stood at over $2.5 billion, which was primarily raised by contributions of member countries. Each individual contribution is determined by the capability of a country, measured through its gross national product. In addition to membership fees, countries are also assessed for peacekeeping operations' costs, which added up to approximately $2 billion in 2000.

According to its various functions, the UN is divided into six principal organs:

1) The General Assembly is the legislative arm of the UN and is broken down into six committees: Disarmament and International Security; Economic and Financial; Social, Humanitarian and Cultural Issues; Special Political and Decolonization; Administrative and Budgetary; and Legal Matters.

2) The Security Council has 15 members: 10 elected by the General Assembly for two-year terms and 5 permanent members. Each member of the Security Coun-

cil has one vote. Decisions on procedural matters require at least 9 of the 15 members voting in favor; substantive issues require 9 positive votes, including one from each of the permanent members. There are two standing committees in the Security Council: one dealing with rules and procedures and another with admission of new members. There are also a number of ad hoc committees that are established as needed, as well as working groups on various issues.

3) The Economic and Social Council is responsible for promoting higher standards of living, employment, and economic and social progress around the world. It facilitates cultural and educational cooperation, deals with social and health problems, and encourages respect for global human rights and fundamental freedoms. The council coordinates the work of 14 specialized UN agencies, 10 functional commissions, and 5 regional commissions.

4) The Trusteeship Council was established to supervise and administer trust territories. These were independent nations, formerly part of Western colonial empires, for which the UN wished to aid their development toward full and effective self-governance. The council suspended its operations as of November 1994, with the independence of Palau, the last remaining UN trust territory.

5) The International Court of Justice, headquartered in the Hague, Netherlands, is the principal judicial organ of the UN. The court is charged with settling legal disputes submitted to it by state parties, as well as giving advisory opinions on questions referred to it by international entities. It is composed of 15 judges, elected to nine-year terms by the General Assembly and the Security Council.

6) The Secretariat is composed of an international staff carrying out the day-to-day maintenance work of the organization. It is headed by the Secretary-General, who is appointed by the General Assembly for a five-year term.

THE NORTH ATLANTIC TREATY ORGANIZATION (NATO)

Shortly after World War II, on April 4, 1949, the United States and Canada signed the North Atlantic Treaty. This entered them into a political and military alliance with 10 European nations: Denmark, France, Iceland, Italy, Portugal, Norway, Great Britain, Belgium, the Netherlands, and Luxembourg. The North Atlantic Treaty Organization (NATO) was essentially created to protect Europe from potential Soviet aggression and create a balance of power between the Communist and Democratic states. In 1952 Greece and Turkey acceded to the treaty, followed by the Republic of Germany, which joined the alliance in 1955. In 1982 Spain became a member of NATO, and by 1999 member states also included the Czech Republic, Hungary, and Poland. At the Prague Summit in 2002, Bulgaria, Estonia, Latvia, Lithuania, Romania, Slovakia, and Slovenia were also invited to join the new, "transformed" NATO. The seven new countries are expected to join the organization by 2004.

NATO is primarily a multinational alliance, promoting collective defense while allowing states to maintain their individual sovereignty. According to the NATO handbook, NATO has the following fundamental tasks:

• It provides an indispensable foundation for a stable security environment in Europe, based on the growth of democratic institutions and commitment to the peaceful resolution of disputes. It seeks to create an environment in which no country would be able to intimidate or coerce any European nation or to impose hegemony (leadership or dominance of one state over another) through the threat or use of force.

• It serves as a transatlantic forum for allied consultations on any issues affecting the vital interests of its members, including developments that might pose risks to their security.

• It provides deterrence and defense against any form of aggression against the territory of any NATO member state.

• It preserves a strategic balance in Europe.

These security undertakings have gone through somewhat of a transformation in the past decade or so. With the collapse of the Soviet Union, NATO has had to redefine its security goals to fit the changing security environment. After the Prague Summit of 2002, it came up with a list of points that helped the organization shift its strategies to better fit the new millennium. The main highlights of the list, as posted on the NATO Web site, include:

• The NATO Response Force will be a technologically advanced, flexible, deployable, interoperable (able to operate between different branches and locations), and sustainable force including land, sea, and air elements ready to move quickly to wherever needed.

• NATO's command structure will be made leaner, more efficient, more effective, and more deployable, in order to meet the operational requirements for the full range of NATO missions. There will be two strategic commands: one operational (the strategic command for Operations in Europe) and one functional (the strategic command for Transformation in the United States).

• In the Prague Capabilities Commitment, individual allies have made firm and specific political commitments to improve their capabilities in areas key to modern military operations, such as strategic air-and-sea lift and air-to-ground surveillance.

• To defend against new threats like terrorism, five specific initiatives in the area of nuclear, biological, and chemical weapons defense were endorsed to enhance NATO's defense capabilities against such weapons. NATO's defense against cyberattacks will be strengthened, and a missile defense feasibility study will be initiated.

MIDDLE EAST: ISRAEL AND THE PERSIAN GULF

Israel

Preserving the security of the state of Israel while supporting the Arab-Israeli peace negotiations has been, and continues to be, an important policy for the United States. The United States has been a strong ally of Israel since the birth of the country, because of the two countries' shared political values, a historical relationship, and shared cultural and personal ties. Over time, the two states have also shared similar security threats, including Soviet aggression and, more recently, threats from radical Islamic fundamentalists and WMD.

The Persian Gulf and the Gulf Cooperation Council (GCC)

Perhaps one of the most significant regions for U.S. foreign policy is the Persian Gulf (also known as the Arabian Gulf). The only political and strategic bloc in the region is the Gulf Cooperation Council (GCC).

Both Iran and Iraq have always been heavyweights in the Persian Gulf region in terms of size, population, resources, and military capabilities. The Iranian Revolution in 1979, the subsequent oil crisis, and the Iran-Iraq war (1980–88) left many of the other Gulf states feeling vulnerable. On May 25, 1981, the State of Bahrain, State of Kuwait, Sultanate of Oman, State of Qatar, Kingdom of Saudi Arabia, and the United Arab Emirates met in Abu Dhabi in the United Arab Emirates to form an alliance known as the Cooperation Council for the Arab States of the Gulf, or the Gulf Cooperation Council (GCC). The six GCC countries are tied together by their religious, cultural, and social mores. The GCC is headquartered in Riyadh, Saudi Arabia, and holds meetings annually. The main bodies of the organization are the Supreme Council, the Ministerial General, and the Secretariat General.

The Peninsula Shield Force, created in 1982, was designed to increase the interoperability of GCC states' militaries, but its strength and validity were strongly questioned during the 1991 Gulf War. Interestingly, a defense pact was never mentioned in either the charter or the framework of the GCC. It is generally believed that the states specifically chose to omit the terms "defense alliance" or "military cooperation" in order not to upset Iran or Iraq.

Instead, the purpose of the GCC, as stated on its Web site (http://www.gcc-sg.org/index_e.html), is:

> [To bring about] inter-connection between Member States in all fields, strengthening ties between their peoples, formulating similar regulations in various fields such as economy, finance, trade, customs, tourism, legislation, administration, as well as fostering scientific and technical progress in industry, mining, agriculture, water and animal resources, establishing scientific research centers, setting up joint ventures, and encouraging cooperation of the private sector.

More recently, however, especially in the aftermath of the Iraqi invasion of Kuwait in the early 1990s, the GCC countries adopted a pact underlining the interconnectivity of their security. On December 31, 2000, at their annual meeting in Bahrain, the six countries resolved to come to each other's defense if necessary, stating that aggression against one meant aggression against all. Even though GCC states agreed to come to each other's aid in the face of aggression, this pact has yet to be ratified.

Overall, the GCC aims to strengthen its political, economic, and strategic position in the region. Its member states seek to alleviate economic and population problems and increase trade flow to the area. Commercial, social, and even political alliances cannot be achieved if there is strategic regional instability. As a consequence, increasing military cooperation and securing defensive capabilities are definitely priorities for the GCC.

U.S. INTERESTS IN THE GULF. Since the decline of British authority in the Persian Gulf in the early 1970s and the end of the Cold War in the early 1990s, the United States has played a strong role in the Persian Gulf theater. Its primary regional interests include protecting its national interests, protecting allies' security, and guarding the international oil supply.

The U.S. military is actively involved in providing deterrence in the region, as well as supporting UN Security Council resolutions dealing with Iraq. Under the umbrella of a coalition that includes France and Great Britain, the U.S. has pre-positioned military equipment and forward military presence all over the region. Pre-positioned equipment is that which is positioned in a tactically useful region for the sake of deterrence or for quick defense against any unforeseen threat in a nonhostile environment (a "just in case" scenario). Forward military presence refers to the presence of the U.S. military in various theaters/regions around the world (including the Persian Gulf) for a variety of reasons, including as training or in defense of U.S. or allied strategic interests.

In 2002 there were approximately 17,000–25,000 U.S. military personnel, along with numerous ships, carriers, and aircraft deployed in the Persian Gulf, though as talk of war with Iraq escalated in late 2002 and early 2003, these

numbers increased. The U.S. Naval Fifth Fleet is based in Bahrain and is primarily responsible for all naval activities in this theater. Protection of U.S. military personnel and infrastructure is one of America's top priorities.

GCC INTERESTS IN THE GULF. As of 2001 the cumulative strength of personnel in the GCC militaries (273,730) fell far short of Iraqi and Iranian totals, which stood at 513,000 and 424,600, respectively. In addition to the as-yet unratified interconnectivity pact and the Peninsula Shield Force, each of the GCC states relies heavily on the United States for military protection. Oman retains strong military ties with the United Kingdom, but hosts U.S. airbases in Seeb, Thumrait, and Masirah. Qatar has alluded to its willingness to allow a forward presence of the U.S. Central Command, currently based in Tampa, Florida.

The United States has individual formal defense agreements with each GCC state except Saudi Arabia. Because of internal opposition, Saudi Arabia has not signed a formal defense pact with the United States, but continues to have strong defense ties (including weapons procurement and training exercises) to its Western ally. Maintaining strategic stability in the six GCC states is of great importance to the United States, since these countries' support is vital to U.S. presence in the region.

ENERGY SECURITY: THE IMPORTANCE OF OIL AND GAS

An important element to consider while studying U.S. alliances and the global dynamics of national security is the heavy Western dependence on energy resources emanating from around the world. After World War II, security analysts concluded that resources shortages could pose a real threat to U.S. national security. They, like economists, look at changes over time in the real (inflation-adjusted) price of products such as oil, to seek evidence of their relative availability or scarcity. A falling price indicates more availability, while rising real prices warn of increasing global scarcity.

For oil in particular, the United States and the world received price "shocks" during the Arab oil embargo of 1973–74, along with more mild spikes as recently as the year 2000. However, excepting these bumps, shocks, and upticks of several months or even years (such as those corresponding to the typical rise in raw material prices during a business boom or to a fall in those prices during a recession), only a real price rise, persisting over years and not attributable to economic expansion or recession, would indicate potential long-term scarcity of a previously more easily available commodity. Figure 9.1 shows some of the events that have influenced petroleum prices paid by the United States between 1970 and 2000.

The investments that the U.S. defense and intelligence communities have made to protect the country against

FIGURE 9.1

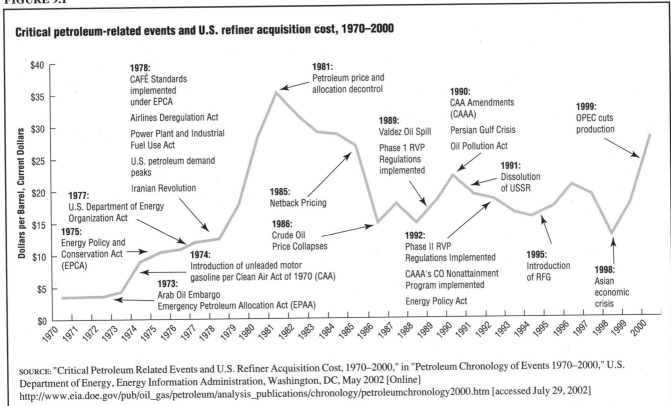

Critical petroleum-related events and U.S. refiner acquisition cost, 1970–2000

SOURCE: "Critical Petroleum Related Events and U.S. Refiner Acquisition Cost, 1970–2000," in "Petroleum Chronology of Events 1970–2000," U.S. Department of Energy, Energy Information Administration, Washington, DC, May 2002 [Online] http://www.eia.doe.gov/pub/oil_gas/petroleum/analysis_publications/chronology/petroleumchronology2000.htm [accessed July 29, 2002]

potential resource shortages have been questioned by some as unnecessary, since commodity prices have been relatively stable for 200 years. Still, U.S. policymakers feel the supply of certain energy resources, especially oil and natural gas, is an important part of U.S. foreign policy and, consequently, the U.S. national security agenda.

The Oil Wild Card

Despite the remarkable price stability of natural resources historically, oil continues to be troublesome for U.S. defense planners. The world oil trade has a high value—more than $200 billion annually, equal to more than 5 percent of the world's total exports of goods and services (though less than 1 percent of its gross domestic product). In addition, demand for oil around the world continues to increase each year.

The U.S. Department of Energy (DOE) projects that world oil consumption between 1999 and 2020 will increase by 2.2 percent annually, and will increase by almost 60 percent total, from 74.9 million barrels per day (mbd) in 1999 to 118.6 mbd in 2020. (See Figure 9.2.) The industrialized world will still use more oil than the developing world, but oil use in the industrialized world will grow much more slowly than the world average, at about 1.3 percent per year. By contrast, developing countries, including the swath of growing, unstable regions from North Africa to Oceania, will be increasing their consumption faster than the industrialized areas and the world aver-

age. The highest growth in oil demand among developing regions, 3.7 percent per year, or over 15 million mbd, is projected for developing Asia. (See Figure 9.3.) The data show that from 1996 to 2020 the projected average annual percentage increase in oil consumption of developing countries will be more than three times that of industrialized countries. However, the total amount of oil consumed per day in the developed world is still projected to exceed that of the developing countries until at least 2020.

Among the industrialized nations, an intensive user is the United States. North American barrels-per-day oil consumption between 1999 and 2020 is projected to be second only to that of developing Asia, and more than double that of the former Soviet Union. The U.S. reputation as a high energy user in general has led to some resentment throughout the world, in part because of the harmful environmental effects such consumption creates. Many developing countries feel that they are being unfairly pressured to sign off on environmental agreements designed to clean up problems caused by industrialized nations (such as the United States) that have reached their current state of prosperity in part through the relatively unrestricted use of natural resources. According to DOE projections, the United States will remain the largest importer and user of oil through 2020, accounting for more than one-fourth of total demand. This could potentially raise tensions in U.S. relations with other countries and regions, complicating national security issues.

FIGURE 9.2

FIGURE 9.3

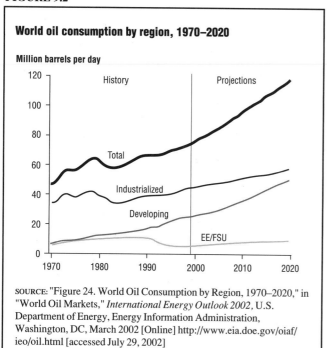

World oil consumption by region, 1970–2020

SOURCE: "Figure 24. World Oil Consumption by Region, 1970–2020," in "World Oil Markets," *International Energy Outlook 2002*, U.S. Department of Energy, Energy Information Administration, Washington, DC, March 2002 [Online] http://www.eia.doe.gov/oiaf/ieo/oil.html [accessed July 29, 2002]

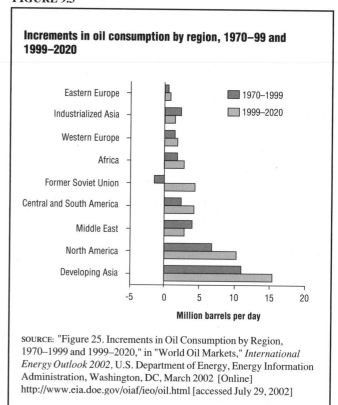

Increments in oil consumption by region, 1970–99 and 1999–2020

SOURCE: "Figure 25. Increments in Oil Consumption by Region, 1970–1999 and 1999–2020," in "World Oil Markets," *International Energy Outlook 2002*, U.S. Department of Energy, Energy Information Administration, Washington, DC, March 2002 [Online] http://www.eia.doe.gov/oiaf/ieo/oil.html [accessed July 29, 2002]

Continued U.S. Oil Supply and the Strategic Petroleum Reserve (SPR)

Certainly petroleum reserves are vital to modern economies, but controlling them hardly guarantees prosperity or security. As with other mineral resources and raw materials, petroleum is distributed within a well-developed market, one that allows almost any country access to the commodity, even during times of conflict, as long as adequate worldwide supplies exist within a reasonable and customary price range. Once the oil-supply chain is upset by events such as civil wars in developing countries, however, prices may become volatile. Additionally, increased production can destroy land and the environment, and eventually, overdevelopment may cause large migrations of displaced population, for example in Africa. A widely accepted summary of the state of oil in the future is that this resource is finite, production will be peaking well before the middle of the century, and an alternative must be found to avoid widespread dislocations in modern life.

One strategy for dealing with the risk or threat of disruption in petroleum supplies has been to encourage public and private stocking. Planners generally give the government the role of creating its own strategic reserves and establishing incentives for such stocking. Because the stocks would tend to ensure the flow of oil, they could reduce the U.S. need to intervene during a crisis—or at least the need to intervene quickly. These stocks could provide the time interval needed to bring alternative energy sources on-line—to shift, say, from oil to coal for electricity generation in dual-fuel-capable boilers, or to start pumping oil wells that were temporarily lying idle. This has been the strategy adopted by the U.S. government and the International Energy Agency (IEA).

The Arab oil embargo of 1973–74, and subsequent price spikes, motivated the United States to create the Strategic Petroleum Reserve (SPR), a series of underground salt caverns along the Gulf of Mexico coast with a capacity of 560 million barrels. The SPR was authorized in 1975 and began operation in 1977. It is the first line of defense against an interruption in petroleum imports. If necessary, the reserve can be drawn down at a rate of 4.2 mbd, equal to about 40 percent of daily U.S. oil imports.

At the same time as the reserve was established, the industrial nations agreed to hold reserves equal to 90 days' imports. They also agreed to coordinate their responses, in the event of an interruption in oil supplies, through the IEA, which has 23 member countries.

In 1985 the SPR's inventory peaked, in terms of days of net imports, at 118 days. However, coverage has since diminished as imports have increased and inventory has been sold to raise revenue to help balance the federal budget. As of early 2003, no oil had been purchased to replenish the reserve since 1995.

The only emergency use of the SPR occurred in January 1991, at the start of Operation Desert Storm, the U.S. military campaign to oust Iraqi forces from Kuwait. According to the Institute for National Strategic Studies

(*Strategic Assessment 1999: Priorities for a Turbulent World,* Washington, DC, 1999), "The mere announcement of SPR sales had a considerable stabilizing effect on world markets. Only 17 million barrels were actually sold before market conditions returned to normal."

U.S. Internal Oil Production vs. Conservation

The ultimate exhaustion of the world's oil reserves—which would be preceded by hefty price increases that could occur well before the year 2050—definitely constitutes a long-term national security problem. Since oil is a nonrenewable resource (i.e., there is only a limited amount of it), many feel that Americans should begin to seriously reduce their use of energy, particularly energy from oil-based sources. Although recent public-opinion polls have shown that most Americans support the idea of decreasing our dependency on foreign oil, especially in the wake of the terrorist attacks of September 11, 2001, Americans also continue to use great amounts of energy—one illustration of this is the continued popularity of heavily gas-consuming sport utility vehicles (SUVs).

Conservation efforts, while one option, are not the only route to decreasing U.S. dependence on foreign oil. Increasing production by exploiting known reserves in various regions of the United States has also been proposed. Such regions include the Great Lakes, the Gulf Coast, and, particularly, the Arctic National Wildlife Refuge (ANWR), the largest national wildlife refuge in the United States. Oil companies have long been interested in ANWR and, along with their political supporters, have challenged its protected status. Conservationists and others who feel the ecological and environmental damage caused by drilling would be significant, even disastrous, have been fighting off these challenges.

Until September 11, 2001, public support has tended to be on the side of the conservationists, but immediately after the terrorist attacks, U.S. opinion changed radically. When asked in July 2001 whether the positives of producing oil and natural gas by drilling in ANWR outweighed the negatives, only 39 percent of Americans surveyed agreed. When asked the same question soon after September 11, however, 61 percent felt the positives outweighed the negatives. (See Figure 9.4.) Still, public opinion seems to have swung once more back to the conservation side. In August 2001 the House of Representatives passed a bill that would have allowed drilling within ANWR, but the Senate rejected this proposal in April 2002, thereby continuing the area's protected status. It is likely that drilling in ANWR will continue to be a matter of debate for some time.

China, Oil, and U.S. Interests

In recent years, China has gone from a net petroleum exporter to a net petroleum importer. It has taken vigorous steps to grow its economy and, as part of that goal, has

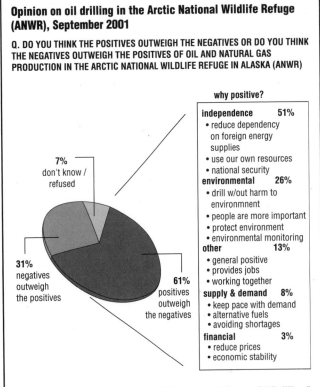

FIGURE 9.4

Opinion on oil drilling in the Arctic National Wildlife Refuge (ANWR), September 2001

Q. DO YOU THINK THE POSITIVES OUTWEIGH THE NEGATIVES OR DO YOU THINK THE NEGATIVES OUTWEIGH THE POSITIVES OF OIL AND NATURAL GAS PRODUCTION IN THE ARCTIC NATIONAL WILDLIFE REFUGE IN ALASKA (ANWR)

why positive?

independence 51%
- reduce dependency on foreign energy supplies
- use our own resources
- national security

environmental 26%
- drill w/out harm to environment
- people are more important
- protect environment
- environmental monitoring

other 13%
- general positive
- provides jobs
- working together

supply & demand 8%
- keep pace with demand
- alternative fuels
- avoiding shortages

financial 3%
- reduce prices
- economic stability

7% don't know / refused

31% negatives outweigh the positives

61% positives outweigh the negatives

SOURCE: "Weighing the Positives and Negatives of Alaskan Oil Drilling," in *The Wirthlin Report,* vol. 11, no. 9, October 2001

tried to promote private automobile ownership by individuals since 1993 (which could lead to 25 million more cars in the country by 2015). Even if it develops the oil fields located in its isolated interior regions, it is likely to import at least 2 mbd by 2015.

China's discomfort with reliance on world markets for this vital resource could translate into a political alliance with one or more oil-exporting states, in the hope that this would mean a more secure source of oil. The problem for the United States with such an alliance is that China's partners in the Middle East will most likely not be American allies, but those considered rogue states, such as Iran. China's friendly relationship with Iran has given Iran plenty of access to Chinese advanced-weapons technology. One worst-case scenario for the United States would be that Iran would take an aggressive stance, armed with nuclear weapons obtained from the Chinese, or enter into some sort of defense pact with the Chinese.

The Persian Gulf Peril

SHARE OF WORLD OUTPUT. The main issue for national security planners in the early 21st century regarding oil is less that the world is running out of oil than that there is an increasing concentration of supply from one region: the Persian Gulf. The Persian Gulf producers work through the Organization of Petroleum Exporting Countries (OPEC) to control oil prices. OPEC membership includes

TABLE 9.1

Global reserves and production of petroleum, 2001

Producer (in order by reserves)	Estimated Reserves (bbl)	Percent of World Reserves	Production, 1998 (mbd)
Saudi Arabia	261.8	24.9	8.8
Iraq	112.5	10.7	2.4
United Arab Emirates	97.8	9.3	2.4
Kuwait	96.5	9.2	2.1
Iran	89.7	8.5	3.7
Venezuela	77.7	7.4	3.4
Russia	48.6	4.6	7.0
United States	30.4	2.9	7.7
Libya	29.5	2.8	1.4
Mexico	26.9	2.6	3.6
Nigeria	24.0	2.3	2.1
China	24.0	2.3	3.3
Norway/United Kingdom (North Sea)	14.3	1.4	5.9
Total	**933.7**	**88.9**	**53.8**

bbl = billion barrels
mbd = million barrels per day

SOURCE: Adapted from "Oil: Production," *BP Statistical Review of World Energy 2002*, BP Amoco, London, England. Reproduced by permission.

TABLE 9.2

Oil production and reserves in the Persian Gulf area, 2001

Country	Production, mbd	Percent of World Total	Proven Reserves, bbl	Percent of World Reserves
Iran	3.688	5.1	89.7	8.5
Iraq	2.414	3.3	112.5	10.7
Kuwait	2.142	2.9	96.5	9.2
Oman	.959	1.3	5.5	0.5
Qatar	.783	1.0	15.2	1.4
Saudi Arabia	8.768	11.8	261.8	24.9
Syria	.551	0.8	2.5	0.2
UAE	2.422	3.2	97.8	9.3
Yemen	.458	0.6	4.0	0.4
Other	.049	0.1	0.1	–
Total	**22.233**	**30.0**	**685.6**	**65.3**

bbl = billion barrels
mbd = million barrels per day

SOURCE: "Oil production and reserves 2001," in *BP Statistical Review of World Energy 2002*, BP Amoco, London, England. Reproduced by permission.

the following countries: Algeria, Indonesia, Iran, Iraq, Kuwait, Libya, Nigeria, Qatar, Saudi Arabia, United Arab Emirates, and Venezuela. The primary mission of OPEC is to coordinate and unify the petroleum policies of its member countries and to determine the best strategy for protecting their individual and shared interests.

World oil reserves (yet-to-be-tapped sources of supply) in 2001 were 933.7 billion barrels. (See Table 9.1.) The Persian Gulf producers and OPEC, while sitting on top of mammoth untapped supplies, have occasionally held back production, as they did noticeably in the year 2000. Indeed, they have usually output their reserves at a rate lower than the maximum possible to limit supply and bolster prices. By contrast, the American oil industry's goal is to produce a full 7 percent of an oil field's underground capacity each year. Industry analysts have said that if this practice were applied worldwide, it would, in theory, yield a capacity of 190 mbd, more than twice the expected worldwide demand in 2010.

As calculated by BP Amoco in its *Statistical Review of World Energy, 2000,* the eight main Middle East/Persian Gulf oil-producing states—Saudi Arabia, Iraq, United Arab Emirates, Kuwait, Iran, Qatar, Yemen, and Oman—were responsible for almost 30 percent (21.40 mbd) of the world's daily production in 1999. Proven Middle Eastern reserves (685.6 bbl) accounted for 65.3 percent of the world's unproduced sources of supply at the end of 2001. (See Table 9.2.)

Nearly two-thirds of the world's global petroleum supplies lie in the Persian Gulf. Should the price of oil remain relatively low, U.S. dependence on Persian Gulf oil may

increase—historically, Gulf oil has been the cheapest oil to produce. In the future, non–Persian Gulf producers, such as Venezuela, Russia, and Mexico, may supply as much as 47–57 mbd, or 62–65 percent of demand. Still, if world oil demand comes in at its DOE estimate of about 95 mbd by 2010, and if non–Persian Gulf production remains at 47 mbd, then the Persian Gulf states might be supplying 50 percent or more of world oil demand by the end of the 21st century's first decade. Such a high level of dependence on one region, and especially Saudi Arabia, would leave the world and U.S. economies vulnerable.

As resource-conflict specialist Michael T. Klare notes (*Resource Wars,* Metropolitan Books, New York, 2001), "A significant share of the additional petroleum will have to come from the Gulf—there is simply no other pool of oil large enough to sustain an increase of this magnitude. All projections of future supply and demand assume that the Persian Gulf will account for an ever-expanding share of the world's oil requirements: from 27 percent in 1990 to 33 percent in 2010 to 39 percent in 2020."

ARMS, WAR, AND SECURITY CONCERNS. That such large reserves of oil are present in the Persian Gulf actually increases the likelihood of interstate conflict there. It gives the nations in the region the means to procure huge quantities of sophisticated modern weapons, and so when warfare breaks out, the scale and intensity of the fighting are elevated. For example, the war between Iran and Iraq of 1980–88 yielded an estimated 1 million casualties and over $100 billion in property damage.

The arms that Gulf States have acquired from the United States alone have been substantial. According to the Congressional Research Service (*Conventional Arms Transfers to Developing Nations, 1990–1997*), between 1990 and

1997 the value of U.S. arms-transfer agreements with the Persian Gulf states of Bahrain, Kuwait, Oman, Saudi Arabia, and the United Arab Emirates came to $42 billion. The Arms Control Association's *Register of Arms Transfers* (Washington, DC, May 1997) also notes major U.S. arms transfers to Persian Gulf states between 1990 and 1998. What is noticeable from these data is the wide variety of armaments transferred at a wide range of monetary values.

WORLD OIL TRANSIT CHOKEPOINTS. U.S. national security concerns regarding Persian Gulf oil extend to those areas that do not themselves hold large petroleum supplies. These are sea passages and straits that are used for the shipment of oil by tanker or pipeline. Because several of these areas adjoin areas of recurring conflict, the DOE has dubbed them "world oil transit chokepoints." Table 9.3 provides details on each of these chokepoints, including the major concerns should closures occur. These six passages carried almost 30 million barrels of oil per day in 1998—more than 40 percent of global consumption. This list illustrates the importance of the volatile Middle East and Persian Gulf to petroleum supplies—four of the six chokepoints (the Strait of Hormuz, Bab el-Mandeb, the Suez Canal and Sumed Pipeline, and the Bosporus/Turkish Straits) lie in these regions.

The Former Soviet Union: A Challenge to the Persian Gulf?

Some industry experts have suggested that Russia may be in a position to pose a challenge to Saudi Arabia's role as top worldwide oil producer. As Edward L. Morse, executive adviser at Hess Energy Trading Company and former assistant secretary of state for international energy policy, and James Richard, portfolio manager at Firebird Management, point out in "The Battle for Energy Dominance" (*Foreign Affairs,* March/April 2002), before the breakup of the former Soviet Union, state-owned oil production had reached 12.5 mbd, well beyond the largest amount reached by Saudi Arabia at its production height. Currently, Russia keeps a much larger amount of its oil for internal use than does Saudi Arabia, so Saudi exports are still substantially higher than Russia's.

There are substantial, and so far unresolved, difficulties associated with Russian oil production, including issues of sufficient investment, management, construction and maintenance of pipelines, and ownership/development disputes among the countries bordering the oil-rich Caspian Sea. Morse and Richard predict that the Caspian area could become the source of enough oil to supplant Saudi Arabia as the West's primary source of oil within four years, but the DOE is more cautious. It predicted in *International Energy Outlook 2002* that the former Soviet Union's net oil production would increase to 14.9 mbd by 2020, as compared to the 22.1 mbd the DOE projected Saudi Arabia would produce in the same year. Total pro-

jected OPEC production in 2020 would be 60.2 mbd, an increase of nearly 50 percent over the 2000 figure.

Although Russia had agreed, in a deal with OPEC, to cut its output, in mid-2002 it announced that it would abandon that agreement. Russian President Vladimir Putin also promised to keep Siberian oil flowing during any Middle East crisis.

POTENTIAL CONFLICTS OVER WATER

According to some national security experts, water is more of a potential source of strife than it may at first appear. Early civilizations relied heavily on systems of dikes and canals, and such waterworks were often the first attacked during outbreaks of hostilities. Conflicts over water even occurred during the Cold War between the United States and the Soviet Union. For example, the closing of the Straits of Tiran to Israeli shipping by Egyptian president Gamal Abdel Nasser on two separate occasions was one of several triggers attributed to the start of both the Sinai Campaign of 1956 and the Six-Day War of 1967.

About 200 river basins are shared by two or more countries. Five or more countries share 13 of those basins, and nine or more countries share 4 rivers: the Danube, Nile, Congo, and Niger. River basins in which conflicts have flared include the Nile, Jordan, Euphrates, Ganges, and Mekong.

As the new century wears on, conflicts over critical water supplies are increasingly likely. This is especially the case in the vast area stretching from North Africa to the Near East and South Asia, where water demand is quickly outstripping supply. Disputes are likely to become increasingly common and heated in these regions. Rarely have the states involved agreed to procedures for sharing the available supplies.

Dangers are especially apparent in areas where there is little rainfall and only a single major source of water. These would include the Nile River, Jordan River, and Euphrates River. Each provides at least two countries with their basic, and increasingly insufficient, needs. A state with a high per capita use of a shared water supply runs the risk that, if another state drawing on the same supply greatly increases its use of the water system, the first state may risk water scarcities, thus increasing tensions between the two countries.

Experts label countries water-stressed or water-scarce depending on the amount of renewable water available to their residents. Water-stressed countries have a per capita availability of not more than 1,700 cubic meters of water per person per year. In these countries, water is often temporarily unavailable at many locations. Difficult choices must be made among uses of water for personal consumption, agriculture, or industry. Water-scarce countries have

TABLE 9.3

World oil transit "chokepoints"

The following presents information on major world oil transit centers. Over 30 million barrels/day pass through the relatively narrow shipping lanes and pipelines discussed below. These routes are known as chokepoints due to their potential for closure. Disruption of oil flows through any of these export routes could have a significant impact on world oil prices.

	Location	Oil flows	Destination of oil exports	Main concerns
Bab el-Mandab	Djibouti/Eritrea/Yemen; connects the Red Sea with the Gulf of Aden and the Arabian Sea	3.3 million barrels/day (1997)	Europe, United States, Asia	Closure of the Bab el-Mandab could keep tankers from the Persian Gulf from reaching the Suez Canal/Sumed Pipeline complex, diverting them around the southern tip of Africa (the Cape of Good Hope). This would add greatly to transit time and cost, and effectively tie up spare tanker capacity. In December 1995, Yemen fought a brief battle with Eritrea over Greater Hanish Island, located just north of the Bab el-Mandab. The Bab el-Mandab could be bypassed by utilizing the East-West oil pipeline, which traverses Saudi Arabia and has a capacity of about 5 million barrels/day. However, southbound oil traffic, which totaled about 1,000,000 barrels/day in 1997, would still be blocked. In addition, closure of the Bab el-Mandab would effectively block non-oil shipping from using the Suez Canal, except for limited trade within the Red Sea region.
Bosporus/Turkish Straits	Turkey; this 17-mile long waterway divides Asia from Europe and connects the Black Sea with the Mediterranean Sea	1.7 million barrels/day (0.2 million barrels/day eastbound) (1998)	Western and Southern Europe;	Only half a mile wide at its narrowest point, the Turkish Straits are one of the world's most difficult-to-navigate waterways. Many of the proposed export routes for forthcoming production from the Caspian Sea region pass westwards through the Black Sea and the Turkish Straits en route to the Mediterrean Sea and world markets. The ports of the Black Sea, along with those in the Baltic Sea, were the primary oil export routes of the former Soviet Union, and the Black Sea remains the largest outlet for Russian oil exports. Exports through the Turkish Straits have grown since the breakup of the Soviet Union in 1991, and there is growing concern that projected Caspian Sea export volumes exceed the ability of the Turkish Straits to accommodate the tanker traffic. Turkey is concerned that the projected increase in large oil tankers would pose serious navigational safety and environmental threats to the Turkish Straits.
Panama Canal and Trans-Panama Pipeline	Panama; connects the Pacific Ocean with the Caribbean Sea and Atlantic Ocean	0.6 million barrels/day (1998)		The Panama Canal extends approximately 50 miles from Panama City on the Pacific Ocean to Colon on the Caribbean Sea. Petroleum was the second largest commodity (by tonnage) shipped through the Canal after grain, and accounted for 16%-17% of total canal shipments during fiscal years 1996-1998. Over 60% of total oil shipments went south from the Atlantic to the Pacific, with oil products dominating southbound traffic. Some coal is shipped through the canal as well, accounting for 5%-6% of total Canal traffic. If transit were halted through the Canal, the 860,000 barrels/day Trans-Panama pipeline (Petroterminal de Panama, S.A.) could be re-opened to carry oil in either direction. This pipeline is located outside the Canal Zone near the Costa Rican border, and runs from the port of Charco Azul on the Pacific Coast (near Puerto Armuelles) to the port of Chiriqui Grande, Bocas del Toro on the Caribbean. Interest has been shown by Caribbean producers in plans to reverse the pipeline to go southbound from the Atlantic to the Pacific. This reversal would allow increased oil production from Caribbean producers to find outlets on the West Coast and other Pacific markets.

TABLE 9.3
World oil transit "chokepoints" [CONTINUED]

The following presents information on major world oil transit centers. Over 30 million barrels/day pass through the relatively narrow shipping lanes and pipelines discussed below. These routes are known as chokepoints due to their potential for closure. Disruption of oil flows through any of these export routes could have a significant impact on world oil prices.

	Location	Oil flows	Destination of oil exports	Main concerns
Russian Oil and Gas Export Pipelines/Ports	Russian oil and gas exports transit via pipelines that pass through Russia, Ukraine, Belarus, Hungary, Slovakia, the Czech Republic, and Poland Major Oil Export Ports: Novorossiisk (Russia); Ventspils (Latvia); Odessa (Ukraine), Tuapse (Russia)	Major Oil Pipeline: Druzhba (1.25 million barrels/day) Major Natural Gas Pipelines: Brotherhood, Progress, and Union (1 trillion cubic feet each); Northern Lights (0.8 tcf); Volga/Urals-Vyborg, Finland (0.1 tcf).	Eastern Europe, Netherlands, Italy, Germany, France, other Western Europe	Russia is a major supplier of crude oil and natural gas to Europe. All of the ports and pipelines (with the exception of the Druzhba oil pipeline) are operating at near capacity, leaving limited alternatives if problems arose at Russian export terminals.
Strait of Hormuz	Location: Oman/Iran; connects the Persian Gulf with the Gulf of Oman and the Arabian Sea	15.4 million barrels per day (1998)	Japan, United States, Western Europe	By far the world's most important oil chokepoint, the Strait consists of 2-mile wide channels for inbound and outbound tanker traffic, as well as a 2–mile wide buffer zone. Closure of the Strait of Hormuz would require use of longer alternate routes (if available) at increased transportation costs. Such routes include the 5 million barrels/day capacity Petroline and the Abqaiq-Yanbu natural gas liquids line across Saudi Arabia to the Red Sea.
Strait of Malacca	Location: Malaysia/Singapore; connects the Indian Ocean with the South China Sea and the Pacific Ocean	9.5 million barrels/day (1997)	Japan, South Korea, China, other Pacific Rim countries	The narrowest point of this shipping lane is the Phillips Channel in the Singapore Strait, which is only 1.5 miles wide at its narrowest point. This creates a natural bottleneck, with the potential for a collision, grounding, or oil spill. If the strait were closed, nearly half of the world's fleet would be required to sail farther, generating a substantial increase in the requirement for vessel capacity. All excess capacity of the world fleet might be absorbed, with the effect strongest for crude oil shipments and dry bulk such as coal. Closure of the Strait of Malacca would immediately raise freight rates worldwide.
Suez Canal and Sumed Pipeline	Egypt; connects the Red Sea and Gulf of Suez with the Mediterranean Sea	3.1 million barrels/day (1998). Of this total, the Sumed Pipeline transported 2.4 million barrels/day of crude oil northbound (2.2 million barrels/day from Saudi Arabia). The Suez Canal transported 0.7 million barrels/day of petroleum in 1998. Southbound trade consisted of 0.1 million barrels/day of petroleum products. Northbound trade consisted of 0.6 million barrels/day of petroleum, half of which was crude oil.	Predominantly Europe; also United States	Closure of the Suez Canal and/or Sumed Pipeline would divert tankers around the southern tip of Africa (the Cape of Good Hope), adding greatly to transit time and effectively tying up tanker capacity.

SOURCE: Adapted from "World Oil Transit Chokepoints," U.S. Department of Energy, Energy Information Administration, Washington, DC, August 1999 [Online] http://www.eia.doe.gov/emeu/security/choke.html [accessed January 30, 2003]

---

a per capita availability of not more than 1,000 cubic meters per year. At this level, there may not be enough water to provide adequate food, economic development is hampered, and severe environmental difficulties may develop. About 1,000 cubic meters is considered the minimum amount necessary for healthy human life.

The tightness of water supplies is most evident in the Middle East and Southwest Asia. Most countries in those areas have great problems meeting the basic water needs of their growing populations. Data from the World Bank indicate that average annual per capita runoff—or renewable fresh water—in these areas in 1995 was 1,250 cubic meters. That amount is just enough to meet the most basic of human needs.

According to the UN, 508 million people lived in 31 water-stressed or water-scarce countries in 2000. By 2025, 3 billion people will be living in 48 such countries. The number of people living in conditions of scarcity will

FIGURE 9.5

Nile River basin

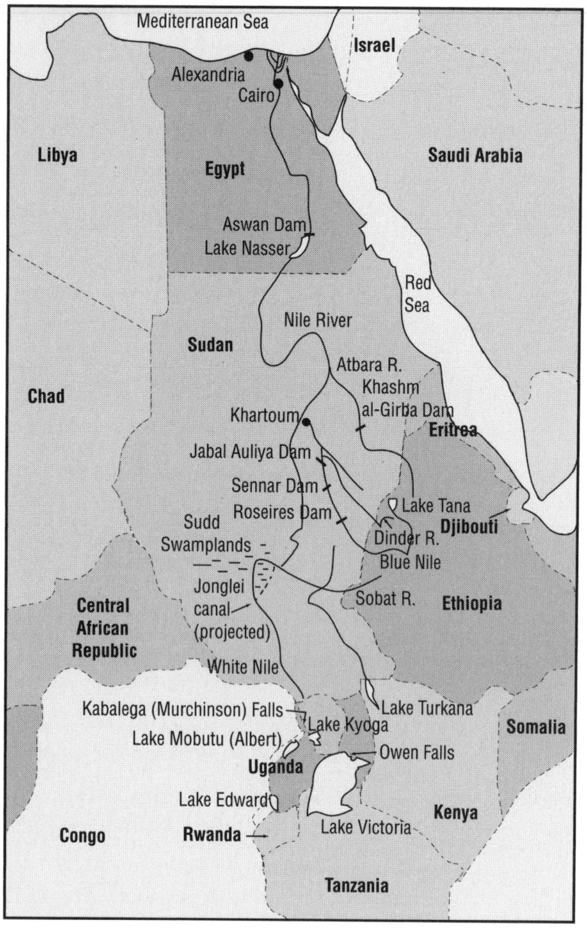

SOURCE: "Nile River Basin," map from *Resource Wars: The New Landscape of Global Conflict* by Michael T. Klare, ©2001 by Michael T. Klare. Reprinted by permission of Henry Holt and Company, LLC.

The Nile is the world's longest river, stretching more than 4,000 miles from its headwaters in equatorial Africa to its outlet in the Mediterranean. (See Figure 9.5.) Traveling northward, it spreads its tributaries in nine countries: Burundi, Congo, Egypt, Ethiopia, Kenya, Rwanda, Sudan, Tanzania, and Uganda. The Nile basin boasts an area of 3.35 million square kilometers—about one-tenth of the total land area of Africa. Within this area, one finds climates indicative of the Nile's unique hydrology: deserts, marshlands, savannahs, and tropical rainforests.

Egypt's past and present security strategy with regard to the Nile is to exploit its privileged position at the mouth of the river. Through repeated military forays into the areas of the river's headwaters, continued into modern times, Egypt ensures that no foreign power tampers with the river's flow. That is because all of the Nile's water is supplied by areas lying outside of Egyptian territory, and there is no other significant source of water in Egypt. To get water, Egypt must dominate and coerce its neighbors, the other lands and powers adjoining the river, also called "upstream riparians."

This strategy gives Egypt the ability to take the great bulk of the Nile's waters for its own exclusive use, while contributing nothing to the Nile's annual flow. The upstream riparians are basically subjugated to Egypt's wishes. Unlike Egypt, they have lacked the money and machines to build extensive dams and waterworks, and Egypt has always had sufficient military potential to deter its neighbors from proceeding with aggression in its direction. With the need for water becoming so dire throughout the region, the temptation of the other powers to draw from the Nile—to dam and otherwise appropriate more of its flow—just grows.

Thus there is a considerable likelihood of future conflict based on the upstream powers' level of desperation. Thus far, those powers have been occupied by internal conflicts and border disputes less directly related to natural resource shortages. Once the violence in this region ends or slows considerably, these countries will be able to focus on such concerns as water supply. Some of these countries will soon proceed with hydroelectric and irrigation improvements on the upper Nile. Ambitious new plans to divert waters from the Blue Nile tributary (see Figure 9.5) to new agricultural uses were lately announced by Ethiopia. Uganda is also considering new hydroelectric improvements.

All this will be problematic for Egypt. Egypt's annual water requirements are skyrocketing along with its population. When Egypt became independent in the 1920s, it had a population of 13.5 million; the population had more than doubled to 30 million by 1960; and by 1998 it had grown to 66 million. If the Egyptian population continues to grow at the rates expected, by 2025 it will reach 95 million people and, by 2050, 115 million.

double, and those living in water stress will increase sixfold. There are currently 11 water-scarce countries: Algeria, Egypt, Israel, Jordan, Libya, Morocco, Saudi Arabia, Syria, Tunisia, the United Arab Emirates, and Yemen. These countries have lately begun to augment their modest rain-fed supplies with desalinated seawater or water newly discovered in old aquifers. However, most of them are finding that meeting the basic water needs of their growing populations is an impossible task.

Potential Conflict Along the Nile

When two or more countries share key water resources, and the sources shared are large river systems like the Nile and Euphrates, the situation can be precarious. Nine countries share the Nile. Ideally, these states need to work out agreements for fairly distributing the annual water flow. Instead, stronger states appropriate an excessive share of the flow.

Meanwhile, other countries along the Nile are experiencing even greater population increases than Egypt. The World Resources Institute (*World Resources 1998–1999*, 1998) projects, for example, that Ethiopia's population will increase 243 percent from 1998 to 2050. The data show that in 2050, Ethiopia's population, at 212.7 million, will be almost twice that of Egypt's 115.5 million. Population growth is proceeding in this region at some of the highest rates of growth in the world—2.2 percent per year in Kenya and Sudan, 2.6 percent in Uganda, and a huge 3.2 percent in Ethiopia. The average global rate is 0.8 percent.

As Michael Klare observes in *Resource Wars*, "It's hard to imagine how Ethiopia, Sudan, and Uganda will be able to feed an additional 225 million people without irrigating more land, and the only major source of water in this area is the Nile and its tributaries. Clearly the leaders of these states will seek to proceed with long-delayed plans to build new dams and divert additional Nile water to domestic irrigation schemes."

THE FUTURE OF RESOURCE CONFLICTS: THE AFRICA PATTERN

Resource stresses abroad will keep the United States on its toes in the next few decades, especially because they may make conflicts among regional powers more likely and more intense. Though involved parties may seek economic sanctions before resorting to military force, transborder resource conflicts are likely to occur.

Two of the regions in which there could well be transborder resource disputes are of intense concern to U.S. security planners. The first is the Persian Gulf, where great oil riches have inflamed border disputes involving the states of the Arabian Peninsula. The second is the Middle East, also known to planners as the Arab-Israeli theater, especially along the Jordan and Nile Rivers. Here, national populations will soar in size, water supplies will be increasingly scarce, and existing political ill will between nations and groups may easily be exacerbated. It is possible that the shortage of some resource, such as oil, could tempt one nation to grab part of the territory of another.

Now that the United States is maintaining a presence in these regions, the low likelihood of success of an outright resource or territorial grab will hopefully discourage sovereign states from contemplating aggression. On the other hand, civil wars in some of the African states have been caused by wars over natural resources, including water, land, diamonds, oil, minerals, and timber. These wars have taken their toll in the form of millions of deaths. For example, coltan is a mineral used in cell phones, DVDs, and other electronic products. Mined in the Democratic Republic of Congo and other African nations, it has created problems as conflicts arise over ownership of rights. Governments, rebel factions, and other entities have confronted Americans and others involved in importing coltan, diamonds, and other resources with increasing resentment.

In Nigeria, where several U.S. oil companies have operations, there have been serious conflicts involving protestors concerned with environmental and health damages they say have been caused by oil-related activities. Protestors also feel that, despite what they were told about the economic benefits of oil production for their villages, corrupt local governments and the oil companies have been the only beneficiaries. In the meantime, they have received little or no compensation for environmental and health-related damage that has resulted from oil-production activities.

Additionally, human-rights abuse charges have been made by Nigerian citizens and by international human-rights organizations, which feel that the oil companies have been complicit in the violent repression of protestors. If not directly involved in such abuses, the oil companies have failed in their duty to prevent, or even speak out against, such abuses, opponents say. In one particular incident on January 4, 1999, for example, Nigerian soldiers using a Chevron helicopter attacked villagers in two communities, killing at least four people and destroying most of the village structures and homes. More recently, on July 9, 2002, Nigerian women protested by taking over a Chevron-Texaco oil plant. Other protests, including kidnappings of foreign workers in oil-producing areas, continue to present threats to Americans. Such incidents only fuel resentment and hatred toward the United States, adding to the potential threat to U.S. citizens and interests abroad and potentially affecting future support for U.S. antiterrorist activities.

CHAPTER 10

NEW ARENAS:
ORGANIZED CRIME AND EMERGING TECHNOLOGIES

The concept of U.S. national security is constantly evolving and adapting to the changing global security environment. There are a variety of emerging trends and threats with which America has not had to deal before. At the same time, the domestic national security infrastructure itself is changing.

ILLICIT MARKETS AND TRANSNATIONAL CRIMES

Transnational threats to American national security include not only hostile states and terrorism but also organized crime, which is associated with a host of illicit activities. Drug trafficking, financial fraud, environmental crimes, and contraband smuggling, to name just a few, are not only threats to Americans and their communities but to U.S. business and financial interests as well as global stability and security. (See Figure 10.1 for a National Security Council diagram of which arena or arenas various international crimes fall into.)

Such crimes are of special concern to U.S. policymakers because in most cases there is no clear identifiable enemy to target. This is quite different from interstate conflicts, in which parties have well-defined targets, and wars, in which armies and rules of engagement are obvious to all sides. Any battles waged against the generic front of "drug trafficking" or "money laundering" are extremely hard to fight and require significant international cooperation.

The head of the organized crime group for the International Criminal Police Organization defines organized crime as "Any group having a corporate structure whose primary objective is to obtain money through illegal activities, often surviving on fear and corruption" (Paul Nesbitt, cited in *Interpol,* London, 1993). *The New Encyclopedia Britannica* (1986) labels the phenomenon as a ". . . complex of highly centralized enterprises set up for the purpose of engaging in illegal activities." Additionally, the *Report of the UN Seminar on International Crime Control* refers to organized-crime groups as "continuing and controlled criminal entities that carry out crimes for profit and that seek to create a protective system against society by illegal means such as violence, intimidation, corruption, and large-scale theft."

Organized-crime groups have several characteristics in common. Much as it does with business, financial gain drives and sustains organized crime. Most groups carry out more than one type of crime. Although not an absolute requirement, many groups require their members to be of the same family or ethnic background, in order to ensure loyalty and to pursue a common goal or scheme. Most organized-crime groups have become successful in one way or another through the corruption of government officials. Another common characteristic is a hierarchical structure, with defined leadership/subordinate roles. In many cases, organized-crime groups are permanent and do not depend on the participation of one or a few individuals to exist, and the groups usually have influence over large areas of a region, country, or countries.

Organized-crime groups undertake a wide range of illicit global activities. They traffic in explosives, arms, narcotics, humans, metals, minerals, endangered flora and fauna, and Freon gas. They conduct extensive money laundering, fraud, graft, extortion, bribery, economic espionage, smuggling of embargoed goods, multinational auto theft, international prostitution, industrial and technological espionage, bank fraud, financial market manipulation, counterfeiting, corruption, and contract murder.

Of these activities, corruption is perhaps the biggest threat to states. Crime groups greatly compromise and jeopardize governments when they use corruption to achieve their aims. Organized criminals co-opt officials and leaders with a combination of bribery, graft, collusion, and/or extortion. Organized crime has successfully targeted such countries as Colombia, Italy, Thailand,

FIGURE 10.1

International crimes affecting U.S. interests, 2000

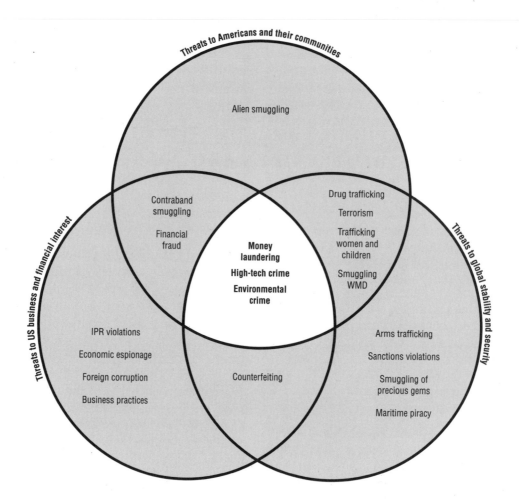

Threats to Americans and their communities

Alien smuggling

Threats to US business and financial interest

Threats to global stability and security

Contraband smuggling

Financial fraud

Drug trafficking

Terrorism

Trafficking women and children

Smuggling WMD

Money laundering

High-tech crime

Environmental crime

IPR violations

Economic espionage

Foreign corruption

Business practices

Counterfeiting

Arms trafficking

Sanctions violations

Smuggling of precious gems

Maritime piracy

SOURCE: "International Crimes Affecting US Interests," in *International Crime Threat Assessment,* National Security Council, Washington, DC, December 2000

Mexico, Russia, and Japan with payoffs or threats to justice officials to alter charges, change court rulings, lose evidence, or even lose interest. By undercutting justice systems, these groups undercut society. Sometimes when organized crime targets members of police forces and armed forces, and those members do not cooperate, they become targets of hired assassins.

There is increasing interdependency among crime groups. The now largely defunct Medellin drug cartel in Colombia at one time joined with Russian and Italian mobsters to smuggle cocaine into Europe. In addition to conspiring with one another, crime groups are also often fighting with one another, which can be equally disruptive to the state. The Colombian and Mexican drug-smuggling rings have clashed more with each other than they have collaborated. Rival drug dealers and middlemen wage wars of attrition in New York, south Florida, and many European cities.

The international networks that underpin the drug trade can be complex arrangements of drug producers, processors, traffickers, and street vendors, orchestrated by organized-crime groups—often more than one. For example, one network arranged for hashish originating in Pakistan to be transported to Mombasa, Kenya. There, it was added to a cargo of tea and reshipped to Haifa, Israel, by way of Durban, South Africa. Then the drugs went to a ship that took cargo to Constanza, Romania, every two weeks. From there, via Bratislava, Slovakia, it went to Italy, where it was sold. The head of the network was a Ugandan native who became a German citizen and worked for a Romanian company. When some of the perpetrators were apprehended in Constanza, they revealed the network.

Drug use has mostly plateaued in the United States, but narcotics trafficking worldwide continues to grow because of foreign demand. In 1997 international narcotics dealings brought in more than $400 billion in profits, making up over 8 percent of the world economy. The U.S. government estimates that drug-related costs for law enforcement, corrections, and public health reach $67 billion annually. Governments of countries like Colombia, Peru, and Bolivia have largely been unable to significantly reduce their countries' production and export of drugs.

Drug trafficking also affects American citizens. El Paso, Texas, which borders Juárez, Mexico, has long been an entryway for drugs controlled by the Carillo Fuentes drug-trafficking organization. In a December 2000 statement for the record before the House Judiciary Committee, Subcommittee on Crime, Steven C. McCraw, Deputy Assistant Director of the Investigative Services Division of the Federal Bureau of Investigation (FBI), noted that "during the past few years. . . . In El Paso, there have been 120 drug related homicides and 73 drug related disappearances."

Leaders of countries often view international crime, such as drug production, as domestic legal concerns. Because criminal groups are mostly trying to make money, their political objectives, if any, may not seem significant. Leaders also can view transnational criminals, because they operate across international borders, as other countries' problems. Up to now, national security has rarely considered law enforcement issues; many political leaders continue to view organized crime as a lower-level law enforcement issue, not a major national security threat.

However, the U.S. government has become increasingly aware that international organized crime is much more than an extension of domestic crime. Highly organized illegal enterprises operate internationally, with scant regard for state boundaries. They become larger, more complex, and grow in number. They penetrate borders and operate with relative impunity in several states. Within national borders, they pollute the integrity of domestic governments. Their willingness to use violence is often more destabilizing than the activities of revolutionary or terror groups alone. In fact, there is a fine line between the two, and occasionally organized-crime groups may operate as both, or have ties to terrorist groups like the Revolutionary Armed Forces of Colombia. (See Table 5.1 in Chapter 5.) Most of the time, the only apparent difference between organized-crime and terror groups is that most terrorists have political or religious feelings, rather than profit, as motivation for their attacks on government or infrastructure.

Organized-crime groups originating in Russia and areas nearby are a growing concern. There are 8,000 Russian/Eastern European/Eurasian criminal groups, 150 of which are ethnic-oriented. These include Chechens, Georgians, Armenians, and Russian-ethnic Koreans. These groups maintain close ties to established American criminal groups such as the American La Cosa Nostra, Italian organized-crime groups, and drug-trafficking organizations. However, these groups particularly participate in complex criminal activity such as gasoline tax fraud, cybersecurity breaches, bankruptcy fraud, insurance fraud, and health care industry fraud.

Countering money-laundering efforts has also gained significant importance in the wake of the September 11, 2001, terrorist attacks on America. Money laundered through legitimate companies and nonprofit organizations has been tracked to various terrorist activities. In January 2001 the U.S. Treasury Department issued a new money-laundering guidance system. The system primarily calls for private businesses and citizens to be more aware of their banking practices and to "apply enhanced scrutiny to their private banking and similar high dollar value accounts and transactions where such accounts or transactions may involve the proceeds of corruption by senior foreign political figures, their immediate family or close associates." This issue gained increasing importance in late 2002, when money was believed to have been laundered for terrorist organizations through the bank of a Saudi Arabian princess. Efforts to tighten lax regulation of financial institutions around the world are a top priority for the administration of President George W. Bush.

Widely publicized policies for countering transnational threats like terrorism and organized crime have been adopted by the United States. These include Presidential Directive 62, signed in May 1998, which establishes a systematic approach to counterterrorism. An International Crime Control Strategy has also been created. Each year, a U.S. National Drug Control Strategy is adopted. Other legislative steps undertaken by the U.S. Congress to counter various transnational threats include: the 2001 USA Patriot Act ("Uniting and Strengthening America by Providing Appropriate Tools Required to Intercept and Obstruct Terrorism"), Civil Asset Forfeiture Reform Act of 2000, Money Laundering and Financial Crimes Strategy Act of 1998, and the Controlled Substances Trafficking Prohibition Act of 1998. The challenge now is to implement these strategies effectively.

In response to international crime, the FBI has three distinct points of strategy: first, provide an active overseas presence, in order to establish relationships with foreign law enforcement agencies; second, train foreign law enforcement officers in both basic and advanced investigative techniques and principles, in order to promote cooperation; and third, build an institution to help promote the rule of law in newly democratic republics, which will protect U.S. interests and citizens in these countries and bring stability to their regions.

INFORMATION TECHNOLOGY (IT) AND NATIONAL SECURITY

Many functions of national security, including the use of computers and communications to thwart or attack an

TABLE 10.1

Potential threats to critical computer-related infrastructures, 2002

Threat	Description
Criminal groups	There is an increased use of cyber intrusions by criminal groups who attack systems for purposes of monetary gain.
Foreign intelligence services	Foreign intelligence services use cyber tools as part of their information gathering and espionage activities.
Hackers	Hackers sometimes crack into networks for the thrill of the challenge or for bragging rights in the hacker community. While hacking once required a fair amount of skill or computer knowledge, hackers can now download attack scripts and protocols from the Internet and launch them against victim sites. Thus, while attack tools have become more sophisticated, they have also become easier to use.
Hacktivists	Hacktivism refers to politically motivated attacks on publicly accessible Web pages or e-mail servers. These groups and individuals overload e-mail servers and hack into Web sites to send a political message.
Information warfare	Several nations are aggressively working to develop information warfare doctrine, programs and capabilities. Such capabilities enable a single entity to have a significant and serious impact by disrupting the supply, communications, and economic infrastructures that support military power—impacts that, according to the Director of Central Intelligence,[1] can affect the daily lives of Americans across the country.
Insider threat	The disgruntled organization insider is a principal source of computer crimes. Insiders may not need a great deal of knowledge about computer intrusions because their knowledge of a victim system often allows them to gain unrestricted access to cause damage to the system or to steal system data.
Virus writers	Virus writers are posing an increasingly serious threat. Several destructive computer viruses and "worms" have harmed files and hard drives, including the Melissa Macro, the CIH (Chernobyl), and Nimda viruses and the Explore.Zip and CodeRed worms.

[1]Prepared Statement of George J. Tenet, director of central intelligence, before the Senate Select Committee on Intelligence, February 2, 2000.

SOURCE: "Table 1: Observed Threats to Critical Infrastructure," in *Critical Infrastructure Protection: Federal Efforts Require a More Coordinated and Comprehensive Approach for Protecting Information Systems*, GAO-02-474, U.S. General Accounting Office, Washington, DC, July 2002

enemy, are evolving rapidly. With each new improvement in information technology (IT), information warfare (IW) and computer security become more important issues for security planners. Federal, state, and local agencies involved in national security rely extensively on computer systems and electronic data. All computer systems, however, contain weaknesses and vulnerabilities that put critical operations and security assets at risk of compromise or disruption.

An infrastructure-protection strategy was outlined in Presidential Decision Directive 63 to safeguard government and privately controlled systems from computer-based attacks. However, although many have sought to implement the directive, in key areas there has been limited progress. The approach of federal agencies has been to develop cooperative relationships with private firms and nonfederal agencies in order to raise awareness and share information, but analysis of vulnerabilities across certain sectors has been limited. Nor does a national plan exist that clearly spells out the roles and responsibilities of federal, state, and local agencies and their contractors, or which defines interim objectives, in strengthening the security of their systems.

The Growth of IT: Processor/Chip Development

The fundamental driving force of the information revolution continues to be the rapid and consistent rate at which silicon-based devices, like computer chips and microprocessors, are developing. Since 1981 processor speeds for personal computers have risen several hundredfold. This phenomenon came to be called "Moore's Law," after Gordon Moore, one of the engineers who founded Intel, the world's dominant microprocessor manufacturer. Specifically, Moore's Law describes a general truth of IT development: thanks to miniaturization and the use of continually better materials, the number of transistors that can be placed on an integrated circuit doubles approximately every 18 months.

Personal computers experienced similar increases in standard memory configurations, hard drive storage system capacities, and modem speeds. Bandwidths—communications line capacities—have also increased. Increased bandwidths have enabled leaps in the speed and convenience of common software functions such as scrolling text and transferring graphics. In addition, this type of technology has become more and more accessible to the general public, making life convenient but also creating dangerous tools.

These increased capabilities have transformed the way the U.S. government and military use technology and the way in which enemies of the United States are able to access information and potentially cause the country harm. In addition, the spread of technology has created an increasing interconnectivity between computer systems, which, though useful for many purposes, also creates substantial risks. According to the U.S. General Accounting Office (GAO) report *Critical Infrastructure Protection: Federal Efforts Require a More Coordinated and Comprehensive Approach for Protecting Information Systems* (July 22, 2002), the interconnectivity of government computer systems allows individuals or groups to launch attacks across a span of these systems or computers, making it easy to disguise identity, location, and intent. In turn, this can make it difficult to find the attackers. Potential risks include the compromise of confidential material, disruption of communications and computer-assisted operations, and corruption of the integrity of data. Table 10.1 lists some of the computer-related threats to the U.S. government that the GAO has observed.

The terrorists that struck the United States on September 11, 2001, made use of easily obtained technology, such as e-mail and cell phones, to orchestrate the attacks. By using public computers, such as those in Internet cafés and public libraries, and cell phones, potential attackers

TABLE 10.2

Types of computer attacks

	What is it?	How does it spread?	Who is at risk?	What damage can it do?
Code Red	Code Red is a worm, which is a computer attack that propagates through networks without user intervention. This particular worm makes use of a vulnerability in Microsoft's Internet Information Services (IIS) Web server software— specifically, a buffer overflow.	The worm scans the Internet, identifies vulnerable systems, and infects these systems by installing itself. Each newly installed worm joins all the others, causing the rate of scanning to grow rapidly.	Users with Microsoft IIS server installed with Windows NT version 4.0 or Windows 2000.	The program can deface Web sites, and was designed to perform a DoS attack against the www.whitehouse.gov Web site. It can also decrease the speed of the Internet.
Code Red II	Code Red II is also a worm that exploits the same IIS vulnerability. However, the worm also opens a backdoor on an infected server that allows any follow-on remote attacker to execute arbitrary commands.	Code Red II spreads like Code Red; however, in doing so, it selects addresses that are in the same network range as the infected computer to increase the likelihood of finding susceptible victims.	Users with Microsoft IIS Web server software Internet installed with Windows 2000.	Like Code Red, Code Red II can decrease the speed of the Internet. Unlike Code Red, it also leaves the infected system open to any attacker who can alter or destroy files and create a denial of service. It does not deface Web pages.
SirCam	SirCam is a malicious computer virus that spreads through E-mail and potentially through unprotected network connections. Once the malicious code has been executed on a system, it may reveal or delete sensitive information.	This mass-mailing virus attempts to send itself to E-mail addresses found in the Windows Address Book and addresses found in cached browser files. It also attempts to copy itself to specific Windows networked computers.	Any E-mail user or user of a computer with unprotected Windows network connections to the infected computer.	SirCam can publicly release sensitive information and delete files and folders. It can also fill the remaining free space on the computer's hard drive. Furthermore, it can lead to a decrease in the speed of the Internet.

SOURCE: "Table 1: High-level Comparison of the Attacks," in *Information Security: Code Red, Code Red II, and SirCam Attacks Highlight Need for Proactive Measures,* GAO-01-1073T, U.S. General Accounting Office, Washington, DC, August 29, 2001

can decrease law enforcement and intelligence agencies' ability to find or stop them.

The Expanding Scope of Information Warfare (IW) Against the U.S. Government

The scope of IW can be defined by the "players" and three dimensions of their interactions: their nature, level, and arena (means of interaction). (See Figure 10.2.) Nation-states or combinations of nation-states are not the only players. Nonstate actors (including political, ethnic, and religious groups; organized crime; international and transnational organizations; and even individuals, empowered by laptops and fast Internet connections) are able to engage in information attacks and to develop information strategies to achieve their desired ends. They can pose information threats, engage in information attacks, and develop digital warfare strategies, such as the introduction of digital "viruses" and "worms," to achieve their ends. (A digital virus is usually passed from computer to computer via e-mail in attachments sent to unsuspecting people. Digital worms are a type of computer attack that propagates through networks without user intervention.) Some examples of particularly problematic attacks are shown in Table 10.2.

Attacks on information systems are a fact of life in the information age. Only a small portion of these

FIGURE 10.2

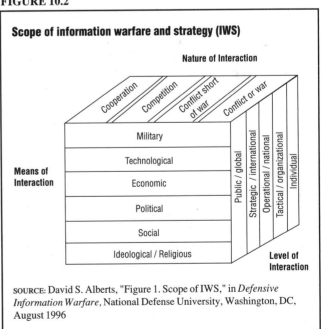

Scope of information warfare and strategy (IWS)

SOURCE: David S. Alberts, "Figure 1. Scope of IWS," in *Defensive Information Warfare,* National Defense University, Washington, DC, August 1996

attacks result in significant loss or damage—the vast majority do not. These are the computer equivalents of crimes such as trespassing, public nuisance, minor vandalism, and petty theft. Yet large companies and the government are at risk from attacks against their computer

FIGURE 10.3

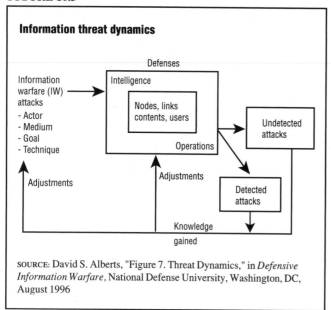

Information threat dynamics

SOURCE: David S. Alberts, "Figure 7. Threat Dynamics," in *Defensive Information Warfare,* National Defense University, Washington, DC, August 1996

systems and networks, as well as espionage committed with IT.

CLASSIFYING THREATS. As with any national security concern, the first task of those who would undertake information warfare defense (IWD) is to identify and classify threats. Some planners refer to such threats within a spectrum known as "the threat space." There are isolated and limited consequences associated with the failure to counter attacks in the range of threats on one end of the spectrum, but there are potentially catastrophic consequences in failing to counter threats on the other end. Planners divide the threat space into three main areas, or regions: 1) everyday—troublesome challenges that exact a price in vigilance but do not pose a threat to national security; 2) potentially strategic—may or may not have national security implications; and 3) strategic—have definite national security implications.

In the category of everyday threats are attacks on commercial targets, which include information age versions of fraud, theft, and white-collar crimes, combined with some transformations of violent crime into virtual form. Some of these attacks can amount to bank robbery, when digital money, in the form of assets and services, is transferred out of accounts. However, attacks by competing commercial organizations typically do not target money but rather vital information, also known as trade secrets. Still, theft of trade secrets has the potential for more serious consequences than isolated thefts or embezzlement. Such attacks may constitute "economic spying" or commercial espionage, and can become a potential strategic threat (part of the middle area of the threat space) when key industries are targeted by foreign companies.

The second area of the threat space is potentially strategic threats, attacks on the country's national or inter-

national physical/monetary infrastructures. These include attacks on systems and services related to public safety, energy, finance, and communications. Hackers mount the vast majority of these attacks. Their motives run the gamut from financial to entertainment to sociopathy to terroristic.

Only a small number of such lone-perpetrator attacks are likely to have strategic consequences, though they can clearly result in significant data loss, interrupted services, and stolen assets. It is conceivable that a hacker attack could somehow mushroom into a national security concern, though unlikely. A well-planned and coordinated infrastructure attack would be another matter, however, and would probably qualify as digital warfare, with strategic consequences.

The strategic category of the threat space contains a relatively small number of threats that must be defended against with great vigor. These would include attacks against U.S. systems that control and safeguard weapons of mass destruction and the country's minimum essential emergency communication network. Other systems and/or networks in this category would be associated with the National Command Authority; command, control, communications, and intelligence; and intelligence, especially information regarding sources and methods.

Figure 10.3 is a diagram showing how information threats and defense work. Attackers have their choice of the time, place, medium, and method of attack. The technology edge also goes to the attacker—it is difficult to perfect defenses at an affordable cost. Defense planners know that IW is a learning environment, with attackers learning from undetected attacks, whether successful or not, and both sides learning from detected attacks, whether successful or not.

In 1988 the Defense Advanced Research Projects Agency, a Department of Defense (DOD) agency, established a Computer Emergency Response Team (CERT) to address the computer security concerns of research users. Based on incidents reported to CERT, an estimated 90 percent of IW attacks are perpetrated using readily available tools and techniques. Only 1 attack in 20 is noticed by the victim. Corresponding results of a Defense Information Systems Agency study show that only 1 in 20 IW attacks may even be reported, and similar findings have been reported by others.

Despite the lack of reporting, in a small number of cases IT technology used against major corporations and the U.S. government can cause major financial and national security costs. According to CERT (in the GAO report *Critical Infrastructure Protection*), the number of cyberattacks against critical infrastructure has risen remarkably since the terrorist attacks of September 11, 2001. In the first six months of 2002 alone, information-security incidents had risen to almost 45,000, with all

FIGURE 10.4

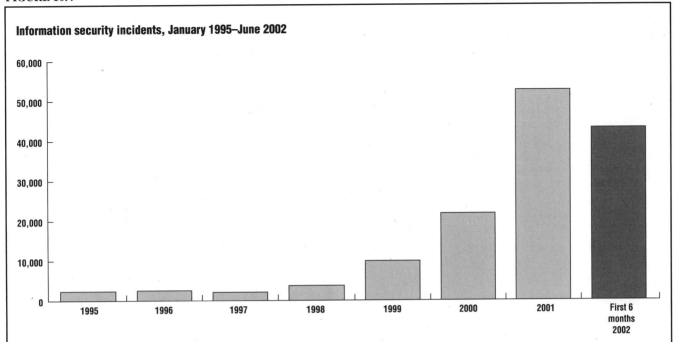

Information security incidents, January 1995–June 2002

SOURCE: "Figure 2: Information Security Incidents Reported to Carnegie-Mellon's CERT Coordination Center: 1995-the first six months of 2002," in *Critical Infrastructure Protection: Significant Challenges Need to Be Addressed,* GAO-02-961T, U.S. General Accounting Office, Washington, DC, July 24, 2002. Data from the CERT Coordination Center, Carnegie Mellon University, Pittsburgh, PA

incidents for the entire year of 2001 numbering about 55,000. (See Figure 10.4.)

COMPUTER CRIMES AND THE GOVERNMENT. By the 1990s computer-assisted crime became a major part of white-collar crime and it has had an impact on the way the government works. Computer crime is faceless and bloodless, and the financial gain can be huge. The National Institute of Justice defines different types of computer criminal activity as:

- Computer abuse—A broad range of intentional acts that may or may not be specifically prohibited by criminal statutes. Any intentional act involving knowledge of computer use or technology . . . if one or more perpetrators made or could have made gain and/or one or more victims suffered or could have suffered loss.

- Computer fraud—Any crime in which a person uses the computer either directly or as a vehicle for deliberate misrepresentation or deception, usually to cover up embezzlement or theft of money, goods, services, or information.

- Computer crime—Any violation of a computer-crime law.

A common computer crime involves tampering with accounting and banking records, especially through electronic funds transfers. These electronic funds transfers, or wire transfers, are cash-management systems that allow the customer electronic access to an account, automatic teller machines, and internal banking procedures, including on-line teller terminals and computerized check products. Money could potentially be taken from the U.S. government through these methods.

Computers and associated technology (printers, modems, computer bulletin boards, e-mail) are used for credit card fraud, counterfeiting, bank embezzlement, theft of secret documents, vandalism, and other illegal activities. Experts place the annual value of computer crime at anywhere from $550 million to $5 billion a year. Even the larger figure may be an underestimate because many victims try to hide the crime. The government and businesses may not want to admit that their computer security has been breached and their confidential files and accounts are vulnerable. No centralized databank exists for computer-crime statistics, and computer crimes are often written up under other categories, such as fraud and embezzlement.

In 1986 Congress passed the Computer Fraud and Abuse Act (PL 99-474), which makes it illegal to carry out fraud on a computer. The Computer Abuse Amendments of 1994 (PL 103-322) make it a federal crime "through means of a computer used in interstate commerce or communications . . . [to] damage, or cause damage to, a computer, computer system, network, information, data, or program . . . with reckless disregard" for the consequences of those actions to the computer owner. This law refers to someone who maliciously destroys or changes computer records or knowingly distributes a virus that shuts down a computer system.

The 2002 Computer Crime and Security Survey was conducted by the Computer Security Institute in San Francisco, California, with the participation of the FBI's San Francisco Computer Intrusion Squad. According to the survey results, of 503 computer security practitioners, government agencies, major U.S. corporations, financial and medical institutions, and universities, some 90 percent had detected computer-security breaches in the last 12 months. Some 80 percent of respondents stated that their institution had suffered financial losses because of computer breaches. About 44 percent of respondents (233) reported collective financial losses of over $455 million.

According to the survey, the most serious financial losses resulted from the theft of proprietary information, with 26 respondents reporting total losses of over $170 million. Still, despite the significant amount of financial losses, only 34 percent of respondents stated that the computer intrusions were reported to law enforcement. This low level of reporting may have to do with an unwillingness to reveal the proprietary information stolen.

Survey respondents reported various types of attacks on, or unauthorized uses of, their computer systems. Some 78 percent of respondents stated they had detected employee abuse of Internet access privileges, such as downloading pornography or pirating software. More than 4 out of 5 respondents (85 percent) reported the detection of computer viruses, and 70 percent stated that computer attacks had resulted in vandalism to their system or Web site. Twelve percent of respondents reported the theft of transaction information through computer attacks, and 6 percent reported financial fraud (up from only 3 percent in 2000).

For the government, one type of computer crime involves the sabotage or threatened sabotage of its computer systems and networks. It is almost impossible to determine how often this happens, since very few incidents are reported. In the computer age, several new scenarios of sabotage involving employee threats have come into being. A disgruntled employee might want to take revenge on the government. A systems administrator responsible for running computer systems might feel unappreciated. A discontented employee might create a "logic bomb" that explodes a month after he or she has left and destroys most or all of the computer records, bringing operations to a halt.

Although infrequent, charges have sometimes been brought against those who destroy a company's computer system. In February 1998 the U.S. Department of Justice (DOJ) brought charges against a former chief computer network program designer of a high-tech company that did considerable work for the National Aeronautics and Space Administration (NASA) and the U.S. Navy. The designer had worked for the company for 11 years. After he was terminated, it was alleged that in retaliation he "intentionally caused irreparable damage to Omega's computer system by activating a 'bomb' that permanently deleted all of the company's sophisticated software programs." The loss cost the company at least $10 million in sales and contracts. Such crimes committed directly against government agencies could have the potential for even greater damage.

COMPUTER HACKING: EASY ENOUGH FOR KIDS? Illegal accessing of a computer, known as hacking, is a crime committed frequently by juveniles. When it is followed by manipulation of the information of private, corporate, or government databases and networks, it can be costly. Another means of computer hacking involves creation of a "virus" program. The virus resides inside another program and is activated by a predetermined code to create havoc in the host computer. Virus programs can be transmitted either through the sharing of disks and programs or through e-mail.

Cases of juvenile hacking have been around for at least two decades and have included: teens getting into more than 60 computer networks, including the Memorial Sloan-Kettering Cancer Center and the Los Alamos National Laboratory in 1983; several juvenile hackers accessing AT&T's computer network in 1987; and teens hacking into computer networks and Web sites for NASA, the Korean Atomic Research Institute, America Online, the U.S. Senate, the White House, the U.S. Army, and the DOJ in the 1990s.

In 1998 the U.S. Secret Service filed the first criminal case against a juvenile for a computer crime. Computer hacking by the unnamed perpetrator shut down the Worcester, Massachusetts, airport in 1997 for six hours. The airport is integrated into the Federal Aviation Administration's traffic system by telephone lines. The suspect got into the communication system and disabled it by sending a series of computer commands that changed the data carried on the system. As a result, the airport could not function. (No accidents occurred during that time.) According to the DOJ, the juvenile pled guilty in return for two years' probation, a fine, and community service. U.S. Attorney Donald K. Stern, lead attorney for the prosecution, observed: "Computer and telephone networks are at the heart of vital services provided by the government and private industry, and our critical infrastructure. They are not toys for the entertainment of teenagers. Hacking a computer or telephone network can create a tremendous risk to the public and we will prosecute juvenile hackers in appropriate cases."

On December 6, 2000, 18-year-old Canadian Robert Russell Sanford pled guilty to six felony charges of breach of computer security and one felony charge of aggravated theft in connection with cyberattacks on U.S. Postal Service computers. Sanford was placed on 5 years' probation, but could have been sentenced to up to 20 years in prison. Sanford was also ordered to pay over $45,000 in restitution fines for the cyberattacks.

On September 21, 2000, a 16-year-old from Miami entered a guilty plea and was sentenced to six months' detention for illegally intercepting electronic communications on military computer networks. The juvenile admitted that he was responsible for August and October 1999 computer intrusions into a military computer network used by the Defense Threat Reduction Agency (DTRA), an arm of the DOD. The DTRA is responsible for reducing threats against the United States from nuclear, biological, chemical, conventional, and special weapons.

THE VULNERABILITY OF THE U.S. DEPARTMENT OF DEFENSE (DOD). Investigators from the GAO, in a report prepared for two congressional committees, observed that the Pentagon experienced as many as 250,000 "attacks" on its computers in 1995, probably from computer hackers cruising the Internet. In 65 percent of the attempts, hackers were able to gain entry into a computer network. The investigators warned, "The potential for catastrophic damage is great, especially if terrorists or enemy governments break into the Pentagon's systems." The report concluded that the military's current security program was "dated, inconsistent and incomplete."

Even after this warning, in 1998 hackers broke into unclassified Pentagon networks and altered personnel and payroll data, in what Deputy Defense Secretary John Hamre called "the most organized and systematic attack the Pentagon has seen to date." In 1999 there were a reported 22,124 cyberattacks against the DOD alone, costing the government an estimated $25 billion to bolster computer-security procedures in order to ward off future attacks.

IT ESPIONAGE. In a computerized global economy where any advantage given to the competition can mean success or failure for a company, trade secrets, copyrighted information, patents, and trademarks become very important. The collapse of a large corporation because of the loss of such information could have widespread effects on the U.S. and world economies. In addition, companies that create military supplies, weapons, and the like for the government may have information that could be deadly in the wrong hands. Though most major companies have developed sophisticated security systems to protect their secrets, in 2001 the GAO reported that the American Society for Industrial Security, which surveys *Fortune* 500 companies, estimated that potential losses to American businesses from thefts of proprietary information were $45 billion in 2000.

The theft of classified corporate information has become a major issue for national governments worldwide. Many governments have begun to use their national intelligence organizations to protect local companies from espionage by foreign companies or governments. In the United States the Central Intelligence Agency has tried to convince Congress that the agency could be useful in protecting American companies from foreign industrial spies. The Economic Espionage Act of 1996 (PL 104-294) made it a federal crime to steal trade secrets for another country.

OTHER THREATS. Most of the crimes listed above were committed with readily available tools. Of most concern to the U.S. government are attacks that might move beyond these easily available tools and techniques to cause significant damage and disruption to the U.S. information infrastructure, compromising the integrity of vital information. Analysts have been able to identify groups, domestic and global, with the motivation and opportunity to launch such attacks. Given the present vulnerabilities of many U.S. computer systems, a well-planned, coordinated strategic IW attack could have major consequences. Such an attack, or the threat of such an attack, could thwart U.S. foreign policy objectives, degrade military performance, result in significant economic loss, and/or undermine citizens' confidence in government. In light of such threats, the U.S. government is taking a proactive approach to defense.

Finding Solutions: Protecting the United States

Because both attackers and defenders make adjustments after every IW attempt they make or perceive, defense against such threats is not a one-time effort but a continuous activity. Collection and analysis of information about attacks is vital if defenders are to stay on par with the attackers. Defenders must be proactive and anticipate future methods of attack so that timely defenses can be developed.

Several executive orders, presidential directives, and acts have focused on, or mentioned activities related to, cyber-critical infrastructure protection. (See Table 10.3.) Other methods of protection using new and emerging technology include facial recognition software, which might be used to identify suspect criminal aliens at ports of entry or in other places. In 2001 alone three government agencies (the State Department, DOJ, and DOD) had received over $10.6 million by June to research such technology. (See Table 10.4.)

Experts at the National Defense University have developed a defense-in-depth strategy against IW attacks to deal with the previously mentioned threat levels. (See Figure 10.5.) The strategy suggests three successively stronger defensive levels corresponding to everyday threats, potentially strategic threats, and strategic threats. Basic to this thinking is that more sophisticated threats will come from fewer sources. The first two lines of defense are designed to identify and separate the most skilled, resourceful, and persistent adversaries. The last line of defense is meant to fully repel them. Intelligence and monitoring efforts are concentrated on a smaller population, increasing the chances of a successful defense. Layered on top of these lines of defense are "information first" and "security first" approaches: for everyday

TABLE 10.3

Key executive orders, Presidential decision directives, acts, and directives that mention activities related to cyber critical infrastructure protection, 1974–2001

Law or regulation	Description
Executive orders	
Executive Order 12472, "Assignment of National Security and Emergency Preparedness Telecommunications Functions"	Signed in 1984, this order established the National Communication Systems and assigns national security emergency preparedness responsibilities for telecommunications.
Executive Order 12656, "Assignment of Emergency Preparedness Responsibilities"	Signed in 1988, this order assigns federal national security emergency preparedness responsibilities to federal departments and agencies for various sectors.
Executive Order 13231, "Critical Infrastructure Protection in the Information Age"	Signed in October 2001, this order establishes the President's Critical Infrastructure Protection Board to coordinate the federal efforts and programs associated with protecting our nation's critical infrastructures. A special advisor to the President for cyberspace security chairs the board. This order also tasks the board to recommend policies and coordinate programs for protecting information systems for critical infrastructure protection. The executive order also established 10 standing committees to support the board's work on a wide range of critical information infrastructure efforts.
Executive Order 13228 "Establishing the Office of Homeland Security and the Homeland Security Council"	Signed in October 2001, this order establishes the Office of Homeland Security, whose mission is to develop and coordinate the implementation of a comprehensive national strategy to secure the United States from terrorist threats or attacks. The office will coordinate the exective branch's efforts to detect, prepare for, prevent, protect against, respond to, and recover from terrorist attacks within the United States.
Presidential decision directives	
PDD 39, "Presidential Decision Directive on Terrorism,"	Signed in 1995 this directive sets forth the U.S. general policy to use all appropriate means to deter, defeat, and respond to all terrorist attacks against U.S. interests. More specifically, PDD 39 directs federal departments to take various measures to (1) reduce the vulnerabilities to terrorism, (2) deter and respond to terrorism, and (3) develop effective capabilities to prevent and manage the consequences of terrorist use of weapons of mass destruction. The directive charges the FBI as the lead investigative agency to reduce U.S. vulnerabilities to terrorism.
PDD 62 "Combating Terrorism"	Signed in 1998, this directive established the Office of the National Coordinator for Security, Infrastructure Protection and Counter-Terrorism. PDD 62 also reinforces the mission of many of the agencies charged with roles in defending terrorism by codifying and clarifying their activities in the range of counter-terrorism programs including the protection of the computer-based systems that support critical infrastructure sectors.
PDD 63, "Protection America's Critical Infrastructures"	Signed in 1998, this directive expanded the NIPC at the FBI, and established ISACs in cooperation with the federal government, private sector, and the CIAO to support work in developing a national plan.
PDD 67, "Enduring Constitutional Government and Continuity of Government Operations"	Signed in 1998, this directive required federal agencies to develop continuity of operations plans for essential operations.
PDD 75, "U.S. Counterintelligence Effectiveness-Counterintelligence for the 21st Century"	Signed in 2001, this directive establishes a counterintelligence board of directors, the National Security Council Deputies Committee, and a National Counterintelligence Executive.
Other directive/acts	
National Security Directive 42, National Policy for the Security of National Security Systems	Signed in 1990, this directive designates the Director, NSA the national manager for national security telecommunications and information systems security and calls upon him or her to promote and coordinate defense efforts against threats to national security systems.
The Stafford Act	Enacted in 1974, this act enables the Federal Emergency Management Agency (FEMA) to provide supplementary federal assistance to individuals, state and local governments, and certain private nonprofit organizations to assist them in recovering from the devastating effects of major disasters.
The USA PATRIOT Act	Enacted in 2001, this act enables law enforcement entities to apply modern surveillance capabilities to new technologies, such as the Internet, and execute these devices in mulitple jurisdictions anywhere in the United States.
The Aviation and Transportation Security Act	Enacted in 2001, this act created the Transportation Security Administration (TSA) in the Department of Transportation. The act gives TSA direct responsibility for aviation and all other transportation security.

SOURCE: "Table 2: Key Executive Orders, Presidential Decision Directives, Acts, and Directives That Mention Activities Related to Cyber CIP," in *Critical Infrastructure Protection: Federal Efforts Require a More Coordinated and Comprehensive Approach for Protecting Information Systems*, GAO-02-474, U.S. General Accounting Office, Washington, DC, July 2002

threats, the goal is to protect against access to information; for more strategic threats, the goal is to keep hackers out by restricting access and/or connectivity.

PRIVATE- VERSUS PUBLIC-SECTOR APPROACHES. IWD strategy also calls for a division of responsibility between the public and private sector, along with, in higher-threat contexts, collaboration between them. (See Figure 10.6.) Primary responsibility for everyday threats would be the private sector's, as handling of such threats is simply a cost of doing business in today's information society and low-

cost defenses are available. Responding to strategic threats is the responsibility of the government, coordinating somewhat with the private sector and international organizations (especially in the case of attacks on networks providing vital services). In general, the "potentially strategic" region is one intended to be a zone of collaboration.

Commercial organizations treating everyday attacks as a cost of doing business can implement countermeasures if their costs will be less than the potential loss posed by the threat. For example, insurance can be

TABLE 10.4

Amounts obligated by federal departments for facial recognition technology, 1987–June 2001

Dollars in thousands

Department/Agency	Pre-1997	1997	1998	1999	2000	2001 (through June 30)	Total
State	$0	$0	$0	$12	$450	$100	**$562**
Energy	125	0	0	400	0	0	**525**
Justice	3,668	4,843	5,500	787	784	5,709	**21,291**
Defense	5,730	744	3,171	2,872	7,330	4,843	**24,690**
Total	**$9,523**	**$5,587**	**$8,671**	**$4,071**	**$8,564**	**$10,652**	**$47,068**

SOURCE: "Table 1: Amounts Obligated by Federal Departments for Facial Recognition Technology, by Fiscal Year," in *Federal Funding for Selected Surveillance Technologies,* GAO-02-438R, U.S. General Accounting Office, Washington, DC, March 14, 2002

FIGURE 10.5

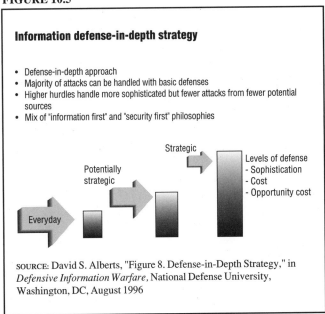

Information defense-in-depth strategy

- Defense-in-depth approach
- Majority of attacks can be handled with basic defenses
- Higher hurdles handle more sophisticated but fewer attacks from fewer potential sources
- Mix of "information first" and "security first" philosophies

Everyday → Potentially strategic → Strategic

Levels of defense
- Sophistication
- Cost
- Opportunity cost

SOURCE: David S. Alberts, "Figure 8. Defense-in-Depth Strategy," in *Defensive Information Warfare,* National Defense University, Washington, DC, August 1996

FIGURE 10.6

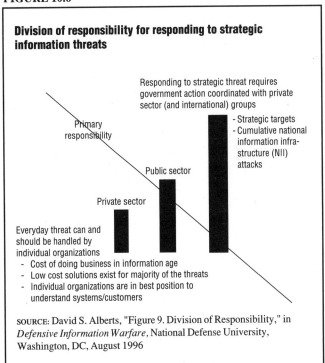

Division of responsibility for responding to strategic information threats

Responding to strategic threat requires government action coordinated with private sector (and international) groups

Primary responsibility

Public sector

Private sector

- Strategic targets
- Cumulative national information infra-structure (NII) attacks

Everyday threat can and should be handled by individual organizations
- Cost of doing business in information age
- Low cost solutions exist for majority of the threats
- Individual organizations are in best position to understand systems/customers

SOURCE: David S. Alberts, "Figure 9. Division of Responsibility," in *Defensive Information Warfare,* National Defense University, Washington, DC, August 1996

purchased to protect against relatively low-probability events with large potential costs.

Public organizations entrusted with national security functions must take a different approach. The cost of a breach in their information defenses includes not only the actual costs of the particular incident or intrusion but a potential loss of faith, trust, and confidence in the nation's security and information systems.

USING IW TO PROTECT THE UNITED STATES. U.S. national security strategies now recognize and utilize IW as an instrument of national power either independent of or complementary to U.S. military operations. American-initiated IW against an adversary usually bears a resemblance to classic methods of competition, conflict, and warfare, but also uses more recent methods. It can run the gamut from propaganda campaigns (including media war) to attacks (both physical and nonphysical) against commanders, their information sources, and their means of communicating with their forces.

The Persian Gulf War of 1991 has become known as America's first information war. In that war, the power of IT was used to leverage information, significantly improving all aspects of warfare, including logistics, command, control, communications, computers, intelligence, surveillance, and reconnaissance. The victory of the United States and its allies in the Gulf War deterred potential adversaries from taking on the United States in the same manner as Iraq, and fostered much thinking about new strategies for countering conventional forces. Thus, IW has become a strategy for our time: potential adversaries want to engage in it, as the United States does, to achieve some of the objectives of conventional warfare.

IWD embodies actions taken to defend against information attacks, especially those against decision-makers, their information, and their communications. These attacks can be launched during peacetime at nonmilitary targets by nonmilitary groups, both foreign and domestic. National security planners attempt to defend against many different kinds of information attacks, with a focus on attacks against the U.S. information infrastructure.

IW has some potential characteristics that traditional military planners strive for, including low-cost precision and stealth. IW can threaten the ability of a state's military to interpose itself between its population and "enemies of the state," causing what defense planners term a "loss of sanctuary"—just what the United States strives to achieve with its air, sea, and missile defense systems. Sanctuary can be defined as a working space, or buffer, between the population and territorial intrusions by alien enemies.

Information attacks can be very effective in destroying the image of sanctuary. Repeated attacks create a perception of vulnerability and loss of control and can cause a loss of public confidence in the state. These impacts can far exceed any actual damage. This makes the problem of IW challenging.

How will the United States respond to information attacks? Currently there is no consensus. Yet, given that IW can be an instrument of power for niche competitors and nonstate actors, it needs to be taken seriously. Says expert David S. Alberts (*Defensive Information Warfare,* National Defense University, 1996): "If we do not [take the threats seriously], if we rely solely on traditional weapons and concepts of war, we may be building our own 21st Century Maginot line [the ill-fated World War II frontline of the French] that can be outflanked with the speed of light."

Some software engineers and others believe the country is not as vulnerable to information attacks as has been claimed. They point to overlaps and duplications that would make it very hard to completely disrupt a given set of services or functions. But unruly "legacy" systems—those in use now but installed some years ago—also carry big disadvantages. As experts from the National Defense University reiterate, the issue is not whether an attack could totally destroy or disrupt a particular system or type of service, but whether it might result in the perception of a failure. Redundancies in most American military systems are neither complete nor reliable. Legacy systems were designed and built with little or no attention to security; thus they are difficult to protect and secure. As the need for interconnectivity and interoperability increases, more and more systems are being lashed together with "workarounds." These patches, in many cases, compromise security. As David S. Alberts says, "It should be clear that the disadvantages of our current collection of legacy systems are not a blessing in disguise but rather the source of problems that need to be addressed."

Battlefield Systems Technology

NEW TECHNOLOGY AND ITS LIMITS. The roots of information-based battlefield and computer warfare go back several decades, along with technical and signals intelligence collection by satellites and sensors. Digital information of many kinds is of increasing importance in battlefield warfare, including command and control, mission planning, simulation, intelligence, and psychological operations. Indeed, every aspect of physical war and of gauging the threat of war is being transformed by the ever-quickening speed and ever-lessening cost of collecting, processing, and transmitting information.

The most important new battle technologies of the last few decades have been precision-guided munitions, long-range airborne and space-based sensors, tandem global positioning systems (GPS), and inertial navigation systems (INS). With these new technologies, almost any target or source of information that can be located and identified can be engaged and disabled.

Because of this, a military offense must spend more time seeking targets than it previously did, and a military defense must spend more time and resources hiding them. Hiding can be done through getting them to mimic background or civilian objects and masking their "signatures"—the distinctive visual, radar, or spectroscopic profiles that, when sufficiently recognized by a weapons system, enable it to identify the object as the target and destroy it. Traditional principles of battle warfare, such as firepower and maneuvering, lessen a bit in importance with these new technologies.

GLOBAL POSITIONING SYSTEMS (GPS). National security specialists know that it will be very difficult to maintain the current American advantage in IW in coming decades. Relevant technologies increasingly spring from the commercial marketplace, not the military, often becoming available without restriction to prospective enemies. Sophisticated, well-funded opponents may be able to buy or lease an array of advanced communications and control technologies from around the world: for example, GPS, surveillance, communications, direct broadcast, internetworking, cryptography, and air-based imaging systems. The costs of such purchases will likely decrease, as will the costs of IW in general.

GPS, in particular, is rapidly becoming commercially and universally available, with devices costing just a few hundred dollars able to receive signals. For example, accurate GPS data can enable rocket attacks against U.S. forces deployed in smaller contingents. In addition, GPS, coupled with sufficiently good surveillance data and other equipment, can place virtually any fixed facility at risk, including most U.S. logistics dumps, barracks, and command headquarters. These cannot be well hidden and thus can be identified and located if someone knows their general vicinity. If the facilities are public, a terrorist with a portable GPS device on-site would suffice to target it.

Overhead surveillance can locate fixed facilities with an accuracy of within a meter or two. With the fall of the

Soviet Union, a vigorous market developed in such Russian imagery. In the next few decades, the sale of satellites with similar capabilities will permit many countries to acquire and transmit such imagery nearly in real time.

It is conceivable that in a time of crisis, the American military could degrade GPS signals worldwide so that U.S. forces could determine locations far more closely than their adversaries. However, as a practical matter, three factors make this option difficult to implement. First, the U.S. government has promoted the use of GPS for civilian purposes, most notably commercial aviation. Only a major and prolonged crisis could justify the global degradation of information upon which others rely for their safety. Second, GPS may be complemented by other navigation systems, or what specialists call "communications constellations." Third, the development of differential GPS means that if a set of fixed points near a target can be ascertained with precision, the target itself can be located with similar precision. So-called differential correction systems have also come on-line throughout North America, Europe, and East Asia. Their accuracy often exceeds that of military specification systems without differential correction.

UNMANNED AERIAL VEHICLES (UAVs). Additional information-gathering capability comes from the use of digital video cameras on unmanned aerial vehicles (UAVs). UAVs, also known as drones, do the battlefield and reconnaissance tasks usually assigned to manned aircraft, but without a pilot aboard. Instead, they are piloted remotely from the ground by radio links. The advantages are that human life is not placed in harm's way, and the vehicle can be designed without having to safeguard and support an onboard human pilot.

Since the mid-1990s commercially available digital-imaging systems mounted on UAVs have been able to collect high-resolution imagery 50 miles to each side of themselves with real-time data links to ground locations. Although the initial resolution of such systems was relatively imprecise, higher-resolution digital cameras are becoming more widely available. In addition, digital cellular telephony is already available through several technologies. Within several years, it appears such technology will be widely available globally and capable of sufficiently high bandwidth to transmit imagery directly.

BLOCKING COMMUNICATIONS AND HIDING TROOP MOVEMENTS. In UAV and satellite imaging American forces might attempt to deny an enemy communications capability by blocking access to third-party satellites. Such an attempt, however, could present several political obstacles. Commercial satellites have a variety of corporate owners in different countries, and not every satellite owner would necessarily cooperate with U.S. forces. If cooperation were incomplete, an opponent's access to satellite links would not be entirely blocked. Jamming signals to and from geosynchronous satellites also usually requires being in their line of sight; thus it is probably not feasible for the United States to jam all signals to and from them.

Global low-earth-orbit cellular systems would make it even more unlikely that the United States could block an adversary's communications that were handled by a third party. System managers could refuse to transmit signals into or out of a region, but doing so would limit or eliminate local service and service to nonbelligerent neighboring states. It would be very hard to shut down a system used by a terrorist group operating inside a friendly country or to interrupt a more primitive system they were using, based on, say, a citizen's band (CB) radio. Similarly, in any attempt to disrupt another nation's air traffic control network, it would be very difficult not to interfere with international air traffic control operations in the general vicinity.

Increasing global satellite connectivity also decreases the chance for military activity to go undetected. Daylight infantry movements can now only be kept secret to the extent an area is not electronically connected to the outside world. But as even the most remote sites become ever more tied to the global communications network, such movements are more likely to be noticed—and counteracted. The predicted marriage between digital video cameras and digital cellular means that many more military movements will potentially be liable to detection.

The communications and information revolutions have tended to knit the world together. More than ever, to disrupt an enemy's communications is to disrupt those of one's friends. Increasing global communications connectivity—thanks to new technologies such as advanced semiconductors, advanced computers, fiber optics, cellular technology, satellite technology, and advanced networking (including the Internet)—has empowered individuals, governments, and armies, making U.S. national security tasks in this area much more difficult and complex.

FINAL THOUGHTS

Given the current host of emerging threats and shifting alliances, the United States is cautiously stepping into the new millennium armed with a new outlook on its national security goals and needs. The Cold War no longer provides a balance of power in the global arena and regional alliances are becoming increasingly important from a geostrategic perspective. Ideological and philosophical bonds are being replaced with ties that emphasize commerce and other elements of national security. Also of importance is ongoing technological innovation and growth in communication. Each member of the community of nations has its own national security agenda, and the United States, as a leading global power, must maintain relations with the rest of the world without compromising its own national security priorities.

IMPORTANT NAMES AND ADDRESSES

Carnegie Endowment for International Peace
1779 Massachusetts Avenue NW
Washington, DC 20036-2103
(202) 483-7600
FAX: (202) 483-1840
E-mail: info@ceip.org
URL: http://www.ceip.org

Center for Defense Information
1779 Massachusetts Avenue NW
Washington, DC 20036-2109
(202) 332-0600
FAX: (202) 462-4559
E-mail: info@cdi.org
URL: http://www.cdi.org

Center for Nonproliferation Studies
460 Pierce Street
Monterey, CA 93940
(831) 647-4154
FAX: (831) 647-3519
E-mail: cns@miis.edu
URL: http://www.cns.miis.edu

Center for Strategic and International Studies
1800 K Street NW
Washington, DC 20006
(202) 887-0200
FAX: (202) 775-3199
E-mail: webmaster@csis.org
URL: http://www.csis.org

Centers for Disease Control and Prevention
1600 Clifton Road
Atlanta, GA 30333
(404) 639-3534
(800) 311-3435
URL: http://www.cdc.gov

Central Intelligence Agency (CIA)
Office of Public Affairs
Washington, DC 20505

(703) 482-0623
FAX: (703) 482-1789
URL: http://www.cia.gov

Chemical and Biological Arms Control Institute
1747 Pennsylvania Avenue NW, 7th Floor
Washington, DC 20006
(202) 296-3550
FAX: (202) 296-3574
E-mail: cbaci@cbaci.org
URL: http://www.cbaci.org/

Computer Security Resource Center
Computer Security Division
National Institute of Standards and Technology
100 Bureau Drive, Mail Stop 8930
Gaithersburg, MD 20899-8930
(301) 975-2934
URL: http://csrc.nist.gov

Congressional Research Service
The Library of Congress
101 Independence Avenue SE
Washington, DC 20540-7500
(202) 707-5000
URL: http://www.loc.gov/crsinfo

Council for a Livable World
322 4th Street NE
Washington, DC 20002
(202) 543-4100
E-mail: clw@clw.org
URL: http://www.clw.org

Federal Bureau of Investigation (FBI)
935 Pennsylvania Avenue NW, Room 7972
Washington, DC 20535
(202) 324-3000
URL: http://www.fbi.gov

Federation of American Scientists
1717 K Street NW, Suite 209
Washington, DC 20036

(202) 546-3300
FAX: (202) 675-1010
E-mail: fas@fas.org
URL: http://www.fas.org

Institute for Defense & Disarmament Studies
675 Massachusetts Avenue
Cambridge, MA 02139
(617) 354-4337
FAX: (617) 354-1450
E-mail: info@idds.org
URL: http://www.idds.org/

Institute for Science and International Security
236 Massachusetts Avenue NE, Suite 500
Washington, DC 20002
(202) 547-3633
FAX: (202) 547-3634
E-mail: isis@isis-online.org
URL: http://www.isis-online.org

International Institute for Strategic Studies—U.S.
1747 Pennsylvania Avenue NW, 7th Floor
Washington, DC 20006
202 659-1490
FAX: (202) 296-1134
E-mail: taylor@iiss.org
URL: http://www.iiss.org

The International Policy Institute for Counter-Terrorism
Interdisciplinary Center at Herzlia
P.O. Box 167
Herzlia, Israel 46150
FAX: 972-9-9513073
E-mail: info@ict.org.il
URL: http://www.ict.org.il

Joint Chiefs of Staff
Public Affairs Office
9999 Joint Staff Pentagon, Room 2E857
Washington, DC 20318-9999

(703) 697-4272
URL: http://www.dtic.mil/jcs

National Defense University Press
300 5th Avenue
Ft. McNair, DC 20319-6000
(202) 685-4210
FAX: (202) 685-4608
E-mail: ndupress@ndu.edu
URL: http://www.ndu.edu

National Guard Bureau
1411 Jefferson Davis Highway
Arlington, VA 22202-3231
URL: http://www.ngb.army.mil

**Nonproliferation and National
Security Institute**
U.S. Department of Energy
Wackenhut Services, Inc.
P.O. Box 18041, KAFB
Albuquerque, NM 87185
(505) 845-5170
FAX: (505) 845-6147
URL: http://www.nnsi.doe.gov

**North Atlantic Treaty Organisation
(NATO)**
Blvd. Leopold III
1110 Brussels, Belgium
E-mail: natodoc@hq.nato.int
URL: http://www.nato.int

Nuclear Control Institute
1000 Connecticut Avenue NW, Suite 410
Washington, DC 20036
(202) 822-8444
FAX: (202) 452-0892
E-mail: nci@mailback.com
URL: http://www.nci.org

Nuclear Threat Initiative
1747 Pennsylvania Avenue NW, 7th Floor
Washington, DC 20006
(202) 296-4810
FAX: (202) 296-4811
E-mail: contact@nti.org
URL: http://www.nti.org

RAND
P.O. Box 2138
1700 Main Street
Santa Monica, CA 90407-2138
(310) 393-0411
FAX: (310) 393-4818
E-mail: correspondence@rand.org
URL: http://www.rand.org/

**Stockholm International Peace Research
Institute (SIPRI)**
Signalistgatan 9
SE-169 70 Solna, Sweden
46-8-655 97 00
FAX: 46-8-655 97 33
sipri@sipri.org
URL: http://www.sipri.org

United Nations (UN)
Public Inquiries Unit GA-57
New York, NY 10017
(212) 963-4475
FAX: (212) 963-0071
E-mail: inquiries@un.org
URL: http://www.un.org

U.S. Air Force
Office of the Secretary of the Air Force
Public Affairs Resource Library
1690 Air Force Pentagon, Room 4A120
Washington, DC 20330-1690
(703) 697-4100
URL: http://www.af.mil

U.S. Army
Chief of Public Affairs
1500 Army Pentagon
Washington, DC 20310-1500
(703) 602-5201
URL: http://www.army.mil

U.S. Coast Guard
2100 2nd Street SW
Washington, DC 20593
(202) 267-2229
URL: http://www.uscg.mil

U.S. Department of Defense
Director for Public Inquiry and Analysis
1400 Defense Pentagon, Room 3A750

Washington, DC 20301-1400
URL: http://www.dod.gov

U.S. Department of Homeland Security
Nebraska Avenue Complex
Washington, DC 20393
URL: http://www.dhs.gov

U.S. Department of State
2201 C Street NW
Washington, DC 20520
(202) 647-4000
E-mail: askpublicaffairs@state.gov
URL: http://www.state.gov

**U.S. House Permanent Select Committee
on Intelligence**
c/o Congressman Porter J. Goss, Chairman
H-405 U.S. Capitol Building
Washington, DC 20515
(202) 225-4121
URL: http://intelligence.house.gov

U.S. Marine Corps
Director of Public Affairs
2 Navy Annex
Washington, DC 20380-1775
(703) 614-6251
URL: http://www.usmc.mil

U.S. Navy
Office of Information
1200 Navy Pentagon, Room 3E335
Washington, DC 20310-1200
(703) 697-9020
URL: http://www.navy.mil

**U.S. Senate Select Committee on
Intelligence**
211 Hart Senate Office Building
Washington, DC 20510-6475
(202) 224-1700
URL: http://intelligence.senate.gov

The White House
1600 Pennsylvania Avenue NW
Washington, DC 20500
(202) 456-1111
URL: http://www.whitehouse.gov

RESOURCES

The U.S. government provides useful nonclassified information on national security. Government sources include the U.S. Departments of State and Defense, along with government agencies such as the Central Intelligence Agency (CIA), the Federal Bureau of Investigation (FBI) and the former Immigration and Naturalization Service (INS), which has now become the Bureau of Citizenship and Immigration Services in the U.S. Department of Homeland Security.

The U.S. Department of State's annual *Patterns of Global Terrorism* report, mandated by Congress and issued every Spring (the latest version being *Patterns of Global Terrorism 2001*, May 2002), offers detailed assessments of significant terrorist acts. The report also highlights terrorism watch list countries—those that have repeatedly provided state support for international terrorism.

In addition to the *Patterns* report, the State Department's *Foreign Terrorist Organizations Designations* are compiled every two years when the Secretary of State designates, by mandate of Congress, approximately 30 groups as global terrorist organizations. *Significant Incidents of Political Violence Against Americans* is another State Department report, published annually by the Bureau of Diplomatic Security, Office of Intelligence and Threat Analysis. It examines terrorism-related acts and other instances of violence affecting Americans.

The U.S. Department of Defense (DOD) has an excellent educational institution that serves as a resource: the National Defense University (NDU), and in particular the NDU's Institute for National Strategic Studies (INSS). The INSS's *The Global Century: Globalization and National Security* (2001) is a two-volume anthology on global security and defense issues. The much shorter executive report of the project is entitled *Challenges of the Global Century: Report of the Project on Globalization and National Security* (June 2001). INSS's series of books

titled *Strategic Assessment*, published every four years (the latest being *Strategic Assessment 1999: Priorities for a Turbulent World*) examines basic trends, U.S. interests, and consequences for U.S. policy in the international security environment, followed by an assessment for key regional areas. The institute's 2015 Project, which forecasted global defense and national security conditions through the year 2015, yielded the anthology *2015: Power and Progress*, a good source on the implications of the great powers; demographic, pollution, and resource stresses; coalitions; and information technology and warfare.

An extremely useful report from the DOD is *Proliferation: Threat and Response* (2001). The report updates information about the worldwide proliferation of nuclear, biological, and chemical weapons with good figures and tables, especially concerning ballistic missile ranges, and focuses on DOD policies and programs countering such threats. The DOD's congressionally-mandated Quadrennial Defense Review (QDR), also known as the *Report of the Quadrennial Review* (May 2001) broadly describes future defense policies.

The U.S. General Accounting Office (GAO), the investigative arm of Congress, produces many documents relating to national security, especially those addressing domestic threats. One such document used in this book is *Bioterrorism: Public Health and Medical Preparedness* (2001), the testimony on October 9, 2001, of Janet Heinrich, Director of Health Care-Public Health Issues, before the Senate's Subcommittee on Public Health, Committee on Health, Education, Labor and Pensions.

On preparations for potential domestic bioterrorism, the premier government source is the U.S. Department of Health and Human Services' Centers for Disease Control and Prevention (CDC) in Atlanta, Georgia. CDC sources used in this book include "Report Summary: Public Health Assessment of Potential Biological Terrorism Agents," in *Emerging Infectious Diseases* (February

2002), and "Biological and Chemical Terrorism: Strategic Plan for Preparedness and Response: Recommendations of the CDC Strategic Planning Workgroup," in *Morbidity and Mortality Weekly Report* (April 2000).

U.S. sources provide abundant information on illegal immigration that could affect national security. Some titles available from the GAO in this area include *Alien Smuggling: Management and Operational Improvements Needed to Address Growing Problem* (2000) and *Illegal Immigration: Status of Southwest Border Strategy Implementation* (1999).

Another source of information in this area is the former U.S. Immigration and Naturalization Service (INS), until early 2003 an agency of the U.S. Department of Justice, but now rolled into the new U.S. Department of Homeland Security. Its annual *Statistical Yearbook of the Immigration and Naturalization Service* (2001) is a complete statistical resource on immigrants, illegal aliens, and refugees who come to the United States. Another such report published by the INS is *Illegal Alien Resident Population* (1999). Demographic data on the foreign-born population in the United States is available from the U.S. Census Bureau in *The Foreign-Born Population in the United States, March 2000* (2001).

The Congressional Research Service (CRS) is the research arm of the Library of Congress in Washington, which serves members and committees of Congress but makes many of its findings available to the public as well. The CRS reports consulted in preparing this book included *Intelligence Issues for Congress* (Richard A. Best, updated July 2002), *Homeland Security Office: Issues and Options* (Rensselaer Lee, May 2002), *The USA Patriot Act: A Legal Analysis* (Charles Doyle, April 2002), and *Weapons of Mass Destruction: The Terrorist Threat* (Steve Bauman, March 2002).

Information Plus sincerely thanks all of the organizations listed above for the invaluable information they provide.

INDEX

House Committee on Un-American Activities (HCUAA), 132–133
House Permanent Select Committee on Intelligence (HPSCI), 129
H.R. 3162. *See* U.S.A. Patriot Act
Hughes-Ryan amendments, 129
HUJI (Harakat ul-Jihad-I-Islami), 92*t*–93*t*
HUJI-B (Harakat ul-Jihad-I-Islami/Bangladesh), 93*t*
HUM (Harakat ul-Mujahidin) (Movement of Holy Warriors), 74, 78*t*–79*t*
Human intelligence, 127
Human rights, 158, 169
Humanitarian interests
  defined, 2
  in peacekeeping, 151
  priority of, 2*f*
Hussein, Saddam, 7, 46, 72

I

IAA (Islamic Army of Aden), 93*t*
IANSA (International Action Network on Small Arms), 20
Ibrahim, Abu, 72
ICBL (International Campaign to Ban Landmines), 20
ICBMs. *See* Intercontinental ballistic missiles (ICBMs)
ICT (International Policy Institute for Counterterrorism), 118
IEA (International Energy Agency), 161*f*
IGOs (International government organizations), 19
IIS (Iraqi Intelligence Service), 72
Illegal aliens, 139
Illegal immigrants, 138
Illicit markets, 171–173
Imagery intelligence, 127, 183
Immigration, 138–139
Immigration and Naturalization Service (INS)
  duties/goals of, 138–139
  need for, 137–138
  restructuring, 139
  U.S. Border Patrol, activities/accomplishments of, 138*t*
  U.S. Border Patrol agents, 139*f*
Imports
  of arms, by country, 15
  of conventional weapons, 9–10, 10*f*
  countries receiving major conventional weapons, 16*t*–18*t*
  countries supplying weapons to other countries, 13*t*–14*t*
  of major conventional weapons, volume of, 12 (*t*2.2)
IMU (Islamic Movement of Uzbekistan), 74, 80*t*
In-Q-Tel, 127
Incubation period, 34
India
  arms imports of, 15
  landmines of, 20
  population/GNP of, 5*t*
  as transition state, 5, 6
  weapons of mass destruction programs of, 36, 37 (*t*3.7)

Individual contributors, 104
Industrialized world, 161
Information
  as intelligence, 126–127
  security incidents, 177*f*
  sharing of FBI, 136
Information technology (IT), 173–183
  computer attacks, types of, 175*t*
  computer-related infrastructures, potential threats to, 174*t*
  information warfare against U.S. government, 175–183, 175*f*
  national security dependent on, 173–174
  processor/chip development, 174–175
Information warfare (IW)
  battlefield systems technology, 182–183
  classifying threats, 176–177
  computer crimes and the government, 177–178
  computer hacking, 178–179
  Department of Defense, vulnerability of, 179
  division of responsibility for responding to strategic information threats, 181 (*f*10.6)
  facial recognition technology, 181*t*
  as important security issue, 174
  information defense-in-depth strategy, 181 (*f*10.5)
  information security incidents, 177*f*
  information threat dynamics, 176*f*
  key executive order on, 180*t*
  scope of, 175–176, 175*f*
  solutions for U.S. protection, 179–182
Information warfare defense (IWD)
  classifying threats to, 176–177
  defense-in-depth strategy for, 179–180, 181 (*f*10.5)
  legislation related to, 180*t*
  private- *vs.* public-sector approaches, 180–181
  to protect U.S., 181–182
Innovision Directorate, NIMA (National Imagery and Mapping Agency), 148
INS. *See* Immigration and Naturalization Service (INS)
Inspections
  for CFE treaty compliance, 21–22
  of OPCW, 49
  UN weapons inspections, 43, 45, 48
Institute for Physics and Power Engineering (IPPE), 48–49
Intelligence
  information as, 126–127
  National Security Agency for, 148
Intelligence community
  bolstered after 9/11 attacks, 104
  budget secrecy of, 128
  Central Intelligence Agency, 128–129, 130*f*, 131
  covert action, 127–128
  Federal Bureau of Investigation, 131–137
  information as intelligence, 126–127
  as national security policymakers, 7–8, 8*f*
  organization of, 124, 126, 126*f*
Intelligence Directorate, 129
Intelligence Oversight Board (IOB), 129

Intelligence Report (Southern Poverty Law Center), 119
Intercontinental ballistic missiles (ICBMs)
  launchers, 50
  START I treaty and, 51
  START II treaty and, 51–52
  See also Ballistic missiles
Interdependence, 157
Interests, national security, 2, 2*f*
The Interim Agreement Between the United States and the Union of Soviet Socialist Republics on Certain Measures with Respect to the Limitation of Strategic Offensive Arms (SALT I), 50
International Action Network on Small Arms (IANSA), 20
International Campaign to Ban Landmines (ICBL), 20
International Court of Justice, UN, 158
International Crime Control Strategy, 173
International crimes
  affecting U.S. interests, 172*f*
  organized-crime groups, 171–173
International Criminal Police Organization (INTERPOL), 19, 171
International Energy Agency (IEA), 161*f*
International government organizations (IGOs), 19
International Policy Institute for Counterterrorism (ICT), 118
International terrorism, 65–111
  active duty military personnel strengths, by regional area/country, 102*t*–103*t*
  American public opinion after September 11, 2001, 107–111, 109*f*, 109*t*, 110*f*, 111*t*
  citizen casualties caused by, 68 (*f*5.3)
  directed against United States, 100–101, 103–104
  facilities struck by international attacks, 68 (*f*5.2)
  financing, 104
  international terrorist attacks, total, 67*f*
  international terrorist attacks, total, by region, 108*f*
  motivations/trends, 66–67
  other terrorist groups worldwide, 90*t*–100*t*
  State Department-designated foreign terrorist organizations, 75*t*–89*t*
  state-sponsored terrorism, 68–74
  substate terror groups, 74
  terrorism around the world, 74, 100
  terrorism, defined, 65–66
  U.S. reaction to September 11, 2001, 104–107
"International Terrorism: A New Mode of Conflict" (Jenkins), 65
International threats, 134–135
International treaty, 49
  See also Legislation and international treaties
INTERPOL (International Criminal Police Organization), 19, 171
Investigations, 134–135, 137
Investigative Technologies Division, FBI, 137

IOB (Intelligence Oversight Board), 129
IPPE (Institute for Physics and Power Engineering), 48–49
IRA (Irish Republican Army), 74, 93*t*–94*t*
Iran
  alliance with China, 163
  Gulf Cooperation Council and, 159
  Iran-Contra affair, 14, 131
  Iranian hostage crisis, 69
  nuclear cooperation with China, 36
  response to September 11th attack, 70
  as state of concern, 7
  as state sponsor of international terrorism, 72
  support of fundamental Islamic groups, 104
  weapons of mass destruction programs of, 36–37, 37 (*t*3.8), 38*f*
Iran-Contra affair, 14, 131
Iran-Iraq war, 45–46
Iraq
  American public opinion on military action against, 110, 110 (*f*5.7)
  ballistic missiles, estimated range of, 47*f*
  Congress grants Bush authority to use force against, 121
  Gulf Cooperation Council and, 159, 160
  as state of concern, 7
  state sponsorship of international terrorism, 72
Iraq, WMD program of
  biological weapons program of, 46
  chemical weapons program of, 45–46
  continuation of, 4
  missiles of, 46, 48
  nuclear weapons program of, 45
  UN weapons inspections in, 43, 45
  WMD programs of, 43 (*t*3.13)
Iraqi Intelligence Service (IIS), 72
Irish Republican Army (IRA), 74, 93*t*–94*t*
Islam, 70, 71
Islamic Army of Aden (IAA), 93*t*
Islamic Group (Al-Gama'a al-Islamiyya), 77*t*–78*t*
Islamic Movement of Uzbekistan (IMU), 74, 80*t*
Islamic Resistance Movement. *See* Hamas (Islamic Resistance Movement)
Israel
  alliance with U.S., 159
  Israeli/Palestinian conflict, 70, 71
  U.S. weapons sales to, 14
  weapons of mass destruction programs of, 37
Israeli/Palestinian conflict, 70, 71
IT. *See* Information technology (IT)
IW. *See* Information warfare (IW)
IWD. *See* Information warfare defense (IWD)

J

Jaish-e-Mohammed (JEM), 80*t*
Japan
  chemical weapons attack in Tokyo, 33–34
  nuclear weapons dropped on, 25, 34
Japanese American internment, 132

Japanese Red Army (JRA), 94*t*–95*t*
JCS. *See* Joint Chiefs of Staff (JCS)
Jefferson, Thomas, 123
Jemaah Islamiyah network, 74
Jenkins, Brian Michael, 65
Jewell, Richard, 133
Jews, 71, 118
Jiang Zemin, 6
Jihad ("holy war")
  Osama bin Laden's call for, 103
  Palestine Islam Jihad, 71, 84*t*
  against Soviet Union, 101
Joint Chiefs of Staff (JCS)
  in Department of Defense organization, 141
  organization of, 144, 144*f*
  Sequoia Study by, 3
Joint Chiefs of Staff (JCS) chairman
  as advisor to NSC, 123
  powers of, 144
  as principal advisor, 141
  transmission of National Command Authority orders, 146
Joint Compliance and Inspection Commission, 51
Joint Consultative Group of Vienna, Austria, 21–22
"Jointness," 141, 146
Jordan, 71
Jordan River, 165
JRA (Japanese Red Army), 94*t*–95*t*
Judicial branch, 122*f*
Juvenile hacking, 178–179

K

Kaczyinski, David, 114
Kaczyinski, Theodore, 114
Kahane Chai (Kach), 81*t*
Kamel, Hussein, 45
Kashmir, 6
Kennedy, John F., 3, 127
KFOR. *See* Kosovo Force (KFOR)
Khamenei, Ayatollah Ali, 7
Khatami, Mohammad, 7, 72
Khomeini, Ayatollah, 69
Kim Jong-Il, 6
Klare, Michael T., 164, 169
KMM (Kumpulan Mujahidin Malaysia), 95*t*
Korean War, 3
Kosovo Force (KFOR)
  cost of, 153–154
  national security strategy and, 151
  number of participants in, 150
Kosovo, U.S. operations in, 155 (*t*8.4)
Ku Klux Klan
  Anti-Defamation League and, 118
  birth of, 115
  Southern Poverty Law Center and, 119
Kumpulan Mujahidin Malaysia (KMM), 95*t*
Kurdistan Workers' Party (PKK), 81*t*–82*t*

L

La Belle Discotheque bombing, 72
Laboratory Division, FBI, 137
Laboratory response network, 61–63
Landmines, 20
Laquer, Walter, 65

Lashkar-e-Tayyiba (LT), 82*t*
Latin America
  NGOs combating small weapons sales, 20
  state sponsorship of international terrorism, 74
  terrorist attacks in, 107
Law enforcement powers
  Patriot Act expansion of, 106
  public opinion on increases in, 111, 111 (*t*5.5)
Left-wing organizations, 115
"Legacy" systems, 182
Legislation and international treaties
  1961 Foreign Assistance Act, 14
  Anti-Terrorism Law, 133
  Antiballistic Missile (ABM) Treaty, 50
  Arming Pilots Against Terrorism Act, 106
  Arms Export Control Act, 14
  Biological and Toxin Weapons Convention, 27, 32*t*, 49
  Central Intelligence Agency Act of 1949, 128
  on chemical/biological weapons, 27
  Chemical Weapons Convention, 27, 32*t*, 49
  Computer Fraud and Abuse Act, 177
  Controlled Substances Trafficking Prohibition Act of 1998, 173
  Conventional Armed Forces in Europe 1A (CFE 1A) Treaty, 22–23, 23*t*
  for countering transnational threats, 173
  for cyber-critical infrastructure protection, 180*t*
  for domestic terrorism, 119
  Economic Espionage Act of 1996, 179
  Executive Order 12333, 128
  Executive Order on Terrorist Financing, 104
  Freedom of Access to Clinical Entrances Act, 118
  Goldwater-Nichols Department of Defense Reorganization Act of 1986, 141, 146
  H.R. 5710 for Department of Homeland Security, 105
  Hughes-Ryan amendments, 129
  International Campaign to Ban Landmines treaty, 20
  Money Laundering and Financial Crimes Strategy Act of 1998, 173
  National Security Act of 1947, 123, 126
  nonproliferation regimes/treaties, 49–52, 51*t*
  Panama Canal Treaty, 144
  Patriot Act of 2001, 106
  Presidential Decision Directive 25, 151
  Presidential Decision Directive 63, 174
  Presidential Directive 62, 173
  Treaty on Conventional Armed Forces in Europe (CFE), 21–22, 21*t*, 22*t*
  UN Resolution 1373, 104
  UN Security Council Resolution 1284, 43
  UN Security Council Resolution 1441, 43

Totalitarian governments, 3

Toxins, 34

   See also Biological agents; Chemical agents

Toyoda, Toru, 34

Trade secrets, 176

Trafficking

   drug, 171, 172–173

   of nuclear and fissile material, 48–49

Transborder resource conflicts, 169

Transition states, 5–6, 5*t*

Transnational crimes, 171–173

Transnational threat, 66, 107

Transnationalism, 5

Transparency, 19, 23*t*

Transportation Security Administration (TSA), 106

Treasury Department, U.S., 104, 173

Treaties. *See* Legislation and international treaties

The Treaty Between the United States and the Russian Federation on Further Reduction and Limitation of Strategic Offensive Arms (START II), 51–52, 51 (*t*3.15), 144

Treaty Between the United States and the Soviet Union on the Limitation of Antiballistic Missile Systems (ABM Treaty), 50

The Treaty Between the United States and the Union of Soviet Socialist Republics on the Limitation of Strategic Offensive Arms (SALT II), 50, 144

The Treaty Between the United States of America and the Union of Soviet Socialist Republics on the Reduction and Limitation of Strategic Offensive Arms (START I), 50–51, 51*t*

Treaty on Conventional Armed Forces in Europe (CFE), 21–22, 21*t*, 22*t*

The Treaty on Open Skies, 51

Treaty on the Principles Governing the Activities of States in the Exploration and Use of Outer Space, Including the Moon and Other Celestial Bodies, 50

Truman Doctrine, 2–3

Truman, Harry S., 2–3, 146

Trust territories, 158

Trusteeship Council, UN, 158

TSA (Transportation Security Administration), 106

Tunisian Combatant Group (TCG), 98*t*

Tupac Amaru Revolutionary Movement (MRTA), 98*t*–99*t*

Turkey, 15, 20

Turkish Hizballah, 99*t*

"Turned" informants, 127

The 2002 Computer Crime and Security Survey (Computer Security Institute), 178

Two-tiered agreement, 49

U

U-2 plane, 127

UAE (United Arab Emirates), 10, 14

UAVs (Unmanned aerial vehicles), 183

UDA/UFF (Ulster Defense Association/Ulster Freedom Fighters), 99*t*–100*t*

Ulster Defense Association/Ulster Freedom Fighters (UDA/UFF), 99*t*–100*t*

UN. *See* United Nations (UN)

"Unabomber," 114

Unclassified sources, 126

Unified combatant commands, 146–147, 147*f*

Uniform Crime Reporting Program, 134

Unipolar hegemony, 4

United Arab Emirates (UAE), 10, 14

United Kingdom, 15, 63

United Nations (UN)

   costs of peacekeeping missions, 151, 153–156

   engaged in collective security, 4

   functions of, divisions of, 158

   opposition to small arms proliferation, 19

   peacekeeping areas of action for, 148

   peacekeeping function of, 148–149

   peacekeeping missions, contributions to, 152*t*–154*t*, 155 (*t*8.3)

   peacekeeping missions of, 149*t*

   peacekeeping missions, U.S. interests in, 150–151

   Programme of Action, 19

   weapons inspections, 43, 45, 48

UN Conference on the Illicit Trade in Small Arms and Light Weapons, 19

UN Monitoring, Verification, and Inspections Commission (UNMOVIC), 43, 48

U.N. Peacekeeping: Status of Long-Standing Operations and U.S. Interests in Supporting Them (GAO report), 150–151

UN Resolution 1373, 104

United Nations Security Council

   members of, 158

   peacekeeping missions set by, 149

   Resolution 1441 and, 43

UN Security Council Resolution 687, 46

UN Security Council Resolution 1284, 43

UN Security Council Resolution 1441, 43

UN Special Commission on Iraq (UNSCOM), 43, 46

United Self-Defense Forces/Group of Colombia (AUC), 88*t*–89*t*

United States

   actions seen as terrorism, 74, 100

   American public opinion after September 11, 2001, 107–111, 109*f*, 109*t*, 110*f*, 111*f*

   arms exports of, 10–11, 14

   arms sales, 14–15

   drug trafficking and, 173

   as global leader, 4

   information warfare to protect, 181–182

   interests in Persian Gulf, 160

   international crimes affecting U.S. interests, 172*f*

   international terrorism directed against, 100–101, 103–104

   Iraq's WMD programs and, 43, 45

   Israeli/Palestinian conflict and, 71

   landmines and, 20

   nonproliferation treaties of, 50–52

   oil consumption of, 161

   oil production vs. conservation, 163, 163*f*

   oil supply and Strategic Petroleum Reserve, 162–163

   peace operations funding, 151, 153–154, 155 (*t*8.4)

   peace operations personnel, 154–156

   in peacekeeping missions, debate about, 150–151

   petroleum-related events/U.S. refiner acquisition cost, 161*f*

   reaction to September 11, 2001, 104–107

   state sponsorship of terrorism in Cold War, 104

   terror attacks, types of targets, 67

   UN peacekeeping operations, contributions to, 152*t*–154*t*

   weapons of mass destruction policy, 27

   See also Federal government

U.S. Air Force, 141, 146

U.S. Army, 141, 144, 146

U.S. attorney general, 132

U.S. Border Patrol, 138*t*, 139*f*

U.S. citizens

   casualties from terrorist attacks, 68

   CIA restrictions on domestic spying, 128

   targeted in foreign countries, 74

   as targets for threats, 2

U.S. Coast Guard, 146

U.S. Department of Defense (DOD)

   computer hacking vulnerability of, 179

   defense agencies related to, 147–148

   definition of terrorism, 65

   intelligence community related to, 126

   military departments reporting to, 144

   organization of, 141, 143*f*

U.S. Department of Homeland Security (DHS)

   APHIS slated to merge with, 63

   departments, responsibilities of, 105

   duties of, 137

   INS functions incorporated into, 139

U.S. Department of Justice, 106, 118

U.S. Department of State

   definition of terrorism, 65

   list of state sponsors of international terrorism, 69–70, 72

   organization chart of, 125*f*

   role in national security, 123–124

   terrorist activities defined by, 66

U.S. embassies, 101

U.S. General Accounting Office (GAO)

   identification of federal departments/agencies with role in combating terrorism, 53

   report on infrastructure protection, 174, 174*t*

United States government. *See* Federal government

U.S. House of Representatives, 8, 121

U.S. Humanitarian Demining Program, 20

U.S. Marine Corps, 141, 146

U.S. military. *See* Military, U.S.

U.S. Naval Fifth Fleet, 160

U.S. Navy, 141, 146

U.S. Postal Service (USPS), 114–115

U.S. property (outside the country), 2
U.S. Secret Service, 178
U.S. Senate
    alliances and, 157
    as national security policymaker, 8
    powers relative to national security, 121
U.S. Treasury Department, 104, 173
Unmanned aerial vehicles (UAVs), 183
UNMOVIC (UN Monitoring, Verification,
    and Inspections Commission), 43, 48
UNSCOM (UN Special Commission on
    Iraq), 43, 46
Uranium trafficking, 48–49
USA Patriot Act
    authorizations of, 106
    to counter transnational threats, 173
    powers of intelligence community from,
    131
USPS (U.S. Postal Service), 114–115
USS *Cole* bombing, 101
Uzbekistan, 74

V

Verification, 51
Versailles Treaty, 27
Vesicants, 32
Vice-president, 123
Vietnam War
    chemical weapons used in, 27
    national security policy and, 3
    War Powers Act and, 121
Violent-crime investigations, 137
Viruses
    as biological weapons, 34
    for computer hacking, 178
    digital, 175, 175*t*
Vital interests
    defined, 2
    in peacekeeping, 151
    priority of, 2*f*
Vomiting agents, 33
VX nerve agent, 46

W

Waco (TX), 133
Waldman, Carl, 25
War
    battlefield systems technology, 182–183
    oil reserves, arms, and, 164–165
War against drugs, 5
War-making

covert action and, 127–128
powers of president, 121
War on terrorism
    American public opinion on, 108–111,
    109*f*, 109*t*, 110*f*, 111*t*
    Department of Defense budget for, 141
    national security issues and, 1
    possible counterproductive results of, 70
    principles and military actions of,
    106–107
War Powers Act, 121, 131
Warheads
    START I treaty and, 51, 51*t*
    START III agreement and, 52
Warsaw Pact Organization countries, 21, 51
Wassenaar Arrangement on Export Controls
    for Conventional Arms and Dual-Use
    Goods and Technologies, 23
Water, potential conflicts over, 165,
    167–169, 168*f*
Water-stressed countries, 165, 167–169
Watergate scandal, 133
Watson, Sharon Ann, 115
Weapons
    oil reserves and, 164–165
    of U.S. military, 146
    See also Conventional weapons
Weapons of mass destruction (WMD),
    25–52
    adherence to international treaties for
    countries of concern, 32*t*
    biological weapons, 34
    chemical/biological weapons, possession
    and programs, 28*t*–31*t*
    chemical warfare agents, common, 33
    (*t*3.5)
    chemical weapons, 27–34
    of China, 35–36, 35*t*
    Defense Threat Reduction Agency
    protection from, 148
    dual use chemicals, 33 (*t*3.4)
    of Egypt, 36
    history of usage and proliferation, 25,
    26*t*, 27
    India's programs, 36, 37 (*t*3.7)
    Iranian ballistic missiles, range of, 38*f*
    Iran's programs, 36–37, 37 (*t*3.8)
    Iraq/Iran programs for, 18
    Iraqi ballistic missiles, estimated range
    of, 47*f*
    Iraq's programs, 43, 43 (*t*3.13), 45–46, 48
    of Israel, 37

Libya's programs, 39, 39 (*t*3.9), 40*f*
national security concern for, 4, 5
nonproliferation regimes/treaties, 49–52,
    51*t*
North Korean ballistic missiles, estimated
    range of, 42*f*
North Korea's programs, 39, 39 (*t*3.10),
    41
nuclear and fissile material, trafficking
    of, 48–49
nuclear weapons, 34–35
Pakistan's programs, 41, 41*t*
Syrian ballistic missiles, estimated range
    of, 44*f*
Syria's programs, 41, 43 (*t*3.12)
White-collar crime, 137
White House Economic Council, 123
White House staff, 123
White supremacists, 116, 119
WHO (World Health Organization), 19
Wilkinson, Paul, 65
Williams, Kenneth, 135
Wirthlin Worldwide National Quorum
    telephone surveys
    American public opinion after September
    11, 2001, 107–108, 109, 109 (*t*5.4)
    on George W. Bush, 111
WMD. *See* Weapons of mass destruction
    (WMD)
Wolfers, Arnold, 1
Working Group in Civilian Biodefense, 58
World Health Organization (WHO), 19
World oil transit "chokepoints," 165,
    166*t*–167*t*
World Trade Center, 65, 100–101
World War I, 25
World War II
    FBI in, 132
    national security policy history and, 2–3
    nuclear weapons used in, 25
Worms, digital, 175, 175*f*

Y

Yassin, Abdul, 72
Yeltsin, Boris, 49, 52

Z

Zangger Committee (ZC), 32*t*
ZC (Zangger Committee), 32*t*
Zionism, 71
Zubaydah, Abu, 131